ROYAL HISTORICAL SOCIETY

STUDIES IN HISTORY

New Series

MASSACRE AT THE CHAMP DE MARS

MASSACRE AT THE CHAMP DE MARS

POPULAR DISSENT AND POLITICAL CULTURE
IN THE FRENCH REVOLUTION

David Andress

THE ROYAL HISTORICAL SOCIETY
THE BOYDELL PRESS

First published 2000
The Royal Historical Society, London
in association with
The Boydell Press, Woodbridge
Paperback edition 2013
The Boydell Press, Woodbridge

ISBN   978 0 86193 247 4 hardback
ISBN   978 1 84383 842 5 paperback

Transferred to digital printing

The Boydell Press is an imprint of Boydell & Brewer Ltd
PO Box 9, Woodbridge, Suffolk IP12 3DF, UK
and of Boydell & Brewer Inc,
668 Mt Hope Avenue, Rochester, NY 14620–2731, USA
website: www.boydellandbrewer.com

A CIP catalogue record for this book is available
from the British Library

This publication is printed on acid-free paper

TO J.

'Massacre des patriotes au Champ de Mars', by Louis Lafitte
(Musée Carnavalet). Reproduced by courtesy of
the Photothèque des Musées de Paris, Paris.

Contents

Publication of this volume was aided by a grant from the Scouloudi Foundation, in association with the Institute of Historical Research. It was further assisted by a grant from the School of Social and Historical Studies, University of Portsmouth.

Acknowledgements

This work has been a long time in gestation, and I must first acknowledge my debt to my doctoral supervisor, Alan Forrest, who shepherded the first version of this project to completion between 1991 and 1994. His never-failing calm reassurance, and certainty of the value of my work, is surely a model for such a relationship. Colin Lucas and Geoff Cubitt, in examining that thesis, were kind enough to praise it also, and Colin especially has been greatly supportive on a number of occasions over the intervening years.

A great immediate debt for this version of the project lies with Colin Jones, who as advisory editor has taken up and guided it, albeit with sometimes brutal honesty, into a more polished form. At different points Sarah Maza and Paul Hanson have also kindly offered supportive help. Likewise, as articles have spun off from it over the years, a substantial number of anonymous readers for *French History*, *European History Quarterly* and *French Historical Studies* have added their comments and criticisms to the evolution of some of the arguments herein. Portions of this material have been previously published, in slightly different form, in the following journals: *French History* ix (1995) and x (1996), *European History Quarterly* xxviii (1998), and *French Historical Studies* xxii (1999). The publishers' permission is gratefully acknowledged. The jacket/frontispiece illustration, Louis Lafitte, 'Massacre des patriotes au Champ de Mars' (Musée Carnavalet), is reproduced by courtesy of the Photothèque des Musées de Paris, Paris.

More recently, Jill Maciak has earned my great gratitude, in lending me her wit and penetration, and in finding a thousand ways to improve a text to which I, as author, was too close to see the many flaws. Christine Linehan, executive editor for the Royal Historical Society, has been both punctilious and understanding, a fine combination in an editor.

Finally, this book is dedicated to the woman without whom I cannot imagine the course of the last decade, or that of those to come. My wife, Jessica.

David Andress

Abbreviations

APP   Archives de la Préfecture de Police, Paris
BL   British Library, London
BN   Bibliothèque nationale de France, Paris
Lacroix, *Actes*   Sigismond Lacroix, *Actes de la Commune de Paris*, 2nd ser. ii–viii, Paris 1902–11

Note on Sources

All quotations from primary sources are the author's translations. At points where a word was illegible, this is noted in square brackets. Some original terms are also noted in square brackets, where the particular vocabulary is pertinent.

Manuscripts from the Archives de la Préfecture de Police are identified by their series followed by two numbers, which indicate for series AA the carton and folio, and for series AB the register and case number; for example, APP, AA85:123 or AB323:1234. See the bibliography for further details.

Where a quotation from a journal of the era has been identified in the text by author or title and date, the reference has not been footnoted, other than to supply supplementary information. Similarly, the year of publications and events is only noted when it falls outside 1791.

Preface to the paperback edition

In the years since this work was first published, my research has developed
further, as of course has writing on Paris and the French Revolution more
generally. In this preface, I hope to indicate how such new material might
influence a reading of this text, while also showing why I believe its conclusions remain valid, and important, observations about the Parisian revolutionary process of the 1790s.

The central catalysing event at the heart of this book is the royal Flight
to Varennes of 21 June 1791. Out of reactions to this emerged the massacre
and the responses to it that form the core of my subject matter. Timothy
Tackett in 2003 produced a study which frames the Flight and reactions to
it on the national stage, as well as offering a counterpoint to the Parisian
situation. He shows that the royal initiative was genuinely traumatizing for
the body politic, occasioning reactions blending fear of conspiracy and of
looming anarchy. Demands to make France secure in its new constitution
helped prompt both a crackdown on radicals – as depicted here in detail –
and also a willingness to pretend, in effect, that the Flight had not happened.
France lurched forward under the banner of amnesty and reconciliation,
but having also taken a decisive step towards political persecution.[1] Unlike
earlier interpretations, which placed much of this dynamic under the aegis
of social conflict, Tackett emphasises the shift in mentality involved.

Such mentalities, and their complex heritage of attitudes from before
1789, are a core part of my argument. David Garrioch, whose earlier work
on the policing of Parisian communities inspired much of my archival meth-
odology, published in 2002 a sweeping yet intimate survey of life in the
eighteenth-century capital. In it he depicts a city caught up in economic and
social change, emerging from an era of relatively closed 'urban villages' into
one of accelerating personal mobility, and also one where life for the working
population was increasingly precarious, becoming distanced from 'bourgeois'
habits as the latter more clearly came to form a new propertied class. Yet it
is also a city in which face-to-face encounters mattered, in which the act
of walking through the urban landscape was still central to everyday life,
along with the interactions such very personal mobility provoked, and where
cafés, taverns and inns still provided the sites of intense and politically-alert
sociability.[2] Garrioch's work can be read with profit alongside that of Robert
Darnton, among the many strands of which is a close attention to patterns of
communication in the pre-revolutionary capital. Darnton notes how avidly

1   Timothy Tackett, *When the king took flight*, Cambridge, Mass. 2003.
2   David Garrioch, *The making of revolutionary Paris*, Berkeley 2002.

people of all conditions sought out gossip and scandal, how alert they were to the potential real consequences of such news for their lives, and how far the royal police were also concerned to track and control such unlicensed political speech, poetry and song. What Darnton's study adds particularly to earlier work such as that of Arlette Farge, discussed in this volume, is a grasp of the complexity of circulation, the many different ways in which individuals from servants and labourers to students and priests might be connected by the transmission of information in both oral and written forms.[3]

Although much of the material Darnton examines suggests that gossip was entertainment as much as it was politics, recent studies by Micah Alpaugh remind us how relatively sophisticated the popular response to upheaval was in 1789 and after. Focusing deliberately on the extent to which many acts of protest were non-violent, Alpaugh shows through contemporary observers' narratives that popular political action, both as the occupation of public space in discussion, and in demonstrations frequently numbering thousands, was an integral part of the revolutionary city.[4] This is an important counterpoint to my own work, which in focusing on those protests that became flashpoints in a narrative of escalation, could be said to have overlooked the significance of those that did not. Alpaugh does a worthy job of reclaiming the Parisians' attempts to have their voices heard without resorting to violence.

However, what has also emerged in recent studies is a clear message about the extent to which revolutionary political culture was primed for such a resort. Whereas a generation ago historians such as Keith Michael Baker and François Furet used 'political culture' as a label to discuss essentially elite preoccupations, and to suggest that revolution marked a break with the past that led on to Terror, there is now a focus – as with Darnton and Garrioch above – on the extent to which revolutionaries were living and thinking within a complex heritage from the Old Regime. At a general political level, Charles Walton has given us an invaluable study of the revolutionary impulse both to launch intolerable verbal and print attacks, and to vacillate in destabilising fashion over authoritarian controls on speech.[5] Walton

---

[3] Robert Darnton, *Poetry and the police; communication networks in eighteenth-century Paris*, Cambridge, Mass. 2010. See also Lisa Jane Graham, *If the king only knew: seditious speech in the reign of Louis XV*, Charlottesville 2000. Arlette Farge herself has also published further, including *Effusion et tourment, le récit des corps; histoire du peuple au XVIIIe siècle*, Paris 2007, a vivid study of the impact of life on the bodies of the poor and workers in the eighteenth century.

[4] See Micah Alpaugh, 'The politics of escalation in French revolutionary protest; political demonstrations, nonviolence and violence in the *grandes journées* of 1789', *French History* xxiii (2009), 336–59; and 'The making of the Parisian political demonstration; a case study of 20 June 1792', *Proceedings of the Western Society for French History* xxxiv (2007), 101–19.

[5] Charles Walton, *Policing public opinion in the French Revolution; the culture of calumny and the problem of free speech*, Oxford 2009. For a study of similar themes, but focused far more on high-political debates, see Jon Cowans, *To speak for the people; public opinion and the problem of legitimacy in the French Revolution*, New York 2001.

locates this problem firmly in an inherited 'culture of calumny', the product of relentless competition within an honour-based society, where defamation was as likely a route to the top as any other, and if accomplished anonymously, was almost risk-free. The only limit was *lèse-majesté*; one dare not be caught attacking the monarchy. Revolutionary politicians would complete the dangerous translation of Old-Regime habits to the 1790s by rebranding this as *lèse-nation*, opening the way to assaults on those who could be accused of criticising this much vaguer object of adulation.

Developments such as these in the wider historiography align with my own further work, one aspect of which focused on the rich records of the Palais-Royal district (known in 1789–90 as Saint-Roch), and how its inhabitants managed the transition to a new 'democratic' order. The propertied citizens who seem to have emerged more-or-less spontaneously as district leaders showed themselves fierce advocates of local autonomy, making them appear from some documents as paragons of direct democracy. But just like the artisanal guild leaderships who had vigorously defended their turf in pre-revolutionary disputes, district officials easily slipped into an enjoyment of power and status for its own benefits, and also developed a role as patrons and providers (albeit frequently cash-strapped ones) in a period of economic upheaval. Moreover, from the very first hours of the Revolution, the street-level narrative that the district papers provide is filled with the complex dreads that would again echo through 1791. District National Guard patrols and civilian commissioners, from Saint-Roch and elsewhere, criss-crossed the city far beyond any rational attribution of jurisdiction, pursuing rumours of nefarious activity in which social discontent and counter-revolution were often indistinguishable. Meanwhile, to their constituents, the district authorities represented 'authority' in what seemed still a very old-regime sense – omnicompetent, paternalist, and to be appealed to over any hiccup in local social relations or wellbeing. While the plain fact of inability to assist in almost all these matters dogged the district's heels, it remained nonetheless part of a complex Parisian response to the new collective situation that owed as much, if not more, to desires for continuity as for change.[6]

A companion piece to this analysis focuses on public discussion in the Palais-Royal, and notably how from the beginning of the Revolution it represented an unstable blend of essential public newsgathering, potential seditious unrest, and spontaneous assertions of justice and authority from a wide range of individuals taking action against such disturbance. Rhetorics of the need for both publicly-expressed surveillance of political action, and a close watch over that very public expression, engineered a fulminating open-air 'public sphere' that was at the same time host to unstable suspicions and endemic potential and actual violence. A case-study of the Palais-Royal

---

[6] 'Neighbourhood policing in Paris from Old Regime to Revolution; the exercise of authority by the district de St-Roch, 1789–1791', *French Historical Studies* xxix (2006), 231–60.

on the day after the 14 July 1790 Festival of Federation illustrates this, as various competing narratives circulated concerning the troubling lack of apparent royal enthusiasm for the oath-taking ceremony at the heart of the celebrations. An examination of what kinds of speech were troubling, what attitudes such utterances were feared to imply, and what level of spontaneous order or disorder arose in response, in a crowd made up largely of uniformed members of the National Guard, offers a complex picture. As with the larger-scale disturbances of the summer of 1791, the line between offenders and guardians of order ran jaggedly through the social landscape, and the space for genuinely free speech was repeatedly squeezed by the threat of violence and the demand for order.[7]

The juxtaposition between a concern for order which is at least partially from the social 'bottom up', and escalatory processes of political violence, links these reflections to two other significant works of recent historiography. Haim Burstin in 2005 offered subtle and thought-provoking reflections on the 'invention of the *sans-culotte*', advancing beyond the questioning of presumed social identities and rhetorical strategies acknowledged in the previous historiography. He identified as one of the key features of the *sans-culotte* identity the 'protagonism' of those who took it up: their eagerness to thrust themselves, as individuals, into leading roles on the local stage, and to broaden the bounds of their personal engagement as far as they could. In a subtle reflection on the dynamic, but also contradictory, relationship between such practices – productive of 'micro-oligarchies' of activists – and the language and structures of direct democracy that they claimed to embody, Burstin indicates the difficulty of assigning any decisive attributes of political or social character to such groups.[8]

Burstin also offers a multi-levelled exploration of how, 'from 1789, Parisian society became progressively saturated with violence', and how earlier precedents, cultural assumptions, and the feverish moods of political confrontation and alarm combined to bring this about.[9] This approach is seconded at the national level by Jean-Clément Martin, whose book-length 'essay' on violence and revolution ably counters both the essentialist demonization of conservative accounts, and the easy circumstantial dismissal of violence as a problem by the Marxist tradition.[10] Both works extend in time and space some of the core themes of this text: the complex web of personal responses to a public sphere that throbbed with the tensions between hope and fear,

[7] 'The micro-physics of Öffentlichkeit? Habermas, Foucault and the administration of democratic space in the Palais-Royal, 1789–1790', *Cultural and Social History* iii (2006), 1–22.

[8] Haim Burstin, *L'invention du sans-culotte; regard sur le Paris révolutionnaire*, Paris 2005; see esp. 116ff.

[9] Burstin, *L'invention*, 197.

[10] Jean-Clément Martin, *Violence et révolution; essai sur la naissance d'un mythe national*, Paris 2006.

the persistent attempts to insist on unity that end up creating further division, and the multiple dimensions of potential and actual violence that flourished on repeated indecisive confrontations of power and the people. In this context, a study of the months leading up to a particularly confused moment of potential political rupture remains, as I hope readers will agree, a significant case-study in the dynamics of the French Revolution.

David Andress
2013

Introduction

On 12 November 1793, a day of wet, numbing cold, a grim and unique ceremony took place on the Champ de Mars, the open space in south-western Paris where the Festival of Federation had been celebrated in 1790, and where today stands the Eiffel Tower. In 1793, for that one day alone, the centre of this vast space was occupied by the guillotine. A single victim journeyed there in the executioner's cart from prison in central Paris, reviled along the route by screaming crowds that twice attempted to break through the cordon of guards and seize him. Jean-Sylvain Bailly, astronomer, academician, doyen of the Third Estate in the Estates-General of 1789 and mayor of Paris from July of that year until November 1791, perished on that dank day for the crimes that the Republic laid against him, crimes that occurred in the summer of 1791.[1]

Bailly was accused of orchestrating, with Queen Marie-Antoinette, executed a scant four weeks earlier, the attempted escape of the royal family in the 'Flight to Varennes' of 21 June 1791. Further, and decisively, he was charged with plotting the massacre of 'patriots' which ensued on 17 July 1791, as they attempted to meet on the Champ de Mars to protest against the National Assembly's decision to reinstate the recaptured monarch. Hence the site of his execution. The tribunal's verdict on his guilt had noted that Bailly had 'thirst[ed] for the blood of the people'. Witnesses at the trial denounced the actions of Bailly's henchmen in the National Guard, who had 'pushed the people aside and showed no compassion for their appeals'. He was labelled as a representative of the upper bourgeoisie, working for a self-interested elite against the people.[2] The rhetoric of the Jacobin Republic here echoes some of the words of those who had themselves been caught up in the massacre and its aftermath.

17 July 1791 had been a day of turmoil in Paris. On the Champ de Mars, thousands of people gathered through the morning to oppose the will of the National Assembly. By evening, popular anger spilled onto the streets, reacting to the violent suppression of that meeting by the National Guard, the revolutionary citizens' militia. One telling incident occurred at around 10 p.m. in the rue Tirechappe, in the central Parisian Section de l'Oratoire. Here a group of journeymen shoemakers was drinking in a doorway when two

---

1 G. A. Kelly, *Victims, authority and terror: the parallel deaths of d'Orléans, Custine, Bailly and Malesherbes*, Chapel Hill 1982, 201.
2 Ibid. 200. Kelly's overall interpretation of Bailly's demise has several strands, including the hostility of Jacobins to the academic world that he represented. It also includes some rather loose usage of 'class' languages, which will be critiqued in a general sense below.

1

members of the National Guard passed by. The drinkers immediately launched into a tirade of insults,

> claiming that they [the Guardsmen] came from the Champ de Mars, where they had committed horrors, that all the National Guard had assassinated people, that they were beggars, villains, that their uniforms must be torn off them and not one left alive. . . . [The Guard say] that it was outsiders [étrangers[3]] spread through Paris who do ill, while it was the National Guard itself that did it, and was paid to do it.[4]

They followed this up, in the absence of further Guards to insult, with a murderous discussion about whether it would be better to stone local Guards with cobbles, or lie in wait and gut them as they left their homes. A group of local women, mostly artisans' wives, argued with them, and received a shower of sexual insults in return. One reported the claim of one journeyman that 'if he had what he had had two years ago, he'd kill several of them at once, that we had been to look for arms [then], that we had returned them, and that today [the arms] were being used against us'. The witness remarked that this was probably a reference to a pistol which the suspect had found during the events of July 1789, though she observed that he had, in fact, sold it.

Here, in the mouths of a group of Parisian 'wage-earners', we find a visceral, albeit alcohol-induced, hostility to the bourgeois of the Parisian National Guard, who had indeed committed a 'massacre' of radical petitioners on the Champ de Mars, killing perhaps as many as fifty.[5] At first glance, this is old-fashioned class-based social conflict with a vengeance, so much so that this view echoed in the normally universalistic language of the Jacobins of 1793 as they condemned Bailly. Moreover, such an interpretation has continued to dominate the historiography of the event, despite the general decline of such views of the French Revolution in recent decades. However, as this book will argue, examination of the hostilities which spilled over into violence on 17 July reveals a far more complex picture of social and political relations amongst the many groups who contested possession of the political arena in Paris in 1791.

The past generation has seen a fundamental shift in the direction and focus of the historiography of the French Revolution. The question of the social identity of actors in the Revolution, both individual and collective, has

---

3 The French *étranger* can equally well mean 'foreigner' and 'stranger', and in the eighteenth century a 'foreigner' could be someone from the next town. In Parisian usage it probably often did imply actual non-nationals, but since the city had an enormous immigrant population, this is of little help in specifying its target. The word 'outsider' will be used throughout to suggest the general 'alien-ness' that is implied.

4 APP, AA153:9–15, case of Louis Oré, 'nicknamed Normand', the only culprit detained from the group.

5 Although one of the oldest critical accounts of this event, the work of Albert Mathiez remains the most detailed: *Le Club des Cordeliers pendant la crise de Varennes et le massacre du Champ de Mars*, Paris 1910, repr. Geneva 1975.

been largely pushed off-stage, driven by impulses both evidential and methodological, and replaced by a concern with such actors' discursive identity. In carrying out this substitution, which is far from being without merit, historians have none the less tended to redirect their attention from those who performed social action towards those who generated discourse, and specifically written discourse as it survives in the archive. Thus the story of the Revolution has 'returned' to politics, and to the educated political elite, putting aside the concern with issues of social identity and interaction that marked the work of historians such as Mathiez, Lefebvre and Soboul.[6]

However, a broader view of this process should see it not as closing off the avenue of social exploration, but rather as opening it to examination from new directions. For, ironically, we now have a much more nuanced appreciation of social existence in the eighteenth century, especially within the great city of Paris, than was deployed by those earlier historians. Moreover, this new awareness has derived from work which consciously untangles the issues of 'social' and 'discursive' existence, in order to present such approaches not as exclusive choices, but as necessary complements to each other in pursuit of an understanding of urban life in this period.

What follows is an examination of the events in Paris that began with the clergy's large-scale refusal to swear allegiance to their new Civil Constitution in January 1791, and ended with the revolutionary National Guard's willingness to shoot and bayonet radical popular protestors on the Champ de Mars six months later. This study will reveal something of the massive disjuncture between the French Revolution's stated beliefs in liberty, equality and social inclusion, and the treatment of those who had most to gain from such beliefs, when they actively attempted to claim what had seemed after 1789 to be rightfully theirs.

The period between January and July 1791 was critical to the course of the French Revolution for a number of reasons. Not least was the growing popular and political realisation that throne and altar were still decisively linked, and by July firmly linked in opposition to the Revolution.[7] At the level of national politics, there can be little doubt but that this was the deci-

6   To select a few of the many works that might be noted here, the 'empirical' breakdown of the Marxist interpretation is documented in W. Doyle, *Origins of the French Revolution*, 2nd edn, Oxford 1988. G. Lewis, *The French Revolution: rethinking the debate*, London 1993, gives a pithy summary of the issues, as does T. C. W. Blanning, *The French Revolution: class war or culture clash?*, London 1998. G. Kates (ed.), *The French Revolution: recent debates and new controversies*, London 1998, presents various key texts, and also suggests that authors such as T. Tackett, W. H. Sewell, Jr, J. Markoff and C. Jones are beginning to sketch out a new 'middle way'. For a further survey of pre-1789 perspectives see V. R. Gruder, 'Whither revisionism?: political perspectives on the *ancien régime*', *French Historical Studies* xx (1997), 245–85.
7   For a detailed exposition of why this link might not have been so clear see D. van Kley, *The religious origins of the French Revolution: from Calvin to the Civil Constitution, 1560–1791*, New Haven 1996.

sive revelation of this year, and that the position in which Louis XVI had been placed by September, accepting a Constitution he had attempted to flee from three months earlier, marked a clear stage in the disintegration of hopes for a 'peaceful' Revolution. The spring and summer of 1791 also marked, however, a critical stage in the evolution of Parisian politics, which had their own convoluted dynamics. The king, as well as feeling himself compromised in his religious duties, also believed himself a prisoner of Paris, and it was from that fate in particular that he fled on the night of 20/21 June 1791, leaving behind an explosive denunciation of the Revolution's works in his own hand.[8]

The king's beliefs about the city, however, were an oversimplification. Parisian politics were sharply divided among a number of groups, whose attitudes to each other and to the capital's population were as antagonistic as any in France at that moment. The events that followed the Flight to Varennes were the climax of a long evolution of political suspicion and social fear, and pitched the city into turbulent uncertainty. On 25 June Louis XVI and his family had returned to Paris under armed guard, their coach watched by perhaps half the city's population as it made its way in sombre silence back to the Tuileries palace. In response to this flight, the standard-bearers of popular radicalism, most notably the Cordeliers Club, had already declared for a republic, and the Parisians seemed to have endorsed this, striking out the royal insignia everywhere from public buildings to coat-buttons. And yet the king was being manoeuvred carefully back onto the throne. From the morning of the flight's discovery, the word had gone out from the municipal and national authorities that the monarch had been kidnapped. Once he was safely back in Paris, a delicate series of interviews between National Assembly representatives and the king and queen negotiated an agreed line, even as others cried out for them to be tried as traitors. The Assembly began to debate the outcome of this process on 13 July, decreeing on the 15th and 16th that Louis was personally inviolable, had been kidnapped, and would resume his full functions upon his acceptance of the nearly-completed Constitution.

The response to this was a wave of radical unrest, expressed by some in violent crowd scenes outside the Assembly, and in more organised fashion by the proposal of a petition for a national consultation on the king's fate. Various texts were put forward, and the movement fell into the hands of those who had already declared for a Republic, the less forthright Jacobin Club withdrawing its support after the National Assembly had definitively voted on the matter. Activists from the Cordeliers Club and the other popular societies that had emerged in its wake since late 1790 gathered crowds on the Champ de Mars over that summer weekend. On the Altar of

---

[8]   This manifesto is reproduced at length in J. Hardman, *The French Revolution sourcebook*, London 1999, 128–36. The events summarised in the following paragraphs will be considered in more detail in later chapters.

the Fatherland, site of the ceremonies of national unity a year earlier, they now invoked the sovereignty of the people to save them from the rule of a traitor monarch. That was the subtext; it was, however, only a petition, and only to make appeal to the wider nation for a decision. Yet the politics of the city did not permit of such an innocent interpretation.

Since the disorders over the Assembly debate began, both the deputies themselves and the Paris municipality had been determined to press on in the face of such resistance. It was to them mere sedition, the product of faction playing on the gullible populace. Others amongst the political class were not so sanguine. Antoine-Joseph Gorsas, who would later serve as secretary to the Convention as it voted on the death of the king (and perish himself as a Federalist rebel), was then a journalist with considerable sympathy for the radical movement. Early in the evening of 17 July he was composing his next day's edition of the *Courrier de Paris dans les LXXXIII Départements*, and reflected on the troubles of the city: 'It is possible that in a few days we shall see the people armed against the National Guard, with which the legislative body surrounds itself, when it ought to surround itself only with [public] confidence.'[9] Gorsas thus envisaged the current crisis as a more radical division between the city and its authorities, and placed virtue on the former side, though he noted that all sides were 'led astray by perfidious suggestions'.

Gorsas went on to note that, 'At this moment, seven in the evening, the general alarm is being sounded from several directions. May the fears that we have expressed not be realised!' Alas, it would seem that they had, and for reasons, at least superficially, that Gorsas had already explored. Around midday, two men had been found in the space beneath the wooden stage that held the Altar of the Fatherland, apparently making holes in the planking. As a crowd of both men and women occupied the stage, it is now commonly supposed that they were little more than peeping-toms seizing an unusual opportunity to spy on female legs. However, such a simple explanation was not in favour in 1791. After being discovered and hauled out, the two men were dragged by an irate crowd to the police authorities of the local Section, where after an interrogation the crowd was assured that justice would be done. The crowd, however, was convinced that the men were plotting to explode a bomb beneath the petitioners. Seized again from the hands of the authorities, they were hanged and then beheaded, victims of the summary justice that had been a feature of revolutionary life since the *Prévot des Marchands* first antagonised a crowd before the fall of the Bastille. This violence was the trigger for an investigation by two *commissaires* from the municipality, who found the situation restored to calm, but learnt on returning to the Hôtel de Ville that the alarmed National Assembly had pressured Bailly into declaring martial law after the first reports of the deaths.[10]

9 *Le Courrier de Paris dans les LXXXIII Départements* (hereinafter cited as *Courrier*], 18 July 1791. Hereinafter dates should be assumed to fall in 1791 unless stated otherwise.
10 For accounts of this process see Kelly, *Victims*, 189–92, and Mathiez, *Club des Cordeliers*,

Gorsas clearly knew of the lynching as he wrote, and indeed was able to elaborate on the character of one of the victims: a military pensioner, his sources said, living in the nearby Invalides, and 'for a long time very suspect, even to his comrades'. Several of these latter were said to have observed him with large sums of money, and to have noted 'that he passed for being paid by the aristocrats [l'aristocratie]'. Moreover, the tale went on, 'he has often been seen in the groups where inflammatory speeches [motions incendiaires] are made'. This convolution of suspicion was entirely characteristic of the politics of 1791.

Upon the declaration of martial law, the National Guard was rallied to the colours, and marched in considerable force to surround the crowd on the Champ de Mars, which was in the region of 20,000 strong. It was here that, as Gorsas was noting the sound of the *générale*, the massacre took place. Two hours later Gorsas was able to record the first news he had of the affair: 'The first shots which are destined to divide the National Guard and the people have been fired on the Champ de Mars. Several citizens are killed or wounded. Paris is in the ferment which must foretell the unforeseen and truly incredible coalition of the two parties of the National Assembly.'[11] Turbulence went on into the night, though Gorsas found time for one last note before going to press: 'Midnight. Paris is fairly calm at the moment; all the streets are illuminated.'

We have already here an array of political judgements sufficient to warrant unpicking. Gorsas clearly believed that there was strong evidence of nefarious intent on the part of the men who died at the hands of the crowd, and that such intent was fomented by *aristocratie*. That necessarily counter-revolutionary force was one of the two *partis* that he saw reconciling themselves in the Assembly, for the king and against Paris. The National Guard, in his view, was also setting itself against the city, in some ways an extraordinary judgement, as some 80 per cent of its rank and file were volunteer part-time troopers from the better-off Parisian classes. The 'people' they confronted, and whom earlier in the evening Gorsas had predicted would arm themselves against the Guard, were of course the 'revolutionary people', whose identity might also be conveyed in the phrase 'all the good citizens', like the several reported killed or wounded above. Gorsas is suggesting a deep and complex rift in the revolutionary body politic, even as he piously hopes that his fears of this are ill-founded.

When we counterpose these views with the statement of the *Révolutions de Paris*, made some days later, about the lynching that precipitated the massacre, we find a further, more troubling, dimension of alarm: 'The true

---

132. G. Rudé, *The crowd in the French Revolution*, Oxford 1959, 89, is content to give the 'peeping-tom' account without mentioning the interplay with the authorities.
11 There is, of course, something 'writerly' about this hour-by-hour account of fears and alarms, but it is wholly untypical of the *Courrier's* usual style, and seems more likely to be an extraordinary response to an extraordinary situation.

people were those who wished to place the presumed guilty men [our two unfortunate voyeurs] under the blade of the law; brigands alone assassinated them.'[12] The *Révolutions*, which in general was more overtly radical than Gorsas, appeared weekly, and its views had been coloured by the reaction to the Champ de Mars events that had swept across the city, and more particularly across its press, from the 18th onwards.

The effect of that reaction on Gorsas's views was to be dramatic. After the breathless prose of the 17th, he was able the next day to compose a more studied account of that day's events, from which a fundamentally different interpretation emerges:

> The popular execution which took place in the morning, had pierced the good citizens with horror and disquiet. They saw with pain that the thousands of brigands that the aristocracy suborns in the heart of the capital, and who have for their lairs, not lodging-houses [hôtels garnis], but the town-houses [hôtels] of our emigrants, had mixed themselves with the multitude, whose sole object was to sign a petition, and they led them astray with inflammatory and fatal speeches.[13]

It was an 'infinity' of such brigands which had penetrated the crowd, and which posed resistance to the National Guard. They cried out 'that [they] must burn the Tuileries, storm the National Assembly, cut off some heads, slaughter the Bluecoats [the National Guards], and a thousand other horrors found on every page of Marat'. The Guards had endured a 'hail of stones' from such agitators before finally opening fire. In the aftermath, various events reinforced the element of deliberate agitation: 'a troop of vagabonds [gens sans aveu]' had carried a body through the city to provoke alarm, crying that fifteen hundred were dead; six workers were arrested wearing white cockades, symbols of Bourbon counter-revolution. Overall, Gorsas wrote, the events had been a plot conceived by 'enemies of the public good', intent on a restoration of despotism by means of unleashing anarchy. Gorsas saluted the Guard he had been so fearful of the previous day: 'Parisian National Guard, of which I congratulate myself for my membership, I should have accused you if you had been guilty. I must vindicate you when you have done nothing but your duty.'

With one stroke, as it were, the suborned aristocratic brigands that Gorsas feared had moved from plotting to blow up the petitioners to being an integral part of the crowd, albeit that many innocents remained within that crowd. The Guard, however, had undergone a decisive metamorphosis, from villain to hero. The *Révolutions de Paris* was less happy about the role of the Guard. In the same passage where it observed that the lynching had itself

---

12 *Révolutions de Paris*, 16–23 July. This account is attributed to Chaumette, Cordeliers Club member and future Hébertist *procureur de la commune*: Kelly, *Victims*, 193.
13 *Courrier*, 19 July.

been the work of brigands, it placed such men at the centre of the plot in provoking the wider violence. It observed none the less that

> if force had been provoked by brigands, it is against the brigands that it needed to be used. But no, they knew them, the brigands, and had them left alone, and the blind fury of the National Guard was directed against the authors and subscribers of a petition which was going to have its effect, and which is a crime that the committees of the National Assembly find it impossible to pardon.

The following issue of the *Révolutions*, which would emerge after the repression had been going on for almost two weeks, devoted page after page to pursuing this theme, and noted that 'the National Guards applaud their transformation into Janissaries'.[14]

This account retains ambiguities: for example, that the Guard's actions emerged from a 'blind fury [fureur aveugle]', directed by others onto an innocent crowd. The ultra-radical Marat's account in his journal, the *Ami du Peuple*, was more direct. In his view the crowd had been 'set up' by the authorities and the Guard themselves. Brigands lurked amongst the crowd, and a few stones and blank pistol-shots when the Guard arrived was enough to make the crowd 'appear to be so many mutineers, seditious rebels, assassins'. The brigands themselves were 'in the pay of Mottié', that is, the marquis de Lafayette, the general commanding the Parisian National Guard.[15] Ironically, of course, Marat has already been mentioned as providing fuel for the confrontation itself. A more conservative publication, the *Feuille du Jour*, felt no need to be ambiguous in its reporting. The entire episode was an offence against law and order, and it reported at length the deaths of two guards in the confrontation before noting laconically: 'On the side of the seditious are counted nine persons killed and about as many wounded. Twelve have been taken prisoner.' It concluded bluntly: 'Factious men! The end of your successes approaches; they have lasted too long; but tremble!'[16]

With this we come close to the unambiguous view of the authorities themselves, which will be explored in more depth later. All that we have reviewed so far is, of course, journalistic commentary, and it is possible, through the records of investigations at the time and in the following weeks, to get much closer to what actual participants told of what they saw and thought. Amongst the first to do so was Philippe Chapelle, aged thirty-three, maker of felt cockades, arrested in the early evening of the 17th near the Pont-Neuf by

---

[14] *Révolutions de Paris*, 23–30 July. The story of the two men killed was capable of further involutions. A sixty-six-year-old neighbour of the Cordelier Legendre testified to the later investigation that he had heard Legendre claim on the 18th that Lafayette had put the men under the *Autel*, and had also arranged for their killing 'to stir up people's feelings [pour échauffer les esprits]': Mathiez, *Club des Cordeliers*, 233–4, statement of Pierre Allemand, 25 July.
[15] *Ami du Peuple*, no. 524, 20 July.
[16] *Feuille du Jour*, 18 July.

a Guard sergeant and a cavalryman of the National Gendarmerie, and accused initially of having cried 'down with the National Guard'. Being 'dressed in the coat of a National Guard with a sergeant's epaulettes' compounded the offence. Two witnesses, a fifteen-year-old apprentice tailor and a twenty-four-year-old journeyman printer, elaborated on the incident. The apprentice had himself been coming from the Champ de Mars when, 'he saw [Chapelle] run from the Pont Royal as far as the Pont Neuf, shouting "down with the uniform of the National Guard, all in[to] bourgeois clothes", and also heard that he said to the public that there had been three thousand men killed on the Champ de Mars, and that his comrade had been killed'. The printer had a different version – Chapelle had said 'that all those who had no uniform were dying; come along and he would have them given arms'.

Chapelle denied any specific words, but said that he 'fled in the fear of being struck'. He had held a sergeant's post in the St-Eustache Battalion, but 'he no longer served at present because his situation no longer allowed him to serve'. He continued to wear the coat 'as having been given to him by the Nation, being a Conqueror of the Bastille [Vainqueur de la Bastille]'. None the less, he was sent to the neighbouring Conciergerie prison.[17] This (ex-) Guardsman at least seems to have had some doubts about the virtue of his colleagues, and similar sentiments were expressed elsewhere.[18]

At around 10 p.m. a Guard patrol coming down the rue St-Honoré, 'after having dispersed by gentle means a great number of gatherings it had met with successively along the said road', was nearing the Palais-Royal when it met a large group coming the other way. One man was in the lead, and he 'gave out great groans, in a very tearful tone, holding in his hand a handkerchief and rubbing his eyes, sobbing as if he were really crying'. The captain of the patrol heard him say 'our brothers, our friends are slaughtered [égorgés], we are all lost', amongst his wailings. Fearing that this would be 'a fatal example' and create 'general alarm' amongst 'the citizens of all ages and sexes' who filled the road, they detained this man, and another who was close behind, carrying a Guard coat beneath his arm, who would turn out to be another *Vainqueur de la Bastille*.

At this point a Guard *chasseur* accused the first man of having said about him, before the patrol arrived, 'he's a National Guard, we have to do away with him'. The *chasseur* now relieved his feelings by punching the prisoner in the face, 'while he was in the hands of the Grenadiers'. So much for 'gentle means'. When the *chasseur* testified to the *commissaire* this punch was not mentioned, and he said that the man had taken him by the lapels and said 'down with the blue coat, we should burn the blue coats'.

The detainee turned out to be Jean François Marie Michel Le Gueulx,

---

17 APP, AA215:460.

18 Most radical leaders were, of course, National Guards, and one at least, Momoro, was present on the *Autel de la Patrie* in uniform: Mathiez, *Club des Cordeliers*, 236–7, statement of Charlemagne Wassal, 25 July.

aged thirty, master innkeeper and a sergeant in the Guard, whose service went back to 14 July 1789. It was on the strength of this that he denied the *chasseur's* allegation – 'he was incapable of saying such a thing'. He had been overwrought, however, due to the sight of 'a dead man, that he had seen carried by four urchins [polissons] on tree-branches going beside the Palais-Royal'. He admitted crying out loud, but 'everyone said it loudly like him'. He denied the phrases the patrol had listed, claiming to have said, again along with everyone, 'that some of our brothers were dead'. After his arrest, his cries continued because of 'ill-treatment', notably the punch in the face.[19]

Whether one takes as more reliable the witnesses' or the detainees' statements in these two incidents, it is immediately evident that there was no simple division between Guard and people, or anyone else, at work on this day. Similarly, exactly where virtue lay is hard to determine. Alexandre Caguy, aged twenty-five, journeyman wigmaker, was chased down and 'battered with blows', according to a witness, by various persons on the Boulevard St-Honoré around 10 p.m. He had merited this by saying in the Place Louis XV 'that the National Guard had acted very badly, that M. de Lafayette was happy to see what happened on the Champ de Mars and that if he had been at Gros Caillou he would have done like the others and thrown stones'. Furthermore, 'all the National Guard were rogues [coquins] and he did himself honour for not having served the nation after such an affair'.[20] While Caguy was being beaten up for this, across the city in the rue de Sèvres most of the violence was on the other side. A Guard cavalryman was pulled from his horse and beaten by a crowd wielding sticks, 'to which he would have inevitably succumbed without the aid of the National Guard'. A patrol rescued him, but only after the mob had made off with his carbine, pistols and scabbard, and had tried to steal his horse. One man had been seized by the patrol, and the horseman confirmed that 'this individual had himself struck him with a stick'. Jean Maurel, aged twenty-six, a journeyman joiner, claimed on the other hand to have been on the scene with three fellows, returning from an inn at Vaugirard, and rather improbably asserted that he had been making 'some observations to defend the cause of the horseman' when the Guard arrived and seized him. It was simply 'not possible' that he should have been recognised as an assailant. None the less, he went into La Force prison.[21]

In all of these incidents, we seem rather closer to Gorsas's vision of a divided city than to his later tale of brigandage, and the incident we began with from the rue Tirechappe can only reinforce this impression. From the mouths of this abusive drunken group had come further ramifications of political suspicion. The brigands, 'the outsiders spread through Paris', who are blamed for disorder are in fact a cover for the misdeeds of the Guard itself.

[19] APP, AA85:85.
[20] APP, AA206:373–4.
[21] APP, AA166:16–17.

The defenders of 1789 are now betrayed. And clearly the level of hostility was sufficiently high for talk, albeit wild talk, of systematic murder. From the very same street, two other incidents further compound the situation. Jean Louis Mirbault, ladies' shoemaker and volunteer National Guard *chasseur*, reported on 18 July that the previous evening he had been dining by his open window at around 11.30 when 'he heard various remarks against the National Guard in general and against M. Lafayette concerning what had just happened on the Champ de Mars'. He recognised the speaker as 'Madame Garpant', his downstairs neighbour, and sought to intervene in the Guard's favour out of his window: 'Garpant replied that if he wasn't paid to support the National Guard and its chiefs he wouldn't take their side, adding that if he had as much trouble as others in getting the bread he ate he wouldn't support them.'

Mirbault was particularly protesting against this allegation of corruption, he noted, though doubtless being told 'he would kiss the arse of M. Lafayette and of his horse' did not salve his dignity either.[22] Having made his declaration and left, he returned only an hour later to record another denunciation of a neighbour in his house, one Londot, 'who calls himself a National Guard volunteer', and who 'had told him several times over several weeks that it was unfortunate that MM. Bailly, Lafayette and Montmorin hadn't been killed; that if they gave them to him he would rip out their hearts with his teeth; that they were traitors and their heads should have been paraded on pikes on 21 June'. Meanwhile, on the 17th, Londot had 'tried to lead off' Mirbault's workers to the Champ de Mars to swear an oath against royalty, and on hearing the call to arms that afternoon, had shed his Guard coat for civilian dress. He was a 'seditionary' who had 'all the vices of a bad citizen'.[23]

If we now pass these various elements and narratives in review, the number of competing versions of events portrays a situation that can best be summed up as political and social turmoil: a crowd which lynches two suspected brigands; news that the crowd itself is composed of brigands; a National Guard force which turns on the people; brigands who turn the people against the Guards; brigands who turn the Guards against the people; Guards who rightly fire on brigands; individuals who are arrested (and beaten up) for accusing the Guards of massacre; individuals who attack the Guards; individuals who threaten the Guards, accuse them of being brigands, and threaten to attack them; and individuals who condemn the Guards, the municipality and the ministry for starving them and conspiring with the king. Such a multitude of attitudes and accusations will clearly require careful unpicking.

---

[22] APP, AA153:7. The verb in question is, of course, 'baiser', which has an even less polite possible translation.

[23] APP, AA153:6, clearly timed, however, an hour after piece 7. Similar denunciations of dangerous figures, notably one Felix, promising death to Lafayette and/or Bailly, are noted by Mathiez, *Club des Cordeliers*, 262, 264–6, 268–9.

However, before beginning to explore more closely some of the ambigui-ties and contradictions that surrounded popular activity, something must be said about the nature and treatment of sources for this period. Like many other histories of the eighteenth-century French, this one relies extensively on the records of the police. It should be noted here that 'police' covers a multitude of archival possibilities, and for this period in particular, we are far from the hackneyed words of paid informers scribbling their prejudices in secret.[24] The primary 'police' documents that concern us are in effect more like judicial records, produced by the offices of the police *commissaires* of the Parisian Sections, who inherited their role from the *commissaires du Châtelet* of the Old Regime. This inheritance will be explored through its historiog-raphy in the following chapter, but we may note here that it was a role less of 'policeman' than of local magistrate and arbitrator. The documents as they survive are polyvocal, and take two main forms.[25] The first, and more straightforward, is the declaration. Here a citizen makes a notarised state-ment before the *commissaire*, perhaps to denounce a crime, or occasionally a political offence, equally often to put on record some minor neighbourhood dispute or odd event that they feel the authorities should be aware of. The declarant will sign the copy of the statement, and it will be deposited in the records of the local Section. More complex in form are the records which result when the police actually have an offender in hand. These commence with the words of the arresting officer, a National Guard, most usually a sergeant or corporal, who may have arrived on the scene only after the fact, but is none the less formally in charge of bringing the offender before the magistrate. Such accounts are usually cursory, and may not indeed indicate the actual essence of the matter. Far more circumstantial, and also frequently far more to the point, are the accounts of witnesses that are recorded next: one, two, perhaps as many as a dozen people of all conditions depose concerning whatever event or incident is in question.

The words of the police do not intrude into these accounts as they appear, and we may speculate as to whether or not they were 'prompted', but they certainly appear to represent what the witnesses desire to say, if we may judge by the marginal additions, deletions and substitutions which take place prior to the signature by each witness. The interrogation of the suspect which follows is definitely in the form of question and answer, however, often revealing in the wording of the questions the interplay between the witnesses' accounts and the police's social prejudices in describing a suspect's actions and motives. But the words of the detainee are given weight, and recorded, even when they dispute the police's interpretations openly, defame

---

[24] The strictures of Richard Cobb about the prejudices of the Parisian police have tended to colour assumptions about the value of 'police evidence' in this period: *The police and the people: French popular protest, 1789–1820*, Oxford 1970, 3–48.
[25] All these documents now form series AA of the Archives de la Préfecture de Police, Paris.

the witnesses and describe a wholly different set of events to that apparently seen by onlookers. The detainee, too, is invited to sign, and if they can, they usually do. The voice of the *commissaire* intrudes again in closing the document, sometimes with a simple decision on detention or release, sometimes with a paragraph of social and political vented spleen.

Do any of these voices tell the 'truth', in some grand sense? Of course not, but there seems no reason to doubt that they reflect what the various parties wanted to say, or felt they should say, in this particular situation, and what is certainly remarkable is the frequency with which self-expression takes a caustic form. Grovelling to authority on the part of detainees is a common strategy, but so is contesting the substance of the accusation, and even occasionally appealing to revolutionary principles. That all parties were busily interpreting events according to their own lights is a given, but that is precisely the interest of these documents, where so many voices are heard, giving so many individual views, and yet building up into identifiable patterns.

Something similar may be said of the discourses of the press in this period, from which our other main body of information is derived. Hugh Gough has noted that 'it is difficult to isolate the influence of the press from that of other forces at work in the revolution'. He goes on to conclude that the press 'reflected the diverse strands of public opinion and, at the same time, helped to form them'.[26] Jeremy Popkin is ultimately more assertive about the role of the press: '[it] served as the Revolution's real "public space" . . . made sense of the great crises of the Revolution . . . represented the diverse groups that were mobilized in the struggle for political power . . . [and] was vital to the functioning of all the other institutions of revolutionary culture'.[27] As Popkin's is the later, and more assertive, interpretation of the press, and as the words of the press will form a substantial part of the evidence deployed here, his statements merit further consideration. This is particularly the case, as they conceal a central problem in the history of the revolutionary press – its relation to its readership. To claim that the press was the Revolution's 'real public space' is thereby to assert that there was no other such space. To say that it 'made sense' of the Revolution's crises suggests that there were no other means of making such sense. And to claim that the press 'represented' mobilised groups implies that they were incapable of self-representation. Popkin is clear on this in his introduction: 'The political press was an indispensable symbol of the public opinion of a people that lacked the means to speak for itself.' It was also, however, 'a babble of voices' that continually disputed its own legitimacy of comment, and continually undermined all leaders' claims to represent 'the people', even as, Popkin asserts, the press was the prime organ of making such claims.[28]

---

[26] H. Gough, *The newspaper press in the French Revolution*, London 1988, 233, 235.
[27] J. D. Popkin, *Revolutionary news: the press in France, 1789–1799*, London 1990, 180.
[28] Ibid. 4–5.

This study will attempt to use the words of the press in a fashion rather more integrated with other potential modes of representation. Paris was the site, nascently in the Old Regime, and explosively in the Revolution, of an intense face-to-face political culture, evident at a variety of levels. In ascending order of concrete organisation, we might cite the street corner, the shop doorway, the pleasure-garden crowd, the café, the political club and the Section assembly as routine sites of politicised sociability, even leaving aside the occasional possibilities for the church congregation or the marketplace to produce such discussions. The press and its output was part of this world, but only part of it. Insofar as we are interested in the people who took part in such sites of politics, then the press can be seen to comment on, and to attempt to comment to, these people. Whether it can be said exclusively to inform them, to give them conceptual tools they would not have otherwise acquired, and to instruct them in the 'right' way to use them, is an impenetrable question, but one towards which our evidence would have to prompt scepticism.

Whether journalists were one-man operators or the mouthpieces of slick commercial enterprises (and we shall meet rather more of the former than the latter), they all projected voices into the wide field of public debate. One of the central points that will interest our study is the extent to which there remains, even after all the journalists' efforts to report and interpret politics, an irretrievable gap between much of what was expressed on the streets and the press's ability to integrate such expression, and the people who undertook it, with their general view of the Revolution. Although journalists did clearly occupy every spot on the contemporary political spectrum, we shall have to examine what notions their writings suggest that they held in common, and seemed unable to overcome, in their relation to the population of the capital and its often violent expression of politics.

Throughout this book, then, the words of police, witnesses, protestors, press, administrators and politicians will be extensively cited. They are all mere words, the babble of voices Popkin observes within the press becoming a deafening cacophony as one tries to encompass the city at large. We shall take individual statements, from whatever source, as we find them, elaborating on the underlying attitudes of some, leaving others for the reader's perusal. What matters in all of them is not generally whether or not a journalist was 'sincere' or 'manipulative', but in what directions that writing might move the ground of debate; not whether or not witnesses might exaggerate, but what view such speech, exaggerated or not, projected back into the public realm. It is this author's personal view that the Parisians who engaged with revolutionary politics were largely too caught up in the terrible importance of it all to make very good liars – they said what they said because at every turn they feared it might be a matter of life and death to figure out what was going on, and to alert others to nefarious possibilities. In the end, however, this book aims to disclose a general pattern of cultural and social beliefs, within which the question of individual veracity fades to insignificance. The documents give us the only picture we can have, and it is the historian's task to persuade the reader that the certain view of that picture put forward here is one worthy of consideration.

The view that we shall present here will be innovatory, not least because the events leading up to the Champ de Mars Massacre have rarely, if ever, been considered outside a fairly set, and limited, form. Early and mid-century accounts emphasised social conflict strongly, and Albert Mathiez concluded his account with the following observation: 'The *sans-culottes* had learnt what fondness the bourgeoisie, who had made the Revolution on their shoulders, nurtured for them, what respect it professed for legality, the word it had constantly at its lips, when its interests or its passions were at stake.'[29] Mathiez, in 1910, had offered a long account that focused on the organised socio-political conflict between the national and municipal authorities and the Cordeliers and other popular societies.[30] George Rudé's 1959 account approached the event from the direction of popular spontaneity, noting the importance of 'wage-earners' in the agitation of the previous days and months as part of a continuing evolution of a popular radical consciousness in the 'revolutionary crowd'.[31]

From these earlier accounts, later historians have retained the element of social conflict, even when modifying the focus of their work. George Kelly, in a narrative which takes mayor Bailly as its central character, has related how bellicose elements in the municipality and the National Assembly, acting to preserve the constitution against a democratic threat, pushed Bailly into deploying a National Guard 'hostile to the plebs', and allowing it to act decisively under martial law.[32] More general summary accounts tend to treat the conflict on the Champ de Mars as a simple, even self-evident, process.[33] Even that arch-revisionist text, the *Critical dictionary of the French Revolution*, sums up its impact with the statement that 'for the first time the bourgeois militia had fired on the people'.[34] One thing that is clear from the accounts of the

---

29 Mathiez, *Club des Cordeliers*, 149–50.

30 Ibid. 107–50.

31 Rudé, *Crowd*, 80–94.

32 Kelly, *Victims*, 182–97, citation at p. 188.

33 See, for example, W. Doyle, *The Oxford history of the French Revolution*, Oxford 1989, 153–5, which deals with the events, their antecedents and aftermath in three paragraphs. J. F. Bosher, *The French Revolution: a new interpretation*, London 1989, 156–7, deals with the turmoil in the capital between March and September 1791 in a similar three paragraphs. D. M. G. Sutherland, *France, 1789–1815: revolution and counterrevolution*, London 1985, 126–30, takes a little longer over the period, and at least recognises some confusion in the actual events of the massacre (at p. 129, largely thanks to a more attentive reading of Mathiez, one suspects), but in the end is pursuing a similar overall interpretation.

34 D. Richet, 'Revolutionary *journées*', in F. Furet and M. Ozouf (eds), *A critical dictionary of the French Revolution*, London 1989, 124–36, citation at p. 128. The events of the summer of 1791 here receive some twelve lines in total. One should add that the cited statement is true

journalists and witnesses quoted above, however, is that the massacre and its interpretations at the time did not fit easily into such a pattern.

Recent work on the politics of Paris before and during the early Revolution has introduced a number of complexities which render older accounts of the massacre problematic, while bringing us closer to an understanding of the dynamics expressed by witnesses at the time. Many of the new accounts themselves, however, do not mesh easily with those contemporaries' views. An important exploration of higher-echelon Parisian politics by Barry Shapiro, for example, concerns itself almost exclusively with machinations within what are described as a network of political factions, some of which had come together to form a 'Fayettist coalition', centred on the leadership of General Lafayette, in late 1789.[35] The text deals with the breakdown of this coalition by the later months of 1790, under the increasingly irreconcilable influences of popular radicalism and overtly 'aristocratic' or counter-revolutionary sentiments. What is most noticeable about this work from our perspective, however, is its insertion of popular pressure into the politics of the capital as a monolithic, self-evident *deus ex machina*, which decisively influenced the thinking of all politicians who were to any extent 'left of centre'. Political figures are here portrayed as rational actors in a mutually-understood power-game, only slowly becoming drawn further apart by apparently inexplicable (and certainly unexplained) external pressures.[36]

Such a view is in contrast to that of Gary Kates, who discusses the ideological differences that cut across municipal politics in the capital. The *Cercle social* group who are his particular focus attempted to advocate representative democracy, and to increase the power of a Municipal General Assembly, but were thwarted by the growing opposition between the authoritarian centralism of Bailly and General Lafayette, and the 'direct democracy' of imperative mandates and surveillance demanded by the more radical of the sixty neighbourhood Districts, prior to their replacement by forty-eight Sections in 1790.[37] Here there is no 'revolutionary crowd' in action, to be sure, but there is a conflict of ideologies and preconceptions which runs far deeper than mere power-plays.[38]

The work of Timothy Tackett on the creation of a revolutionary culture amongst the deputies of the National Assembly is relevant here. The deputies

---

only if one reads 'the people' to mean something like Rudé's 'revolutionary crowd', and then only in the most literal sense. The National Guard had confronted crowds, and driven them off violently, many times since the summer of 1789. See Rudé, *Crowd*, 61ff. for some examples.

[35] B. M. Shapiro, *Revolutionary justice in Paris, 1789–1790*, Cambridge 1993.

[36] Ibid. esp. pp. 77–9, 225–6.

[37] On the evolution of Parisian local institutions under the Revolution see M. Genty, *Paris, 1789–1795: l'apprentissage de la citoyenneté*, Paris 1987, and R. B. Rose, *The making of the sans-culottes: democratic ideas and institutions in Paris, 1789–1792*, Manchester 1983.

[38] G. Kates, *The Cercle social, the Girondins, and the French Revolution*, Princeton 1985.

had felt the influence of both popular approval and pressure in the course of their debates at Versailles, many Third-Estate representatives and budding radicals revelling in their reception by the crowds who flocked to debates. In the October Days, however, when Parisian crowds invaded Versailles, many had received a rude shock concerning the capital's population and its ability to take up arms, and this was manifested in something which was to be a continuing feature of Parisian politics: 'Increasingly, for a great many representatives, all public disturbances, all recalcitrance to authority, virtually any occurrence with potentially negative consequences for the patriot cause were construed as part and parcel of a generalized conspiracy.'[39]

Tackett goes on to say that conspiracy theories had been part-and-parcel of pre-revolutionary political life, in fact a 'cultural constant under the Old Regime at every level of society'.[40] We shall review further elements of this in the following chapter, but the fact of such theories' persistent presence does nothing to vitiate their consequences, both psychological and practical, at any particular juncture, and the situation of Paris in early 1790 seemed to reinforce the reasons for alarm and insecurity. The marquis de Favras, executed on 19 February for a plot to rescue the royal family, was only the most unfortunate of many who seemed to be plotting, almost openly, against the Revolution. In Tackett's reading, by the middle months of 1790 clear ideological 'Jacobin' and 'Capucin' parties had formed in the National Assembly, and the clash between patriots and aristocrats had become effectively institutionalised through clubs, meetings and journals. In this arena, both sides distrusted popular activity, and tended to view it as provoked by their opponents, thus leaving little room for popular pressure to be viewed as an independent force.

It is this approach which clearly underlies the thinking of many of the actors and commentators that we have already seen, but to this observation must be counterpointed the issue of what the people of Paris were actually doing by 1791. If, as appears evident, there was a turbulent popular politics on display in the open spaces of the capital, how did it interact with the equally complex currents of revolutionary political events? If popular pressure was not Shapiro's amorphous *deus ex machina*, what forms did it take, and how were the specifics of these moulded to the assumptions of the educated revolutionaries so as to allow the aggravation of tensions which led to the Champ de Mars Massacre? What was the deep background that made the conspiracy theories that Tackett observes such a 'cultural constant'? To begin to explore these questions, we shall turn in the next chapter to developments in the

---

39 T. Tackett, *Becoming a revolutionary: the deputies of the French National Assembly and the emergence of a revolutionary political culture (1789–1790)*, Princeton 1996, 244–5.
40 Ibid. 245–6. On the evolution and contours of conspiracy theory and its denunciation in this era see G. Cubitt, 'Denouncing conspiracy in the French Revolution', *Renaissance and Modern Studies* xxxiii (1989), 144–58.

broader historiography of the Parisian 'people' in the eighteenth century and the Revolution, before returning to the start of our chosen period, the moment when Paris awaited news of the clergy's response to a basic question: were they for or against the Revolution?

1

The People of Paris and their Historians

Having looked directly at the place of the Champ de Mars Massacre and its actors in historians' writings, several broader dimensions of historiographical development will need to be explored to lay the foundations for the study which follows: work on policing, neighbourhood and culture under the Old Regime; on cultures of the artisanate in the eighteenth century; on the identity of the *sans-culottes*; and on the elite perception of the urban population at the beginning of the Revolution. This will be largely, with some important exceptions, an anglophone historiography, and some comment on this is needed.

It would be unfair to say that French historiography of the people of Paris has not advanced beyond the viewpoint established forty years ago by Albert Soboul, but it is difficult to see developments within this field as substantially revising that position.[1] The presence of the historiographical trend marked most clearly by François Furet, which would dismiss concern with 'the people' (other than in terms of their use as a referent within discourse) as irrelevant to the real meaning of the Revolution, has led to a severe retrenchment by other French historians into defence of the notion of a 'popular movement' in Soboulian or quasi-Soboulian terms.[2] This hinges on the conviction that the artisans and traders who made up the leadership of the politically-radical Parisian Sections in 1793–4 were genuine adherents of a socially radical political philosophy – not yet socialism, but the closest the era could get to that state. Moreover, this schema also requires that these *sans-culotte* cadres emerged from a previously politically-quiescent milieu, learning their politics from the ideals of the Revolution, and that they represented a genuinely 'popular' appropriation of radical republicanism in the face of other political elements simultaneously less radical and less 'popular'.[3]

The continued weight of this view is visible, for example, in the work of Dominique Godineau, which takes Soboul's schema entirely for granted as a concrete basis to compare a female 'popular movement' with its male coun-

1   For which see A. Soboul, *Les Sans-Culottes parisiens en l'an II: mouvement populaire et gouvernement révolutionnaire*, Paris 1958, and the English translation (by G. Lewis) of parts of Soboul's work, *The Parisian sans-culottes and the French Revolution, 1793–4*, Oxford 1964.
2   Furet's critique began with the publication of F. Furet and D. Richet, *La Révolution française*, Paris 1965, and took more developed form in F. Furet, *Interpreting the French Revolution*, Cambridge 1981, before being institutionalised in Furet and Ozouf, *Critical dictionary*.
3   See Soboul, *Parisian sans-culottes*, esp. pp. 45–50, 248, 261.

terpart.[4] Challenges to that schema, most notably by Richard Andrews, have been treated as attacks to be repelled, when they have not simply been dismissed without consideration.[5] Andrews has suggested that the leaders of opinion and action in the Sections during 1793–4 were far closer to being 'bourgeois' than they were 'popular', and he has produced considerable evidence on the backgrounds of a large number of individuals to substantiate this. Further, he argues that the 'terrorist' agenda of price-controls, surveillance of suspects and deployment of armed force to appropriate the food supply was a means of diverting popular anger from a bourgeois Parisian leadership onto an outside, rural alleged counter-revolution. In the face of this, one defence of the Soboulian position, by Raymonde Monnier, was forced to admit the pertinence of Andrews's material commentaries, while quibbling over details and trying in the last instance to restate the identity of the *sansculottes* in terms of their own rhetoric – 'a movement which wished itself to be universal and fraternal'. Since the collapse of this rhetorical mask appears to be a *fait accompli*, it can hardly be reconstructed by pure assertion.[6]

The weight, and distorting influence, of the Soboulian legacy is again visible in the later work of Monnier, where she turns her attention to the 'democratic public space' of revolutionary Paris.[7] This work charts the rise, vicissitudes and survival of an associational democratic spirit within Parisian politics, from the level of the various popular societies that began to appear in 1790–1, through the complex internal politics of the city in the Jacobin period and the Terror, and into the attempts to close down the space for such activism in the later 1790s. Monnier's conclusions highlight the strong linkages between urban life and this political milieu:

> During the Revolution, political societies prospered in a city where communication was a given of daily life, through work-relations, leisure and neighbourhood existence. The geography of the fraternal societies in the spring of 1791 shows that this new sociability was developed through a neighbourhood economy, wedded to the dynamic of urban communication from one part of the city to another. It was grafted onto a set of relations in which the promenades, the public gardens, the cabarets and the cafés played a primary role;

---

4   D. Godineau, *Citoyennes tricoteuses: les femmes du peuple à Paris pendant la Révolution française*, Paris 1988, now translated as *The women of Paris and their French Revolution*, Berkeley 1998. An even more devoted following of a Soboulian schema, in a work claiming wider scope, is Genty, *Paris, 1789–1795*.

5   R. M. Andrews, 'Social structures, political elites and ideology in revolutionary Paris, 1792–4: a critical evaluation of Albert Soboul's *Les Sans-Culottes parisiens*', *Journal of Social History* xix (1985–6), 71–112. See also his 'Political elites and social conflicts in the Sections of revolutionary Paris, 1792–an III', unpubl. DPhil. diss. Oxford 1971.

6   R. Monnier, 'La Garde citoyenne, element de la démocratie parisienne', in M. Vovelle (ed.), *Paris et la Révolution: actes du colloque de Paris I, 14–16 avril 1989*, Paris 1989, 147–59, esp. pp. 152–3.

7   R. Monnier, *L'Espace public démocratique: essai sur l'opinion à Paris de la Révolution au Directoire*, Paris 1994.

they continued to be sites of exchange and discussion under the Revolution, parallel to the societies. The militants came there to inform themselves, to read, and to comment on the news. . . . [I]t was in the public places that the scenes of the conquering Revolution were improvised and acted out.[8]

As we shall see in the course of this book, Monnier's vision is, in many ways, a reasonable one, but the point that must be made here is that, in her work, it is entirely an assumed vision. When we turn to the chapter in which Monnier discusses the popular societies of the spring of 1791, we find neither a sociology of membership, nor an investigation of how society members might be placed within any of the turbulent events of that period. Rather, apparently unwilling to touch on the knotty question of how far the rank-and-file believed in the vision of a 'democratic public space', Monnier shows us how beautiful that vision was in the words of various educated popular-society leaders: François Robert, Lanthenas, Concedieu, Nicolas Bonneville, all lawyers and/or writers.[9] Like other works which have focused on the 'democratic' impulses of the Revolution, Monnier is fixated on the 'porte-parole', the spokesperson, whose discourse allegedly encapsulates (and perhaps guides) the thinking of the less-articulate mass.[10] When this is taken in conjunction with her statement that 'the classic analyses by Albert Soboul of the popular mentality, his portrait of the Parisian *sans-culotte*, have lost nothing of their value', it is clear that this line of analysis has reached an impasse.[11] Such attitudes to Soboul's work, for his followers, constitute a massive blocking formation, beyond which research cannot penetrate if it wishes to offer any other way of seeing the Parisian popular classes.

The extent to which precisely such new ways of seeing are required can be gauged from the work of two historians who have extensively illuminated the artisanal world that has been assumed to underlie the *sans-culotte* movement: Steven L. Kaplan and Michael Sonenscher. In a succession of works, while not always in total agreement, they have largely reconstructed our understanding of this area of the eighteenth-century French economy. Previously

8   Ibid. 232.
9   Ibid. 47–68, followed by a long section devoted exclusively to the thought of Bonneville at pp. 69–82.
10 A similar emphasis is found, for example, in the works of Jacques Guilhaumou: *Marseille républicaine*, Paris 1992, and *La Langue politique de la Révolution française*, Paris 1989. For some indication of the extent to which such figures as the spokesperson and, in a slightly different register, the 'cultural intermediary' have dominated French discussions of popular politicisation across revolutionary France in recent decades see C. Duprat, 'Lieux et temps de l'acculturation politique', *Annales historiques de la Révolution française* ccxcvii (1994), 387–400, introducing a special number on 'political acculturation'. I am grateful to Jill Maciak for drawing the extent of this focus to my attention. There are important distinctions to be drawn between educated figures who claimed to speak for the 'people', and those who set out to speak to them, but as I shall highlight in later chapters, in Paris at least, such distinctions often became fatally blurred.
11 Monnier, *Espace public démocratique*, 10.

assumed to be a collection of small, relatively stable workshop units with a virtually patriarchal authority structure, this can now be seen as a field of intense movement and conflict. Workers and employers existed in complex webs of customary and economic relationships, often complicated by administrative and legal claims. Guild and journeyman identities were only two of numerous pegs upon which self-assertion could be hung, and were themselves not representative of any consistent solidarities.[12]

When relating their work to the origins of the *sans-culottes* these authors have in general confined themselves to cautious speculations. Kaplan ended his article on intra-guild conflicts, for example, with the suggestion that the experience of power-struggles, cabals and corrupt electioneering may have educated men for a later role in the Sections. This, however, is as close as either writer has come to a view on the socio-political origins of *sans-culotterie*. Michael Sonenscher has been drawn into the field of speculations on the conceptual origins of the term and rhetoric of the *sans-culotte*. Suggesting at one point that the language of the popular movement was a political adaptation of a journeyman discourse used to assess their moral worth against their masters, he has also commented upon the creation of the image of the *sans-culotte* by educated politicians out of a stock of theatrical and republican images of the common people.[13] It is clear from this that the space for 'rethinking' these identities is broad.

Alongside the concept of a 'popular movement', the alternative avenue in past years for the study of Parisian popular activity in the Revolution has been the notion of 'the crowd'. The classic study in this area is that of George Rudé, dating from 1959.[14] The book is a clear and convincing refutation of the notion that the actors in the great revolutionary *journées* were no more than disreputable rabble. Beyond that, however, it has little to say. While the work has yet to be superseded as a piece of basic scholarship, its conclusions are remarkable for their simplicity: the 'revolutionary crowd' represented a

---

12 M. Sonenscher, 'Artisans, sans-culottes and the French Revolution', in A. Forrest and P. Jones (eds), *Reshaping France: town, country and region during the French Revolution*, Manchester 1991, 105–21; *Work and wages: natural law, politics and the eighteenth-century French trades*, Cambridge 1989; 'Journeymen, the courts and the French trades, 1781–1791', *Past and Present* cxiv (1987), 77–109; and 'The sans-culottes of the year II: rethinking the language of labour in revolutionary France', *Social History* ix (1984), 301–28. S. L. Kaplan, 'Réflexions sur la police du monde du travail, 1700–1815', *Revue historique* dxxix (1979), 17–77; 'Social classification and representation in the corporate world of eighteenth-century France: Turgot's "carnival" ', in S. L. Kaplan and C. J. Koepp (eds), *Work in France: representations, meaning, organization, and practice*, Ithaca, NY 1986, 176–228; 'The character and implications of strife amongst masters in the guilds of eighteenth-century Paris', *Journal of Social History* xix (1985–6), 631–47; and 'La Lutte pour la contrôle du marché du travail à Paris au XVIIIe siècle', *Revue d'histoire moderne et contemporaine* xxxvi (1989), 361–412.

13 For the former see Sonenscher, 'Sans-culottes of the year II'; for the latter idem, 'Artisans', and *Work and wages*, ch x.

14 Rudé, *Crowd*.

fair cross-section of the lower classes, their primary motivation for riot was hunger, but they were leavened with the political ideas of certain of the revolutionary bourgeoisie, and in the end their actions retained 'an element of spontaneity that defies a more precise analysis'.[15]

Beyond the banality of these observations, Rudé can also be criticised for his conceptual framework. His use of the words 'revolutionary' and 'popular' as virtually synonymous with a radicalising influence on politics masks questions of the actual modes of popular action, and ignores any activities which do not fit into his pattern.[16] Colin Lucas has highlighted these problems, although his retention of the ordering concept of 'the crowd' poses its own difficulties.[17] Lucas proposes a model in which the crowd, in its actions before the Revolution and in the events up to July 1789, looked essentially to the constituted authorities to right the wrongs about which it was protesting. The presence of the crowd was a temporary 'carnivalisation' of the normal modes of authority, even when this went to the extreme of lynching Foulon and Berthier after appeals for them to be tried had met with vacillation.[18]

From the October Days onwards, however, Lucas sees the crowd gradually moving closer to a position of real influence on the structure of power – moving the king to Paris, then in 1792 assisting in his dethroning, and by 31 May–2 June 1793 helping to reshape the legislature. This is a problematic analysis. In concrete terms, it could easily be argued that the true place of 'crowds' in Parisian politics under the Republic was in subsistence riots such as those of 25–6 February 1793, an episode that was roundly condemned by the revolutionaries in power.[19] Moreover, the *journées* of 1792–3 seem to consist of mobilisations by the radical societies and Sections, and disciplined action by a considerable portion of the Parisian National Guard – scarcely spontaneous popular activity.[20] Conceptually, Lucas relies on seeing 'the

---

15 Ibid. 208–9, 228–31.
16 A further observation that might be made on Rudé's analysis is that his sample of detainees for the Champ de Mars period, amounting to some 238 cases, is drawn from the period 14 April to 15 November 1791 (ibid. 82 n. 2, 93). This timespan begins after three months of political and religious agitation, and runs on into the late autumn, by which time a new constitution, a new mayor and a new National Guard commander had completely reshaped Parisian politics. These facts are not mentioned in Rudé's analysis, nor is any particular justification given for his timespan (it being, implicitly, a three-month/four-month slice either side of the massacre). Without such justification, it can only be viewed as arbitrary in the extreme, and liable to distort the picture of events he gives.
17 C. Lucas, 'The crowd and politics', in C. Lucas (ed.), *The French Revolution and the creation of modern political culture*, II: *The political culture of the French Revolution*, Oxford 1988, 259–85 at pp. 260–1.
18 Ibid. 267–9.
19 Robespierre, for example, dismissed the rioters as 'a mob of women, led by valets of the aristocracy', and not 'the people of Paris' at all: cited in C. Blum, *Rousseau and the republic of virtue: the language of politics in the French Revolution*, Ithaca, NY 1986, 198.
20 See, for example, L. Whaley, 'Political factions and the second revolution: the insurrection of 10 August 1792', *French History* vii (1993), 205–24, and the detailed study of the

crowd' as an entity, indeed almost an organism, in which an evolution of behaviour can be perceived. When considered closely this is of course an absurdity.[21] Crowds are composed of individuals who happen to be in a certain place on a certain occasion, and, regardless of whether they gather by chance or intent, their behaviour has to be grasped in terms of the understandings of the individuals present, which is to say in terms of their culture. Psychologists may agree that a crowd situation can liberate people from social restraints, and even carry its own dynamic, but it is unlikely that such a situation can generate new conceptions of sovereignty. If a crowd gathers for such a sophisticated political goal, then what that is must be in the minds of individuals before they 'merge' into the crowd. To look for evolution in crowd behaviour at such a level is a confused and obfuscatory way of probing for changes in political culture, which are surely more easily approached directly.

When Soboul and Rudé wrote their works on the Parisian popular movements and crowds of the Revolution, they seem to have had very little to go on in terms of an understanding of the preceding popular culture that might have shaped later developments. Rudé essentially neglects the issue in favour of a background that is principally historiographical – the history of the 'revolutionary crowd' displacing the Parisians' history.[22] Soboul's remarks on the nature of artisanal relationships clearly show that he envisaged the pre-revolutionary workshop as the patriarchal and essentially static environment that has been so effectively displaced by the work of Kaplan and Sonenscher.[23]

Both Soboul and Rudé assumed that an unmediated, direct concern with hunger was at the heart of popular concerns in this pre-revolutionary environment: crowds that rioted over food, and beggars that were tracked by the police, were the most visible signs of popular action. Twenty years later this continued to be the focus of research, in the work of Jeffrey Kaplow. Here, an admixture of Chicago-School sociology helped to produce a description of a helpless, fatalistic 'culture of poverty' in the Parisian streets and slums, policed into submission, and always on the verge of dissolution. Again, the

preparations for the 31 May–2 June uprisings in M. Slavin, *The making of an insurrection: Parisian Sections and the Gironde*, London 1986.
[21] A similar 'crowd-as-organism' approach is taken by B. Singer, 'Violence in the French Revolution: forms of ingestion/forms of expulsion', in F. Fehér (ed.), *The French Revolution and the birth of modernity*, Berkeley 1990, 150–73. This, however, deals with rather more 'visceral' incidents than Lucas's political turning-points.
[22] See Rudé, *Crowd*, 1–5, for the historiographical approach. His first chapter, 'Paris on the eve of the Revolution', begins as a geographical and socio-economic survey, and ends with observations on the ubiquity of concern over the bread supply: ibid. 11ff., 22–6.
[23] See Soboul, *Parisian sans-culottes*, where he remarks on the *sans-culottes'* hostile, but also ambivalent, relation to property (pp. 33–6), on the generally small size of economic enterprises (pp. 40–1), and comments that 'The small master-craftsman, working and living with his *compagnons* [journeymen], very often a former *compagnon* himself, exercised a decisive ideological influence on the latter. . . . It was the lower middle-class craftsman who fashioned the mentality of the worker' (pp. 50–1). Rudé, *Crowd*, 18–19, echoes the same view.

Revolution stood in the background of this picture as a formative, and trans-forming, event, inventing politics for these people as it seemed to have 'invented' them for the modern age.[24]

Doubts about the enormous condescension that this attitude betrayed surfaced slowly. Daniel Roche took another tack, neglecting (relatively) the records of the police for those of the notaries, examining what lower-class Parisians actually had, and where they lived. He disclosed a world already in transformation before 1789: cottons replacing wool, coloured print fabrics instead of fusty browns; ornaments, painted plates, prints, even books insinu-ating themselves into the lives of artisans and workers; the rapid circulation of a modern consumer economy, with its implications of openness and aware-ness, beginning to show through the Old Regime gloom.[25]

By the time that Roche's work appeared, the first of Arlette Farge's studies, on street-life in eighteenth-century Paris, was already in print.[26] This began to chart a territory of popular assertion, collective assumptions and actions that would be magnified in her study of such people's 'Fragile Lives' in 1986.[27] In some senses, the speed with which the image of Parisian popular life suddenly took on a kaleidoscopic hue suggests that earlier historians must have been wilfully blind, but such speed is of course misleading, and conceals substantial trawling of the pelagic archival depths. Farge's account, and David Garrioch's simultaneously-published analysis of neighbourhood and community, were both based on an in-depth study of police archives, what Farge calls 'the odd scrap, snatch of a phrase, fragments of lives from that vast repository of once-pronounced words that constitute the archives'.[28] These two works build up, from banal incidents recorded by neighbourhood police *commissaires* and, in Farge's case, the more detailed dossiers of the central police records, a picture which is far too intricate to be thoroughly summa-rised here. Suffice it to say that since their publication any consideration of events involving *le peuple* at this time must acknowledge their culture as complex, alert, and aware of the implications of their tense relationship with the elite of French society. Garrioch and Farge demonstrate the intricate interlacing of family and neighbourhood relations, gossip and opinion, work-culture, religion and superstition, along with the impact of adminis-

---

24 J. Kaplow, *The names of kings: the Parisian labouring poor in the eighteenth century*, New York 1972.

25 D. Roche, *Le Peuple de Paris*, Paris 1981, trans. M. Evans and G. Lewis as *The people of Paris: an essay in popular culture in the eighteenth century*, Leamington Spa 1987.

26 A. Farge, *Vivre dans la rue à Paris au XVIIIe siècle*, Paris 1979. This is essentially a collec-tion of contemporary texts, both published and archival, on street-life, with some commen-taries by Farge.

27 Idem, *La Vie fragile: violence, pouvoirs et solidarités à Paris au XVIIIe siècle*, Paris 1986 (cita-tions will be from the English translation, *Fragile lives: violence, power and solidarity in eighteenth-century Paris*, Cambridge 1993).

28 Ibid. 1; D. Garrioch, *Neighbourhood and community in Paris, 1740–1790*, Cambridge 1986.

tration and policing which gave popular life both vitality and perpetual instability.

The relationship with policing is particularly significant for what follows.[29] By the late eighteenth century, the mechanisms for policing Paris were hallowed with age, deriving in the most part from innovations under Louis XIV. Some earlier elements survived, notably in the City Watch [guet] and Guard [garde], based on medieval notions of urban self-regulation and service by lot, but even these had been invaded by substitution, professional service and bureaucratic control. Different elements of the city's economy, such as the ports along the river, the customs barriers and the city markets, had their own para-military police forces, and the regiment of French Guards [gardes françaises], billeted in the city, could lend more concentrated force, as well as manning routine guardposts.

Besides functions of overt public order, there were two other effectively separate elements of the policing function, which overall differed considerably from a modern conception of the term. 'Police' in the eighteenth century meant something like 'social administration', conveying the idea that populations, and especially great urban ones, were something to be actively managed. Thus the police controlled street-sweepers, licensed cabs, even registered wet-nurses. More directly, and this is the most sinister arm of the administration, they watched the population closely. A network of police 'inspectors' were charged with observing, controlling and inhibiting criminal and deviant activity of all kinds, operating through a variety of means, one of which was the enrolment of substantial numbers of paid informers from the criminal milieu itself. Such agents could themselves become actively involved both in the apprehension of criminals, and in the darker side of the more corrupt relationships that easily developed in this secret world. Moreover, this police was charged with the operations of *lettres de cachet*, the 'sealed letters' on the orders of which anyone could be detained at the royal pleasure, often being seized from off the streets. It is this image of the police that prevailed in the literary critiques of the Old Regime and, as we shall see later, was to be perpetuated into the Revolution to the confusion and disadvantage of all.

However, there were also more sanguine sides to the relationship between police and population, particularly in respect of the work of the *commissaires* of the Châtelet court. These men were part of the Old Regime system of venal office-holding: they had purchased their offices and public functions as investments in social status, but as Richard Andrews has recently argued, they were also a dedicated part of the system of 'social administration' with

[29] On this topic in general see A. Williams, *The police of Paris, 1718–1789*, Baton Rouge 1979; D. Garrioch, 'The police of Paris as enlightened social reformers', *Eighteenth-Century Life* xvi (1992), 43–59, and idem 'The people of Paris and their police in the eighteenth century: reflections on the introduction of a "modern" police force', *European History Quarterly* xxiv (1994), 511–35.

which we are concerned.[30] As *commissaires* they resided in the neighbour-hoods, or 'quarters' of the city to which they were assigned, and provided a permanent centre for the reporting and management of issues of public order and criminality, and also for the registering of complaints and grievances, the arbitration of disputes and the swearing of statements for instigation of more formal legal proceedings. Their job was to 'know' their quarter, to provide justice with a local, albeit firmly paternal, face. However, they were also used successfully by the local population for a number of purposes, highlighting the complex reciprocity of the 'policing' relationship. Their function as a taker of statements and depositions was obviously of much use to a litigious and disputatious population, and might also be used simply to make a 'public' statement concerning a dispute with neighbours or business associates. Recourse to the *commissaire*, as Garrioch's studies show, functioned as part of a web of neighbourhood regulation, where state and community norms blended, not ever seamlessly or without tensions, in the interests of the inhabitants. That this was the case in general did not prevent riot from breaking out on occasion, or the existence of long-standing grievances and feuds. It also did not prevent a slow deterioration of these webs of control from mid-century, allied to another dimension of increasing tension between population and authorities.[31]

It is this latter dimension that Arlette Farge elaborated in 1992, through her concept of the evolution of a 'popular' opinion in this era, paralleling the formation of public opinion in a 'bourgeois public sphere' asserted by Jürgen Habermas, but at a level less elevated, less 'enlightened' and less accessible.[32] In order to trace the evolution of the kinds of popular awareness that would be in place by the 1780s, it is necessary to go back almost to the first years of the eighteenth century. Farge begins by noting that in the years around the Orléans Regency in the 1710s and 1720s, the *peuple* was seen by the elite as little more than a source of anecdotes, particularly tales of crime and death. The people collectively appeared to their eyes only as the joyful or afflicted audience to royal ceremonies, as the dark background to criminality, or as a surging mass in formless riot. This is not to say that the police, meaning here the clandestine networks of observation and arrest, took no interest in what was said on the streets of Paris, but their pursuit of sedition was conducted

30 See R. M. Andrews, *Law, magistracy and crime in Old Regime Paris, 1735–1789*, I: *The system of criminal justice*, Cambridge 1994. David Garrioch's works, above, had, of course, already done much to draw the nature of these officers to historical attention.
31 David Garrioch has studied the longer-term evolution and decline of neighbourhood self-regulation amongst an emergent 'bourgeoisie' in *The formation of the Parisian bourgeoisie, 1690–1830*, Cambridge, Mass. 1996.
32 A. Farge, *Dire et mal dire: l'opinion publique au XVIIIe siècle*, Paris 1992 (citations will be from the English translation, *Subversive words: public opinion in eighteenth-century France*, Cambridge 1994), introduction at pp. 1–5. For a critical evaluation of Habermas's formulation, and a survey of recent debates relating to it see B. Nathans, 'Habermas's "public sphere" in the era of the French Revolution', *French Historical Studies* xvi (1990), 620–44.

27

more as the search for the unconditional obedience expected by absolutism than as a hunt for organised opposition. What they began to find by 1730, however, as the long-running dispute between the state and the Jansenist tendency amongst the clergy entered a new phase of rigour, and the 'convulsionaries' of St-Médard responded with apocalyptic prophesies, was a massive popular response, a 'deafening' chorus of comment and protest. The police reports reflect astonishment on two fronts, firstly the sheer determination and firmness with which members of the 'simplest folk' took sides, and secondly that they were capable of expressing themselves with such conviction and reflection on the issues involved.[33] The authorities took refuge, as they were to continue to do, in talk of agitation from 'above', but the opposition of the Parisian people to anti-Jansenist campaigns was likewise to continue through the century.[34]

Discontent in the early part of the century emerged almost exclusively in terms of comment and satire on court life, encouraged by the deliberate publicity of that milieu. As Farge interprets it, the war declared on Jansenism since 1728 was felt by the people as a betrayal by the king, who did not fulfil the role of a monarch as perceived in the memory of the great days of Louis XIV. Every aspect of his personality and actions came under criticism, setting a trend that was to continue throughout his long reign. In the atmosphere of police kidnappings of clergy and the arrest of those who spoke out, Parisian opinion lost all sympathy with the king, and with those who pursued the 'good priests'. From this epoch came a rash of stories, rumours and reported writings against the court and Church, where the episode of the convulsionaries combined with a metaphor of woman as purity: women of the people scandalously abused by clerics, royal officers committing rape in their carriages, a rapist marquis left unpunished while his victim died, and even a servant of the police lieutenant-general impregnating all nine charity-girls brought to his house to do some embroidering. Farge argues that the stories helped to fill in the conceptual gaps left by the tearing of the social fabric this controversy represented – the assault by Church and king on the purity of Jansenist religious feeling.[35]

Beyond the use of metaphor, the Parisians were also quite capable of voicing material and political concerns, which were frequently glossed over by the police observers who wanted only to show a general picture of satisfaction or unreasoned discontent – popular speech in its proper place of sociopolitical vacuum. In September 1729 the birth of the dauphin supposedly 'caused general satisfaction to all', prompted by thoughts of general tranquillity and a possible tax reduction. So one agent summed up, before going on to

[33] Farge, *Subversive words*, 23–5.
[34] For the history of Parisian Jansenism in all its manifold implications see van Kley, *Religious origins*. Garrioch, *Formation*, also offers an account of the impact of these disputes within parish life in the early eighteenth century.
[35] Farge, *Subversive words*, 66–71.

record a whole series of articulated concerns – possible shifts in the court power-balance, economic discontent at the closure of businesses ordered for the celebrations, continued unhappiness with the rule of Chief Minister Fleury, and new dubious royal actions to ponder, such as the brutal rejection of a petition to restore privileges to humbler inhabitants of Versailles. Beneath the bland surface painted by the police, their own reports showed a popular opinion engaged in active discussion of the latest events, shifting with the smallest changes from above, seldom unanimous, but always separated by barriers of suspicion and rejection from what the police apparatus would wish them to think.[36] If at this time 'opinion' was still a matter of direct responses to particular events, its evolution into something wider was to go on at an ever-accelerating rate.

Underlying Parisian discourse were the perpetual themes of material existence – concern over dearth and high prices was 'obsessively present' even in relatively good times.[37] Food shortage could trigger riot, as could the processes of policing and justice – prisons rioted in 1720, 1740 and 1770 when they were packed to overflowing with the destitute victims of hunger, in 1720 a round-up of vagrants caused street-fighting and in 1750 a similar operation that drew into the police net the children of respectable artisans provoked serious disorder, which will be looked at in more detail in a later chapter. The crowd invited to the spectacle of the death penalty inflicted at the Place de Grève was not always an approving witness – 'taking place at the foot of the scaffold was a history of violence and passion which could so easily be turned against the current order'.[38] The forces of order were always on prominent display at these, frequent, events, as the monarchy explicitly tried to take 'history', particular narrative, which might invoke a judgement on the particular justice of this or that condemnation, out of a supposedly timeless ritual expression of absolute power.

Exploring the people's sources of information, Farge comments on the *nouvelles à la main*, manuscript gossip-sheets copied and circulated surreptitiously to subscribers in Paris and elsewhere, for which there was a huge demand in the eighteenth century. News came from the servants of the great for a price, and was recirculated to various markets. The full-length versions tended to have a more elevated audience, due to the cost of a regular subscription, but it was common for the copyists producing them to make an illicit extra copy which they could reproduce in abridged (and sometimes embroidered) form in their own time. For as little as two or three *livres* per month, a subscription would buy several such issues each week, and a policeman noted in 1730 that 'we have seen several shopkeepers and workmen in the rue Montmartre who are receiving them at that price'. Thus

---

[36] Ibid. 71–4.
[37] Ibid. 88.
[38] Idem, *Fragile lives*, 181. A section of this work (pp. 177–204) is devoted to the multiple and ambiguous meanings of popular 'participation' in this display of royal power.

the population was far from the uninformed mass it was still commonly assumed to be, and from around 1745 the police went so far as to create socially useful news to slip into the *nouvelles*, at the same time as their reports continued to milk them for information.[39]

Farge remarks that these products were avidly and universally consumed, even though there was a simultaneous expression of scorn for the possibility of it all being true – not an unfamiliar response to us. In the eighteenth century part of this avidity, argues Farge, came from the conviction that information was continually 'being manipulated by the complex strategies of the court, the police, and the petty hordes of the evil-minded'. Thus the aim was always to try to get ahead of the game, before the news could be distorted in retransmission. As is often the case, the attempt to control information which is basically in the public domain ended by increasing the speed and volume of its circulation. Paradoxically, while both official and more enlightened opinion through the century continued to ridicule the notion that the people were worthy of being informed about public life, or even had the right to opinions on events, there remained a tendency for the elite to believe news just because it was the talk of Paris – even to the extent of crediting some of their own fabrications.[40] All these aspects of the volatility of news, and its contentious quality, would reappear with new emphasis in the Revolution.[41]

Farge also examines the cases of those confined in the Bastille for their seditious words across the century from the start of Louis XIV's reign, observing there, as with the wider public world, a growth in dissent, especially focused on religion, and on the king's body.[42] These two themes would come together when the unemployed servant Damiens, inspired by Jansenist religious ideology, stabbed the king in 1757, an event which produced an explosion of police repression of seditious speech.[43] From this

---

[39] Idem, *Subversive words*, 26–9, citation at p. 29. Two *livres* would equal a day's wages for a skilled craftsman, perhaps two days' for a labourer.

[40] Ibid. 31–3, citation at p. 32.

[41] Production of *nouvelles à la main* continued up to, and into, the Revolution. Benoite DuPrey, a twenty-eight-year-old woman arrested on 11 May 1791 in the Section de la Place-Vendôme, had lived in Paris, disguised as a man, for eight years, working as a public letter-writer, which for over three years had also included copying *nouvelles* for a variety of employers. Eighteen months in the Hôtel-Dieu with a 'slow fever' had left her/him destitute, and a church porter had taken him/her in, a charity rewarded by an attempt to swindle him with forged letters from DuPrey's supposedly wealthy mother: APP, AA206:235. DuPrey was imprisoned, but released with the warning to dress as a woman in future: APP, AB323:717, released 25 May. See also E. Wahl and F. Moureau, 'Les Nouvelles à la main en 1788–1789: idéologie et contrastes des gazettes manuscrites', in P. Rétat (ed.), *La Révolution du journal, 1788–1794*, Paris 1989, 139–47.

[42] The 'body politics' of this era have, of course, become an expanding field of work in recent years. See S. E. Melzer and K. Norberg (eds), *From the royal to the republican body: incorporating the political in seventeenth- and eighteenth-century France*, Berkeley 1998.

[43] Farge, *Subversive words*, 125–75. She contrasts her 'long-term' interpretation with that of

point on Farge detects an acceleration in the evolution of sentiment. She notes that from 1760 the modes of popular speech, writings and placards began to take on 'a life of their own' that the police could no longer keep up with: 'a speed which nothing could halt. . . . The political climate settled into a period of permanent criticism shared by all, great or small'. What is involved here is 'a refinement in cognitive and reflective capacities', a move away from criticism focusing physically on the king, to an engagement with 'another kind of politics, removed from him, which interested everybody'. War and its accompanying dearth and taxes were a central focus in 1760–3, and when an employee at the Hôtel de Ville was warned by a neighbour that he could end up in a dungeon for his comments on royal glory and popular hunger, he replied 'I care not at all, for they will not say that I am a rogue.' Speaking ill of the king still brought its punishment, but it had lost its infamy – indeed the shame seemed to rest in staying silent.[44]

Criticism continued to resound into the dying years of Louis XV's reign, when under the Chancellor Maupeou attempts were made to rein in élite resistance to the state.[45] Reasserted absolute power, and an accompanying clerical reaction, seeming to bring with it a crisis in provisioning, stimulated protest and anonymous pamphlet libels, for which once more the punishments intensified. Against this background Farge paints a further shift in the nature of the sedition pursued between 1768 and 1775:

> [Prisoners in these years] had clearly advanced to a state of mind in which criticising the king seemed such an obvious thing to do that they wasted little time on it before going on to clamour for 'the right to speak and write on any matter of State'. The vocabulary changed, and the political reflection became more sophisticated, day by day.[46]

Even topics of resistance to despotism and popular consent to government made their appearance. For Farge the most interesting element in all this is the assertion that to hold opinions and discuss public affairs was 'not just a legitimate act, but an inalienable right'. The police regarded this as clear evidence that a subject was no longer in the proper relationship of deferential love towards the king (and was perhaps therefore deranged), even if detainees explicitly argued that one could love the king and criticise the court. Perhaps the police were right, at least about the lack of love, since Louis XV's death passed amid indifference, while the subsequent exile of Maupeou was greeted with raptures, only to turn to anger as the dearth

D. van Kley, *The Damiens affair and the unravelling of the ancien régime, 1750–1770*, Princeton 1984, which argues that the juncture of the late 1750s was especially significant for the emergence of such sedition.
44 Farge, *Subversive words*, 179–81.
45 The classic modern study of this episode is D. Echeverria, *The Maupeou revolution: a study in the history of libertarianism, France, 1770–1774*, Baton Rouge 1985.
46 Farge, *Subversive words*, 190.

returned, and violence as widespread shortages prompted riots in the 'flour war'.[47]

Farge noted in her earlier work that the general population of Paris had established by the late eighteenth century 'a kind of tenacious harassment with regard to all forms of authority, or almost'. Des Essarts's *Universal dictionary of police* of 1786 commented that riots, gatherings and sedition were 'only too common, in spite of the active vigilance of the police'.[48] It seems that the problem of insubordination in general was a growing one through the century, matched by an increasing police effort at containment. Observers by the 1780s acknowledged this, but tended to be sanguine about the possibility of serious disturbance – Louis-Sebastien Mercier noted that 'in general, it has become impossible for a riot to degenerate into sedition', due to the heavy repressive forces available.[49] This complacency was perhaps based on the same notion as the tactics of the police, that sedition was caused by outsiders and 'bad elements', who if they were watched closely enough could be contained. Farge demonstrates that this was not so, that riot and disorder came from the heart of a population that lived

> forever on the lookout for what might prove threatening to it and in search of whatever might strengthen it. It was looking for equilibrium at the heart of a fragility by which it was almost totally defined. . . . Not being taken for a fool was one of its passions or rather one of its necessities, and thus the whole of its intelligence was put into not being abused or deceived. From this came its taste for news and gossip; its desire to know and understand; to give things a name; and the speed with which it circulated its information.[50]

As we have seen, from early in the century it was commonplace to expect deceit from the authorities, to resist that deceit through the deployment of alternative understandings and rumours, and to hold in reserve the possibility of overt physical resistance should the situation become intolerable. Moreover, the decades from 1720 to 1770 saw a distinct evolution in senti-ment. The causes behind this change are not discussed by Farge – exploring them would involve venturing into areas far removed from the judicial archives, and any link that could be made with 'enlightened' culture would of necessity be almost entirely speculative.[51] It seems clear, however, from Farge's work, that by the commencement of Louis XVI's reign the unques-

---

47 Ibid. 191–2.
48 Idem, *Fragile lives*, 258.
49 L.-S. Mercier, *Le Tableau de Paris*, textes choisis par J. Kaplow, Paris 1979, 318. (Original publication Amsterdam 1782–6, although this collection contains comments on events of 1787–8 which indicate that a later edition has been used.)
50 Farge, *Fragile lives*, 285.
51 Such speculation may not of course be entirely unjustifiable, but it does not essentially concern us here. For examples of what can be said in this direction see R. Chartier, *The cultural origins of the French Revolution*, Durham, NC 1991, and K. M. Baker, *Inventing the French Revolution: essays in French political culture in the eighteenth century*, Cambridge 1990.

tioned legitimacy of absolute monarchy had been undermined, even at street-corner level, by arguments which point, however hesitantly, towards the development of a self-conscious polity. Farge may be overstating her case to see some autonomous 'popular public sphere' forming, but it is certainly valid to recognise that the possibility of a non-deferential mode of expression was a significant innovation, and an ominous one for the security of the absolutist regime.

The 'famine plot persuasion' of the eighteenth century, documented by Steven Kaplan, offers further evidence of the increasingly intractable problem faced by the authorities in their elaborate efforts to control the population and its thoughts. While no less destabilising in its effects than the scorn poured on the king, this complex of beliefs about the food supply none the less relied heavily on the centrality of the royal role.[52] In every decade from the 1720s on, the same elements of alleged conspiracy reappeared. Underpinning the whole framework was the universal assumption that France was a land of boundless fertility, where any dearth that arose must be due to deliberate agency. This tendency was augmented by the reluctance of the police apparatus to admit that difficulties might be caused by factors outside their control, such as the weather, rather than by miscreants that could notionally be brought to book. When shortages occurred, the first assumption of people from all social classes was that there was some organised body profiting from the resultant price-rise – often such accusations embraced unpopular court factions, royal or ministerial mistresses, bankers or tax-farmers. Failure of government to intervene was seen as a sign of complicity, while if the ministry attempted to ease the shortage by imports and movements of grain, this opened up a panoply of new charges: the grain was spoilt and dangerous, it was French grain exported and now re-imported at a premium, more was stockpiled than the government would admit, any rotted grain thrown into the rivers was actually good stock disposed of to keep the price high, and so on.[53]

Despite the best efforts of government to explain away such fears, the famine plot idea continued to grow, and from the liberalisation of the grain trade in 1763–4 to the 'flour war' of 1775, it was 'a quasi-permanent mental set' among everyone from common artisans and labourers to provincial *intendants* and *parlementaire* magistrates. The liberalisation itself was an obvious gift to speculation, and as the grain price began to rise in the late 1760s, the government's attempt to isolate Paris from the impact of this led to belief in a plot to obtain a 'royal grain monopoly'. The re-imposition of control under Terray in 1770–1 and the vesting of purchasing powers in a public corporation did nothing to allay these suspicions (or rather convictions) – the diarist

---

52 S. L. Kaplan, *The famine plot persuasion in eighteenth-century France*, Philadelphia 1982, 2.
53 Ibid. passim, esp. conclusion and pp. 63–4.

Hardy noted in 1773 that Terray was 'suspected perhaps rightly of favouring the Monopoly and the Export of grain'.[54]

Louis XV died in disgrace, and the famine plot persuasion had no little to do with this. It continued, moreover, to ravage the governments of his successor. Turgot freed the trade again, prices rose and the flour war erupted across the Parisian region.[55] The minister gave a new twist to the plot mentality, blaming popular violence on agitation from the deprived monopolists and disgruntled police, but even after his fall, rumours of further conspiracies in the grain trade continued into the 1780s.[56] Part of the crisis of 1789 was a re-eruption of this theme, as 'aristocratic' speculation and exportation of grain were added to the political crimes of the Second Estate. The Parisians' march on Versailles in October 1789 further illustrates one of Kaplan's main conclusions – the centrality of the king to the complex of beliefs encompassing subsistence issues: 'According to the unwritten compact between king and people, in return for their submission, the king promised to assure their subsistence. . . . If the king failed to act or (it amounted to the same thing) if the subsistence threat persisted or worsened, that was proof enough of some kind of plot.'[57]

The later decades of the century were also marked by government measures in other fields of life which inflicted alarm and bred suspicion amongst the *peuple*. The abolition of the artisans' guilds, engineered by Turgot in February 1776, was greeted and foreshadowed by a storm of protest from guild masters, using every kind of abuse to condemn the character of the journeymen and workers who would be 'freed' from their control, and predicting the breakdown of both law and order and the economic system.[58] In this we can see a continuation of the condemnation of the lower orders as unthinking rabble, who have to be held to their places and tasks by the threat of force. It is curious that this kind of opinion should emerge from bodies whose members had, by definition (or at least in theory), occupied the status of journeymen themselves in previous years. Moreover the guilds were the site of intense factional conflicts, severely undermining the notion of solidarity and control they based their claims on, and in fact often aligning masters and their journeymen together against regulatory controls they saw as usurped by opposing cabals.[59] Whatever reservations we have about the masters' world-view, it has to be acknowledged that the workers themselves

---

[54] Ibid. 53–7, 59.

[55] For a detailed exploration of this episode see C. A. Bouton, *The flour war: gender, class and community in late ancien régime French society*, University Park 1993.

[56] Kaplan, *Famine plot*, 60–1 and n. 316.

[57] Ibid. introduction and conclusion, esp. pp. 1–2, 66–7.

[58] See idem, 'Social classification'.

[59] See idem, 'Character and implications'. Abuse of the system meant that not all masters had actually been journeymen, but their ideology rested on perpetuating that myth.

reportedly fell into an 'insolent rapture', and 'independence' began to be manifest even before the promulgation of the edict.[60]

By mid-March it was felt necessary for the police to begin to crack down on workers 'deserting' their masters without completing agreed work, and orders were given that all 'disobedient journeymen' should be jailed. The diarist Hardy noted the repression with relief, along with a rumour that the king had ordered journeymen to remain with their masters for a year. Police patrols by both day and night were stepped up, and the French Guards had to intervene in several incidents. Meanwhile the police were overwhelmed with people wishing to register in business, and had to resort to pretexts to send them away – asking for proofs of capital or probity nowhere mentioned in the edict, for example.[61]

The whole process of chaotic levelling had clearly undermined the guilds' attachment to a government which could resort to such measures, while on the other side of the dispute the workers' experience was of 'perplexity, frustration and [a] sense of betrayal . . . they found themselves treated as quasi-delinquents and would-be insurgents. . . . Instead of being welcomed into the milieu of commerce, they encountered delays . . . that seemed like tricks devised to fool them and deny them satisfaction'.[62] Which, it must be said, is very much what they were.

Turgot was dismissed in May 1776, the edict was in *de facto* suspension by the next month, and in August a new edict re-established the guilds, and in particular 'the domestic authority of the masters over their workers'.[63] Michael Sonenscher has observed that this reassertion of masters' control was part of a process whereby workers were stripped of much of their independence and power in the eyes of the law during the eighteenth century.[64] In earlier decades, it had been common for collective master–journeyman disputes over rates of pay, working hours and conditions to be arbitrated through the courts, but in later years a growing concern for social discipline allied to a stricter view of the employment relationship to strip away the legal safeguards the journeymen argued for under 'natural law'. The post-1776 Paris guilds were reduced in number by over half to forty-four, and their statutes were based around a series of police decrees standardising corporate forms, thus removing workers' use of particular rights and customs as arguments in disputes.

Control was reinforced in 1781 by royal letters patent ordering all journeymen to register with a guild, and instructing them to carry a *livret*, or work-record book – two issues that had been bitterly fought out, to a stand-

---

60 Idem, 'Social classification', 199–201.
61 Ibid. 201–2.
62 Ibid. 203.
63 Ibid. 210.
64 Sonenscher, 'Journeymen, the courts'.

still, in individual guilds since the previous century.[65] We cannot be certain of the impact of such changes on the popular mentality, as the central police archives Farge exploited for her studies do not exist for the post-1775 period. One thing seems clear, despite the loss of these records: police attention to Parisian life was as intense in the 1780s as it had ever been, if not more so. For example, Lenoir, commander of all the police forces of Paris as *Lieutenant-général de Police* for much of the pre-revolutionary period, had in his possession when he came to write his memoirs after the Revolution the reports of spies concerning 'undesirables' at large in 1781–5. Among these pornographers, hacks and part-time informers were men such as Gorsas, Audouin and Fréron – journalists we shall meet in 1791 – as well as, for example, Marat, Chenier and Mercier himself.[66] There can be no doubt that this intense scrutiny extended to many other milieux.

While Mercier, as we have seen, argued in his work that the police were ultimately able to contain popular Paris, he none the less observed in the late 1780s that insubordination 'has been visible amongst the lower classes [le petit peuple] for some years, above all in the trades'. He saw an 'abandonment of all discipline' which would shortly have 'the most evil effects'.[67] Among the conclusions to Garrioch's work is that

> the very process of centralisation and of breaking down barriers both within the capital and between Paris and its provinces, combined with the demographic explosion and the growing gap between prices and real wages, made the maintenance of order an ever-present preoccupation. The measures taken to assure the supply of bread, the police concern with rumour, and the action against beggars and the ubiquitous vagrants ['gens sans aveu' – which also implied criminality] all testify to the near-paranoid state of the official mind.[68]

Garrioch's emphasis here is an ever-growing policing against an ever-growing perceived threat of disorder, an environment to which the controls over journeymen, for example, would seem to attest eloquently. The level to which this concern was 'near-paranoid' is debatable, given the events of 1789 and after, although it was certainly oriented more towards conspiracy theories than to any appreciation of the forces and perceptions animating the population.[69]

---

65 Ibid. 100–6. See also Kaplan, 'Lutte pour la contrôle'. The bitterness of master–journeyman relations would be reflected in conflicts that erupted in 1791, and which were viewed as suspiciously by the revolutionary authorities as they had been by the Old Regime.
66 See R. Darnton, 'The high Enlightenment and the low-life of literature in pre-revolutionary France', in D. Johnson (ed.), *French society and the Revolution*, Cambridge 1976, 53–87, esp. pp. 75–6. (Original publication in *Past and Present* li [1971], 81–155; also reproduced in R. Darnton, *The literary underground of the Old Regime*, Cambridge, Mass. 1982, 1–40.) See also R. Darnton, *The great cat massacre and other episodes in French cultural history*, Harmondsworth 1985, ch. iv, for similar scrutiny in an earlier generation.
67 Mercier, *Tableau*, 316, 318.
68 Garrioch, *Neighbourhood and community*, 211.
69 A classic interpretation of the Revolution, following figures such as Lefebvre and

Reaching the eve of the Revolution through historiographical survey, we find an environment within Paris of turbulent fear, alarm and suspicion, a population 'forever on the lookout' for plots, and a police apparatus apparently on the verge of psychosis in its scrutiny of that population. With this as a chronological background, the declining historical interest in popular activity in the Revolution itself appears curious. One reason for it, of course, is the devaluing of the agenda which led historians such as Soboul and Rudé to examine such activity in the first place. A strong current of thought around the bicentenary moment strove to discard any reference to violent social change in the revolutionary process, valorising the 'political culture' approach of those such as François Furet, while necessarily eliding Furet's conclusion that that very culture was terroristic from its origins.[70] Within the political culture of the revolutionary elite, 'the people' appear as a cypher, an empty sign ready to be filled with whatever values are desired by those who arrogate the right to speak in the name of 'the people'.[71] In this context, actual popular activity is irrelevant, embarrassing not only to historians who want to disregard it, but to elite political actors themselves, of all shades, whose ability to define 'the people' rests largely on popular passivity.[72]

One of the aims of this study is to problematise this relationship between political leadership and defining 'the people'. For many purposes political leaders throughout the Revolution did require passivity from their followers, but that does not mean that they got it. The pressures of war, and an increasingly ruthless suppression of dissent, made this issue less problematic as time passed, but in the early years of the Revolution real popular activity continued to challenge efforts by elite observers to define an acceptable role for 'the people'. This is true even at the earliest moments of revolutionary uprising, during the taking of the Bastille itself. Here it was not just definitions of who constituted the people that were at stake, but indeed whether the people could be included with 'the citizens'. The opening of Loustalot's

---

Labrousse, would put this rising tension down to a growing long-term economic crisis. More recent historians have become sceptical about the 'objective' evidence for such a crisis, but there is clearly a psychological crisis-mentality emerging in the relations we have documented. For such critiques see D. Weir, 'Les Crises économiques et les origines de la Révolution française', *Annales. Économies, Sociétés, Civilisations* xlvi (1991), 917–47, and L. M. Cullen, 'History, economic crises, and revolution: understanding eighteenth-century France', *Economic History Review* xlvi (1993), 635–57.

70 For which see Furet, *Interpreting the French Revolution*.

71 'Political culture' is of course itself a heavily-laden term, defined by Baker, *Inventing the French Revolution*, 4, as 'the set of discourses or symbolic practices by which . . . [political] claims are made'. See also W. H. Sewell, Jr, 'A rhetoric of bourgeois revolution', in Kates, *The French Revolution*, 143–56, who challenges the 'hint of linguistic reductionism' (p. 146) he finds in Baker's formulation. Sewell's use of 'bourgeois' here is equally questionable, however, and the level of significance attributable to control over definitions under revolutionary circumstances must be acknowledged.

72 This is a vast and possibly unjustifiable generalisation. A great deal of support is given to it, however, by S. L. Kaplan, *Farewell Revolution*, Ithaca, NY 1995.

account of these events in his *Révolutions de Paris* provides an exposition of precisely this contrast, recording the aimless destruction carried out by the former, and the determined and disciplined action of the latter.[73] A National Assembly deputy went further in distinguishing 'the seditious armed through licence' from 'the citizen armed for liberty'.

Colin Lucas has demonstrated that this type of discourse was used to 'free' the revolutionary import of collective violence from its more brutal aspects. By palming these off onto brigands and vagrants, 'the revolutionary contribution of the crowd could remain uncontaminated by frightening violence'. The message was reinforced by turning the deaths of prominent individuals into acts of justice – Loustalot claimed that Berthier, the intendant of Paris lynched on 22 July, was killed by a man whose father he had murdered, and various accounts made de Launay, commander of the Bastille, give verbal provocation or justification to the crowd that butchered him. Meanwhile, this did not stop the commentators slipping into an assimilation of all the poor with the untrustworthy rabble, or even those that Lucas describes as 'potentially more radical' laying the blame for crowd violence on the 'ignorance and gullibility of the poor', who were led by 'others' into their acts.[74] From such highly ambiguous beginnings, a revolutionary culture which claimed to decisively include 'the people' was born.[75] As we have already seen, these ambiguities of attitude were to carry forward through the rest of 1789, and into the development of firmer lines of division between 'patriots' and 'aristocrats' that went on through 1790. With all of this in mind, we can now turn to see how the Parisians reacted to, and interpreted, the alarming news that the clergy had, apparently, rejected the Revolution.

[73] See C. Lucas, 'Talking about urban popular violence in 1789', in Forrest and Jones, *Reshaping France*, 122–36, esp. p. 124.

[74] Ibid. 129–31.

[75] It is worth noting the extent to which that inclusion, flawed as we shall argue it to be, was 'revolutionary', as the Enlightenment had been resolutely 'antipopular' in its conceptions, and the thought of the late eighteenth century was highly ambiguous on this subject. See H. C. Payne, *The philosophes and the people*, London 1976, and Chartier, *Cultural origins*, ch. ii, 'The public sphere and public opinion', esp. pp. 27–30, 'The public or the people'. M. Cranston, 'The sovereignty of the nation', in Lucas, *The political culture of the French Revolution*, 97–104, esp. p. 103, demonstrates the interchangeability of 'nation' and 'people'. However, P. Nora, 'Nation', in Furet and Ozouf, *Critical dictionary*, 742–53, can define that term at length without mentioning the concept of 'the people'. P. Rétat, 'The evolution of the citizen from the *ancien régime* to the Revolution', in R. Waldinger, P. Dawson and I. Woloch (eds), *The French Revolution and the meaning of citizenship*, Westport 1993, 4–15, documents the 'ambiguities and contradictions which surround' that term (p. 13), and its relations to *peuple*, *factieux*, *brigand*, etc. in the press discourse of 1789.

2

Aristocrats, Priests and Brigands:
January–February 1791

In January 1791 Parisian politics were already seething with doubt and fear, most of which was directed towards what had already become the Revolution's principal enemies – the aristocracy and the clergy. Around this time, former *monarchiens* and other royalist elements in the National Assembly coalesced under the leadership of Stanislas de Clermont-Tonnerre to form the 'Society of Friends of the Monarchical Constitution', commonly called the *Club monarchique*, and which in the first weeks of its existence had already become the preferred target of radical accusations concerning aristocratic conspiracy of all types.[1] Meanwhile, in the face of clerical resistance to their new place in the Constitution, the National Assembly had decreed that all clergy should take what amounted to an oath of loyalty to the Revolution and its works – an oath refused by the vast majority of the bishops sitting in the Assembly itself. Across the country this would be one of the great polarising moments of the Revolution, and its effect within the city was no less significant.[2]

The parochial clergy of Paris were to take this oath at their Sunday services in the first two weeks of January. The level of local tension aroused by the potential and actual resistance of the clergy is evident from the circular sent to Section officials on two occasions from the central police administration. On 9 and 14 January, police *commissaires* were asked to patrol their local lodging-houses on the following Saturday evening, to watch for 'extraordinary movements', and to remain at home ready to take action on the Sunday morning. On both occasions nothing in the record suggests that any notable incidents occurred.[3] Clearly, however, the municipal administration was afraid that the 'floating population' might be used to stir up trouble at the oath-taking ceremonies.

In the haze of half-truths and misinformation that made up the blanket-

[1] According to Colin Jones this grouping 'grew out of unofficial aristocratic clandestine gatherings in late 1790', an origin which would permanently cloud its influence: *The Longman companion to the French Revolution*, London 1988, 173.
[2] For the wider picture see T. Tackett, *Religion, revolution and regional culture in eighteenth-century France: the ecclesiastical oath of 1791*, Princeton 1986.
[3] APP, AA82:60, 48, 93, 111, 115, Section du Palais-Royal. To make the link clear, the *commissaire* annotated this request as an 'invitation relative to the installation of priests'. For a full analysis of the operation of neighbourhood policing see ch. 3.

coverage of the press, credulousness and suspicion went hand-in-hand. The journalist Gorsas scorned rumours of an assassination plot by leading politicians against Lafayette on 5 January, but a few days later found himself the victim of false information when he published an account of the taking of the clerical oath at St-Roch, parish church of the Section du Palais-Royal. The next day he had to publish a disclaimer, since by then it was common knowledge that the clergy of the parish were in full resistance to the oath, led by the curé: 'A priest, *claiming to be from this parish*, came himself to abuse our good faith [with the false information].' It is odd that Gorsas should have been so easily taken in, since only a few days before he had accused the clergy of wanting 'to spark off a war of religion'.[4] Like most journalists, Gorsas reproduced rumour and hearsay, sometimes critically, sometimes not, as his prejudices (and perhaps his mood) dictated.

If the authorities feared that the clerical party would raise the mob in its interests, the first signs of trouble over this issue came from the opposite direction, for on 9 January an angry congregation of patriotic citizens had forced the Guard to hide a priest in the marriage-chamber of St-Germain-l'Auxerrois (Section du Louvre) after his sermon had appeared 'as contrary to the principles that all good citizens must have according to the decrees of the National Assembly'. It is unclear just what he had said wrong, since he claimed to be going to take the oath that Sunday, and the text he was reading from appeared innocent to the *commissaire*.[5]

Back at St-Roch we find the curé himself provoking disorder. On the evening of 18 January he interrupted a baptismal ceremony, taking over from the officiating priest at the font. This might have passed off quietly had the sectional general assembly not been in session in the main body of the church. The presence of a considerable number of people created a situation that hovered on the brink of danger, as one Jean Louis Thouvenin, merchant cabinetmaker, testified:

> that being in the general assembly he heard a loud noise from the direction of the baptismal chapel of the said church that he was there at the moment when the trouble grew considerably that he penetrated the crowd and reached M. the curé who was celebrating the ceremony of the sacrament of baptism that believing him to be in danger he invited him like the other good citizens to cease, that M. the curé ceased . . . he the witness helped to protect him to his home.[6]

Another priest was found to conclude the service, and the police recorded this and other accounts later. There is no clear record here of the exact

---

4 *Courrier*, 7, 10, 11 Jan., emphasis in the original. Note that the curé is the equivalent of the English vicar: the priest in titular control of the parish, with a considerable cohort of assistant priests.
5 APP, AA182:24.
6 APP, AA82:126.

nature of the 'trouble', whether a portion of the assembly made itself menacing, or whether word spread to the surrounding streets and a crowd gathered. There was clearly, however, a rapid angry response to the curé's presence. We may presume, since the 'good citizens' led him to safety, that the trouble came from less supposedly respectable elements. The angry popular resistance to the curé was liable, in this incident and later, to be re-interpreted as trouble created by the priests for their own dark purposes.

The aforementioned curé of St-Roch, one Claude Marduel, was in the process of becoming one of the more famous refractories of the capital. Gorsas, who lived in the parish, retailed news of his doings in an unfavourable manner, delving also into his past to allege that he had only obtained his living by fraud and influence; there had been 'a famous trial on the subject', he intimated on 2 March. Ironically, however, Marduel would not be put out of a job until April as the Assembly was forced to ask refractories to continue in their functions until replacements could be found.

Not everyone viewed the situation with such equanimity, and the furore over the oath was such that any hint of unusual behaviour concerned with religion became suspicious. On 25 January a former prosecutor of the Châtelet court felt it was worth reporting to the *commissaire de police* of the Section du Louvre that 'small crosses' were on sale in the rue des Arcis, and that 'these sales and purchases may announce something dangerous'. One of the merchants confirmed 'that he had sold many of them over the last few days, even by the dozen'.[7]

The suspicion that religious resistance had taken on (or indeed had always had) a sinister aspect was further boosted by the interpretation of conflicts which had a wholly secular origin. In the last week of January the whole of Paris was aflame with the news of a 'massacre' at La Chapelle, to the north of the city, on 24 January. The actual incident was a skirmish in confused circumstances between salaried troops of the Parisian National Guard, supporting the work of customs officials, and the locals of the town, in which shots were fired and several people killed. Violence at and around the customs barriers was a serious problem at this point. Part of the structure of Old-Regime taxation so resented by the population, municipal tolls had been retained by the revolutionary authorities after the clean sweep of other taxes in 1790 because of their ease of collection, and the revenues they provided to municipalities for other urgent spending. Few amongst the urban population appeared happy with this rationale, however. On 27 January Bailly himself led cavalry to the Barrière de Sèvres at 10 a.m.: 'I found there neither tumult nor gathering; but the clerks informed me that, the smugglers presenting themselves in groups of sixty or eighty, the officials and troops find themselves too few to be able to resist.' And so the smugglers had worked unhindered, insulting the clerks as they passed. This gives some idea of the

---

7   APP, AA182:54.

opposition the customs men were facing, and one explanation for the violence at La Chapelle.[8] The register of La Force prison at this time contains a number of cases of people arrested for 'having struck' or 'mistreated' the clerks of the tax-farm, 'agitated the people' against them, or even 'raised a sabre', either in arguments over dues, or quite simply 'so that the contrabandists might pass more easily'. The hostility towards the *chasseurs des barrières*, who were the armed branch of the customs service, made itself felt elsewhere too – on 31 January in the Section des Thermes-de-Julien three workers from the municipal relief workshops [travaux publics] tried to start a swordfight with two such soldiers.[9]

The La Chapelle 'massacre', however, generally received a different interpretation. Sigismond Lacroix comments that 'from the first day' the patriotic clubs and journals turned on the *Club monarchique* as instigator of this outrage. Fréron wrote in his *Orateur du Peuple* on 26 January that '30,000 workers are enrolled with Clermont-Tonnerre. . . . All the former royal bodyguards are admitted. . . . Paris is on the eve of the counter-revolution; and, if we lose an instant, a single instant, we are consigned to death.' The actual total registered with the Club for subsidised bread was around 2,500, but the radicals were less concerned with accuracy than with invoking the image of mass brigandage under preparation.[10]

On the day following this claim Clermont-Tonnerre's house was put under siege by an enraged crowd, but Bailly and the forces of order were well able to retain control of the situation, as he reported to the Assembly.[11] The 27th seems to have been a day for suspicious happenings. In the Section du Louvre a baker reported to the evening session of the general assembly that at 6.30 that morning a man 'who appeared to him to be a stonemason' had tried to force him to sell a loaf below the usual price. When he refused the man said that 'he would have him strung up [il le feroit mettre à la lanterne] and . . . said to him again that within four days he would give it [the bread] at six *sous*, and by force'. The Section thought enough of this to inform the National Assembly's *comité des recherches* and the public prosecutor.[12] Again, in the Section du Palais-Royal a half-dozen 'posters of a proclamation of the

---

8 Lacroix, *Actes*, ii. 281.
9 APP, AB322:888 (16 Jan.), 918 (19 Jan.), 1055 (1 Feb.), 1126 (7 Feb.), 1034, for the fight, one of whose proponents was deported from the city for his pains. The dues on goods entering the city were voted out of existence on 19 February, but were not actually lifted until 1 May. As they were one of the great pre-revolutionary grievances of the Parisians, hostility to this dilatory procedure is understandable.
10 Lacroix, *Actes*, ii. 230, 237. Desmoulins's paper echoed the figure for enrolled workers, feeding the 'myth' surrounding this total (see pp. 47–8 below), while the *Révolutions de Paris* was more conservative at 15,000.
11 Ibid. 281.
12 APP, AA182:56.

municipality concerning the functions of priests who have not sworn their oath' were discovered torn down, with no clue as to the culprits.[13]

In the following weeks the *commissaire de police* of the Section du Louvre received further reports of suspicious incidents. On 4 February a tobacco-vendor reported an encounter with a strange man on 16 January who claimed to be taking 700 *livres* to the Faubourg St-Antoine 'to support some house-holds', and who came back on 2 February to offer her and her husband 6 *livres* per day to be ready to take up arms for his 'party', saying 'that the nation would not be the strongest'. On the next day, the Section's secretary and another *bourgeois* reported on nightly meetings in the rue de Chevalier that blocked the road with carriages until 4 a.m., arousing local suspicions that this might be a cell of the *Club monarchique*. On the 9th a surgeon overheard three Germans, including two salaried *chasseurs* of the National Guard, in a billiard-hall saying 'that they hoped to have their revenge for the La Chapelle affair', that the German powers were arming against France and that 'their first blow would be for the Parisians'.[14] Such *prima facie* evidence of aristo-cratic brigandage and conspiracy is suggestive, but unverifiable. Given that the brigands never did rise, we may observe only that such reports show the fear that ran through the streets of Paris, carried by rumour and hearsay.

At this time the *Club monarchique* was attempting to prove its good faith by transferring the money it had collected, for poor relief or brigandage depending on one's point of view, to the Sections. It would seem that the subscriptions of Clermont-Tonnerre's club had had a positive effect on some opinions. On 11 February a man who had come to receive a passport to leave the city (presumably as an indigent) was jailed after making 'threats and invectives' against the judicial and police authorities of the Sections – 'He spoke much of M Clermont-Tonnerre, making a eulogy of him because he had given him bread.'[15] Probably a more typical reaction to the controversy is that of the 'homeless beggar' who was jailed 'as very suspect' on 20 January for having said 'loudly that M. de Clermont-Tonnerre received at his home a quantity of persons that he enrolled for the counter-revolution'. There is no indication that he approved of this concept, but it was dangerous enough that one so lowly should be repeating it, no matter how many times it appeared in the press.[16]

While the Club tried to polish its image, however, Gorsas commented that at the same time it was having free tracts distributed against himself, Lameth, the Jacobin Club and others, and that many Sections had refused its 'cursed'

---

13 APP, AA82:152.
14 APP, AA182:67, 68, 74. The last incident, to less prejudiced ears, sounds less suspicious when it is noted that the men went on to wish they were back home in Germany where 'they wouldn't have to live with these buggering townsmen [bourgeois]'. None the less, the authorities took all these reports seriously, forwarding them to the central administration.
15 APP, AB322:1173, released 19 Feb.
16 APP, AB322:1015, released with *passeport* 31 Jan.

cash, raising their own subscriptions instead. Meanwhile, Clermont-Tonnerre had supposedly been speaking to the officers of the salaried National Guard about the reliability of their men. Gorsas also reported that the Section du Luxembourg had verified the list of paupers in its area that the Club had provided – 'In general all those enrolled were strong, vigorous, and in a condition to work.' Therefore, in other words, they were being recruited for brigandage.[17] The *Révolutions de Paris* reported more rumours which may have come from the activities of the Club:

> Tuesday evening the suburban bakers were warned to be on their guard the next day, Wednesday, market day, and to distribute their goods [inside Paris] at an early hour, because a large quantity of bread below the current price would be delivered, in the hope of insinuating to the people to demand the same reduction from the bakers. However, nothing extraordinary occurred Wednesday; the plot was defused.[18]

By early February the religious issue was being brought to bear on wider issues of public security. It had been mooted that the king's aunts – Mesdames – might travel to Rome on a 'pilgrimage' to consult the pope. On 8 February Gorsas called for them to stay, and indeed for the royal family to be considered 'so many hostages to public tranquillity'. This was necessary considering 'the brigands in the pay of the deposed priests, with which the capital abounds . . . many suspect men, wearing the uniform of the *patrie*; twenty thousand blue coats ready to be put on by our counter-revolutionaries'.

Amongst all this, mid-February saw renewed attacks on customs posts by night, and although Lafayette and the Guard stood by to intervene, no-one was brought to book.[19] When Mesdames did depart for Rome later in the month, there were mass demonstrations of popular disquiet at what was feared to be the first stage in an evacuation of the royal family. A large Guard presence held the crowds in check as they flooded the Tuileries on 22 and 24 February, on the former occasion escorting an uneasy comte de Provence – Monsieur, the king's brother – from the Luxembourg palace to demonstrate his continued presence. The personal attentions of Bailly helped the drama pass off peacefully, but it represented none the less a serious escalation in the tension between the court and Parisian opinion.[20]

The refractory priests and their supporters, meanwhile, continued to disrupt neighbourhood religious life. On 6 February a man was arrested for shouting during the sermon in St-Roch, and a beadle testified that he had been there frequently during the past weeks, harassing the oath-taking priests

---

[17] *Courrier*, 4, 5 Feb. One need hardly add that there were a great many men in Paris that winter who, while fit for work, were none the less going hungry.

[18] *Révolutions de Paris*, 12–19 Feb. Note the reluctance to admit that a rumour may be insubstantial.

[19] Lacroix, *Actes*, ii. 601.

[20] Ibid. ii. 695–6.

and loudly praising Marduel. He proved to be an itinerant beggar, and seemed to have been protesting against the fact that the priest was reading his text rather than speaking from memory. He was sent to La Force prison, where it was noted that he was sent on to the Hôtel-Dieu for treatment, thence to be deported home.[21] The revolutionary authorities gave him the benefit of the doubt, but within a month Gorsas would be alleging that Marduel was paying such men to cause trouble.

In the third week of February religious issues again caused a flare-up of anxiety over counter-revolution, coinciding with the popular agitation over the departure of the king's aunts for Rome. On 20 February the curé of St-Philippe-du-Roule read from the pulpit a pastoral letter from the arch-bishop of Paris which effectively argued against the validity of the clerical oath. Over the next few days copies of the text appeared around the city, distributed by people like Marie Françoise Leclerc, school-mistress in the Luxembourg Section, arrested on the 20th for handing out these 'inflammatory pamphlets'. One of her pupils testified that she had said several times to her class 'that if one received first communion from the new priests one would be damned', while another said she had seen Leclerc receiving the pamphlets from a priest of St-Sulpice.[22] This and later incidents make it clear that the refractories did have a 'party' at their disposal, although women such as Leclerc probably acted out of religious rather than political motives – difficult as that distinction may have been for most Parisians to perceive.

In the Section du Palais-Royal, meanwhile, on 26 February, Jean-Baptiste Suret, artist-designer, reported to the police:

> that on Wednesday morning the 23rd of the present month there came to the establishment of M. Billard innkeeper where he the declarant was reading the papers a woman unknown to him who came to get some coffee, who said to the mistress of the house Mme Billard 'will you give your signature to ask that your new curé not be received', that Mme Billard responded that she did not get mixed up in that, that however the said woman showed a piece of note-paper on which there were around twenty signatures below an invitation to good citizens to sign so that their curé might stay, that M. Billard took the paper and a pen, his wife asked him what he was going to do, and he said that he was going to sign so that the old curé [Marduel] should go, that the woman who carried the paper seeing the pleasantries made to her changed her tone,

---

21 APP, AA82:215; AB322:1111. This beggar, Joseph Augustin Guerin, was arrested again on 21 June, in the Section des Enfants-Rouges, 'for having, being on the corner of the rue des Filles-Dieu, held a discourse tending to trouble public order'. The register went on, 'Through interrogation it appears that this man has a mental abberration [la tête exaltée]', but rather than refer him to the Hôtel-Dieu again, he was simply released on 27 June, again with a *passeport*: APP, AB323:1229
22 APP, AB322:1266. Leclerc was sent before the Police Tribunal, but no sentence is recorded here.

saying that it was a paper that she had taken from the bigots to play a trick by depriving them of it, that her coffee being served she left.[23]

There is no more than this, so we can only hypothesise as to the woman's identity and the authors of the petition. The 'bigots' were probably bourgeois or even artisanal devout women of the parish, since the whole thing seems to have been female-oriented – the woman offered the petition to Mme Billard rather than to the customers. From her behaviour it seems likely she had been paid for her services, but did not herself care much about the project – unless she was an expert at dissembling, but the situation was not yet so tense that a partisan of the curé might not have dared argue back. At this point, Gorsas was accusing the clergy of mobilising prostitutes in their favour – an unlikely alliance, but an accusation well-suited to the moment.[24] The café-owner may have turned this incident into a joke, but that a citizen should report it, and the *commissaire* file it, reflects again the uncertain atmosphere of the city. As usual, journalists like Gorsas only contributed to this instability. On 2 March he embroidered the petition for Marduel into an allegation that the curé 'had arranged for each person, brigands or others, to be given three *livres*, to obtain signatures'. He went on to list a *bourgeoise*, a female haberdasher and a female dressmaker who were acting as his agents – information that was probably accurate, but it is doubtful whether those women saw themselves as agents of a conspiracy.[25]

Some idea of the prevalent mood in the population, or at least among the taxpaying 'active citizens' who sat in the local administrative bodies, can be gained from a motion passed by the general assembly of the Section de la Place-Vendôme on 22 February. They firstly appointed two sets of *commissaires* to investigate the La Chapelle incident (now a month in the past) and Mesdames' departure, and then voted to ask the municipality to proclaim 'in conformity with the former police regulations, a ban on the manufacture and sale of canes and sticks containing offensive weapons'; further, that it should seize such weapons held by dealers, and explore ways of removing them from the possession of individuals. Not only this, but the Section also wanted strict enforcement of the order against non-members of the Guard wearing its uniform, and an order for the police *commissaires* and 'all the good citizens' to investigate the identities of people 'who arrive continually in Paris and live in

---

23 APP, AA82:295.

24 *Courrier*, 26 Feb., commenting on the demonstration of the 24th at the Tuileries: 'For the most part the public functionaries [feminine gender] of the rue St-Honoré . . . in the pay of the non-juring public functionaries [masculine gender].'

25 Ibid. 2 Mar. On 13 March Gorsas alleged that Marduel was plotting to attack the new curé, using 300 children from the Christian Schools. The notion that Catholic clergy had a special hold over women was of course a standard trope of anti-clerical rhetoric now and later. For an intelligent reappraisal of some of these issues see T. Tackett, 'Women and men in counter-revolution: the Sommières riot of 1791', *Journal of Modern History* lix (1987), 680–704.

the houses of emigrated persons'. Last but not least Guard patrols by day and night should be stepped up 'until the disquiet which has given rise to the present deliberation should have ceased'.[26]

Such demands clearly reflect the scare-mongering of the press. While Gorsas himself had written on 12 February that 'we engage all our fellow citizens not to allow themselves to be seduced by the tales that the thirst for disorder brings to birth in the capital', on the 22nd he fulminated, linking Mesdames' departure to a plot by the tax farmers to blow up the customs-barriers (in league, somewhat improbably, with the smugglers,) and to a conspiracy of 30,000 brigands to kidnap the queen and dauphin, dispose of the king as a liability, and have a new St Bartholomew's Day Massacre of the patriots. Meanwhile he alleged that some (unnamed) Guard officers were unreliable and should be removed. None of this could be called in any sense conducive to public tranquillity.

On 26 February the Section de Notre-Dame met in general assembly and voted, as had Place-Vendôme four days before, for the banning of all hidden weapons. They explained this by invoking 'the exposition made to the assembly that there existed in Paris factories and stores of mechanical daggers, spring-loaded stilettos chained to gauntlets, and other hidden and perfidious weapons'. This revelation was supposed to come from the Cordeliers Club, which had 'made the discovery of the model and the manufacture of these daggers', the 'infernal invention' of which ought to be pursued by the rigours of justice.[27] On 28 February Gorsas wrote of these 'subtle daggers', alleging that a factory for them had been found 'in the Cordeliers neighbourhood', the products supposedly bound for Bordeaux, but to someone the worker found in charge could not name. This was the very day that the young aristocrats rapidly dubbed 'knights of the dagger [chevaliers du poignard]' occupied the Tuileries, when the National Guard had rushed off to defend the keep of Vincennes from the wrath of the Faubourg St-Antoine.

It will already be evident from the foregoing incidents that the fears of the Parisian press and population did not merely point 'upwards' to the aristocrats and clergy, but also 'downwards' to the transient, labouring and criminal population of the city, albeit that such fear was largely due to the ease with which such groups were believed to be suborned. Fréron's remark that the *Club monarchique* had recruited 30,000 men, and Gorsas's use of the same total above, was an echo of wider and long-standing fears of 'brigands' in the capital. The word *brigand* was an almost ubiquitous designation at this time for all those low elements susceptible to subornation, and its repeated use made the fears concerning such groups more concrete. The perceived threat of armed and organised brigandage had been central to the 'Great Fear' of 1789, and in Paris in particular it had also acquired a far more precise

---

[26] Lacroix, *Actes*, ii. 723.
[27] Ibid. ii. 796.

meaning by 1791 – the rumoured 30,000 men suborned by *aristocratie* to bring down the Revolution, and 'known' to be hiding in the city.

This was a figure Lafayette had mentioned for the total of 'outsiders [étrangers] and vagabonds [gens sans aveu]' in Paris as early as the week after the fall of the Bastille.[28] In late December 1789, after the arrest of the marquis de Favras, a flyer appeared around the city denouncing him 'for a plan he has made to raise up thirty thousand men to assassinate M. de Lafayette and the Mayor . . . and then to cut off the food supply'. In February 1791, amid renewed rumours of aristocratic plots, the president of the Jacobins would read a denunciation to the Club 'that more than thirty thousand persons of every estate had entered Paris in the past few days to carry out a *coup de main*'. Its relative constancy, as well as its use in varying contexts in 1791, would suggest that the total alone had acquired mythic potency.[29]

The fear of brigands, as we have already seen, would play a leading part in the events of the summer; the repressive decree published by the municipality on 16 July was entitled 'On the factious persons, the suborned outsiders, the aristocrats and other enemies of the public good', and in the official account of the massacre the phrases flew – 'factious', 'seditionaries', 'brigands', exercising 'the most criminal violence' and obliging the authorities to resort to force. On 23 July 1791 Rabaut de St-Etienne would protest in the National Assembly that measures were not being taken fast enough to complete a census of Paris. This was necessary, in his view, to disclose, and thus disarm, 'the brigands, the assassins, the rogues with which Paris is replete' – variously 'outsiders' and 'felons', all 'infinitely suspect'.[30]

Such fears had already led the Municipal Police Department to order a survey of people letting furnished rooms – *logeurs* – in January 1791, in order to gain an overview of the situation of the transient population. This survey was carried out on 18–20 January, and the results transmitted to the administration, where they were lost to us, presumably in the fires of 1871. Gorsas alleged on 27 February that collation of the survey revealed 30,000 people in this form of accommodation, which he regarded as confirmation that these were the brigands everyone believed to be in Paris. One Section's data has survived in the Police Archives, that of Grange-Batellière in the north of the city. Such a small sample alone cannot prove or disprove city-wide tendencies, but we can gain from it some idea of the world of *hôtels garnis* – furnished lodgings – that the press, population and government so feared.

There were twenty-four *logeurs* in this Section, including ten women. Only one man called himself an *aubergiste*, with some justification, since he had forty-four tenants. No-one else approached this total, though one widow

---

28 See Rudé, *Crowd*, 19 n. 8.
29 See N. Ruault, *Gazette d'un parisien sous la Révolution: lettres à son frère, 1783–1796*, ed. A. Vassal and C. Rimbaud, Paris 1976, 174, 221. Note the echo of famine plot in the Favras denunciation.
30 Lacroix, *Actes*, v. 476, 371, 399–400.

had twenty-eight. The other traditional names for innkeepers – *marchand de vin* and *limonadier* – were held by one and five people respectively (including one *limonadière*), but these people had only between one and seven tenants. Six men had artisanal trades, and the others are merely noted by name. Some *logeurs* were clearly specialised – a mason had five of the same trade among his eight tenants, a tailor had eleven cab-drivers among his seventeen, and one who was a cab-driver himself let exclusively to seven of his fellows. One woman had seven joiners among her ten tenants, and another catered for eight unskilled labourers. At a more elevated level, three women shared between them two *bourgeoises de Paris*, with servants, two army officers and a former King's Bodyguard, with families, a *Chevalier de St-Louis*, a barrister, an 'American', a gentleman from London and a 'former ballet-master'.

The total number of tenants was 205, divided as follows – sixteen workers on public relief work; thirty-four unskilled males, plus one dependent female; eighty-four artisanal males, plus one dependent female; fourteen female needleworkers, six female stallholders and sellers [marchandes], fourteen washerwomen and other unskilled females; and twenty-six miscellaneous others with nine dependants, from students at the *École des Ponts et Chaussées* to those already mentioned. Of this total, seventy-two had taken up their present residence before June 1790, ninety-six between June and December of that year, and thirty-seven in the first three weeks of January 1791. Of this last group eleven had moved in between the 17th and 19th – that is, in the previous two days. The eleven covered all the social categories, and five of them had moved in with the *aubergiste* in his large establishment, which none the less also had tenants, including a second-hand dealer and a day-labourer who had been there since 1785.

The thirty-seven arrivals in January compared with none in the previous month, twelve in November and eight in October. However, forty had arrived in September 1790, suggesting that these peaks of mobility could be accounted for by factors such as the quarterly rent-date and the availability of seasonal work. A small peak of eleven in June would seem to confirm this, bearing in mind that in a high-mobility milieu elapsed time will tend to distort such earlier figures downwards.

The fears of the patriots were concentrated on the unskilled and unemployed who were thought easiest to suborn, and who supposedly were flooding the city in unprecedented numbers. Of the sixteen workers on municipal relief-works, it is true that five had taken up residence in January 1791, but four had been in place since 1789, and another five since prior to June 1790. The general unskilled workers present a similar pattern – of thirty-four, twelve dated from 1789 or earlier, three from January–June 1790, no less than seven from September alone, and only six from January 1791.[31]

Such a 'snapshot' view of a highly mobile population is likely to accen-

---

31 APP, AA174:1–5. For reference, the month-by-month arrivals for 1790 (all categories) are as follows: 2, 2, 8, 9, 9, 11, 5, 9, 40, 8, 12, 0.

tuate the significance of recent arrivals, but as can be seen, even without attempting to compensate for this effect, this Section does not seem to have been deluged with undesirables in its lodging-houses. One should scarcely be surprised at this, given the knowledge through hindsight that fears were highly exaggerated, but they were very real to the patriots of the time. Moreover, the suspicion which linked aristocrats and clergy to the dregs of society in collusion against 'all the good citizens' was only one of several dimensions of fear and conflict that were open, and continued to expand, over the early months of 1791.

Returning to the day, 27 January, when Bailly had first to defend the *barrières*, and then to drive off hostile crowds from Clermont-Tonnerre's house, we can move via a riot in the Faubourg St-Antoine into another dimension of revolutionary alarms and suspicions. The counterpoint to the dreaded 30,000 infiltrators in the city was the feared and believed additional presence of spies in the pay of political factions amongst the population. If *brigand* was the favourite word of the authorities and the patriotic establishment for describing their opponents, the cry of *mouchard*, police spy, had long been an insult amongst the people.[32] By 1791 the influence of radical campaigns was turning it more directly into a political accusation. Journalists such as Marat were making accusations of counter-revolutionary subornation in the Guard, supposedly orchestrated by Lafayette to defeat the 'popular' cause.[33] Those targeted in this fashion had several avenues of response, but one tried at this time was recourse to the law.

Three master-artisans and a 'former artilleryman' from the Faubourg St-Antoine tried to bring an action for defamation against Fréron and his paper, *L'Orateur du Peuple*, in January 1791, after he had denounced them as sold to Lafayette. The case came to the *Tribunal de Police* on 19 January, when the Guard had to be used to keep order amongst a large attendant crowd, and the trial was adjourned for a week. On the 26th the case resumed, but the court declared itself incompetent in the matter, and dismissed the suit. Fréron's incendiary style found fuel even in this:

> the sole object [of this move] is to bring things to the point of being able to fire on the people: this shall be for the conspirators the signal to strike, to assassi-

---

[32] The term's longer-term ramifications will be considered below. For a recent account of its importance in the riots of the 'Pre-Revolution' see T. M. Luckett, 'Hunting for spies and whores: a Parisian riot on the eve of the French Revolution', *Past and Present* clvi (1997), 116–43.

[33] Echoes of this can be heard at the lowest level of incident. For example, on 10 February, a labourer begging on the Place Royale was detained after shouting 'mouchard' at a Guard captain who had refused him alms: APP, AB322:1169, released with *passeport* 14 Feb. A cobbler on the quai de Grève was detained in August for his daily habit of crying 'mouchard' after National Guards: AB324:2026, sentenced to eight days detention 'in view of the state of his health'.

nate all the patriots in their homes, and for the royal family, the signal to head for the frontier, through arson, massacre and pillage.[34]

Perhaps, then, it is unsurprising that the next day, 27 January, one of the four plaintiffs, variously noted as Kabert or Kabers, and 'nicknamed Louvain', a merchant cabinetmaker and *Vainqueur de la Bastille*, was attacked by a crowd. Various journalists' accounts give specific triggers for the violence – he had insulted the *Vainqueurs* while drunk, fought a duel and wounded a National Guard, or insulted the Guard in the street, having been expelled from it previously. There can be little doubt, however, that the assault was related to the trial, and to Kabert's identity as a suspected *mouchard*. At around 11 a.m. a crowd fell on him with a rain of blows in the grande rue du Faubourg St-Antoine, knocking him twice to the ground during his flight to the shelter of a Section *comité* house, where he arrived 'drowned in his blood and scarcely breathing'. The alarm had been given to the Hôtel de Ville, and several municipal officers, including the writer of the eye-witness account quoted here, rushed to the scene with the Guard Reserve. The main body was held up at the Porte St-Antoine due to a barricade (or convenient traffic-jam) of several wagons. Thus the officers found themselves obliged to negotiate at first with the crowd:

> Entering the committee-room, the municipal officers mounted on the desk and harangued the people: they observed to them that obedience to the law was the safeguard of liberty and that individuals did not have the right to punish even a criminal with death. . . . They asked that Kabers be placed under the safeguard of the laws; they offered and promised to conduct him themselves to prison. Several voices spoke these terrible words: *No, no, hang him, hang him!* This cry was at once repeated by the people filling the ante-chambers, the vestibule and the courtyard; a crowd of madmen threw themselves into the room.

Kabert was dragged out for another beating before the Guard broke through to the scene and retreated with him all the way to the Châtelet. The same witness meanwhile noted that the majority of the crowd was 'more or less agitated, but unarmed and appearing far from enraged'. This contradicts the conclusion of a report in the *Journal de Paris*, which called the riot a crime 'in which the populace of this faubourg, properly defined, alone took part – since all the people supported, with respect, the efforts of the officers'.[35]

Since the eye-witness report makes no mention of particular divergence of opinion in the crowd, it seems likely that the journalist's attempt to distinguish *peuple* from *populace*, and to blame the latter element, is merely a repeti-

---

34 Lacroix, *Actes*, ii. 285–9.
35 Ibid. ii. 292–4. The crowd had its revenge nearly two years later, on 31 December 1792, when Kabert was lynched in virtually the same spot, having been dragged from the Place Royale after speaking up for the king.

tion of the kind of prejudicial judgement common to the eighteenth century. The *populace*, which we might translate today as an 'underclass' of urban marginals, was a prime source of alarm about social order. The *Révolutions de Paris*, however, sought to turn these perceptions on their head. The writer acknowledged that the *populace* existed, but described it as the breeding-ground not of riots, but of *mouchards*. Education would redeem it for the Revolution: 'Let us arrange moments for them to be instructed, to withdraw themselves little by little from the mire and the shadows of ignorance . . . soon we shall all be brothers, in manners as well as birth.'[36] We shall see later, however, that patriotic journalists could mix good and bad perceptions of the common people to suit any point they cared to make.

The Faubourg had been aroused for several days prior to the court case which triggered this unrest. Placards had been appearing in the streets against English goods, blaming these imports for the difficulties of French industry. Lafayette had ordered the Guard to remove them when they appeared, but the patriots saw in them a plot to discredit the workers – the *Révolutions de Paris* said by making it appear that they were dictating policy to the government – while Tallien of the Minimes Club published an appeal for calm blaming the agitation directly on the *Club monarchique*. Despite their suspicions of popular stirrings on this front, the radical press were happy to gloat over Kabert's fate.[37]

This incident demonstrates the popular support for the views of those who, like Marat, saw treason and plot not merely amongst the aristocracy and clergy, but in the ranks of the National Guard itself. On 6 January the *Ami du Peuple* had published a letter from a grenadier in the Carmes Battalion, alleging that although their blank cartridges were functional, the powder in those supplied with bullets would not fire, even when tossed into flames – implying that this relatively 'patriotic' battalion was being effectively disarmed. In the same issue, Marat reported that the Recollets Battalion had purged itself of suspect elements, and that others such as Henri-Quatre, Filles St-Thomas and St-Roch were in dire need of the same treatment, containing as they did many men 'too rich to have any morals'. On 9 January he reported that the Val-de-Grace Battalion had been purged, but that the Petit-St-Antoine and Pères de Nazareth were still suspect.[38]

Marat also denounced individuals as spies for Lafayette, such as one Plainville, who worked on the staff of the National Guard headquarters, and had worn the insignia of a major until a patriot had threatened to rip them off, and Buot, 'the police inspector, who has the audacity to show off two colonel's epaulettes . . . despite being rejected by the National Guard'. Each of these officers also seemed to control others of lower rank – Bruyant, formerly a sergeant of the *Gardes françaises*, discharged 'for base acts', or a sergeant

36 *Révolutions de Paris*, 22–9 Jan.
37 Lacroix, *Actes*, ii. 289–91, 293.
38 *Ami du Peuple*, nos 332, 335.

from the St-André-des-Arts Battalion, 'hounded out by the citizens for espio-nage'.[39] By mid-February, Marat had gone on to criticise the system of finding replacements to do Guard service – such men 'are always taken by the officers sold to the divine Mottié [i.e. Lafayette] from the band of *mouchards* that the great general . . . has placed in each battalion, to lead the soldiers of the *patrie* astray'. As a result, he claimed, there were universal complaints that men were avoiding their service, but this was understandable, as no 'honest and delicate citizen' would want to spend the twenty-four hours of a tour of duty with 'infamous *mouchards*'.[40] It would be easy to dismiss Marat's warnings as ravings but, as we shall see, he was sometimes in possession of accurate infor-mation on the municipality's spies.[41]

Thus the patriot/aristocrat conflict within the city was cross-cut by a set of political suspicions which linked the activities of the forces of order them-selves to brigandage, spying and collusion with counter-revolution. Moreover, the drive of those such as Marat to highlight this issue was all the more pointed, for they were embroiled in a genuine political struggle with Lafayette and his agents. It was a struggle where views about popular political awareness blended with attitudes to the mob's ignorance and political incom-petence, and to assumptions about the factional nature of opposition, to create dangerous misunderstandings. Threats and intimidation of individuals on one side were met with inflammatory rhetoric, and the potential of crowd violence, on the other.

The issues at stake can be introduced through the case of an individual who was probably a relatively innocent bystander, but who none the less felt the full force of the attitudes involved. Later in the year, on 19 May, Louis Nicolas Hion reported to the police *commissaire* of the Section du Palais-Royal that he was the victim of 'a frightful plot woven against his honour and his life'. He was a lieutenant in the centre (i.e. salaried) company of the Oratoire National Guard Battalion, and deposed information filling six folio pages about the actions of various members of the headquarters staff, who since mid-1790 had taken him for an Orléanist agent and had systematically denigrated him in the eyes of colleagues and the public. On the Champ de Mars in July 1790 the *aide de camp* Desmottes had called him 'the worst man in the army . . . in d'Orléans' party . . . an ingrate who owed everything to M. de Lafayette and yet betrayed him'. Rumours of his 'inflammatory speeches' were spread, and one *aide-major* named Beauregard claimed that Hion had backed out of a duel.

After further incidents like these he had threatened in late 1790 to publish

---

[39] Ibid. no. 329, 3 Jan; no. 361, 4 Feb.
[40] Ibid. no. 373, 15 Feb.
[41] Recent work emphasises Marat's role as more than just an isolated polemicist: O. Coquard, 'Le Paris de Marat', in Vovelle, *Paris*, 173–84. For more general information see J. Massin, *Marat*, first publ. Paris 1960, Aix-en-Provence 1988, esp. pp. 143–73 on the 1790–1 period.

their details, which had eased the pressure, but since Easter the calumnies had recommenced. In April Beauregard had insulted him to his face, and he had recently received an anonymous letter threatening to 'drag him through the mud' if he published. Hion had resolved to do this none the less, following which more threats had been made by the same officer. Now he was lodging this complaint 'persuaded that the Commune of Paris did not award him the rank of officer . . . to make an assassin of him [pour y faire un cours de spadassinage], but on the contrary [for him] to give the example of submission to the laws'.

There is no evidence that any consequences followed from this denunciation.[42] However, if we return to the beginning of the year, we can begin to fit allegations such as those thrust at Hion into a wider pattern. On 7 February Stanislas Maillard, hero of the Bastille and the October Days, was detained by Raphael Carle, commander of the Henri-Quatre Guard Battalion, a man Marat had denounced as receiving 3,700 *livres* to pay his *mouchards*.[43] Carle accused Maillard of alleging publicly that Carle had paid three men to kill him. This dispute seems to have begun when Maillard acted as counsel for Rotondo, a writer, and alleged Orléanist agent, who had been assaulted by agents of Lafayette late in 1790.

Rotondo, who was to play a role in the drafting of the Champ de Mars petition of 17 July, had been in the crowd at a popular assault on the Hôtel de Castries in November 1790, and had accosted Lafayette to protest at the rough treatment the Guard were meting out to the people present. As a result (supposedly) of making a pun on Lafayette's family name, which received some circulation, Rotondo was beaten up by eight armed men on 28 November, arrested three times over the next two weeks, and spent most of December and January in jail. Acquitted of all charges on 20 January, he proceeded to lodge a counterclaim against the general and his men, and hence by this point was already involved in a tangled conflict with the Fayettists.[44]

---

[42] APP, AA84:106, 108. On 24 May Hion returned to complain that he had found a woman in the Palais-Royal offering for sale the pamphlets he had printed for free distribution. Lacroix, *Actes*, iv. 365, notes some details of this case, including that Hion's 'historical précis' of the plot ran to 35 quarto pages: BN 4–Ln27–9810. He cannot trace any repercussions. Hion appears to have survived the calumnies, and went on to serve on the Commune of 10 August and as a *commissaire des guerres*. He was arrested on 27 nivôse II, 'following a denunciation from the popular society of Toulouse', but apparently released, since he was disarmed and detained following the prairial rising, although subsequently rehabilitated: A. Soboul and R. Monnier, *Répertoire du personnel sectionnaire parisien en l'an II*, Paris 1985, 80.

[43] *Ami du Peuple*, no. 343, 17 Jan. 1791. Carle was a figure apparently close to the central Guard leadership, and would command the second Division of the Parisian National Guard at the Champ de Mars on 17 July.

[44] See I. Bourdin, *Les Sociétés populaires à Paris pendant la Révolution*, Paris 1937, 65 n. 2. Lafayette's family name was Motier, often spelt 'Mottié' by the radical press, who used it to taunt him. (Officially, after the abolition of nobility in June 1790, *ci-devant* nobles should

Under questioning on 7 February Maillard said that Carle 'bore a grudge for this and had paid three grenadiers to assassinate him'. These men, however, had thought better of it and told everything to Maillard over some wine. It appears from other sources collated by Sigismond Lacroix that Maillard had been suspected by Marat of Fayettism in December 1790, but had cleared his name at a meeting of the *Vainqueurs de la Bastille* on 19 December. Somehow from here he ended up in the courtroom at the Fréron/Kabert case on 26 January, at which point Carle is said to have personally threatened him, and he responded by publicising the threat. By 4 February things had developed to the point where a procession of over 200 Guards from Carle's battalion went to the Jacobin Club to protest against the latter's support for Maillard's accusation. The president of the Club told them that they could sue if they wished. However, it seems that the intimidation of hauling Maillard into the office of the *commissaire* a few days later was sufficient to end the dispute. Maillard deposed for six pages about the alleged assassination plot, but in the end had to admit that he could give no precise details of the men who had told him about it. Since there was no evidence for a charge on either side, he was sent on his way.[45] Whether he had ever been a 'Fayettist', it is clear that from December 1790 he counted himself amongst those opposing Lafayette's party, a group which the latter had already labelled as the 'Orléanist faction'.

As George Kelly has expressed it, contemporaries felt that they had good reason to see Louis-Philippe Joseph, duc d'Orléans, as a major force in the Revolution:

> [T]he presence of this colossal prince-plutocrat could not be avoided. His 7,500,000 livres of annual rent staggered the imagination; his territorial *apanage* ran to the extent of three or four of today's *départements*; he was the nominal leader of French Freemasonry; his Palais-Royal dominated Paris as Versailles dominated France; he had the temperament and intermittent talents of a *frondeur*; and his ostentatious separation from the politics of the court gave credibility to the notion of a 'revolution from above' where certain shrewd political bankers were investing.[46]

In his youth he had joined his father in protesting the Maupeou *coup*, and been banished from the court; in 1787, he had first helped to co-ordinate opposition within the Assembly of Notables, then suffered temporary internal exile for his famous protest at the royal session of the Parlement of Paris on

---

have reverted to using their family names: Motier for Lafayette, Riquetti for Mirabeau, etc. The rule was not widely observed.) Rotondo was half-Italian, and when Lafayette confronted him and asked whether he was French or Italian, his answer was 'Half one, half the other [Moitié l'un, moitié l'autre]'. One must assume that the tone made of this a mocking insult.

45 APP, AA215:388–93, Section d'Henri-Quatre; Lacroix, *Actes*, ii. 564–5.
46 G. A. Kelly, 'The machine of the duc d'Orléans and the new politics', *Journal of Modern History* li (1979), 667–84 at p. 667.

19 November. His massive popularity, springing also from his turning of the Palais-Royal into a public pleasure-ground earlier in the decade, was further increased by his role in the Estates-General, and it was widely felt that this was being managed as a vast power-play for the throne.[47] Since 1788 Choderlos de Laclos had become his secretary and chief advisor, and there is no doubt that the duke's funds were liberally spent in the name of liberalism.

Figures as diverse as Barère, Duport, Mirabeau, Sieyès, Dumouriez, Desmoulins, Danton and Marat were alleged to have been received into the Orléans 'machine' at points in 1789, although Mounier, Lafayette and Robespierre were not: Kelly describes them as 'bitter enemies and not for hire'.[48] For Kelly, all this, and many of the other allegations raised against the duke, should not be seen as 'conspiratorial', but as 'a new politics that we would judge normal'. In other words, as the gathering of like-minded people around a source of funds for the pursuit of a political agenda – and one which was, in its avowed aims, unobjectionably liberal.[49]

However, in the context of the late eighteenth century, such an open and innocent interpretation of political activity was unlikely, to say the least. It is of course the conspiratorial aspect of all these plans which captured the attention, and alarm, of contemporaries, and continued to do so for many years.[50] Orléans was to be accused, not merely of general democratic agitation, but specifically of plotting the violent overthrow of the monarchy – notably during the October Days, an episode from which his bitter personal enemy Lafayette emerged with flying colours, while the duke fled into exile. He had remarked upon first hearing of the women's march that it was all a plot by Lafayette, but that he would get the blame anyway, and so it largely transpired.[51] By 1791 this 'Fayettist/Orléanist' axis of conflict was clearly present on the streets of Paris. The Fayettist side had established an intelligence 'machine' based in the headquarters of the Parisian National Guard, from where they actively combatted what they saw as Orléanists and their supporters amongst both the press and the rabble, viewed as acting persistently to enflame popular sentiments against public order and in favour of the duke. As well as press coverage, this battle also included tactics such as 'the distribution of cheap bread and of money, and the spreading of rumours and

---

[47] On the Palais-Royal see R. M. Isherwood, *Farce and fantasy: popular entertainment in eighteenth-century Paris*, Oxford 1986, ch. viii, 217ff., and D. M. McMahon, 'The birthplace of the Revolution: public space and political community in the Palais-Royal of Louis-Philippe-Joseph d'Orléans, 1781–1789', *French History* x (1996), 1–29.
[48] Kelly, 'Machine of the duc d'Orléans', 674.
[49] Ibid. 675.
[50] Indeed, until the *Bicentenaire* itself. See H. La Marle, *Phillipe Égalité, 'grand maître' de la Révolution*, Paris 1989, and, for a far more sympathetic approach, A. Castelot, *Philippe Égalité le régicide*, Paris 1991.
[51] For this remark see ibid. 185. For the long-drawn-out (and ultimately unsuccessful) attempt to formally pin the blame for these events firmly on Orléans see Shapiro, *Revolutionary justice*, chs iv, ix, x.

counter-rumours by oral and written means', all in the attempt to excite or calm *le peuple*, particularly those of the feared Faubourgs St-Marcel and St-Antoine.[52]

Evidence to indicate that Lafayette did fund and organise some of the propaganda for social peace that emerged over this period is quite clear, but it is a large step from here to accepting the inverse proposition, that every pamphlet calling on the people to protest against economic or political conditions, and every disturbance that arose, was a product of an organised Orléanist opposition. Such disturbances could be multi-faceted, in response both to major issues, and to everyday concerns. For example, tensions rose dramatically in Paris during the latter half of May 1790, as the National Assembly endured stormy debates over the delicate issue of constitutional rights to make war and peace. Patriotic anger at royalist pamphleteers and journalists led to several attacks on print-shops, and the public burning of publications by crowds – a particularly violent and widespread outbreak followed the final vote for a compromise solution on 22 May. Such incidents were, of course, widely and luridly reported, adding to the atmosphere of confrontation.[53]

Two days after this last disturbance, three men, caught stealing silver plates in a hostelry, were being marched into detention at the Châtelet when one of them is said to have cried out 'that for an *écu* [a coin worth several *livres*] he would be out the next day'. The response to this intimation of police corruption was dramatic:

> The numerous people surrounding them let out a cry of fury, tore the three villains from the hands of the Guard, who could put up no resistance to the immense crowd who had seized them. The thieves were conducted to the St-Antoine market. Two of them were hanged, and the other killed by stoning.[54]

The next day, 'an immense crowd, armed with sticks' attacked a thief in Guard custody on the quai de la Feraille – his fate is unclear from the *Moniteur* report, but he was probably killed. Lafayette himself was passing the area, and plunged heroically into the mob to seize one of the 'assassins'. He berated the crowd, brought it to its senses 'and warned it of the factious efforts being made to arouse them'. The paper editorialised that 'the good people of Paris are not at all guilty of these excesses; they are indubitable proof that the capital is today given over to vagabond outsiders, without domicile, paid to excite disorder'. The next edition reported the municipal decision to double

[52] O. Elyada, 'L'Appel aux faubourgs: pamphlets populaires et propagande à Paris, 1789–1790', in Vovelle, *Paris*, 185–200. One should note that Elyada appears to have no difficulty in taking the actual existence of the Orléanist 'party' for granted.

[53] See W. J. Murray, *The right-wing press in the French Revolution, 1789–1792*, London 1986, 96–102, esp. pp. 96–7, and *Moniteur*, 24, 26 May 1790.

[54] Ibid. 26 May 1790.

the Guard patrols, and preparations for swift intervention in future incidents (which did not occur). It was alleged that 'positive and determined knowledge exists of sums distributed to brigands, mostly outsiders, to desolate the capital'. If one riot was a misfortune, two were 'a plot formed against public tranquillity, factious designs, the project of attacking the laws and the Constitution through the hands of a ferocious and misled multitude'.[55]

As contemporaries in general blamed outbreaks such as these on *factieux* and *brigands*, so the Fayettists were sure that the 'faction' strengthened by such unrest was that of the duke, and that 'since the end of April [1790], agents of the duc d'Orléans [had] appeared again in the popular faubourgs', accompanying the duke's imminent return from his English exile. The sole evidence available for this, however, is that Marat had resumed publishing the *Ami du Peuple*, and between late May and early July made several calls on the people to rise up. This, however, was his standard fare, and there is no particular evidence beyond supposition to link him in any way to Orléans. George Kelly has observed that such figures as Marat may well have received funds from Orléans (or more properly Laclos – it was far too delicate a job for the indolent duke), but that 'if he "bought" talents, he did not need to invent their ideas for them'.[56]

The case for seeing Orléanist propaganda as the sole effective fount of sedition relies on some very feeble foundations, especially when viewed with two centuries of hindsight. Unlike Lafayette, whose party's publications are distinct in tone and style, Orléans is supposed to have used 'already existing journals' to put across his message, a system deduced from the comments of his enemies and the occasional sympathy shown for the duke in certain papers. Even Ouzi Elyada, generally uncritical of the Fayettist assumptions on this issue, recognises that it is difficult to see men such as Marat and Fréron as conscious Orléanist agents, 'but it is highly possible that these latter were paid from time to time'. Moreover, although 'we have no exact details of the financial relationships' linking the duke to various *Père Duchesne* papers, they are supposed to have been associated with him, having made sympathetic gestures around the New Year of 1791. The fact that the same papers continued to support the Cordelier–Jacobin 'Left' is read as evidence of 'a certain co-operation' between these two political forces.[57]

There is no doubt that the war between the agents of Lafayette and the radical press grew more bitter in the early months of 1791, until in late March several of them were reduced to physically destroying the presses of Anne-Felicité Colombe, publisher of an anti-clerical *Père Duchesne*, as well as of Marat's and Fréron's journals.[58] The police records show that on the 11th of that month, Mlle Colombe had already been threatened by a party of *grena-*

---

55 Ibid. 27, 28 May 1790.
56 Elyada, 'L'Appel', 185–9; Kelly, 'Machine of the duc d'Orléans', 677.
57 Elyada, 'L'Appel', 193.
58 Ibid. 196.

diers from the Filles St-Thomas Battalion, who had been calumniated in the *Orateur du Peuple* – when they complained to the Section authorities about this, she counterclaimed that they had threatened 'to follow her all the way to the scaffold'.[59] Several months earlier, on 14 December 1790, Estienne, the chief agent later responsible for destroying her press, had tried to have its products seized pursuant to an action for defamation against Fréron. At the time, Colombe had lodged a protest against the illegality of the search being made: 'she reserves the right to take action against the persons who allowed themselves this visit, before the competent tribunals and in front of the nation, interested in the conservation of the liberty of all its members'.[60] This may be merely bluster, but it does not sound like the talk of a corrupt political agent.

Elyada sees the final assault on Mlle Colombe as an admission of defeat by the Fayettists in the face of a powerful coalition of Orléanists and radicals – the 'authoritarian arguments' that made up Fayettist discourse had failed to reach 'a people who engaged more and more in democratic practices in the Sections and the popular societies'. We might see this conclusion as an admission of defeat in trying to find real evidence for Orléanist propaganda. Elyada admits 'that while serving Orléanist interests [which mainly means criticising Lafayette], the Duchesne papers continued to function as commercial businesses. The alarming headlines . . . were vehicles of manipulative messages . . . but they served equally as a means to invite the crowd to buy the papers'.[61] Given the general explosion of press production (and competition) during the early years of the Revolution, this argument for the dual purpose of such publications would not seem to hold up for long against Occam's Razor.

If it seems reasonable to suggest that the radicals were writing in good faith (or at least what passed for it in a commercial venture), we also have to acknowledge that the Fayettists probably believed what they were saying. Their discourse painted the common people as 'incapable of participating in political life in a democratic fashion, as they lacked the education, the intellectual apparatus, and the experience: they had to recognise their limits and leave the care, management and protection of the popular interest to the "brave general" and "our good king" '.[62] In its conception of the incompetence of *le peuple*, this is scarcely an advance on Old Regime notions, and quite probably ran deeper than a merely intellectual assertion – those who held this position are likely to have genuinely believed in popular political

[59] APP, AA215:409–411, Section d'Henri-Quatre.
[60] APP, AA215:345–7. The Colombe printworks would be raided again in the aftermath of the Champ de Mars, and its entire staff of three taken into custody as they were preparing an edition of the *Ami du Peuple* (APP, AA206:388; AB324:1851, Section de la Place-Vendôme; they were transferred to the Abbaye on 27 July). Estienne was well-known to the radical press as a Fayettist agent, frequently described and caricatured: A. de Baecque, *The body politic: corporeal metaphor in revolutionary France, 1770–1800*, Stanford 1997, 244–5.
[61] Elyada, 'L'Appel', 194.
[62] Ibid.

incapacity, from which the idea of factional agitation followed in 1791 as logically as it did in 1757 at the trial of Damiens.

We might with hindsight pardon the Fayettists for their blinkered viewpoint, but it is none the less clear that, having conceived of the various forces opposing them from below as agents of a faction, they proceeded to create a counter-faction to combat them. Agents such as Estienne did conduct a shady war of attrition against individuals determined to publish their radical views, and figures such as Desmottes and Beauregard persecuted those in the Guard they regarded as insufficiently loyal. Radicals such as Rotondo and Maillard who confronted these forces in various ways received short shrift, even if they could sometimes give as good as they got, in the courts of law and public opinion, if not in various dark alleyways. The determination to single out individuals and to pursue a politics of intimidation actively helped to create the sense within the radical elements of Parisian society that they were being persecuted by forces that were, from their perspective, counter-revolutionary. Unfortunately, no political group was able to truly reconcile its view of the active forces at work with an overall picture of the place of the common people and its actions in the revolutionary drama. The long-term history of the people of Paris, and the attempts of the *ancien régime* to manage them in accordance with its own narrow views of popular capacities, had resulted in a situation of almost universal incomprehension. These failures to match expectations to behaviour would be mapped onto the new revolutionary body politic, with dramatic and tragic consequences in 1791, and beyond.

3

Guards, Spies and Commissaires: Policing the Capital

The tragic incomprehensions that formed the political landscape of Paris would be reflected again in responses to the confused *journée* of 28 February. Before returning to that we need to gain a clearer view of the operations of those charged with public order, an arena within which the Fayettist quest for political order was played out. The multiple demands of the Section de la Place-Vendôme on 22 February give a sense of the alarm that frequently arose in the population at the threat of disorder. The unauthorised wearing of Guard uniforms was a particular concern, considering both the revolutionaries' highly-tuned sense of visual identity and the licence such an imposture gave to go armed. Nor was it entirely an empty fear – on 18 January a man who worked on the fish boats was arrested wearing the full uniform and equipment of a grenadier, and passed nearly a month in prison before being released with a warning. On 5 February a journeyman locksmith dressed as a gunner was arrested, for that fact as well as for 'having spread invective against the National Assembly'. He spent eleven days in prison. The next day a man threatened a deputy with a sabre, which was confiscated. He was allowed to keep the *chasseur* uniform he was wearing, however, so he may have been just an enraged patriot.[1]

Whatever the reason for such impostures (and it is likely that the second-hand clothing trade had something to do with it) there was also a very real undercurrent of popular hostility to the National Guard itself.[2] In the first two weeks of January eight clashes between Guard and population resulted in imprisonments. In most cases the detainee spent no more than two or three days in La Force before being either vouched for or released on his own recognisance. It is probable that some of the unspecified 'insults' and 'affronts' were the result of enforcing closing-time in bars, but two others involved 'having stirred people up' against the Guard, another 'having aroused [ameuté] the public' to the same end, and a fourth arose from the Guard attempting to

---

1   APP, AB322:1013, 1101, 1125. There is no indication of what political colour the *député* was.
2   On the clothing-trade, and its burgeoning development in the eighteenth century, see D. Roche, *The people of Paris: an essay in popular culture in the eighteenth century*, trans. M. Evans and G. Lewis, Leamington Spa 1987, esp. ch. vi, and *The culture of clothing: dress and fashion in the Old Regime*, Cambridge 1994, esp. ch. xii.

'disperse a gathering on the place de Grève'.[3] Several more cases in late January include a public-relief worker who set his dog on a sentry, an unidentified man who included Lafayette in his curses, and a journeyman shoemaker who served two weeks for hitting a Guard.[4]

The cases are fewer in February, but those which did arise seem to have been more serious. On the 7th a man struck a Guard and insulted Lafayette, earning a one-month sentence from the Police Tribunal. On the 19th, a public-relief worker and other unidentified men set upon a Guard seriously enough to earn the worker a six-month sentence. As for opinions, on the 21st a journeyman joiner remarked as a patrol passed, 'that the bayonets wouldn't last for long'. He only spent two days in jail, however, as he was vouched for.[5]

The 'bayonets' that he denounced had inherited a tradition of policing that, as is well-known, was the most organised in Europe. Throughout the eighteenth century the police had spread a continually tightening net of surveillance and control across Paris. Although they had doubtless never planned to encounter a revolution, none the less their perceived enemies were almost ubiquitous. These ranged from the ever-present vagabonds to the servant class and the disorderly troops of women and children, on up into the realm of those who had an 'interest' in encouraging subversion, a realm embracing the highest concerns of state. That such sinister figures existed was axiomatic in the conduct of policing. For years in the 1730s the police had a standing order to locate and detain one Gaspard de Vise, believed to be the principal force behind the convulsionaries of St-Médard, although he was never found. The *Lieutenant-général de Police*, Lenoir, whose service ended in 1785, still believed that Jansenist agitation across the century was part of a plot in alliance with Protestantism 'to destroy the clergy of France and to overturn royal authority'. The pursuit of this was one of the contexts in which Dutch and German ambassadors and tourists were watched, although good reasons could always be found to scrutinise any foreigners.[6]

Jansenism was only one of the many fields in which the *ancien régime* police actively strove to head off a perceived threat to public order. It is an historical commonplace now to invoke their concern with the administration of the food supply, the regulation of the flood of foundlings into the city and the reverse flow of infants put out to wet-nurse, or the maintenance of the cleanliness and lighting of the streets, alongside those tasks which seem more appropriate to modern notions of policing.[7] What is less widely observed, indeed scarcely acknowledged, is that the revolutionary adminis-

---

3   APP, AB322:715, 769, 772, 783, 787, 796, 806, 874. Of these, the *état* of six perpetrators can be identified: a newspaper-seller, an unemployed clerk, a journeyman upholsterer and a journeyman tailor, a worker on public relief and a 'former principal notary's clerk'.
4   APP, AB322:958, 980, 1051.
5   APP, AB322:1132, 1271, 1282.
6   Williams, *Police*, 189–237, esp. pp. 198–200.
7   See, for example, J. Godechot, *The taking of the Bastille*, London 1970, 64–86, where these and other tasks are covered in summary detail.

tration assumed the role of the *ancien régime* police almost in its entirety. The final elimination of the Châtelet police jurisdiction came, along with that of the other courts and parlements, at the end of 1790. On 26 December the new municipal *Département de Police* published a decree setting out the division of tasks among its four administrators.

The first of these, named Thorillon, had charge of all matters concerning the military, such as recruitment and offences by soldiers on leave, along with the fire service, the organisation of the National Guard for routine policing, as well as the following:

> sweeping, clearance of mud and snow, watering, illumination, . . . pleasure-grounds [wauxhalls, panthéon], public balls, clubs, circuses, public promenades, squares, streets, crossroads, edifices, churches, cemeteries, for good order, decency, morals and security, inspection of pharmacies and druggists, execution of current and future regulations.

The second, Jolly, despite the freedom of the press supposedly granted by the Revolution, controlled:

> spectacles, booksellers, printing, engraving, hawkers, . . . markets and horse-post, public carriages and cabs, posts and message-services, open and enclosed markets, workers and domestic servants, wet-nurses and their agents, enumeration of the inhabitants of Paris.

The third area of responsibility went to Perron, a serving member of the municipal investigation committee (*comité des recherches*), making him particularly suitable to watch over:

> furnished lodgings, inns, those letting rooms, cafés, vagabonds, fraudsters, beggars, denunciations of theft, foreigners, jews, gaming-houses, nocturnal assemblies, prostitutes, quacks, passports [along with correspondence with other authorities].

Lastly, one Maugis had the surveillance of:

> guilds and corporations, weights and measures, second-hand clothes dealers, resellers, cloth and fabric markets, butchers and slaughterhouses, bakeries, the stock-market, lotteries, customs barriers, and all that is relative to the collection of dues.[8]

Their names are almost all we know of these men. All were lawyers: Perron had been a barrister to the royal council [*avocat aux conseils du roi*], Jolly a barrister before the Parlement of Paris and Maugis and Thorillon both prosecutors at the Châtelet. Recent work which extensively details the political role of the municipal *comité des recherches* in 1789–90 can only give two para-

---

8   These lists are taken from the *Révolutions de Paris*, 8–15 Jan., but appear in the same form in other journals.

graphs of vague information on Perron, and no personal details. It is known that he continued to serve as a police administrator until 10 August 1792, but was subsequently arrested and killed in the September massacres, having been called in a pamphlet that April the 'grand-master of the *mouchards*' – with some reason, as we shall see. On the other administrators, our information is even more hazy.[9]

If these men must remain relatively faceless, it is none the less clear that they presided over an institution which was intended to maintain a comprehensive grip on Parisian life. Although legislation in early 1791 would remove elements such as the guilds and customs barriers from this panoply, it still stretched far and wide over almost all public activities, and no doubt some private ones. The fact that the chief agents of this police apparatus have remained obscure figures, compared with the renowned pre-revolutionary *lieutenants*, Sartine and Lenoir, is one indication of how far revolutionary politics had moved Paris away from the point at which such a system could have been successfully imposed.

That is not to say that the police system was a complete failure on the ground. By early 1791 day-to-day policing was probably as effective as it had been before 1789, with various elements working in a more co-ordinated version of their predecessors' roles. Neighbourhood guardhouses and patrols were mounted by the volunteer National Guard of the local Sections, in place of the old Guard and Watch, while the paid companies provided the permanent back-up once afforded by the French Guards – frequently with the same personnel. Civil policing was provided by an elected *commissaire de police* in each Section (assisted by up to sixteen part-time *commissaires de section*), performing the same role as the old Châtelet *commissaires* – receiving complaints and declarations, conducting initial interrogations of suspects and those caught red-handed, deciding on referrals to the central authorities or a summary night in a guardhouse cell, and generally monitoring the security of the Section.[10]

The organisation of the National Guard had developed steadily over the first months of the Revolution. Provisional regulations for the *Garde nationale parisienne* were adopted in early August 1789, imposing uniformity on the hurried and sometimes haphazard formation of neighbourhood militias which

---

9 *Moniteur*, 24 Oct. 1790. See also Lacroix, *Actes*, viii. 282; P. Robiquet, *Le Personnel municipal de Paris pendant la Révolution*, Paris 1890; Shapiro, *Revolutionary justice*, 24.
10 The *commissaire de police* system was established by the law of 21 May 1790 which defined the whole structure of municipal government for Paris: Jones, *Companion to the French Revolution*, 210–11. See also Garrioch, *Neighbourhood*, 1–15, for the role of the Châtelet *commissaires*. Andrews, 'Political élites', offers a socio-political breakdown of the *commissaires de police* of 1792–4, who were a different breed from those of 1791. On the National Guard see D. L. Clifford, 'The National Guard and the Parisian community', *French Historical Studies* xvi (1990), 849–78, and 'Command over equals: the officer corps of the Parisian National Guard, 1789–90', *Proceedings of the Annual Meeting of the Western Society for French History* xviii (1991), 152–65.

had emerged from the crisis of 12–14 July. Each of the sixty Districts was to have a 500–man battalion, including 100 paid Guards recruited principally from the French Guards and other defunct military units. The paid guardsmen, living in barracks under full-time discipline, were intended to give the headquarters a reliable core of military strength. They were supplemented by six extra paid companies, one attached to each of the Divisions of ten Districts, and by late October by a corps of paid cavalry, six companies of *chasseurs* at the customs barriers, and permanent guards for the Halles – the main central markets – and the ports. Lafayette, who commanded the Guard from 15 July 1789, also put some energy into establishing the principle that all movements of Guard units outside their own Districts were to be controlled by the headquarters, not District authorities – this was stated definitively by the municipality after the October Days.[11] Although as time progressed Lafayette and the municipality were to impose an increasingly centralised structure on the Guard, every step down this path was hard-fought by the jealous advocates of District autonomy.[12]

Arguments concerning the rights of Districts over 'their' forces continued into 1790, principally in the form of attempts to recall officers for dubious conduct. Although one prominent case involved an accusation of excessive use of force in favour of grain-merchants, others included charges of favouritism and nepotism, and simple dereliction of duty, and still more were quibbles over the form of, or necessity for, written commissions. In a similar way Districts and Battalions continued to resent the overly military manner of the officers of the General Staff. Lafayette had hand-picked these men for their reliability and experience, qualifications which resulted in an exclusively noble, albeit 'patriotic', body. Their attempts to treat the Guard like a regular military force subject to discipline (which on duty it theoretically was) resulted in yelps of outrage at arbitrary and aristocratic ways.[13]

The national authorities' view of the Guard remained one conditioned by absolutes. What they wanted from the Guard was spelled out by Rabaut de St-Etienne on 21 November 1790, reporting to the Assembly on a project for the organisation of the Guard: 'To deliberate, hesitate, refuse, are crimes. To obey, there, in a single word, are all their duties. A blind and purely passive instrument, the public force has neither soul, nor thought, nor will.'[14]

Even those such as Dubois de Crancé, who wanted more acknowledgement of the role of the Guard as a bulwark against despotism and internal enemies, agreed that it should not have the right of deliberation or disobedience. Furthermore, its powers to enforce public order were continually

---

11 Clifford, 'National Guard', 853–4.
12 Ibid. 851, 853–5.
13 Idem, 'Command', 156–60.
14 F. Devenne, 'La Garde nationale: création et évolution, 1789–Août 1792', *Annales historiques de la Révolution française* cclxxxiii (1991), 49–66 at p. 56. Dubois de Crancé later criticised the Parisian Guards for slavishly pledging loyalty to Lafayette after the 18 April 1791 débâcle.

strengthened. Ten days after the Champ de Mars Massacre, a new law was voted that reduced the number of warnings the Guard had to give before firing on crowds. Article ten of this legislation codified the fields in which the Guard could be used against the people:

> Seditious gatherings . . . [against the collection of feudal dues], against the collection of public contributions [i.e. taxes], against the absolute liberty of circulation of foodstuffs and gold and silver currency . . . against the freedom of work and industry, as well as [concerning] conventions relative to the level of wages, will be dispersed.[15]

Within this measure were incorporated the commitments to the freedom of the grain trade and the collection of dues sworn at the Festival of Federation of 14 July 1790, as well as the anti-worker Loi Le Chapelier of June 1791, whose article eight had authorised the Guard to disperse workers' meetings, 'held to be seditious gatherings'.[16] If, as we shall see, the desire of the authorities for an unthinking instrument of public order was far from being fulfilled in practice, no more is it true that the Guard stood up for democracy, whatever its early complaints about 'military aristocracy'.

While enthusiasm for autonomy continued at the District level, the organisation of the Guard reinforced its identity as a 'bourgeois' force, and aided its mission of social order. Even if non-active citizens were only formally excluded in 1791, 'all workers, artisans and non-domiciled citizens' were exempted by the 1789 regulations – which in practice was generally taken to mean excluded, especially as a six-*livre* compensatory bounty was offered to those who left, and specific measures and incentives were in place to disarm workers. It is true that some of the poorer men who had rendered service in the July crisis were allowed to remain, and that some Districts set up uniform funds to help the 'less well-off', but in general the Guard steadily consolidated its nature as a militia of property-holders. Over time, Guard service clearly became less of a revolutionary honour, and more of a routine burden. This was reflected in the regulations, which indicated that the obligation of Guard service fell on all propertied persons, not merely the 400 volunteers, and in District practice, which frequently involved extracting contributions from the non-serving bourgeois to finance the battalion. As early as August 1789, one District made the role of the Guard particularly explicit, ruling that all property-holders were liable to contribute 'for the common defence of the property included within a district'. This included women and clergy, clearly exempt from actual service.[17]

One study has explored the status of 344 Guard patrol-leaders who

---

[15] Ibid. 61.

[16] Ibid. 55, 60.

[17] Clifford, 'National Guard', 854, 865–7. Many of the issues raised by Clifford are also discussed by M. Genty, 'Controverses autour de la garde nationale parisienne', *Annales historiques de la Révolution française* ccxci (1993), 61–88. Genty cites many documents from early

brought prisoners before *commissaires* in July–December 1789. While lawyers were preponderant in elective office at this time, they number only twenty-three in this sample, compared to fifty *bourgeois de Paris*, ninety-three artisans and ninety-eight merchants and shopkeepers. The sample also includes ten clerks or *employés*, six workers and one unemployed domestic servant, a status normally associated with the dangerous *populace*. None the less, despite a few survivors of the popular mobilisation of July 1789, the Guard was clearly predominantly the domain of those who, by 1791, would be defined as active citizens. The records of battalion and company officers in comparison show an unsurprising shift up the social scale, signifying in part the importance of those with prior military experience. Relating the Guard figures to those of militiamen in Petit St-Antoine in the July crisis, and to citizen activists in St-Germain l'Auxerrois in 1790, it can be said that 'The active National Guard was more similar to the broadly representative group of citizens who turned out to defend the Revolution in Petit St-Antoine than it was to the district leadership.' In particular, the tendency for lawyers and professionals to be over-represented in political activism emerges clearly.[18]

The author of this study, Dale Clifford, has also argued that the Guard became a more politicised force over time, and that towards 1791, hostility to 'military aristocracy' in the Guard grew, and the contests over officer elections increasingly emphasised the autonomy of the Districts and citizens' rights. She also notes that in this changing and radicalising political climate, there was a 'surprising' lack of change in the officer corps: 'instead of alteration by "new men", the officer corps slowly became more radical because its members did'.[19] Although men of military background declined from around 36 per cent of battalion commanders to 20 per cent, to be replaced by men of business, this was a relatively small shift, and the vast majority of officer elections confirmed existing positions, or merely juggled the hierarchy.

There is one sense in which the National Guard was clearly becoming more 'political' – almost half its battalion commanders in late 1790 held another local office. Clifford argues that this reflected the politicisation of the population as a whole, not a shift in social composition, but it could equally be suggested that control of the Guard and the Districts was falling into the hands of a more concentrated group with the time to devote to a long-term administrative commitment.[20] The organisation in May–July 1790 of the forty-eight Sections as a replacement for the sixty Districts, which assigned the new administrative units a much smaller role in politics, also cut the direct link to the sixty battalions. This was intended as a measure to combat the political independence of the Guard, and to undercut the general

debates on the Guard, although this work does not ultimately seem to add anything not already said by Clifford.

18 Clifford, 'National Guard', 876–8.
19 Idem, 'Command', 153.
20 Ibid. 160–1.

rebelliousness of some Districts. It seems to have succeeded in quelling the ardour of a few radical assemblies, but the reorganisation left many of the old boundaries unchanged, so the intended fragmentation was largely ineffective.[21]

While this explains why the Guard might have clung to its autonomy, it is not hard to find flaws in a simple model of the 'politicisation' of the guard-mounting classes. If it is true, as Clifford indicates, that the rhetorical intensity of disputes grew over time, none the less she has also demonstrated that the tensions over command practices in the Guard had been present from its origins. Further, we may observe that if the militia 'turned out to defend the Revolution' in July 1789, they were also deeply concerned for their property. As Jacques Godechot's account of the July events makes clear, the maintenance of public order and respect for property was a prime concern of militia patrols, to the extent of lynching looters in some areas.[22]

Such attitudes were to remain firmly on display in the months following those events. In his account of 1789, George Rudé notes, for example, that various trades petitioning the municipality late in the summer for improvements in pay and conditions were rebuffed as brusquely as they had been by the old order, 'sometimes with the help of the National Guard'. The hostility that the Guard was already engendering is evident in the outburst of one domestic, who received no less than two years' imprisonment in August for having said in the Palais-Royal, after municipal refusal to grant citizens' rights to servants:

> that all the bourgeois guard and all the people who wore the uniform were all f—ers ['j.f.', for 'jean-foutres'] and that 10,000 domestics were capable of f—ing over all the f—ers who wore the blue coats . . . and that there were 60,000 domestics in Paris who could unite with the workers of various conditions [états] and they would see all these f—ers hide at home with their f—ing coats.[23]

Hostility such as this would continue to be part of the public landscape in 1791, and the anti-clerical protest which aggravated the opposition between Guard and people had already been present in 1789. At the end of September a dispute over burial-fees led first to a riot in which a curé was forced to carry out a funeral service, then to another which threatened the life of the curé of a neighbouring parish who had dismissed his choir-leader for taking part in the funeral – reinstatement under the auspices of the National Guard, along with a ringleader's arrest, calmed the crowd.[24]

Thus the Guard was already embroiled in multifaceted conflicts, and an

---

[21] See Rose, *Making of the sans-culottes*, 77–82, 87–93, on the abolition of the Districts.
[22] Godechot, *Bastille*, 199.
[23] Rudé, *Crowd*, 65. His original sentence had been branding and nine years in the galleys, but this was commuted.
[24] Ibid. 66.

accelerating cycle of subsistence disturbances through August and September would see their relations with the population further strained, as they found themselves arresting individuals for accusing Lafayette of complicity in shortage. Guards had to be stationed in bakeries from the beginning of September, and by the 18th the Hôtel de Ville was experiencing its third minor siege by angry crowds.[25]

The October Days themselves demonstrated the continued complexity of social relations, and placed the Guard in opposition to a Parisian people determined to deal with their perceived enemies. As well as the various issues mentioned above, popular discontent had also turned on political events in Versailles. Such demonstrations as had taken place, including an unarmed march by 1,500 people from the Palais-Royal towards Versailles on 30 August, had been broken up by the Guard. By September radical patriots were contrasting their position with the *patrouillotisme*, 'patrol-otism', of Lafayette's militia.[26] As was only to be expected in the circumstances, the accusations of famine-plotting that had condemned the previous administration again fuelled denunciations of the new one. As Barry Shapiro points out, the *journée* of 5 October actually began with a crowd assault on the Hôtel de Ville itself, which was narrowly prevented from escalating into lynching and wholesale arson. Women in the crowd proclaimed that 'the entire Commune was composed of bad citizens who all deserved to be hanged, beginning with M. Bailly and M. de Lafayette'.[27] This crowd was turned aside from its municipal targets towards seeking culprits at Versailles, and at this point the Guard demonstrated that it was not yet devoid of 'soul, nor thought, nor will', by obliging Lafayette to lead them virtually at gunpoint.

Shapiro demonstrates that by turning the focus of hostility from municipal to national authority, Lafayette eventually managed to achieve a considerable victory over a potentially dangerous insurrection, while at the same time further securing the constitutionalists' power-base against the aristocrats. Events appeared to vindicate the crowd's actions after the transport of the royal family to Paris, as the Assembly acted to ensure that bread reached the capital in adequate quantities, at a lower price than in the summer.[28] However, in line with the notion that the October Days were a victory for the moderates in the city, a crackdown on radicals followed. This began with the press – a warrant drove Marat into hiding, and on 8 October a decree zealously enforced by Guard patrols restricted what newspaper-hawkers [*colporteurs*] could cry in the streets.[29] Furthermore, the third week of October

25 Ibid. 67–9.
26 Shapiro, *Revolutionary justice*, 89.
27 Testimony of Stanislas Maillard, ibid. 90. This episode was of course one of the greatest demonstrations of female political initiative during the revolutionary decade, as re-emphasised recently by D. Garrioch, 'The everyday lives of Parisian women and the October Days of 1789', *Social History* xxiv (1999), 231–49.
28 Rudé, *Crowd*, 78.
29 Shapiro, *Revolutionary justice*, 100–1

saw a clash which ended this series of food protests. On the 21st a baker who had hoarded bread (allegedly for the Assembly, widening the import of the crime) was subjected to the classic fate of the people's enemies. Dragged first to the Hôtel de Ville, where officials promised that he would be tried, he died hanged from a streetlamp on the Place de Grève as the crowd's patience rapidly expired. His head toured the city on a pike. Lafayette's response was a full mobilisation of the Guard, breaking up the parade of the trophy and various associated disturbances, and clearing the Place de Grève itself with the threat of cannon fire. Later the same day, the Assembly was moved to pass the martial law provision that would be invoked on 17 July 1791, and within twenty-four hours two protestors had been executed to drive home the point. One of these was probably guilty of complicity in the baker's death, but the other had done no more than attempt to rouse a crowd in the Faubourg St-Antoine.[30]

In keeping with his general theme of the leniency of revolutionary justice in 1789–90, Shapiro points out that rioters arrested prior to this incident received light custodial sentences or brief periods in the pillory. It could equally be argued, however, that the judicial response to the 21 October riot was almost as severe as that to the Reveillon riots of April 1789, for which three men were hanged and five branded by the *ancien régime* authorities.[31] Certainly, it was part of a general administrative offensive which also targeted excessive autonomy in the Districts, and some individual activists.[32] Thus the October Days and their aftermath demonstrated that although in a crisis the Guard could put political goals above blind obedience, it was ready and willing to crack down on popular unrest once the 'bigger' issue of the king had been settled.

If the events of 1789 suggested on the whole that Parisian National Guards could ultimately be relied on to behave as a force for public order, evidence from more everyday policing suggests that their definition of order could be somewhat arbitrary. For example, on 4 January 1791 a Guard patrol led by a *commissaire de police* was in the Palais-Royal confiscating obscene material from hawkers. A scuffle resulted in a bystander being arrested for insulting the Guard. This twenty-two-year-old confectioner said,

> that he had not at all insulted them, that he had seen one of the National Guards who were assisting us [i.e. the *commissaire*] push back a gentleman [un Monsieur] by the arm, and that he, the respondent, had said 'one moment, don't push people so hard', at which the National Guard had said to him that he would f— his sabre through his belly, that he the respondent observed to him that it was no part of his duties to be able to do that.

---

30 Ibid. 103–5.
31 Rudé, *Crowd*, 34–43. The April events, however, had also led to at least several dozen deaths in the direct repression of the riots.
32 Shapiro, *Revolutionary justice*, 106–7, 108–14.

The *commissaire* got him to admit that he had used the word *polisson*, 'rascal', in talking to the Guard, but he did not question the substance of the exchange.[33]

What also contributes to a sense of unease at the ability of the Guard to manage the duties it had been given are incidents such as the shot fired at a sentry on 26 January. The investigators found a Guard volunteer in a third-floor apartment who admitted that he had taken up his gun, which he habitually kept loaded, but that 'inadvertently he had discharged it through the window, perhaps excited by a little drink'. On 2 March a shot went through a boutique on the quai de la Megisserie, narrowly missing the two people inside. It was traced to another bourgeois volunteer, who admitted 'that it was indeed true that he had fired that shot, but that he didn't know that a musket carried so far'. On 28 June two artisans, a journeyman innkeeper, two labourers and a water-carrier declared that they had seen a shot come from the apartment of a jeweller on the rue St-Louis, and felt obliged to say something 'as misfortunes occur every day from shots fired imprudently and without precaution; that last Friday . . . the water-carrier Etienne Meunier was dangerously wounded' by another accidental shot.[34] Mirabeau's funeral service in April was marred when a *fusillade* was fired in his honour, and a shot from a gun which had been left loaded brought down a piece of masonry from the ceiling of St-Eustache onto the head of a Guard.[35]

Men capable of these everyday incompetencies, buoyed up by a sense of aggressive righteousness, were sent out on twenty-four-hour shifts to police a city that had for centuries been regarded as a sink of iniquity, a reputation now accentuated by the threat of counter-revolutionary co-optation of the *populace*. How far these factors added to the escalation of social tensions in 1791 is a question we shall address later, but there can be no doubt that the potentially aggressive insecurity and enthusiasms of the Guard need to be appreciated in order to understand what occurred in those months.

The basic volatility of the Guard as a police force added to a situation in which justice and public order were already in a precarious state. The normal processes of justice had been effectively suspended since 1789, and by early 1791 it had become necessary to create six Provisional Criminal Tribunals alongside the new regular courts, to get the backlog under control.[36] The prisons were clogged with defendants awaiting trial, while the ongoing econ-

[33] APP, AA82:29, Section du Palais-Royal. The man was released when he was vouched for by his employer.

[34] APP, AA215:372–4, Section d'Henri-Quatre; AA182:103, Section du Louvre; AA215:453, Section d'Henri-Quatre. In no case was any observable action taken, except to relieve the inebriated man temporarily of his weapon, and to file a report with the police administrators.

[35] See Lacroix, *Actes*, iii. 538. On 11 April, as a result of this incident, the municipality banned such indoor firing.

[36] The records of these institutions can be found in series Z3 of the Archives nationales, and have been used to good effect in A. Wills, *Crime and punishment in revolutionary Paris*,

omic crisis continued to cast more unfortunates athwart the law. The overall result was a constant procession of petty (and not-so-petty) criminals passing into and out of the prisons. A glance at the register of the prison of La Force shows that the vast majority of detainees were remanded for a few days and then released, while those that reached the lower jurisdiction of the Police Tribunal could expect no more than a small fine or a few weeks' jail sentence.[37]

The result of all this is evident in the note appended by *commissaire de police* Deneux of the Section des Arcis, when he sent a violent drunk into custody at midnight on 11 May 1791:

> We observe simply that for some time we have seen the National Guard insulted, ourselves outraged in our duties, that several times we have forwarded well-founded complaints from various patrols, that to their complaints we have joined our own, and we have asked for visible punishments that bear a character able to inspire respect and submission . . . that these troublemakers have nothing else to say but that they will be let off with a few days in prison.

The very next piece in the records confirms this – a *colporteur* who 'for want of being able to live otherwise' had been running an illegal street-lottery, arrested on 11 May, was sent to La Force, rearrested in the same place ten days later, and three days after that was back with the *commissaire* again, with a note requesting the return of his property, since he had paid the required twelve-*livre* fine.[38]

Within a month Deneux had become so sick of this game that he had begun to confiscate all money found on gamblers for the Section's poor-fund – 'because the prison of La Force does not correct them'. He managed to continue this policy for a week before the arrestees began returning from prison, accompanied by notes from the administrators reminding him that he was exceeding his powers, and ordering the return of the money.[39]

It should not be thought, however, that the judicial system was in the hands of starry-eyed humanitarians. When the machinery finally creaked into action, it could still be rigorous. On 22 April 1791 a man found lurking

Westport 1981. This study, however, remains within the relatively narrow bounds of 'legal history' and does not venture into the politics of law and order.
[37] See APP, AB322–4, passim, sentences noted on prisoners' records. La Force was the standard destination of prisoners remanded by the police, and for the serving of brief sentences imposed by the Police Tribunal; those sentenced by other courts went to Bicêtre, while the Conciergerie and Châtelet were used for prisoners on trial and those detained on various kinds of warrants. The Abbaye was for 'political' cases.
[38] APP, AA56:164, 165–7.
[39] APP, AA56:232, arrest of a dice-player, 8 June; 241–2, 245, arrests 9, 10 June, all returned 15 June. On 3 July Deneux encountered a prisoner who, having been found lurking in an alley, 'responded with insults' to all questions, and 'told us to go f— ourselves'. He sent him to La Force, without comment, but doubtless with black thoughts: APP, AA56:314.

in a house was arrested 'as very suspect having been flogged and branded several days ago on the Place de Grève'. He rapidly received a three-month sentence for the crime of having stayed in Paris after this punishment.[40] A journeyman printer who repeatedly stole type from his employer was arrested on 17 March; the sentence handed down, after six months' incarceration, was a public whipping, plus two days in the pillory for his female accomplice.[41] On 29 July five men who had robbed a house on the night of 28 December 1789 were hanged on the Place de Grève, and a sixth branded and sent to the galleys for life. Although the crime had been 'without violence to persons', this had not restrained the elected judges, nor was it to temper approving press coverage of the execution.[42] It should be noted that the new penal code which the Assembly had been elaborating made both acting in concert and during the hours of darkness aggravating factors in crime, but it still did not permit the death-sentence for theft of any kind. It also abolished all forms of corporal punishment.[43] Such systematic leniency was clearly not part of the assumptions of any part of the police and judicial system as it actually operated in 1791, and the apparent laxity we see must be put down to the literally overwhelming volume of petty crime. Certainly the police were constantly alert for signs of suspicious activity, and were prepared to read much into small incidents, as a further case from the Section des Arcis shows.

The document is a declaration received by *commissaire* Deneux from one L'hermitte, a process-server from the Châtelet and *commissaire de section*. In that latter function L'hermitte had received at 5 p.m. on 11 January 1791 a young man named Daponnier, seeking a certificate to enable him to get a job in the public workshops or a passport to leave Paris. He presented a certificate of residence signed by a Pierre Bourre, a *logeur* supposedly living in the same street as L'hermitte. Seeing this, the latter was 'astonished', since he took care to know the Section, and particularly his own neighbourhood, but the name was 'absolutely unknown' to him.

As L'hermitte carried out further investigations, the young man fled, and Deneux was left to record the declaration, and to add his own deductions, which show the heights to which suspicion could rise:

> persuaded as we are that the Police Department will believe with us that a man is always guilty when he lies, that he must have great reasons for lying about his domicile, and that the said Daponnier may be amongst the young people that burglars send in advance to study the means of entry into houses, see how they are secured, who lives there, and whether they are watchful; that

---

40 APP, AB323:420.
41 APP, AB322:1534.
42 Lacroix, *Actes*, vi. 145. The *Révolutions de Paris*, 30 July–6 Aug., was an honourable exception: 'do they fear to make the benefits of the Revolution felt too soon, and do they wish to prolong the horrors of the *ancien régime*?'
43 See *Moniteur*, 1 July.

for these reasons Daponnier is a highly-suspect young man who should be arrested.[44]

On the other hand he was perhaps a young man without a home who wanted a job thereby denied to him, but we have already seen that the police faced sufficient pressures to justify a certain lack of charity on their part.

Furthermore, the pursuit of felons might involve greater risks than merely being insulted. Two 'observers' employed by the police *commissaire* of the Roi-de-Sicile Section, charged with tracking down four known criminals, came to Deneux on 13 May to report what had happened when they spotted them on the Place de Grève. One of the policemen followed them into a bar, where three of them and a fourth man in their company recognised and attacked him, one carrying two pistols and another an open knife. A bystander stepped in to help the observer, and was hit over the head by the 'fourth man', who was seized by the Guard while the three wanted men made good their escape.

This man, Jean François Delahaye, called himself a merchant bonnet-seller, and offered receipts to prove he had done 102 *livres* worth of trade in the last month – a touch perhaps of protesting too much. He only added to the suspicions of the police when he went on to describe Bidot, the unem-ployed journeyman goldsmith who had stepped in, as 'a worthless rogue, a gambler and a professional fraud' whom he knew to have tricked a 'country-man' out of 1,400 *livres* a few days before, and to allege that Bidot had insulted him and leapt at him to start the affray. (The innkeeper himself was present to confirm the denials of Bidot and the policeman on this point.) Delahaye also denied all knowledge of any of the other participants in the fight. He got little advantage for himself out of these stories, but managed to place enough suspicion on Bidot to have them both sent to La Force 'as trou-blemakers and persons of bad conduct'. The *commissaire* noted: 'we observe to M. the administrator that these two individuals having accused each other of theft and brigandage' – an injustice to Bidot, who accused no-one of anything, except hitting him – 'it may perhaps be appropriate to place them in his hands to produce useful information'.[45]

It is initially hard to fathom how a man who steps in to help a police employee (and there can have been little doubt over his identity, the men were calling him a *mouchard* as they struck) could be thought to be a criminal on the word of the man he helped to arrest. We might see here possible grounds for agreeing with Richard Cobb's cynical view of the workings of the revolutionary police, placing the basis for many of their assumptions and

---

[44] APP, AA56:35. This report was passed to the Police Department and to the passport and public works administrations; Deneux was taking no chances.
[45] APP, AA56:170.

decisions less on investigation than on the standard forms and lists of 'usual suspects' provided by treatises on policing and similar manuals.[46]

It is certainly the case that the perception of brigandage that we have previously noted was an extension of a perception of the lower orders as a whole. To be undomiciled [non-domicilié], that is, without a permanent address (often defined as being 'in one's furniture [dans ses meubles]'), placed a person in a lower juridical category than otherwise. Quite simply, a commissaire de police could order the imprisonment of a non-domicilié on his own authority, whereas for a domicilié the signatures of two notables adjoints (fellow Section officials) were required.[47] Moreover, to be sans aveu – that is, to be unable to produce a respectable citizen to vouch for you – was to invite almost automatic imprisonment upon falling foul of the police; such people, gens sans aveu, being essentially identified as vagabonds. The mobile and disreputable elements of the Parisian population were effectively guilty until proven innocent, and easy prey for social prejudice coloured by political fears.

If such views may help us account for some apparently odd attitudes and unjust decisions, it remains true that, as we have seen, men like commissaire Deneux had minds of their own. However, the outcome of the Bidot/ Delahaye incident may seem less bewildering once we have explored some further complications in the relationship between policing and crime. Another case from the files of commissaire Deneux, a few months later on 27 August, reveals more of this new dimension.

The tale began when a Mme Vidu, logeuse, came to report that one of her tenants, one Cudot, 'an employee of the department of police', and his mistress had attacked her the previous day, passing from vicious insults to spitting in her face, and preparing to take a stick to her when her daughter intervened, and 'was in turn mistreated'. She noted further 'that this Cudot never stops saying that he couldn't give a f— for her, as he is employed by the police, and has, according to him, the ear of M Perron, one of the administrators'.

As she completed her statement, Cudot himself burst into the office, and after the commissaire informed him of what was going on, 'instead of responding, he behaved before us in an infinitely indecent manner, threatening us with M. Perron, whose man he said he was, allowing himself even to say that a commissaire like myself was not a man to be feared at the police department, where he was sure to be listened to more favourably'. He fled, however, when Deneux called the Guard. Mme Vidu was advised to call them herself next time she saw him, and the commissaire sent copies of this encounter to the Département de Police and the municipal prosecutor.

46 Cobb, The police and the people, 14–37.
47 Dozens of procès-verbaux make this clear, and, as the Courrier reported on 18 May, the commissaire of the Section du Faubourg-Montmartre was fined 54 livres for committing two young domiciliés to La Force without this procedure.

This was not the end of it, however. As Mme Vidu and her daughter were walking home, Cudot accosted them, repeated his various threats and insults, and banged the daughter's head on a wall, after which his mistress punched her, threw her on the ground and kicked her about the head before they made off. For some reason the Guard, when summoned, refused to hunt for the two culprits, so the women went back to Deneux. He personally led a patrol which cornered the mistress, detaining her after she had been restrained from assaulting him – she was Marie Jeanne LeBrun, aged twenty, 'calling herself a laundress' (and probably a part-time prostitute, he implies by this). She had nothing to say but 'invective', and the clearly wearying Deneux noted 'we have ceased to interrogate her, preferring to leave that care to M. the administrator'.

Meanwhile two journeyman tailors came to testify that they lived in the same lodging-house, and had kept out of Cudot's way because he 'had threatened them with the municipality where he said he was employed in a very trusted role, he could make them pass for thieves and obtain an order for their arrest and detention in La Force'. LeBrun, at least, could now be sent there. About Cudot, all that could be done was tell Mme Vidu to have him arrested if he showed up again, and to add a very strong note to the minutes sent to the *Département de Police*, calling Cudot 'infinitely guilty' and noting 'our astonishment that an undomiciled vagabond should have obtained in preference to other citizens a place of trust'. Deneux is sure to make clear in the report that he scorns the threats against himself, but does display a rather naïve attitude to the current practices of criminal detection, as we shall see.[48]

In the records of the *Bureau municipal*, the confidential inner government of the city, there is a clear record of police espionage. We find, for example, that on 30 April 1791, 'on the report made to the Bureau of the services rendered by one Doublet for the discovery of a large number of thieves, and the ill-treatment he has suffered from those who feared his activities', a grant of 200 *livres* was made in addition to 150 he had already received. On 5 May six different agents received grants of between forty-five and 600 *livres* 'for services to the public good'. Sigismond Lacroix, who published these records at the turn of the century, cannot identify Doublet, but says that the six others were 'all secret agents of the municipal police'. All the claims were submitted on their behalf by Perron, the administrator for whom Cudot had claimed to work. On 12 May one Deschamps, again unidentified, was given 514 *livres* 'as reimbursement of police expenses' since December. On 17 June claims were made for a Lenoir and for a Morel – 240 *livres* in back-pay for the last two years, and 600 *livres* for services rendered. On 8 July 300 *livres* were reimbursed to the *commissaire de police* of the Section de Ste-Geneviève, which he had paid out 'in salaries to various persons charged by him with checks and information-gathering on objects of concern to public security'.

[48] APP, AA57:95.

The municipality was not undiscriminating, however, and they also turned down a request for payment by two men who had served as 'police inspectors for the District of St-Jacques-l'Hôpital', though without giving a reason.[49]

It should not be imagined that the espionage activities of the police were confined to tracking down thieves. Perhaps the most striking single piece of evidence we have of 'political' policing is a note of a decision taken just before the midnight conclusion of the emergency session of the *Corps municipal* on 17 July. A total of 20,000 *livres* of expenditure was authorised to the *Département de Police*, 'destined to provide for the concerns required by public safety . . . and for which the Mayor and the four police administrators will not be held to give any detailed accounts'.[50]

We can only speculate as to possible uses for this money, but it may have been used to pursue the leaders of the 'plot' the authorities assumed was behind the agitation of July.[51] Certainly when it came to activities more overtly linked to the *émigré* counter-revolution, the secret police were actively working for the *comités des recherches* of the municipality and the National Assembly. On 5 June an *inspecteur* with a warrant from the latter committee arrested a nineteen-year-old journeyman innkeeper 'accused of having designs or intentions to engage with other individuals in the [counter-revolutionary] army of the Prince de Condé'. Scraps of paper found in his room linked him to one Medard, 'former doorman of the convent of St-Roch, whose current location is unknown'.[52]

When, after the promulgation of the Constitution, Bailly tired of the mayorship and resigned, he spoke of espionage in his resignation address of 12 November 1791. 'The espionage which conducted an inquisition into words and even into thoughts was detested with good reason', he said. At the same time, however, spies were a 'safeguard of our fortunes and our morals' when used to hunt down 'brigands . . . their haunts and their shadowy activities'.[53] The radical press brought a hurricane of opprobrium down on him for these remarks, but if anything he was minimising the administration's use of spying, and there is no sign that such methods were abandoned under later regimes.

Until this statement, however, the municipality had vigorously denied the employment of *mouchards*. On 26 January the deputy municipal prosecutor, Cahier de Gerville, had stood up in court and made just such a denial during

---

49 Lacroix, *Actes*, iv. 71, 107–9, 234, 590–1; v. 296. By August the municipality was getting round to fulfilling less urgent requests for payment, such as to the inspector of the horse-market (vi. 79) and the 400 street-sweepers controlled by the Police Department (vi. 203.)
50 Ibid. v. 410.
51 Mathiez, *Club des Cordeliers*, pt ii, reproduces and comments on the police and judicial records of this pursuit.
52 APP, AB323:1012. The prisoner was transferred to the Abbaye, where the records for 1791 have been lost. We have already noted the extent to which the St-Roch parish was a centre of clerical non-juring in 1791.
53 Lacroix, *Actes*, viii. 39.

the Fréron/Kabert trial. Marat, who as we noted saw the *mouchards* as agents of a plot to put France in the hands of Lafayette, responded on 3 February by publishing a certificate from 'the inspector in charge of the security department', which one man offered as proof that he was not a spy. For Marat, however, this showed that Cahier de Gerville 'lied like a hangman's valet . . . since espionage forms a department'. He correctly identified Perron as the administrator in charge of espionage, alleging on 4 February that he drew 200 *livres* per month for the man who had offered this certificate.[54]

Such indirect proofs were not Marat's only weapons; on 10 April he published a letter denouncing the *commissaire de police* of the Section du Louvre for supporting spies, which named as *mouchards* 'the individual Doublet and his wife' – the same man we have already seen named in secret municipal records. Their task was to identify thieves, and they had been given a certificate to identify them to other police officials: 'provided none the less that they are not taken *in flagrante delicto*', it read, 'this due to their conversion'. They were 'turned' criminals themselves, in other words – the classic tools of the eighteenth-century police.[55] Doublet's position, and character, is further confirmed in two other incidents. On 19 May one Alexis Doublet was arrested 'for having repeatedly made a scene on the square of the porte St-Martin where he sought arguments with various individuals, declaring to them that he was a police observer [observateur de la sûreté]. This avowal drew around him a considerable gathering and some individuals wished to hang him'.[56]

Such indiscretion may have taught him a lesson, and a case which came to light on 2 September 1791 reveals Doublet attempting to put his position to more systematic advantage. One Marie Magot, *femme* Bertaud, as a consequence of what appeared initially to have been an unmotivated assault on a man in her company, gave evidence that 'M Doublet and his wife' were running a protection-racket against the merchants of second-hand goods on the Quai de l'Infante. Two months previously Doublet had ordered her to close her boutique after she refused to buy a handkerchief from a man accompanying him. Doublet, insisting, claimed 'to have his orders from the municipality and the Hôtel de Ville'. Having finally closed her boutique, Magot walked home, and Doublet and his wife followed her, announcing who he was, and threatened that 'if he wished he could do a great deal of harm to the sellers, and he would send them merchandise from thieves'. Those who did not co-operate would subsequently be denounced to the authorities as receivers, those who did would find the arrangement mutually profitable. Magot's indignant refusal to have anything to do with such schemes had resulted in Doublet following her repeatedly, loitering around her shop and

---

54 *Ami du Peuple*, nos 360, 361.
55 Ibid. no. 425. On the character of such spies in the eighteenth century see Mercier, *Tableau*, 84–5, 203, and pp. 80–3 below.
56 APP, AB323:793, Section des Gravilliers. Released 20 May.

finally ordering a companion to assault a neighbour who had been accompanying her. Joseph Malaux, the nineteen-year-old unemployed domestic servant who actually made the assault, had been arrested, and stated that he lived with Doublet, who was 'attached as an observer to the Hôtel de Ville'. He was lodged by Doublet, in return for which 'he lent him his support when there was someone to arrest'.[57]

Malaux claimed that the neighbour had started to assault him, after Doublet had pointed him out as a receiver of stolen goods. The *commissaire* ordered him to be detained until a domiciled citizen, other than Doublet, could be found to vouch for him. He further noted that if Malaux 'should carry out the threat that he has just made to us to collect a crowd if we have him taken anywhere except to the municipality', he should be taken directly to prison. No-one did vouch for him, despite Malaux's attempt to obtain a reference from the secretary of the Section de l'Oratoire. This worthy wrote back that he did not know Malaux, but that 'it is enough that he knows Doublet for [the secretary] to suspect dishonesty, and that if his approval is needed to send [Malaux] to La Force, he would give it gladly'. Early in the evening Malaux was transferred to La Force, where he later served a one-month sentence for the assault.[58]

In the activities of such *mouchards* and their accomplices, we can find all too much justification for the actions of those who had assaulted Kabert in January, taking him for a *mouchard* of Lafayette. The police spy was evidently an odious creature, and one who might himself exhibit all the characteristics that were held against brigands. On 22 May a 'former observer' was detained as a common pickpocket, and on 15 August it was noted about one Jean Deveaux, arrested trying to strangle a woman whom he said had taken a banknote from him, that he 'has been a police observer: this is a bad character who has been imprisoned a number of times'.[59] Despite this latter note, in both cases the men were released within a few days, following the pattern we have already noted for this time. In this context, the suspicion that fell on Bidot after having voluntarily participated in the operations of such *observateurs* begins to make sense.

The examples of Cudot and Doublet show that some of these men were ready to abuse their position, even in the face of the elected authorities, but it would also seem that these same authorities sometimes abetted such actions. On 29 December 1790 one Hutte, 'employee in the security of Paris' was detained, accused of picking the pocket of a polisher. The laconic prison record is not clear on what happened next, but while Hutte went free, his accuser was driven into a fury which cost him a spell in La Force. As for the consequences of being denounced, the register of La Force notes for 21 April 1791 the names of five women held since 23 January 'as suspects according to

---

57 APP, AA86:3, Section du Palais-Royal, 2 Sept.
58 APP, AA86:4; AB324:2470, sentence of Tribunal de Police noted, 10 Sept.
59 APP, AB323:835, released with *passeport* 25 May; AB324:2286, released 23 Aug.

the denunciation of an individual known by the name of the Wooden Leg, and after this interrogation they have been released'. They had been held for three months apparently without even being questioned.[60]

The truth was, as all Paris knew, that *mouchards* had been the scourge of the city for decades. In the 1780s Louis-Sebastien Mercier commented at length in his *Tableau de Paris* on their work in the capital, concluding that 'this inquisition, which can have its abuses, produces public security', which was an 'inestimable advantage' due solely to these spies, whose number was in any case inflated by public opinion – an 'error useful to the police'. He observed, however, that police *inspecteurs*, 'believed ordinarily on their word', were not a disciplined body — 'Some obey their moods, their whims; but who knows whether motives of greed do not also enter into their activities?'[61] That these remarks were no mere empty speculation can be seen in the 'Child-Kidnapping Affair' of May 1750, which the Parisian glazier Jacques-Louis Ménétra recorded in the 1790s as one of the clearest memories of his childhood, and which has been explored through detailed use of police records by Arlette Farge and Jacques Revel.[62] Like Kabert, the victims of riot here were *mouchards*; instead of political plotting, the reason was the abduction of children, occurring as the clandestine police machinery twisted a policy designed to reduce begging and street crime into little more than a licensed extortion racket.

On 23 May 1750, in the neighbourhood of St-Roch, a police agent (*exempt de police*) named Labbé was hounded and done to death in a riot with remarkable parallels to the Kabert incident. Labbé too was an inhabitant of the district which turned on him, after he had tried to seize a child on the Pont Marie. He proved a more vigorous fugitive than Kabert, running through a market and an apartment house as well as several streets, captured more than once and re-escaping after beatings. The crowd pursued him at last to the house of a *commissaire du Châtelet*, the equivalent then to Kabert's place of shelter. Here the offer to see justice done was made by this official, and at first there seemed more chance of it being accepted. However, the Watch broke the truce by trying to clear the crowd from the house, shots were fired and the forces of order found themselves under siege. The *commissaire* escaped, and Labbé was surrendered to the crowd for punishment; he was beaten to death in the street and his body paraded in front of the house of the *lieutenant de*

---

60 APP, AB322:711 (the *frotteur* was released two days later, but fined 24 *livres*); AB323:411. The 'Wooden Leg' was evidently a famous spy, as later that year one Henri Poligni succeeded in getting himself incarcerated for drunkenly denouncing various individuals to the Guard as criminals, having claimed to be 'a second wooden leg': AA57:110, 3 Sept. 1791.

61 Mercier, *Tableau*, 203, 335.

62 A. Farge and J. Revel, *Logiques de la foule: l'affaire des enlèvements des enfants, Paris 1750*, Paris 1988. See also J.-L. Ménétra, *Journal of my life*, ed. and comm. D. Roche, trans. A. Goldhammer, New York 1986, 21–2.

police, whom the people blamed, rightly as research shows, for the kidnapping policy and its abuse.[63]

It transpired in the official enquiry, although it was never made public, that the new *lieutenant de police*, Berryer, a favourite of Mme Pompadour, had ordered his men to be particularly rigorous in their normal pursuit of vagrants and vagabonds. He felt no need to keep any particular control over his men, other than that of paying by results, that is, arrests. Since the police agents also had to fund transport and the pay of their subordinates out of this 'head-money', they began to look for new ways of increasing their income under the cover of this policy of rigour. Berryer's lax discipline allowed them to begin taking children and ransoming them back to their parents, and he took no notice of individual complaints, so long as he could boast of his men's zeal and energy at court.[64]

This episode marked without doubt a low point in the prestige and discipline of the Parisian police, and under men such as Sartine and Lenoir, a tighter rein would be kept on such abuses. None the less, the essential organisation remained the same. Not only that, but even in 1750 the forces of order rallied behind a version of events which served both their preconceptions and the maintenance of social order. In setting out to seek culprits the police spoke of 'a company of brigands formed in order to make the people rise up', demonstrating that this concept was well-established long before the Revolution.[65] When punishment was finally handed down by the parlement, three young marginals went to the gallows, while for the kidnappings, four policemen received largely symbolic punishments. None of the hanged had even been involved on the 23rd, but in other, less dramatic incidents. Farge and Revel suggest that the investigation was guided by an 'intuitive sociology' which produced a list of likely suspects, all 'bad boys' surviving in marginal employment, no women and no artisans, that all witnesses agreed had been present on the 23rd right up to the kill. Farge and Revel note that not only did the bourgeois and artisans have their status to protect them, and a greater ability to manufacture an alibi, but that 'once the drama had ended, and the tension relaxed, they were ready to forget everything and share in the version of the affair given by the authorities', not least because the violence reminded them of a kind of 'other culture' that they wished to ignore in themselves.[66]

Whatever kind of self-defence mechanisms the artisanate employed, their basic hostility to the police spies remains evident. As we have already seen, the personal character of some of these men in 1791 could only have added to this antipathy, and the same can be said of those in 1750. Labbé's immediate superior was the *inspecteur de police* Poussot, who lived with his mistress

---

[63] Farge and Revel, *Logiques*, 69–84.
[64] Ibid. 41, 52–3.
[65] Ibid. 22.
[66] Ibid. 59–62.

Geneviève Dion, 'nicknamed la Maréchale', an ex-thief who had found more profitable employment spying on pamphleteers and prostitutes. She habitually resorted to violence, false denunciation and blackmail to obtain money and the sexual services of prostitutes that took her fancy. The couple and their 'mouches' were known as the 'bande de la Maréchale', a gang as feared as any robbers, with no redeeming glamour. It is little wonder than in the popular mind the police were held guilty of 'every compromising act' imaginable.[67]

The police meanwhile, at the highest levels, viewed all disturbances through blinkers – their observation that 'the underworld is thus indeed at the origin of public disturbance' sums up their attitude, and they were capable of moulding all social tensions into a model of banditry and subversion. Two workers who chose 23 May 1750 to pick a fight with their master over their wages found themselves arrested in the round-up after the Labbé riot, while at the same time the police were hunting for evidence of the continued influence of the great criminal gangs of the early decades of the century – Cartouche, Rafiat and others. Through the following months, many women were questioned in the hunt for the 'support network' such a band was sure to have.[68]

Viewed solely in terms of such assumptions, the Parisian police appears as an instrument of repression, and one which was perpetuated into the Revolution to serve ends only slightly altered. However, such a view is not the complete picture, and we must recognise that the presence of the police was also an integrated part of local life for Parisians in the eighteenth century. David Garrioch shows that the Châtelet *commissaires* in particular were linked to the modes of neighbourhood communal self-regulation. Although they remained outside and 'above' the community, an appeal to them also functioned as a tactic within community disputes.[69] Despite the repressive aspect of their task, during the Revolution the Section *commissaires de police* played an essential role as local elected officials, and the records they have left are filled with declarations concerning minor incidents, which illustrate that this form of police remained the instinctive first resort of the community in a wide variety of circumstances.

Even some of the more repressive police devices, such as the *lettres de cachet* dreaded and denounced by the *philosophes* and their lesser fellow-writers, could find a role in everyday social relations. Arlette Farge and Michel Foucault have compiled an entire volume of documents showing the desire of ordinary families to have their offspring or relatives disciplined by a spell in a royal prison.[70] The glazier Ménétra's autobiography, while doubtless

---

[67] Ibid. 51–2, 56.
[68] Ibid. 46, 48–50.
[69] Garrioch, *Neighbourhood*, 53–5.
[70] A. Farge and M. Foucault, *Le Désordre des familles: lettres de cachet des Archives de la Bastille*, Paris 1982.

elaborating on some incidents, illustrates the ambivalent attitudes behind such practices. In the early years of his marriage he records that his persistent adultery led his wife's family to plot his confinement 'for a quarter at St-Lazare'. Warned by another relative, Ménétra recounts that he first threatened his father, whose signature was necessary to complete the warrant, and then after talking to a contact in the police, he borrowed a gun and hid in his room, ready to shoot the first man through the door. The arrest, he notes, was never carried out. Despite this scare, real or imagined, Ménétra has no difficulty observing that in later life he thought it only proper to have his own son-in-law arrested and put away for six weeks, for very similar reasons. The man in question was a thoroughly bad character, and the families involved considered a more permanent seclusion, although they finally decided that this was unnecessarily extreme.[71]

We can see an interesting contrast between the 'ordinary' attitudes of Ménétra and those of Mercier, who along with all other 'enlightened' writers, had denounced the arbitrary powers of the police. He wrote of witnessing a police abduction – 'four henchmen leapt on him, held him by the throat, dragged him away, pressed him to the wall'. A passer-by warned him not to bother interfering, and the scene was set for Mercier to condemn such practices.[72] The more robust Ménétra, who told a tale of having personally experienced such treatment one night by the porte St-Denis, seized from behind and carried off to the Bonne-Nouvelle guardhouse in a darkened coach, was moved to remark, when the mistake was realised, only 'that many a crook looks a lot like an honest man'.[73]

None the less for many Parisians the secret police, as opposed to the network of *commissaires*, was a repressive force always on the brink of violating the law itself – and when it did so, it was with impunity, as the events of 1750 had proven. Such sentiments persisted into the pre-Revolutionary period. Thomas Luckett has shown that, when the court–parlement disputes of the summer of 1787 had raised the political temperature high enough, crowds led by the *Basoche* of law-clerks and other young men began to hunt out *mouchards*. A riot around the Palais de Justice on 17 August had seen the *Basoche* capture a 'well-known spy', who was then forced 'on pain of death to reveal his comrades, and each one he indicated was surrounded and chased out or, if he resisted, attacked and knocked out on the spot'.[74] Three days later, in the streets close to the Palais-Royal and the church of St-Roch, neighbourhood apprentices were 'hunting for spies and

---

71 Ménétra, *Journal*, 185, 210.
72 Mercier, *Tableau*, 201–3.
73 Ménétra, *Journal*, 208.
74 Luckett, 'Hunting for spies and whores', 116–43 at p. 125, quoting directly from the *Mémoires secrets* of Bachaumont. Note that Luckett views these and subsequent events as a significant innovation in Parisian popular practice, contrary to the thesis that I am developing here.

whores', eventually targeting an unpopular innkeeper, invading and vandal-ising his premises. When the innkeeper seized one participant and carried him off to the local Châtelet *commissaire's* office, the crowd returned to besiege the building, demanding the handing-over of the innkeeper and a known *mouchard* who was also present, with the express intention of lynching them. Although the crowd lacked the temerity of the Labbé or Kabert mobs, and never breached the doors, windows and furniture were smashed by repeated stonings, until as the evening grew late they began to disperse. The City Guard finally made a prudent appearance after the trouble had died down.[75]

One of the first acts of the July 1789 uprising in Paris was an assault on a *mouchard* on 9 July, after he had tried to make an arrest in the Palais-Royal.[76] Seen from a certain perspective, nothing had changed by 1791; indeed the situation appeared to have worsened. Some of the old police personnel had faded away, but others were presumably still employed, since an espionage network cannot be created from nothing, and they would, no doubt, have been ready and willing to stay in service. Meanwhile, a whole new breed of *mouchard* had emerged, whose role was to support the administration against radicals, and, if one went along with Marat and Fréron, to plot the day when all the evils of the old order would be restored. On the other side of the fence, just as in 1750, a shadowy underworld, now rebaptised as aristocratic brigan-dage, was blamed for all popular agitation. Since both sides viewed the other as being in league with the same third party, the situation could not have been more absurd, but a glance back into the eighteenth century makes it all too comprehensible. The *ancien régime's* repressive relationship to its people was too twisted to be straightened out in one great heave, and many of its worst features – the mutual suspicion of police and population, the use of criminals as agents, a general air of secrecy, arbitrariness and deceit – lingered on, in the streets and in the minds of men on both sides. These warped perceptions would continue to influence politics, to the detriment of all concerned. As we shall see in the next chapter, one agency by means of which these concerns were spread was the press, although this institution also bred disquiet for many other reasons.

---

[75] Ibid. 120–2 and passim for Luckett's own analysis of such events.
[76] Godechot, *Bastille*, 183. This spy may or may not have been the 'sieur Zezzi' who unsuc-cessfully petitioned the municipality in January 1791 for 'aid and indemnity', claiming to have been 'suspected of being a spy' and assaulted on 8 July 1789: Lacroix, *Actes*, ii. 452.

4

Plots, Pamphlets and Crowds:
February–April 1791

The events of the *journée* of 28 February 1791 would offer every side in the revolutionary political equation the chance to validate its own interpretation of the forces at work. Several thousands of the ordinary population of the Faubourg St-Antoine chose that day to march to the château of Vincennes, a few miles to the east of the city. They were moved by a growing concern over the previous week that the municipality's recently-begun refurbishment of the château as an overflow prison had sinister connotations. It appears that on the 25th the Cordeliers Club had sent a deputation to the Jacobins to propose just such an expedition, but had been rejected. Gorsas subsequently linked this overture to the machinations of the *Club monarchique*. Popular concern, however, was noted, and to some extent shared, by the authorities of the Sections des Quinze-Vingts and de Montreuil, the latter Section's *commissaire de police* informing the municipality that a general sentiment to undertake a demolition had arisen within the Section by the 26th.[1] Upon reaching the site 3–4,000 people occupied the courtyard, while a substantial number of men entered the keep, and began to demolish the building work which had been started.

When news that the march was getting under way reached the Hôtel de Ville, the general alarm was sounded, and substantial contingents of the National Guard, along with the headquarters staff, marched to intercept the crowd. Some of the Guards of the local Faubourg-St-Antoine Popincourt battalion, while at Vincennes, showed their disapproval of Lafayette, but their colleagues maintained discipline (and later repudiated this disloyalty in a printed deliberation). Desmottes, the *aide-de-camp* involved in the persecution of Hion, would subsequently accuse the Enfants-Trouvés battalion commander Santerre, a popular leader of political life in the Faubourg, of having ordered his men to fire on him on the road to Vincennes, an accusation which would lead to further factional confrontation in the courts.

At Vincennes, despite manifestations of defiance from the marchers, the overwhelming armed presence took control. Sixty-four men were arrested inside the keep, but the confrontation continued, and a hostile armed crowd made a show of force at the Barrière du Trône when the Guard attempted to bring the detainees into the city. The Guard, however, forced its way through

---

1 Lacroix, *Actes*, ii. 763–4.

without needing to open fire, and the only confirmed casualty was a caval-ryman shot in the leg as they passed through the Faubourg. This incident was clearly a significant mobilisation by the workers of the Faubourg for 'patriotic' motives, and the reported fears of the population about the erection of a 'new Bastille' show that the municipality was as widely distrusted in some quarters as the overtly aristocratic party. However, at the time this incident was swept up into the mêlée of anti-aristocratic accusation.[2]

The Vincennes events were only half of this *journée*. News of the distur-bance there reached the streets of central Paris at about the same time as news that a *Chevalier de St-Louis* had been arrested in the Tuileries palace carrying a dagger. It seems that popular and aristocratic elements alike saw in this a possibility of harm coming to the king, and both sides rushed to the Tuileries, each to guard him from the other. The result was a further tense confrontation, this time between crowd outside and aristocrats inside, which was only resolved when Lafayette returned with the Guard, dispersed the crowds and arrested several dozen young army officers and other court gentlemen.

Several of these were questioned by Section authorities, with attention focusing particularly on links to the *Club monarchique*, but the interrogations did not appear to have disturbed their aristocratic *sang-froid*.[3] It is clear from another case that the hysteria over 'subtle daggers' had penetrated official circles. The man whose arrest had sparked the disturbances, Mathieu Jean-Baptiste de Court de la Tonnelle, 'major of the militia of St-Domingue', was held at the Abbaye while the Police Department tested his knife by wounding a pigeon and shutting it in a box for two days, with some food. Its survival seemed at least to satisfy them that the blade was not poisoned, but de Court was also under suspicion for having been seen making 'the most inflammatory remarks' in the Palais-Royal and elsewhere, and remained in custody until the general dismissal of such cases on 13 March.[4]

Everybody blamed everyone else for the events, and on 3 March the Section des Quinze-Vingts protested that the detainees were 'citizens seduced by the enemies of the public good, shut up like vile criminals in dungeons', and offered 'certificates of probity' for all of them, as they had been led on by 'a too-great zeal for the public good'.[5] The *Révolutions de Paris* of 26 February–5 March expressed the difficulties that even the most radical patriots had with such events. It remarked that 'as for the expedition to

2 Ibid. ii. 774–5; iii. 10.
3 See especially APP, AA206:130, Section de la Place-Vendôme, where the marquis de la Motte, captain in the Regiment Royale Cavalerie, stonewalled with some elegance before being dispatched to the Abbaye.
4 APP, AB322:1377. De Court's position in the colonial militia may well explain his vehe-mence: the colonists' position vis-à-vis their non-white fellows was a live political issue at this time. AB322:1372, 1375, 1407, lists eight other aristocratic detainees from these events who passed through La Force, but all were held ultimately in the Abbaye.
5 Lacroix, *Actes*, iii. 14.

Vincennes, it is evident that it was provoked by the aristocrats' to enable them to seize the Tuileries. On the other hand, 'the good sense of the people is worth a hundred times more that all that of those who govern them. They felt, this people, that a citadel placed half a league from the capital . . . could be dangerous for the success of the revolution'.

In other words, its destruction saved it from being used for aristocratic plots, while at the same time its destruction was an aristocratic plot! This bizarre argument hints at the potentially traumatic effect that a constant interpretation of events by an avid press might have had on the developing social and political situation, an issue we must now examine in more detail.

Press discourse and destabilisation

Once freed from the restrictions of the *ancien régime*, the Parisian publishing industry had boomed, and its production both maintained the popular aware-ness of events evident in 1789, and created its own agitations.[6] As we have seen, in May 1790, events had led the sober *Moniteur* to fulminate against the subversives, *factieux*, brigands and others who were suborning the people. One of the most consistent features of the press, however, was its inconsis-tency. November of that year saw a major clash when a crowd wrecked the Hôtel de Castries, after its owner had wounded Charles de Lameth (at that time still a hero in popular and radical eyes) in a politically-calculated duel. This provocation prompted the *Moniteur* to be more neutral in its treatment of the rioters: 'The people, which had assembled in some order, gathered without tumult, and went to the rue de Varennes, into the dwelling of M. Castries. All the furniture, mirrors and trinkets were thrown out of the windows.'[7] The people, for the press, would always be whatever it was most convenient for them to be at any given moment, be it the heroes of insurrec-tion, avengers of insulted patriotism or a sheep-like, corruptible mob.

These problematic attitudes would influence even the radical press, as we have just seen in the case of the *Révolutions de Paris*. Ambiguities of response such as this must modify the definition of underlying assumptions within the radical press offered by Jack Censer. He proposes that a central tenet of the radical journalists can be summarised as a belief that 'a moral, egalitarian *peuple* had developed, who were opposed by a selfish and self-indulgent *aristo-cratie* [committed to keeping power, including by violence]. . . . To oppose the

---

6   For general histories of the press see Gough, *Newspaper press*, and Popkin, *Revolutionary news*. See also the brief essays on many aspects of the revolutionary press collected in Rétat, *Révolution du journal*.

7   *Moniteur*, 15 Nov. 1790. This was the incident that brought Rotondo and Lafayette face-to-face, no doubt to the former's subsequent regret. An engraving of the destruction, including men wielding axes and picks, and the hurling of furniture and sacks of documents from windows, is used, a little anachronistically, as the cover illustration for W. Beik, *Urban protest in seventeeth-century France: the culture of retribution*, Cambridge 1997.

"aristocratic" menace to the social ideal of the *peuple*, the radicals suggested a literal adherence to popular sovereignty'. The 'infallible' people would keep its rulers from getting out of hand by 'vigorous action' if need be.[8] In general Censer calls these attitudes 'Cordelier politics', defining them in relation to the position on popular sovereignty taken up by the District des Cordeliers, and after May 1790 by the Club which replaced it as the focus for extreme Parisian radicalism. We may note now, however, that such radicalism did not easily align itself with all popular action. It clearly opposed the national and Parisian authorities by 1791, but even that attitude was the fruit of a complex evolution.

Censer's study indicates that the hostile radical attitudes to Bailly and Lafayette which would dominate in 1791 had emerged in the course of 1790. Between May and August of that year, all six of the journals he studied had swung in opinion from admiration of the revolutionary authorities to deep distrust, amounting to a conviction of their counter-revolutionary intentions. In early April 1790 Desmoulins could still praise Lafayette for co-ordinating espionage efforts against plots, but Lafayette's approval of the suppression of the Nancy mutiny in August was enough to confirm a new picture of him in the eyes of Parisian patriots as an egotistical aspiring military dictator. It was also from this point on, spurred by attempts to increase the powers of the National Guard, that suspicion of its officers, and particularly the headquarters staff, began to take firm root.[9]

Attitudes towards Louis XVI took a similarly decisive hostile turn, resulting from events in April–June 1791 that we shall survey below, but following on from doubts perceptible in late 1790. Censer sees political evolution, however, rather than reaction to specific events behind these changes: he finds that a progressive disillusionment with all power-holding persons and institutions took place, for reasons he cannot wholly elucidate.[10] It is suggested, however, that such a process was implicit in the doctrine of popular sovereignty itself. If this is by its nature hostile to strong government, its adherents will perceive attempts to 'govern' in a negative light, especially when behind the figures initially admired are others – queen, court and clergy – consistently reviled as a threat to the *peuple*. The longer government under this system went on, the more hostile opinion would grow. In this sense, Censer confirms our observation on political attitudes at this time, that from the initial premises there was no hope of compromise – what we could call the 'brigands and *mouchards*' mentality. However, we might suggest that he undervalues the role of the elimination of the Districts in breeding anti-

---

[8] J. R. Censer, *Prelude to power: the Parisian radical press, 1789–1791*, London 1976, pp. xii–xiii.
[9] Ibid. 100–10.
[10] Ibid. 111–23. Raised against Censer's interpretation is the view of Barry Shapiro that the disenchantment of the radicals with Lafayette was a more pragmatic divorce: see p. 16 above.

municipal hostility in mid-1790, and likewise neglects the impact of specific events and situations in the following year.

Part of the attack launched by radicals involved accusations of corruption and conspiracy, bringing us back again to the question of faction and suborna-tion. Not only did such allegations serve as political explanation and justifi-cation for both authoritarian and radical positions, but they were also part of the mental framework of nearly all contemporary writers. As Norman Hampson observed in his biography of Danton, 'The former Grub Street hacks had not lost their old habits when they became the journalists of the Revolution and the air was thick with insinuations against almost everybody worth buying.'[11] Of course, in the case of Mirabeau, for one, it has been convincingly demonstrated that he was paid by the court, but it is equally evident in this case that in his actions he remained consistently loyal to his own opinions.[12]

Although it is quite possible that the Parisian air was thick not only with insinuation, but with Orléanist, Fayettist, British, Prussian and Austrian gold and its purchases, there remains no solid evidence to tie any of this either to outbreaks of popular violence, or to those who wrote for and encouraged popular radicalism. If some, like Fréron, were rakes, others were respectable intellectuals, like those at the heart of the *Cercle social*, pillars of the arti-sanate like Santerre or the butcher Legendre, or indeed apparently genuine idealists, as Louise and François Robert, journalists and exemplary popular society activists, seem to have been.[13] Of course, for those opposed to radical opinions, this social diversity was in itself evidence of corruption, since in a conservative world-view nothing else could have brought such elements together.

Robert Darnton famously put forward a counterpoint to this, suggesting that the future revolutionaries had formed a 'low-life of literature' in pre-revolutionary Paris, a kind of frustrated literary rabble, forced to peddle smut and co-operate with the police to survive, and who therefore brought to revo-lutionary journalism and rhetoric a visceral hatred of the *ancien régime* which coloured its whole development. Elizabeth Eisenstein has demonstrated the inaccuracy of this perception of pre-revolutionary conditions, at least for certain figures, and thus of the inevitable progress to the outburst of pent-up hostilities.[14] None the less, she cannot argue that the hothouse discourse of the revolutionary press did not exist, and other work has suggested that, as

11 N. Hampson, *Danton*, London 1978, 40. See pp. 26–66 for an overview of Danton's early revolutionary career against a constant background of such accusations.
12 See B. Luttrell, *Mirabeau*, Hemel Hempstead 1990, 208–10, for his arrangement with the court; pp. 213–78 for his performance as its defender.
13 For the first and last of these see Censer, *Prelude*, 31–3, 14–15. For the intellectuals see Kates, *Cercle social*.
14 See Darnton, 'High Enlightenment', and E. L. Eisenstein, *Grub Street abroad: aspects of the French cosmopolitan press from the age of Louis XIV to the French Revolution*, Oxford 1992, ch. v, esp. pp. 145–52.

early as Sieyès's *What is the Third Estate?*, the revolutionaries had become caught in an ascending spiral of rhetorical excess.[15]

Clearly the output of the press was affected both by this combination of apparently self-generating rhetorical aggravation with an inflammatory political context, and by the socio-political assumptions underlying the conflicts that it entered into. None the less, it is also evident, and significant, that the basic market conditions of its production and distribution drove it towards material that was inherently provocative. The most blatant examples of this kind are of course in the new genre of the 'Père Duchesne', utilising burlesque figures and a ripe vocabulary, and aimed at the very bottom of the market, a genre which grew dramatically in volume from late 1790 onwards.[16] The assumption must be that there was a popular readership for such texts, although they were clearly also a vehicle for a wide range of political viewpoints attempting to capture the popular mind, including right-wing writers using a 'Mère Duchesne' to debunk the radical pretensions of her male counterpart. Hébert's publication, later to become an epitome of Parisian radicalism, was at this time a relatively moderate work, compared to others such as the one written by the abbé Jumel, and produced in partnership with the forthright Mlle Colombe.[17]

However, there was no particular relationship between political opinions and mode of address. One newspaper which was commonly reported among the wares of inflammatory hawkers in 1791 was Audouin's *Journal Universel*. Censer comments on this publication – its prose was 'dull', its opinions of a 'subdued tone', and its critique of Lafayette and Bailly 'respectful, even apologetic'.[18] Although it was, apparently, a very successful publication, turning out a daily eight pages for a good number of years, a reading of it over January–August 1791 none the less confirms this impression of tedium. What Audouin did give was reports of daily political events, especially Assembly debates and news from the frontiers, in a handy format, laced with the straightforward expression of radical opinions. If this did manage to appeal to the very people that the moderates were most afraid of, then perhaps it says something about the political sophistication of some of *le peuple* that all the purveyors of caricature *sans-culottes* were failing to grasp.

None the less, even Audouin's publication could not do without a little inflammatory 'spice'. Each issue had on its front page between three and six headlines, set above the start of the text, and ostensibly indicating the content of the issue. These were the *titres* cried by the *colporteurs* as they

---

15 Guilhaumou, *Langue politique*. Guilhaumou covers the same ground more briefly in his 'Discourse and revolution: the foundation of political language (1789–1792)', in G. Levitine (ed.), *Culture and revolution: cultural ramifications of the French Revolution*, College Park, MD 1989, 118–33.
16 See O. Elyada, 'La Mère Duchesne: masques populaires et guerre pamphlétaire, 1789–1791', *Annales historiques de la Révolution française* cclxxi (1988), 1–16.
17 Ibid. 5–7. See also J.-R. Hébert, *Le Père Duchesne*, repr. in 10 vols, Paris 1969, i–iii.
18 Censer, *Prelude*, 18.

90

hawked their wares in the streets, cafés and open spaces of Paris. However, in the case of the *Journal Universel*, they are so different in tone from the text that one cannot help suspecting that they were added by the publisher to put some life into the text (and the sales).

For example, over 6–13 January 1791 the *titres* included:

Details on the project of counter-revolution which should have occurred at Marseille on Christmas day. . . . Important discovery of all the bad priests dishonouring religion and recognised as enemies of the Nation and the king. . . . Infamous letters addressed to curés to engage them not to swear the civic oath. . . . Infamous manoeuvres of the Aristocratic Priests to excite tumult. . . . Great Tumult at Saint-Sulpice, over the civic oath refused by the curé. . . . Frightful manoeuvres employed by the priests in the seminaries of Paris. . . . Great fury of the Aristocratic Priests against the National Assembly. . . . Notice given to all good citizens to unite to halt the cabals of the priests who refuse to swear the oath.[19]

Between 23 and 30 March 1791, the clergy were no longer quite so central, and the loudest headlines were:

Denunciation of several attacks on the liberty of citizens [an article on imprisonment for debt, it transpires]. . . . Important details on the money spent by the court and its creatures. . . . Notice to citizens concerning the false papal brief, spread about by the enemies of the public good. . . . Notice to citizens on the general Revolution which is being prepared with great activity. . . . Plot of the bishops and rebel prelates, to excite a War of Religion in France. . . . Notice on the infamous conduct of the Counter-Revolutionaries and on their criminal projects. . . . Announcement to good citizens concerning the preparations of our enemies, and the negligence of the French ministers towards putting the Kingdom in a state of defence.

By early June the tone remained the same, but priests continued to decline in prominence relative to more secular counter-revolution:

Notice to good citizens, on the subject of the troubles excited purposely by the enemies of liberty, to later accuse the people of them [another variation on the subornation and brigandage theme]. . . . Motion tending to launch a decree against the emigrants who cowardly desert their fatherland and carry off our gold. . . . Reflections on the conduct and the projects of the enemies of our liberty. . . . Great details at the National Assembly, on the subject of the gathering of the Malcontents on the frontiers, and on a crowd of vagabonds which is accumulating in Paris. . . . Important notice to citizens on the efforts employed by the enemies of the Constitution, to lead astray and seduce the people [further variations on the same theme].[20]

19 *Journal Universel, ou Révolutions des Royaumes, par P.-J. Audouin.*
20 Ibid. 4–14 June.

We have already recognised that sensation sold newspapers then as now, and the violence of Audouin's headlines clearly reflects an attempt to compete in this field. The practice of *colportage* in Paris, like all other public activities, had been closely controlled by the *ancien régime* police, but after the Revolution and the tacit, later explicit, abandonment of controls over the press, the incidence of such public hawking exploded to keep pace with the booming press industry. Even given the Parisian avidity for news, this boom was bound to saturate the market eventually. Between May 1789 and October 1791 515 newspaper titles came out in the city, 53 per cent of which lasted no more than a month, including 107 which printed only a single issue. The first half of 1791 was second only to the post-Bastille period in the number of new titles emerging. Censer suggests that this reflected 'both a rising popular interest in daily news and national politics and a growing number of people who wanted to publicize their own opinions'.[21] We should add to this the observation that, perhaps more significantly, those opinions were becoming ever more violently divergent.

Regardless of its political motivations, the burgeoning of press production, especially in 1791, also coincided with a growing army of the unemployed, for whom *colportage* might have been a last resort before crime and destitution. The police records of the Sections du Louvre and des Arcis, covering the right-bank quaysides and the Place de Grève, show something of the extent of this practice. From April to mid-July 1791, ninety-eight people were detained in these two Sections for what might be called crimes of desperation – petty theft, pickpocketing and low-stakes open-air gambling. Of this number, no less than thirteen had been, or were, *colporteurs* or 'paper-sellers [vendeurs de papiers]'. They took their places alongside an array of unemployed artisans and other impoverished workers, including those who had suffered a gradual descent to the point of crime – a servant who had gone on to sell vegetables, a locksmith who became a message-runner, a journeyman pork-butcher who worked as a mason's labourer – and those who had never been more than errand-runners or casual labourers (the only single category, at fourteen, to outnumber the *colporteurs*).[22]

Under such circumstances, Paris must have rung with the cries of such hawkers, who were of course obliged to buy their stock, and thus had even more incentive to recoup a meagre profit. The arrest of one man in the Section de la Place-Vendôme on 27 June 1791 illustrates the hand-to-mouth existence led by many news-peddlers. Having sold two men in a café a copy of Audouin's *Journal*, he went on to offer them an *Orateur du Peuple*, which they read, and, finding it inflammatory, arrested him. He was a twenty-seven-

21 Censer, *Prelude*, 9.
22 APP, AA56; AA182. As we shall later see, even some of those arrested while selling papers preferred to record their former *état*, rather than this new occupation, so the number of detainees who had tried their hand at *colportage* may have been even higher than indicated.

year-old errand-runner, and admitted buying six copies of the *Orateur* in the Faubourg St-Germain, and four of *Louis XVI and Antoinette treated as they deserve* at 'rue de la Parcheminière no. thirteen in the house of the innkeeper on the second floor at the front', from a man whose name he did not know. He also admitted knowing 'that these were the two sheets . . . which should not be sold'. The tiny quantities of stock indicate clearly the meagre resources of this seller, and his willingness to risk arrest suggests desperation – there is certainly no bravado or evidence of political commitment in his answers.[23]

Under such difficult economic circumstances, *colporteurs* were tempted to elaborate on what may already have been fairly 'hot' material in pursuit of potential clients. On 1 March in the Section des Tuileries, one was imprisoned 'for having hawked inflammatory material and having announced it under a false title, which was the "Great Anger of the Père Duchesne about a man who went to the queen's chamber to kill her" '. Clearly, this was a fabrication of new sensation from the *journée* of 28 February, as stale news was passed off under a more enticing label. His reward was a week in La Force.[24]

The arrest of a *colporteur* of unidentifiable previous trade on 24 April, in the Section des Enfants-Rouges, is known to us by a near-illegible record. The hawker had attempted to sell the *Journal du Soir* with the cry 'M. Delafayette has retaken command, down with the aides de camp . . . throw out the headquarters that gives false orders.' A Guard noted that this paper did not, in fact, contain these incendiary phrases, but the man repeatedly defied warnings to stop his cries – 'this individual told him several times that no-one could stop him selling his papers'. The Guard proved him wrong, and the *commissaire*, noting that he had 'neither plaque nor medal' that would mark him as an official *colporteur*, was about to order his imprisonment when a local citizen vouched for him.[25]

The action taken against this *colporteur* came after events on Palm Sunday and the following Monday (to be explored in the next chapter) had marked a significant escalation in the political confrontation between court and people, and confirms the intensification of police vigilance against *colporteurs* in times of tension, as after the October Days. This is also apparent in the Champ de Mars episode. At 10 a.m. on 17 July a *colporteur* was brought to the Enfants-Rouges *commissaire* by two sergeant-majors and a volunteer of that battalion. They had heard him crying 'the order of march for going to the Champ de Mars, citizens assemble!' and had arrested him, 'judging that this was an inflammatory writing and very dangerous in the present circumstances'.[26] The vendor, Jacques Chenon, aged thirty-eight, an unemployed stonemason, had been selling papers 'for around eight months'. Asked why he sold 'inflammatory papers', he answered 'that he was not the only one that

23 APP, AA206:328. He was sent to La Force.
24 APP, AB322:1402.
25 APP, AA157:103.
26 APP, AA157:143.

sold them, that he thought that they were in order, the name of the printer being at the bottom'. Despite this attention to one rule, he was, not surprisingly, devoid of 'the permission and the medal' officially required, thus offering further excuse to detain him. He was sent to La Force.[27]

The pamphlet that Chenon had been hawking when he was arrested was entitled, in the clerk's rendition, 'Great detail of the gathering of more than two hundred thousand citizens of the capital and its environs, on the space [terrain] of the Bastille, in order to go to the Champ de Mars today Sunday seventeenth July: the order of march of the citizens.' It had been printed by 'l'imprimerie de Tremblay, Rue Basse St-Denis no. eleven'. Although the collection of the Bibliothèque nationale does not include a copy of this particular pamphlet, its title, tone and publisher place it in a well-established series. The Tremblay shop, home also of Hébert's *Père Duchesne*, had been producing its 'Great Detail' pamphlets for some months. This series constitutes one example of a genre of publication apart from the periodical press and the burlesques of Hébert and his ilk, which reported news of sensational events anonymously (thus seeking perhaps to avoid the impression of being mere opinion), and appeared in clouds around any significant incident. The first identifiable one in this series in 1791 is *Great detail of the revolution that took place yesterday in the Faubourg St-Antoine, in which a mouchard was massacred by the people*, which is a brief polemic on the Kabert riot of 27 January. This lauded the action of the people, 'against whom so many rogues weave so many iniquitous projects'. It seemed unaware of the fact that Kabert had survived the ordeal, and attempted to cover its evident approval of the 'massacre' with petty equivocation: 'We are far from approving these movements of fury into which the people is sometimes led; but what renders this in some way excusable, is the impunity of the brigands, who daily escape the prosecution of the laws.'[28]

From around the same period comes a report of a counter-revolutionary sermon which nearly ended in a lynching – *Great detail of a sedition caused by a vicar of Paris*. This account describes an unidentifiable incident in which a priest preaching at the Hôpital de la Pitié – a 'madman foaming with rage' – was finally prevented from continuing his series of sermons, which had blamed the ills of society on the Assembly, and advocated a return to the *ancien régime*.[29]

Although the tone of these works was fairly wild, even at this date, presumably around January-February, when priests were still big news, it was not until after Easter that they began to grow truly rabid. Oddly, no Tremblay pamphlet on the Passion Week events appears to have survived, but others, including one in a very similar series by 'l'imprimerie de Labarre', show that

[27] Among his wares again appeared Audouin's *Journal*.
[28] BN, 8-Lb41-2553, *Grand détail de la révolution arrivée hier au faubourg St-Antoine, dans laquelle un mouchard a été massacré par le peuple*.
[29] BN, 8-Lb39-8172, *Grand détail d'une sédition occasionnée par un vicaire de Paris*.

the general pamphlet coverage of those days was extremely inflammatory. Concerning the king's communion with a non-juring priest, the Labarre pamphlet had this to say:

> On such a folly, what must one think of a monarch over whom the refractories have an inconceivable ascendancy, which all the citizens well know, since all the public papers declare him the sworn enemy of the revolution, and of which his ill-considered conduct gives authentic proofs.[30]

By mid-May, the tone had grown considerably more radical, as the opening paragraph of the Tremblay pamphlet on a minor riot over hoarders shows:

> Poor people, tormented always in a thousand fashions: you, the prop, the support of the state, until when shall you let so many unchained monsters subsist to make eternal war on you; do not think that your greatest enemies are those that menace the frontiers; the most terrible are close to you. So crush at the first chance these serpents that surround you, otherwise you shall soon be the victim of your indulgence.[31]

However, while 'vile monopolists' were the target of this attack, the writer also denounced

> the rogues who trouble your rest by plunging you into continual disquiet, who wish to excite you to revolt through the force of oppression, to have an occasion to slit your throats and quench their thirst in your blood, who treat as factious men your true supporters, and who wish to make the revolution odious by abusing the authority you have confided in them to vex you.

One may readily ask what message such accounts wished to send – to revolt or not to revolt? Perhaps it was some fine legal scruple that constantly infused these writings with the cautionary idea that a general rising was just what the people's enemies wanted; more likely it was just involuted revolutionary conspiracy-mongering. But it must be asked if such a constant production of material that managed to be inflammatory without offering any radical solutions did not indicate a profound conflict in radical minds. Even the most radical of activists (always excepting Marat) clung to the forms of constitutionality, albeit in their Rights-of-Man-oriented understanding of it, suggesting that such an approach signified more than mere timidity or lack of commitment. The confusion at the heart of the radical approach to politics, where activists lacked any genuine alternatives to the constitutional structures whose manipulation was repressing them, must thus be constantly

---

30 BN, 8–Lb39–9869, *Détail de la grande révolution arrivée aux Thuileries pour le départ du roi.* See also BN, 8–Lb39–4826, 4827, 4867, 4868. The Labarre pamphlet, and others, printed as fact the supposed death of a journeyman wigmaker at the hands of the Guard, a completely false rumour: Lacroix, *Actes*, iii. 631–2.
31 BN, 8–Lb39–4925. The people is addressed throughout in the familiar 'tu' form.

borne in mind. The press, particularly in its ephemeral pamphlet variety, was the shallowest manifestation of this general mindset, offering instant reporting of suspicious and inflammatory events without political reflection, and leaving the people enraged, but stymied. The whole experience of the Champ de Mars Massacre only offers tragic confirmation of this.

Another case from the July events, in spite of its occasional farcical air, leads us further into the production and distribution of ephemeral literature. At 11 a.m. on 20 July two men were brought in to the *commissaire de police* of the Section de l'Oratoire by a lieutenant of cavalry, who had arrested them in the street, for standing amidst a group of people and calling out 'The law is atrocious, let us make a well-reasoned petition, it shall soon be zero.' While the *commissaire* heard the first witness, one of the two accused, Jean Pierre François Chardon, 'nicknamed la Panache', offered to take the Guard to the printer and author of the pamphlet from which he had read. After consultation this was agreed, and he went off with a patrol which returned to make a long report on its successful hunt.[32]

The *commissaire* began by questioning Chardon, aged twenty-four, a native of Paris, and a *colporteur* by trade. He said he had bought the pamphlets at seven that morning, speaking to the shorter of the two printers. He claimed to have read it out 'between his comrade and him' out of simple curiosity as to the contents. He confused the *commissaire* by saying he could not read when asked if he knew of the martial law decree posted two days before. The second seller cleared this up by admitting to doing the reading at the request of someone else, but only in order to encourage sales. He was Louis François Dufour, also a Parisian by birth, aged thirty-six, and a journeyman papermaker who had been reduced to *colportage* for the last few days for lack of work. He, too, was unaware of martial law, he said, but recalled that the printer had said there was no risk in selling the pamphlet.

Following this, one of the printers was called for questioning. Jacques Dumoulin was seventy-one, and owned the printworks at 7, rue Thibotaudé jointly with a M. Libron, upon whom he placed all the blame for any trouble, having himself merely done the work of printing the sheets without reading them, even when he was handing them out to sellers. The second printer announced himself as Louis Livron, but signed as Delivron. He claimed that, knowing the purity of the writer's principles, he had not troubled to read the copy before it was set in type, and in correcting the proofs he had missed the offending phrase. Like all the others, he was in ignorance of any new law on the freedom of the press, as he phrased it. He had sold thirty-six dozen copies that day to *colporteurs*, but denied telling any of them that it was safe to sell, or otherwise. He added that the copy had come in partly on Monday 18th and partly on Tuesday 19th, and the print-run had been finished at around 9 p.m. that day.

[32] APP, AA153:16

The writer was then questioned, Charles Foulhioux, aged thirty-six, a Lyonnais resident in Paris since 1776. Like the others he stressed his lack of firm association with his fellow defendants. He claimed to have written the piece, 'The Great Sickness of the Père Duchesne', on the 17th 'during the morning', and had it collected at 6.30 a.m. on the 18th, before he could have known of the new law – if he had, he assured the *commissaire*, his love for the Constitution and his devotion to the *patrie* would have made him respect it. On the other hand he had absolutely nothing to do with printing and distribution, and it was up to the printer, he said, to be sure of what he was selling. He added that he had written several works on 'the spirit of the Law and the Revolution', and that having been three times a victim of the *ancien régime* (in unspecified circumstances) he had more motive than anyone for loving the Constitution.[33]

Faced with this parade of buck-passing, the *commissaire* referred the matter to the *Département de Police*, where, in consideration of the remorse and love for the law shown by all concerned, they were released with a stern warning. The haphazard and fragmented world of printing and *colportage* is here clearly on display. The work of Foulhioux (or Fouilhoux) can be traced in the Bibliothèque nationale. He published a total of twenty *Père Duchesne* pamphlets in 1791, a series of six in July and fourteen in September. The printer's address is that of Dumoulin and Livron, but while in the July editions it is 'L'imprimerie du véritable père Duchesne' – the habitual notation on the at least six different versions then circulating – by September it has become 'L'imprimerie de Sallière'. Dumoulin perhaps sold out after his brush with the law.[34]

The pamphlet seized on the two *colporteurs* is bound fifth in the July collection, but there is scant internal evidence to date the others precisely.[35] The piece in question is entitled 'The great sickness of the père Duchesne, caused by all that has happened on the Champ de Mars, Sunday the 17th'. It is a typical *Père*, more diatribe than sense, interrupted by torrents of oaths as the readership had come to expect. The passage its sellers were reading out comes on the second page:

> Everyone is wrong, *foutre*, except the law, even if it is atrocious: let us make a well-reasoned petition, and that law of blood [evidently the decree reinstating the king] shall become, if not a paste of ink, at least nearly zero. But also, let us behave with such cohesion, that the buggering beggars who wish us ill, shall never be able to penetrate the thickness of our columns, *sacré mille jean-foutres*.

---

33 Charles Foulhioux went on to a later revolutionary career as an adjunct to the Jacobin *représentant en mission* Roux-Fazillac: J.-P. Gross, *Fair shares for all: Jacobin egalitarianism in practice*, Cambridge 1997, 24, 187.

34 To continue the digression, 7 rue Thibotaudé is the address from which the *Mercure National* of François and Louise Robert was published up to January 1791, and it was then identified as 'L'imprimerie de Roland'.

35 BN, 8–LC2–517.

In other words, the Assembly seems to have done wrong, but will come around, and the primary danger is that of being swept away by dangerous agitators. Foulhioux obviously had the news of the two lynchings of the 17th when he began to write, since he blames them on 'a heap of gallows-fodder sent into Paris, who take atrocious care to calumnify your civic feelings'. If his readers were to meet such agitators, he urges them to offer short shrift: 'stuff them for me with blows of your sticks'. He calls for unity between the people and the Guard and the promotion of tranquillity. The idea of forming a petition seems to have been dropped after being mentioned only once, and the rest of the pamphlet concentrates on driving home the message of reconciliation. The obvious reason for this switch would be that he heard some news of the Champ de Mars events after he had begun to write, and was unsure as to how to continue, so completed the piece in the most bland style he could manage, buried under further heaps of the *Père's* oratory. Clearly his printer's deadline carried more weight than discovering exactly what was going on.

Foulhioux's opinions are less restrained in his other pamphlets from the same month. There are rants against financial speculators, and against the Assembly which lets such things happen under its nose, because it, too, is in the hands of intriguers and serves the rich against the people. This class of popular enemy extends as far as the Section committees, who are all working to do the people out of the wealth that should be theirs – the church property being sold off was held, originally, for the poor, and so, Foulhioux demands, that is who it should go to now. Alongside this is a stream of indignation against the king subsequent to his flight, and demanding his trial.

Such may be his opinions, sifted from some fifty pages of verbiage, but when it comes to putting them into practice, Foulhioux hedged his bets so far that it is impossible to find one call for positive action in the whole series, with the exception of the hastily-regretted example above. His standard ploy for calming the ire he may have stirred in his readers is, as with this example, to warn them against falling into the hands of agitators, and to state that, paradoxically, they must ultimately put their trust in the Assembly. Foulhioux reveals himself as someone whose contribution to the revolutionary atmosphere was even more shallow than that of the Tremblay writer(s) – a man without decided opinions of his own, making a living in the 'Père Duchesne industry' without attaching much significance to what he writes. Fortunately for him, neither did the *Département de Police*.[36]

The administrators, however, found justification in the general post-Champ de Mars situation for a prohibition, in a municipal decree of 27 July,

---

36 C. Hesse, *Publishing and cultural politics in revolutionary Paris, 1789–1810*, Berkeley 1991, considers in some depth the careers, politics and circumstances of some of the more successful Parisian printers, but she cannot approach the ephemeral world apparently inhabited by men such as Foulhioux and Dumoulin, still less the scavenging existence of their vendors.

of the *colportage* of 'inflammatory sheets', naming particularly the works of Marat and Fréron. On the 30th they imposed a blanket ban on the verbal embroidering of headlines, justifying it as follows:

> Colporteurs often allow themselves to announce sheets and journals in a manner contrary to their real contents and always disturbing to the public. They are, no doubt, guided by the hope of more considerable sales. But, as such an infidelity is always in opposition to the law and cannot but induce error in an infinity of citizens, the Department of Police has felt it to be its duty to put an end to this abuse.

Confiscation and imprisonment were ordained as punishment for crying anything apart from the title of the piece for sale.[37]

The Guard headquarters supplemented this crackdown with its own orders, sometimes leading to confusion. On 12 August a patrol brought to *commissaire de police* Deneux of the Section des Arcis a *colporteur* arrested while reading aloud from the *Thermomètre du Jour* – very far from a radical organ. The arrest was in accordance with 'today's order . . . to arrest . . . all public readers'. The *commissaire* was nonplussed with the prospect of enforcing such a general directive, which moreover had not been communicated to him. Touched in his revolutionary sensibilities, he wrote 'we do not think that such an insufficient instruction can authorise us to pronounce the detention of a citizen, a detention which appears to us arbitrary and hence tyrannical'. He released the *colporteur*, although just to be on the safe side he warned him not to read from his wares in public again, and confiscated his stock. Given the doubts Deneux had just expressed, this outcome demonstrates the authoritarian nature of police practice, subverting the revolutionary rhetoric of its practitioners.[38]

The Parisian press operated in an intensely competitive market, a fact which oriented its output towards sensationalism. This drift was reinforced by the pre-revolutionary 'apprenticeship' of many of the writers, by the inclinations of its readership, and simply by the intensely hostile political atmosphere. All of these elements contributed to a revolutionary press discourse that appears thoroughly 'overdetermined' in its resort to bloodthirsty rhetoric and denunciation of involuted conspiracy. We may allow the possibility of political subornation and subsidy, but its effect on the products of the press in such an environment is moot. The already inflammatory nature of much output was then reinforced by the prevalent method of sale – public hawking – itself made more competitive by the desperate economic situation of many *colporteurs*. Overall, therefore, even without taking account of the deeply

---

37 Lacroix, *Actes*, vi. 22–3, 28–30. The decree of the 27th was withdrawn after Condorcet and others protested at its implied pre-publication censorship of the two journalists, but the general ban on incendiary materials was restated, and the decree of the 30th went unchallenged.
38 APP, AA57:34.

troubling nature of events themselves in 1791, we can already see that many factors pointed to the escalation of public tensions through the diffusion of the press, regardless of whether we credit journalists and their sales-force with political motives. Furthermore, we have begun to suggest that, even where radical views are clearly apparent in the press, the tide of inflammatory production concealed a fundamental flaw in such an outlook – its lack of a viable political alternative.

Tensions after the Vincennes *journée*

The alternative generally suggested by the people was to hang their perceived enemies. The municipality of Paris itself increasingly fell into that category as time wore on, and its various individual actions gradually came to seem like a pattern of oppression. One such action was the decision to keep the Vincennes detainees of 28 February locked in the Abbaye after the Tuileries culprits had been released – Gorsas noted on 15 March that placards had gone up in the Faubourg St-Antoine calling for the people to march and hang Lafayette, although there is no sign of real disturbance.[39] Popular feeling was certainly aggrieved at the release of the 'knights'. The Fayettist *Feuille du Jour* ironically offered its version of the views of the crowd at the Tuileries, remarking that 'lacking an accuser was just a technical issue', and that 'the useful habit of hanging first' was necessary 'for the interest and the glory of the state'.[40]

On 16 March a sixty-seven-year-old ex-mason was arrested for tearing down the official *affiche* of the aristocrats' release. The *commissaire* questioning him was intent on discovering his connection to the affair – did he think them innocent, or had he been 'inspired' by someone to tear the notice? No, he said, he had done it because he viewed their names 'with pain' and thought them 'very guilty'. None the less, he was sent to La Force with a note that 'he appears to us to have done it by design and perhaps through some outside suggestion', once again making it clear that the authorities doubted the possibility of genuine popular interest in political events.[41] They were willing to accept less ambiguous actions, however, such as the report of a female linen-worker on 2 March, which she made 'through the patriotism which animates her and the great interest that she takes in all that may interest the public good'. She stated that the previous night, as she walked home, she had overheard two men bemoaning the failure of what had clearly been a planned *coup* in the Tuileries, saying that 'M. de Buisa [De Brisac?] had a load of pistols hidden in *l'oeil de boeuf* [an audience chamber with a round

39 The same notices are remarked on by the *Feuille du Jour* of the same date.
40 *Feuille du Jour*, 14 Mar.
41 APP, AA182:119, Section du Louvre. Once in La Force it was not long before the incon-sequence of the matter was perceived: AB322:1524, release ordered 18 Mar.

window] to arm his hundred Swiss, but that he had not dared propose to arm them, seeing so many National Guards.'[42]

None the less, the first two weeks of March passed relatively peacefully, since aristocratic plotting seemed to have been brought under control on 28 February. According to the general press coverage, concern for the health of the king perhaps also dampened public fervour in the second week, and a certain amount of relief is reported to have greeted his recovery from fever by the 18th.[43] On the 17th, however, the authorities succeeded in stirring the hornets' nest themselves by publishing an *ordonnance* from the Police Department, one of the aims of which was clearly to counter the fears that had existed in February about concealed weapons. It did so, however, in terms so ineptly draconian that the outcry from the popular societies and the Jacobin Club forced its withdrawal only four days later.[44] The document, which covered various measures against disorder and theft, had gone so far as to ban the sale of old keys, and to order that new ones could only be made in the workshops of recognised master locksmiths. A mere two weeks after the Assembly had voted the final abolition of guild mastership (Loi d'Allarde, 2 March), it is not surprising that the *Révolutions de Paris* remarked that the measure was 'astonishing' in its stupidity. Gorsas observed that in any case, no-one would obey the prohibition on going armed, 'at least while the very nonchalant and very pusillanimous police does not sweep the capital of the brigands that they have allowed to accumulate there'.[45]

The capital's tensions over aristocracy (and brigandage) thus clearly remained, despite the general decline in counter-revolutionary activity that was perceived after 28 February. The continuation of additional fears about the clergy is reflected in a letter from the municipal prosecutor to all *commissaires de police* on 18 March: 'I am assured, Monsieur, that tomorrow morning, perhaps from before six, there shall take place, in one or more churches of Paris that are not firmly designated to me, a ceremony demanding the presence of a bishop; which is commonly carried out only in cathedral churches or those of seminaries, and which it is in the public interest to prevent.'[46] Hence all *commissaires* were advised to take all possible measures to prevent such ceremonies taking place, and further to hold curés personally responsible for any illicit usage made of their churches. There is no indication from *commissaires* of any secret ceremonies being discovered. The wording of the warning suggests that the prosecutor was fearful of illicit ordinations, but there is no other evidence of such concerns.[47]

---

42 APP, AA206:147, Section de la Place-Vendôme.
43 See all journals for this period, some of which, predictably, were more sardonic about the daily reports of the royal motions and sputum than others.
44 See Bourdin, *Sociétés populaires*, 205–7.
45 *Courrier*, 21 Mar.; *Révolutions de Paris*, 19–26 Mar.
46 APP, AA82:436, Section du Palais-Royal.
47 Lacroix, *Actes*, iii. 197, notes the sending of the circular, but cannot clarify its subject.

On the same day, however, Martin Sylvestre Boulard, 'printer-bookseller of the commune of the section du Palais-Royal', testified to the shocking discovery he had made in the church of St-Roch, where the names of the confessors were habitually posted:

> they had suppressed with scandalous affectation, and covered either with white paper, or another name, all the names of the priests who had taken the civic oath, which cannot be the result of the ill-will of one individual, since the lists, of which there are at least three, are covered by glass, and hung fairly high, so that one could not easily reach them. I also saw that the glass and the frames were freshly washed, which indicates a premeditated design to insult those who have given proofs of patriotism.[48]

It would certainly seem that way, and the Section committee went *en masse* to note the alteration – which amounted to the defacement of only four out of twenty-seven names, indicating something of the scale of non-juring. However, they chose not to take action, a laxity rewarded two days later by a minor riot when a full congregation noticed the changes, and ended by smashing at least one of the glass plates.[49] At a service later on that day, there were complaints that the text chosen for the sermon was clearly designed to reflect negatively on the issue of the oath. Four parishioners recorded their protest, while a fellow-priest backed up the preacher in his plea of innocence. *Commissaire* Toublanc obviously found the theological question beyond his scope, and referred it to the *Département de Police*, who took no observable action, as they had not done in the Section du Louvre in January.[50]

As troubles with the clergy continued, so too did hostility to the aristocrats. A patriotic mob carried out another assault on the meeting-place of the *Club monarchique* on 28 March. Clermont-Tonnerre later wrote to Bailly to protest that the mob had been allowed to penetrate the building by the forces of order, and had broken or stolen various objects, while 'the Guard in the house threatened several members, instead of protecting them'.[51] Evidently not all the Guard could be accounted tools of counter-revolution. There seem to have been generally fewer reports of aristocratic goings-on as the spring wore on, although they did not disappear completely. On 4 April a salaried Guardsman reported to the Place-Vendôme *commissaire* that he had been at the Hôtel de Ville at 11.45 the previous night, and had seen three men lurking in the shadows, keeping the sentry outside the entrance to the headquarters under observation. They were 'in civilian clothes and without cockades'. But what had really 'excited his disquiet, was that . . . he had recognised them as former officers of the French Guards'. They made off after seeing him

---

48 APP, AA82:438, Section du Palais-Royal.
49 APP, AA82:452, Section du Palais-Royal. Overall over half the *curés* of Paris were in refraction – 28 as against 24 jurors: Lacroix, *Actes*, ii. 462.
50 APP, AA82:455.
51 Lacroix, *Actes*, iii. 609, letter of 14 Apr. to municipality.

go up to the sentry to alert him.[52] On the theme of popular hostility to the authorities, it must be similarly acknowledged that March and early April saw fewer day-to-day skirmishes recorded than the previous two months. However, what incidents there were once again seem to indicate an escalation in feelings. For example, on 4 April again, at Mirabeau's funeral, the Guard was lining the route when a tailor raised the cry 'down with the bayonets', which the charge said had 'exposed the said Guard to being abused by the crowd of people who repeated the same phrase'.[53] These sentiments would only gain in strength with the passage of time.

Early April saw a flare-up of another kind of suspicion linked to counter-revolution, illustrated by a letter published in the *Bouche de Fer* on 1 April from 'S.G., National Guard': 'The least things are important in revolutions, and I am astonished that no-one remarks upon the *variations* in the colours of the national cockade, a sacred rallying-sign to which patriots should never permit any disfigurement.'[54] The writer went on to report the subtle variations in colour and design of cockade he had seen 'with indignation', and concluded that their wearers 'appear suspect to me; and who assures us that these modifications are not the means of recognition amongst enemies of the public good?'.

Whether as a result of reading this, or by his own independent inspiration, the thirty-eight-year-old servant Louis Jean Gobrou was to be found two days later in the Palais-Royal garden tearing off various peoples' cockades, crying 'here's another who has a white cockade from the *Club monarchique*', while 'enveloped in a circle of women' who seconded his efforts. Under questioning, he stated that among the crowd were some, 'who wear cockades on a white ground with a small addition in the centre, which announces in these cockades a difference with the national cockades, and that his goal, along with that of the several people who were at his side, was to try to prevent gatherings of suspect people through this mixture [sic; perhaps read 'distinction']'.[55] This obsession with the minutiae of visual symbolism was not confined to isolated alarmists. The registers of La Force show that it was not unknown for a person to be arrested 'at the public clamour' and jailed 'as suspect' for wearing a non-standard cockade, or for not wearing one at all – the Guard sentries around the Tuileries appear to have made a habit of

52 APP, AA206:181.
53 APP, AB323:202, released 6 Apr. The death of Mirabeau exposed again the inflammatory tone of pamphlet literature. His secretary apparently attempted to commit suicide during Mirabeau's final illness and, despite his lack of success, at least two pamphlets immediately appeared announcing an 'assassination attempt' against him. See Lacroix, *Actes*, iii. 414–15. On 4 April Marat's *Ami du Peuple* accused the man of poisoning Mirabeau, and denounced a cover-up.
54 *Bouche de Fer*, no. 37. This was an organ of the *Cercle social*, whose political views are discussed in ch. 5.
55 APP, AA83:54, Section du Palais-Royal, 3 Apr., 5.30 p.m.

arresting those whom their enquiries about missing cockades had prompted into insults.[56]

From the same period, a note from the minutes of the Municipal General Council indicates that one of the public schoolteachers present on 12 April to take the civic oath had tried to amend its wording. 'General disapproval' followed, and 'the noise grew again when it was remarked that this individual, dressed in a National Guard coat, wore buttons different from those of the Parisian uniform'. Thanks to this, he was detained and questioned personally by Bailly. The detail of his uniform seems to have absorbed concerns to the exclusion of any mention of the act which had first drawn attention to him. The difference arose, he said, 'because he had bought his uniform second-hand and his fortune had not allowed him to substitute other buttons'. His release, however, depended on three active citizens from his Section who were found to vouch for him.[57] Lacroix recorded this episode as a 'bizarre incident', but it clearly fits into the pattern of excessive suspicion that enveloped Parisian life.

The resistance of the clergy, meanwhile, continued, entering a new phase as replacements for the refractory curés were finally found. On 3 April a priest complained that, acting on the instructions of the new curé, M. Legrand, he had tried to gain access to the church of the Convent of Ste-Anne in the Section du Palais-Royal, where he was to catechise a group of children. The Mother Superior of the convent had refused to admit him, saying she recognised no other curé but M. Marduel. Two lay witnesses confirmed her words. *Commissaire* Toublanc went to the convent on rue neuve St-Roch, to find there that word had spread, and that 'there was a large gathering of persons of both sexes' in front of the doors, which he managed to partially disperse before knocking.

He spoke to the Superior, who went into a long explanation of how the convent had no obligation to lend its church for the catechism, and that although they had done for the last twelve years at the request of M. Marduel, it was no longer possible for them to do so. She felt bound by her conscience to admit that she could not bring herself to recognise the new curé, but none the less she had 'for a long time' asked his predecessor to find a new site for the catechism. That was that, as far as the issue of the church went, but meanwhile the trouble had been growing outside, fomented by some suspicious bedding that had been thrown from a window. Toublanc investigated, and found two women, guests in the convent, who had acted 'out of the fear

---

[56] See APP, AB322:1300, a nineteen-year-old arrested by the Bastille labourers for wearing a red cockade (21 Feb., released 1 Mar.); AB323:387, an unemployed journeyman innkeeper wearing a yellow and black cockade (19 Apr., vouched for 21 Apr.); AB322:1478, two men, including the 'secretary to the colonial committee', arrested for insulting the sentry (12 Mar., released 14, 15 Mar.); AB322:1522, a servant detained for the same offence (16 Mar., vouched for 18 Mar.)
[57] Lacroix, *Actes*, iii. 543.

they felt, seeing the trouble grow in the street, having the intention to get out by jumping from the window, which was around ten to twelve feet up'. This ends the record, and we must assume that the crowd was pacified, or drifted away.[58]

Let us note, however, what Gorsas reported of this incident. He described how the enraged parents of the excluded children had battered down the door of the convent after the first refusal to admit the priest, and seized two nuns who tried to resist – 'Their garments resisted less than the doors, and vigorous hands were applied several times to their anti-constitutional buttocks. They were chased off after this beneficent and public correction.'[59] This is a far cry from the rather dignified exchange Toublanc noted, which we may assume to be a more reliable account of events. Such reports as that of Gorsas, whether emerging from journalistic malice, exaggeration for effect or the uncritical acceptance of gossip, contributed to a slide towards the real violence that followed.

On 6 April the authorities of this Section were again confronted by clerical stonewalling. At 11 a.m. a deputation of 'neighbours and parishioners' came to the Section committee to complain that the monks of the Brothers of the Christian Schools, contrary to normal practice, had sent their children home from classes that morning without taking them to mass. The president of the committee himself summoned the monks to offer an explanation, and seven of the eight brothers arrived, the last being occupied with his 'functions'. Brother Boniface, their Superior, explained

> that believing their conscience to be involved, and wishing to conserve this in all its purity, they had unanimously agreed not to conduct the children confided to their care to the services celebrated either by the new curé or his vicars, recognising no other pastor of this parish than M. Marduel and the priests delegated by him.

All the president could do was send a copy of this to the mayor, just as Toublanc could only inform the *Département de Police* when, the next day, the servants of the marquise de Vibraye were found emptying a chapel inside St-Roch of furniture she had provided, once the lady had proved this with a document dating from 1763. The following day, the *commissaire* of the Section de la Place-Vendôme recorded that the Brothers of the Christian Schools of the Madeleine parish had disappeared overnight.[60]

Incidents such as these seem to have been taking place across the city, and by 7 April, no doubt aided by the inflammatory press coverage, they had raised tensions to the level at which open violence was committed. Women reportedly went on a rampage in the rue St-Antoine, breaking into several convents and leaving their occupants 'charitably beaten', as one journal put

[58] APP, AA83:52.
[59] *Courrier*, 6 Apr.
[60] APP, AA83:66, 77; AA206:185.

it.[61] The municipality at once banned gatherings in front of ecclesiastical buildings and ordered the Guard to defend religious property and personnel. In its passage through the bureaucracy this became an order to religious communities to close their churches 'to give no pretext for the contraventions of ecclesiastics and the excesses of the people', as *commissaires de police* were told by a letter on 8 April ordering its enforcement. This measure was officially confirmed by the municipality on 14 April.[62]

The growing confidence of the refractory clergy, sure now of papal support and the sympathy of the king, may well have provoked this disorder, as it was widely believed they were now concentrating their efforts on corrupting the young in convent schools. The public caning of nuns combined a violent and painful assault with a heavily symbolic chastisement, and such measures had the less sober of the Parisian patriots in a frenzy of titillated glee – pamphleteers went to town on the theme of *culs*.[63] This episode evidently entered the popular consciousness, for on 17 April two nuns who refused to donate a pickaxe to a man for use in the public workshops were threatened that he would 'have them whipped like the others'.[64] Although it seems to have been a brief explosion, fears of its repetition lingered, and on 27 April an order came to Toublanc to watch over the 'sisters of charity' of St-Roch, who were threatened with being 'insulted' by persons unknown.[65] The attacks, it should be noted, were no light matter. On 7 May the municipality approved funds to hospitalise two nuns, 'fallen into dementia, apparently through the fear caused to them by ill-treatment from the people'.[66]

Meanwhile, however, on Palm Sunday, 17 April, a congregation of the non-jurors' supporters who had hired the church of the Théatins monastery on the Left Bank for a service were attacked and driven out by a large crowd.[67] This incident, not widely reported by journalists caught up with the king's activities on this day, seems to have been an unqualified victory for the crowd, which broke up the mainly female congregation, assaulted some of the women, and hung a placard announcing their triumph over the door of the church. They then remained in possession of the conquered ground for the rest of the day, twice forcing the replacement of the sign, the second time after its removal on municipal orders.[68]

At this point the king's choice of a refractory priest for his communion would help to shift the focus of Parisian agitation onto secular affairs, but the

---

[61] Lacroix, *Actes*, iii. 475.

[62] APP, AA83:82; Lacroix, *Actes*, iii. 475, 565.

[63] Lacroix notes that lists of alleged victims of the attacks ran to over 300 – all 'pure fantasy': ibid. iii. 481.

[64] APP, AB323:334, Section des Thermes-de-Julien. Released 22 Apr.

[65] APP, AA83:196. Evidently Toublanc did so successfully, as his laconic note reads 'Calm'.

[66] Lacroix, *Actes*, iv. 159.

[67] Ibid. iii. 622.

[68] See BN, 8-Ld4–7094, a sympathetic and somewhat hyperbolic account, but one to which Lacroix gives credence.

religious issue did not die away completely. The months from January to April had seen the refractories steadily defeated in a war of attrition, pushed back from defiant repudiation of the clerical oath to attempts to hold on to their jobs, then to petty resistance to the new priests and a retreat to the interior of religious houses, and finally into a vain attempt to worship openly apart from the new order. Nor was there to be any let-up in the control over priests. In late May authorities in the Section de la Bonne-Nouvelle faced disorders when they were ordered to amalgamate their parish with that of St-Sauveur. On 16 May female parishioners 'suspended by the bell-ropes' reportedly caused mayhem as they resisted attempts to remove the parochial regalia to its new home.[69] On 22 May the *commissaire de police* hurried to the church to find 'a large assembly of women and some citizens' being addressed by the priest, the abbé de Damalix. Some two to three hundred women were present, along with about a dozen men, as Damalix said

> that among the decrees of the National Assembly there were some that were recognised as bad, and that as the enemies of the public good sought to lead the people astray about its true interests, he proposed to that assembly [i.e. his audience] to meet each Sunday after the service as an elementary assembly of citizens, to explain to them the decrees.

Damalix here clearly shows his familiarity with revolutionary discourse, but its implied content, and context, made such an aim highly suspicious. After this proposal had been warmly applauded, some of the women began to voice complaints that the administrators of the parish, one of whom was a Section *commissaire* present, had not done enough to resist its demise. Before the situation could turn ugly, the *commissaire de police* persuaded Damalix to close the meeting and leave. The next week, armed with a municipal order prohibiting these meetings, the *commissaire* went to the church with a Guard detachment and detained the priest in front of some 250 women who had again gathered to hear him. This arrest shows how determined the authorities had become by this time to contain dissent with a religious basis, as well as hinting at their fear of unruly women – the observation that the gathering was 'composed almost wholly of women' seems to have had equal place with the unconstitutional words of the priest as reason to prohibit it.[70] Damalix was detained until the municipal prosecutor had examined his case, then released on his own recognisance, although he was reported to the public prosecutors 'as a disturber of the public peace'. This decision had twice involved the Municipal Council, showing the strength of concern over this issue.[71]

It would seem that the authorities were not Damalix's only enemies. On

---

[69] See *Feuille du Jour*, 19 May.
[70] APP, AA76:7, 8–13, 22, 29 May.
[71] See Lacroix, *Actes*, iv. 437, 466; *Corps municipal* sessions, 30 May, 1 June. Although recording these decisions, Lacroix was ignorant of Damalix's identity and offence.

2 May two men had been arrested 'for having stirred up the public in front of the residence of the former curé of Bonne-Nouvelle and sought to do harm to the said curé by calling him a begger and a rogue that must be hanged'. Once again, the authorities had been firm, and the second man was also marked down 'for having excited the same people against a patrol which came to restore order, by saying that it was going to fire on the people'. This latter offence sufficed to earn him a one-month prison sentence while the other man was released three days later.[72]

Much of the evidence we have looked at suggests that popular hostility to the refractory clergy was a significant feature in their defeat, although as this incident demonstrates, alongside the efforts of *commissaire* Toublanc and others through previous months, the authorities were anxious to prevent the expression of this hostility. This may be due in part to the kind of response that emerged when a crowd again broke up a Théatins congregation on Ascension Day, 2 June. Although the municipality had refused the congregation any special protection, the general press reaction was to blame the refractories themselves, suggesting that the disturbance had been arranged to add force to abbé Raynal's polemic against the Revolution, delivered in the National Assembly on 31 May.[73] Once again, we are faced with the consequences of a complex political field. Two men were arrested in the course of this disturbance, one of whom was later convicted of having shouted, 'We must hang the chasseurs, let's hang the chasseurs. We must disarm the grenadiers and stab them with bayonets. The National Guards are traitors, they protect the aristocrats.' His sentence, perhaps coloured by being passed in the aftermath of the Champ de Mars repression, was firstly to do public penance with a sign saying 'violator of the law, and insulter of the National Guard', and then, for a crime of mere words, to be flogged, branded and sent to the galleys for nine years.[74] Whatever else occupied their minds, the revolutionary authorities were determined to enforce respect for the National Guard amongst the people. That is not to say, however, as the following chapters will show, that the relationship of the Guard itself to authority was entirely unproblematic.

[72] APP, AB323:562, 564. The released man was a public workshop worker; no *état* is recorded for the other.

[73] See Lacroix, *Actes*, iv. 473–7.

[74] APP, AB323:1001, 5 June, Section des Quatre-Nations. Sentence reported in *Feuille du Jour*, 6 Aug. The man was François Paré, a journeyman saddler, who may not have been entirely sober at the time of his outburst.

5

The Saint-Cloud Affair and the Wages Movement

Events during Passion Week were to further expose the fault-lines in the constitutional settlement, and would help to turn radical attitudes toward the authorities from muted hostility to outright opposition. This process, and its impact on popular opinion, was exacerbated by the city's economic difficulties, raising the spectre of famine plot through accusations of official collusion in currency speculation. At the same time, a series of clashes over the control of artisans' work practices set official *laissez-faire* on the side of former masters, while workers claimed that revolutionary justice and the Rights of Man backed their arguments for regulations and collective bargaining. Outbursts from the population suggested a similar attitude, despite a continuing crackdown in the name of social order, as both indigence and alleged sedition grew through May and June, and attitudes hardened among both moderates and radicals. However, there still remained ambiguities about popular consciousness and activities, underlying this evolving conflict, and becoming crucial in later events.

The Easter crisis

On Palm Sunday, 17 April 1791, perhaps at the very moment that *dévotes* were being whipped out of the church of the Théatins, Louis XVI gave in to his conscience. In a two-pronged move to preserve his spiritual purity, he took communion at the Tuileries from a 'real', non-juring, priest, while making plans to avoid his normal, and more public, Easter communion at St-Germain l'Auxerrois, where he would have had to be served by a juror. Unfortunately, one of the salaried grenadiers on duty in the royal chapel on the 17th was outraged to see the non-juror's participation, and felt bound by patriotic duty to spread this sentiment. Concern and rumour fermented overnight, placing a new interpretation on the king's declared intention to leave the capital the next day for his summer residence at St-Cloud. When he attempted to leave the Tuileries by carriage with his family on Monday the *Moniteur* reported the result in euphemistic style: 'A large number of citizens surrounded him and observed to him that, in the present circumstances, it was with pain that they saw him leaving Paris. The king, not wishing to increase the disquiet occasioned by his departure, consented to delay it for some days.'[1]

For many people, there could have been little doubt but that this trip was intended to be the first stage of a longer flight. Gorsas reported on the 20th that Louis had been bound 'despite himself' for Rouen and a royalist army. Not only did the crowd blockade the royal convoy, but the National Guard on duty, and some brought as reinforcements, stood with them. A volunteer from the Carmes battalion later told the Cordeliers Club how officers from the headquarters had harangued them:

> We heard this handful of individuals provoke the horrors of carnage and a universal massacre: they continued to threaten us; but we swore firmly that they should have to trample our corpses before our souls gave way, and we abandoned a man to the capricious whim that exposes the safety of the father-land.[2]

The waving of swords in the troops' faces had no effect, nor did the later presence of both Lafayette and Bailly.

The next two weeks saw the fervour previously directed at the refractory clergy turned on secular politics. Lafayette tendered his resignation within days, since he could no longer, he said, command obedience. Gorsas noted that 'the rumour is current . . . that the king's departure was merely a planned ruse, and M de la Fayette's resignation the next stage of a plan', all designed to lead up to a massacre.[3] The majority of the Guard rallied to their general, not only persuading him to withdraw his resignation with a mass meeting at the Hôtel de Ville on the 24th, but also circulating a pledge of loyalty that was signed by thousands. Radical opinion was outraged, firstly since it asserted that Lafayette's reappointment was constitutionally a matter for the Section assemblies, and secondly by the display of slavish and aristocratic spirit involved in this oath. The *Révolutions de Paris* was forthright: 'Only the Sections . . . had the right' to reappoint the general, 'he is thus a criminal guilty of *lèse-nation*'. The implications were clear:

> In his system, visibly combined with that of the court, it is necessary for the citizen-soldiers to submit to the same yoke as the line troops, and to obey without thinking. How to bring them to this point? Profit from the still near-universal enchantment, and require, as a condition of his return, the oath of blind fidelity to his orders.[4]

New permutations of the alarm over 'military aristocracy' that had dogged

1 *Moniteur*, 19 Apr. M. P. Fitzsimmons describes the event in *Remaking France: the National Assembly and the Constitution of 1791*, Cambridge 1994, 114, although he makes no allusion to the subsequent popular and radical unrest.
2 Lacroix, *Actes*, iii. 631–2.
3 *Courrier*, 22 Apr.
4 *Révolutions de Paris*, 23–30 Apr.

the Guard since its formation thus clearly continued to emerge. Ordinary people spoke out, such as Jean Louis Jupin, an unemployed servant arrested on 23 April, 'for, by his expressions of disapproval towards the battalion's swearing of the oath to obey M Delafayette and having said that he should only be obeyed when he commanded well, having sought to spread disorder amongst the people in making them share his sentiments'.[5] More bluntly an unemployed journeyman glazier employed in the public works attacked the sergeant-major of the Notre-Dame Battalion on the same day, tearing off his epaulettes – decorations commonly used as a symbol of military authority in press and public comments.[6] The majority of the Guard evidently rallied rapidly to the defence of order, but seeds of political doubt had been sown, which would re-emerge in the harsher conflict of July.

Immediately after the events of 18 April, the Cordeliers had led the radical attack, first turning on the king. They published a decree in unprecedentedly strong language, condemning 'the first functionary of the state', accusing him of authorising rebellion and provoking civil war, and denouncing him before the Nation. The publicity this text received was remarkable, for not only did the Club have it plastered across the city, but it would seem that a number of publishers seized on it, reprinting it with accompanying texts, some of which were genuine commentaries, others merely a thin cover for their piracy.[7] Most reported Lafayette's resignation in tandem with the Cordeliers' proclamation, as the two items of news seem to have burst upon the Parisians on the same day, 21 April. Both public interest and political suspicion surrounding these issues were intense, as the following incident in the Section de la Place-Vendôme that day illustrates.

Groups of people were reading the freshly-posted Cordeliers' *affiches* near to the Madeleine guardhouse when the sergeant on duty attempted to disperse them and take down the inflammatory material. He claimed that a servant had then 'aroused the people against him by calling him a *mouchard* of M. delafayette [and said] that they had to string up [the sergeant] from the lamppost'. As two other Guards would testify, these words endangered the

---

5 APP, AB323:423, Section des Arcis, released 27 Apr., vouched for.

6 APP, AB323:427, Section de Notre-Dame, released 27 Apr. A witness giving testimony after the Champ de Mars Massacre noted a conversation between two men, one a National Guard captain himself, which began 'Is it not true, captain, that on the Champ de Mars they make speeches against the epaulettes?': Mathiez, *Club des Cordeliers*, 257.

7 There are two versions in the Bibliothèque nationale, 8–Lb39–4867 and 4868, and another in the British Library, F.R. 118(19). Also, at APP, AA83:166 is a text identical to BN, 8–Lb39–4867, with a slightly altered title, seized from a sixteen-year-old *colporteur* in the Palais-Royal on 21 April. This document in particular is a very rough production, untrimmed and smudged, apparently printed from worn type. These two texts preface the Cordeliers' document with a spurious account of Lafayette's resignation and subsequent transatlantic flight to the arms of his 'papa Waxingthon'.

sergeant, who retreated to the guardhouse and gathered men to arrest the culprit.[8]

The man they arrested was François Geoffrenet, aged forty-eight, a servant of the former Genevan *chargé d'affaires*. His version of events was rather different:

> Leaving the d'Aguesseau market this morning at around eight o'clock he saw a group of people . . . [he approached] . . . he heard everyone complaining that an individual in a riding-coat had torn down a poster of the Cordeliers Club that he had declared them to be inflammatory. Seeing everyone angry against [this man, Geoffrenet] approached him and said that he must not know the Rights of Man and the Citizen, after the illegal infraction he had committed, that only a *mouchard* could do such a thing.

The *commissaire* ignored this version of events, notably that the sergeant had been in civilian dress, which would perhaps have modified Geoffrenet's approach to him, and the latter's denial of any incitements to violence. He pounced on his admission of a link to the Cordeliers – 'he was not a member there, but through patriotism he had attended sessions' – and interrogated him about the origins of the *affiche*. The case was taken very seriously, and Geoffrenet was led to the Police Department and then into La Force, where his dossier was forwarded to the public prosecutor. The Section du Théâtre-Français officially protested against this arbitrary oppression, and complained to the Jacobin Club, to no evident effect.[9]

The *Société fraternelle* that shared the Jacobins' quarters was meanwhile voicing its own opinions on recent events. After 18 April the Directory of the *département* of Paris had published two addresses, one to the king and one to the people of the city. The *Société* commented:

> The society, having heard the reading of an address to the king presented by the administrators . . ., has applauded the zeal and firmness with which the mandatories of a free people have spoken to the king of the French. But how great has been the surprise of the society at the reading of a decree of the *département* posted today, a decree in which this same administrative body seems to reproach the Frenchmen who inhabit Paris for exaggerated or deceitful fears! If our fears were exaggerated or deceitful two days ago, those that you took to the king the next day on the same subject were thus likewise![10]

In the interchanges revealed here, we can see once again the difficult double position of the authorities. As revolutionaries themselves, they were fearful of

---

8   APP, AA206:217–9.
9   See APP, AB323:403; Lacroix, *Actes*, iii. 717. The *affiche* itself was briefly the subject of a referral to the prosecutor by the *Corps municipal*, but the full *Conseil municipal* quashed this a few days later: ibid. iii. 706, 719.
10   *Observations sur la journée du 18 Avril*, ibid. iii. 641–3.

the possibility of aristocratic plots and the flight of the king, but they still viewed the *peuple* as a body prone to panic and to primitive reactions, and of course to subornation, fit only to be lectured to and ordered around. The radicals had quite different ideas. They had no particular reason to trust the authorities, whose behaviour was often questionable, whereas the people, in their idealised view, had solid revolutionary credentials. As the *Société fraternelle* went on in the same pamphlet to observe: 'when the people of Paris attacked the Bastille, they had received no powers from the rest of the French: they marched ahead, they conquered, and they were not disavowed. . . . The powers that were given to us implicitly to conquer liberty are given to us very positively to conserve it, and we shall be most faithful to those mandates'.

The events of the following days show a pattern of attitudes that would intensify through the months to come, as the words and actions of ordinary people clashed with those of the authorities, and with their apparent compromises with counter-revolution. The forces of order continued to respond with unhesitating repression, which did not even need a political statement to set it off. In the Section de Beaubourg on 23 April the Guard were clearly taking no chances, arresting one man 'for having, through his drunkenness and the absurdity of his face, which he had blackened, amassed a crowd of people which could have become dangerous'.[11] Meanwhile, one of Lafayette's *aides-de-camp* caused a scuffle in the Palais-Royal by seizing inflammatory material from a *colporteur*. Following the arrest of a man who threatened the officer with a stool, another man caused a disturbance by following the Guard, saying that, 'you must not mistreat him'. He was also seized, and severely dressed-down by the *commissaire* when he turned out to be an active citizen – it was 'astonishing' that he should stir up discontent against the Guard 'at a moment when all minds are in ferment'. His rather acid response was to recall that the Guard had handled him 'with a great deal of brutality' and dragged him into the guardhouse.[12]

At first glance it appears curious in this context that the first arrested man, another *colporteur*, when questioned should observe that seizing material such as the 'Ami and Orateur du Peuple' was done 'with great reason'. He went on to claim, however, that he could show them others 'equally dangerous, such as those entitled "D'orléans shall not reign", "The letter of Mr Laclos to Mr D'orléans", "To yourself Laclos", "Regicide D'orléans", and finally that entitled simply "D'orléans" '. Such anti-Orléans material was reported by the *Journal* of the *Club monarchique* as being burned at this point by *colporteurs* belonging to the pro-Orléans party, while anti-Orléans men burned the publications of Marat and Fréron. Events of this kind, if they took place, would no doubt appeal to the *monarchiens'* image of the Revolution as a plot,

[11] APP, AB323:425, worker in the public workshops, released 27 Apr.
[12] APP, AA83:184.

but declarations such as this one demonstrate that this street vendor, at least, could stand outside this supposed fray.[13]

Publications such as those listed above were none the less part of an ongoing stream of material dedicated to the thesis that the duc d'Orléans was behind every new crisis of the Revolution – at this point one pamphlet had already blamed the 18 April *journée* on a signal from the Palais-Royal fountains, coinciding with the Cordeliers' decree, which in reality had come several days later.[14] Respectable right-leaning newspapers such as the *Feuille du Jour* mentioned such things as the tale about the fountains without quite seeming to give them credence – 'we are assured that this signal is that which rallies the seditious'. The same journal, however, made dark hints in this direction when explaining unrest over a municipal decision on 26 April to disband a company of salaried grenadiers – the company of the sixth Division, quartered at the Oratoire – for their disobedience on the 18th. 'Groups instructed by the infamous motors of the troubles that agitate us' were using the opportunity to pour scorn on Lafayette for this supposed assault on liberty, it reported. Even when the duke seemed to be in public disfavour, this was grist to the mill, as on 2 May – 'We warn M. d'Orléans . . . that his agents are neglecting to maintain the public in a good disposition towards him.'[15]

Amid this maelstrom of event and comment, the authorities continued to strive for order. On 26 April the municipality and the departmental Directory addressed a joint plea to the National Assembly, asking for urgent action to complete and implement the new penal code, and to regulate the right of petition and the freedom of the press. Their reasoning was plain:

> For a long time, the enemies of the constitution have placed their hopes in anarchy; they have counted on the exaggeration of patriotism and on the excess of that impatient ardour produced by the rapid conquest of liberty. They have calculated on the habit of mistrust in a people always abused; that so-long repressed hatred of an oppressive government; those movements of fear and of scorn inspired by all acts of authority, when it is usurped. They have employed these sentiments, which they must have found everywhere, with the most fatal cunning against all the legitimate powers conferred by a free people.[16]

In other words, patriotism is not patriotism when it does not do what the authorities want, and the people, damned with faint (albeit remarkably perceptive) praise, cannot be trusted.[17] We should note that, despite their

---

13 *Journal de la Société des Amis de la Constitution Monarchique*, no. 20, 30 Apr. The items reported burned were the papers of Marat and Martel (Fréron's cover-name), and 'No, D'orléans, you shall not reign' and 'to yourself Laclos'.

14 BN, 8–Lb39–4828. The British Library has a pamphlet collection on d'Orléans, the vast majority hostile, running into hundreds: BL, F.255–63.

15 *Feuille du Jour*, 28 Apr., 1, 2 May.

16 Lacroix, *Actes*, iv. 6–7.

17 Note that certain elements of this analysis seem to prefigure more modern interpreta-

insistence that all this trouble was fomented by the enemies of the Constitution, the authorities could not put names, or even clearer labels, to these forces. In the revolutionary atmosphere, to invoke shadowy enemies seems to have served well enough, and the municipality was soon to have its extra powers. Meanwhile, regardless of any such convenient explanations, troubles continued to accumulate. Following the king's apparently unsuccessful example, emigration accelerated, while rumours of mutiny and disaffection in the frontier garrisons reached the city in growing numbers.

On 29 April the Cordeliers posted some 'Reflections' on the Guard's oath to Lafayette, and as the press reported, the Palais-Royal in particular was a battleground between those putting them up and those tearing them down.[18] The arrest of two men in the Palais-Royal involved the depositions of no fewer than thirteen witnesses. One detainee, Joseph Chaney, a Swiss merchant and Cordeliers member, said that he had observed the tumultuous groups trying to read the posters, and had thought to aid the cause by sticking up a spare one he had in his pocket. After doing this, he read it out, and in response to a sympathetic question, had said that he would strike the hand from anyone who tried to remove it – this was the cue for the Guard to intervene, as they made their round systematically taking down these posters. His attempt to invoke the Rights of Man and the Citizen earned him a rough handling (the Guard appears to have been predisposed to intolerance on this topic), and he ended up being transferred to the Châtelet.[19]

Both civilians and Guards had clearly learnt to expect trouble over such 'political' issues. Pierre Lenoble, a nineteen-year-old self-declared 'author', was seized for defaming the arresting Guard and attempting to raise a mob to rescue Chaney. Several people testified to this effect, but Lenoble claimed to have managed to say no more than 'it's frightful' before being seized. He observed that people in the crowd who had arrived after Chaney's arrest were calling the Swiss a beggar and villain who should hang, not even knowing what he had done, while the Guard had prepared to use their bayonets just upon hearing someone say that the arrested Lenoble was 'a good and excellent patriot'. Cooler heads prevailed in the *commissaire's* office, and Lenoble was released when an Assembly deputy vouched for him.

The events of this day enraged the writer of the *Révolutions de Paris*, who described

> The vexations committed on the 29th in the Palais-Royal, at the Tuileries and in several other areas. . . . Ill-treated citizens, heaped with insults by the oath-taker soldiery, have been, in scorn of all the laws, dragged into the prisons, at

tions, such as those of Arlette Farge already explored, and Isabelle Bourdin: see p. 119 below.
18 See *Courrier*, 30 Apr.; *Feuille du Jour*, 1 May.
19 APP, AA83:207–12. He was even accused of passing a false *écu* to buy the glue to stick up the poster, but this claim seems to have been opportunism on the part of the shopkeeper.

the pleasure of the municipality. . . . Never was oppression so manifest, and the circumstances which have accompanied it are a recital of atrocities.[20]

The same issue also reported that Lafayette had disavowed the oath that had stirred all this trouble, going on to allege that this was because too many Guards had themselves renounced it to make them an effective force for counter-revolution. Repercussions, however, continued to reach the streets. Gilbert Pinot, a hatter's labourer, went on a drinking-spree on 2 May, and ended up perorating to 'a very great quantity of persons'. In his possibly flustered state he confused Lafayette's behaviour with the issue of the ending of customs dues on imports to the city, asking why wine had not fallen in price since their removal the previous day. He knew what he thought of the general, though – he 'deserves to be f—ing strung up [foutu à la lanterne]'. Pinot had then 'threatened to stick his knife, which he had opened, in the belly of any who would say good of the general'. The *commissaire* noted that he 'must be regarded as a disturbing element [un perturbateur] and a dangerous man, above all in present circumstances'.[21]

At a slightly more sophisticated level, there is the tale of Edmé Champigny, a printer, who had produced a *Père Duchesne* pamphlet praising the Guards who had backed Lafayette. The *colporteurs* he had sold it to, upon discovering its message, returned to his shop on 4 May and put it under siege – a rare instance of concerted political action by such men, perhaps driven by the sentiment that the pamphlet's contents had put them in danger from crowds themselves. Champigny had to be taken into protective custody by the Guard. The plot thickened when Fréron and the *Révolutions de Paris* alleged that the authors of the pamphlet had been two municipal officers, and there was a brief flurry of activity amongst this group as various of them denied it.[22] On 5 May Gorsas also chose to paint Champigny as at least partly a villain, but the fact that his position was slightly closer to the views of the municipality led him to put the blame for the text on the *aristocrates*.

The *Club monarchique* itself intervened in the debate, with an *affiche* 'To our comrades' denouncing false patriots trying to exalt the patriotism of the Guards and 'push it beyond the bounds'. Two men were arrested in the following days for tearing down copies of this, one of whom appears to have been a messenger for Marat – the *Ami du Peuple* reported his arrest, for 'an act not merely licit, but meritorious' when, as it noted, the 'prevaricators' of the municipality were sending men round night and day to remove Cordelier's

---

20 *Révolutions de Paris*, 30 Apr.–7 May.
21 APP, AA56:134; AB323:561, Section des Arcis. He was released from La Force on the 6th. The abolition of the dues presented problems for the Section de Bondy, which had just arrested seventeen men for breaching the customs-wall and extorting fees for smuggling; they were released without charge on 4 May: APP, AB323:536, 29 Apr.
22 See APP, AB323:593 for Champigny's brief stay in La Force. Lacroix, *Actes*, iv. 143–7, contains various notes on this matter, including Lacroix's own conclusion that the authors were municipal officers who also produced the *Journal des Clubs et Sociétés Patriotiques*.

posters. The records of La Force note that the man in question was carrying 'a letter addressed to Marat signed Ducieux, Grenadier of the Battalion of the Oratoire, member of the Jacobins Friends of the Constitution, which contains the greatest invective against M delafayette etc'.[23]

With this letter, we return to the other contemporary *cause célèbre* concerning the Guard. Marat must finally have received the letter, or another copy, since on 12 May he published 'The shameful acts of General Mottier, or denunciation by François Ducruix [*sic*], grenadier of the Oratoire, one of the fourteen victims of the day of 18 April.' The 'fourteen victims' were those members of the dismissed Guard company who had been refused readmission to the re-formed unit, supposedly for misconduct, allegedly for their patriotism. To thicken the plot further, on 17 May Marat reported that Ducruix had disappeared, and called for patriots to search the prisons for him.[24] Gorsas noted on the 15th that a rumour was spreading that one of the fourteen 'has drowned himself, they say, from despair', but no conclusion to this appeared in the press.

This matter agitated patriotic opinion for several weeks. The Jacobin Club, as well as a number of Sections, made official representations to the municipality in favour of the dismissed men, receiving short shrift in return, while rumours about the character and fate of the 'fourteen' ran wild. Gorsas reported on one occasion that a coincidence of names was being used to accuse them of a robbery.[25] As early as 28 April a group of ten or twelve young Savoyards had set upon two National Guard cavalrymen, 'on the pretext that they were amongst those who had made the grenadiers of the Oratoire Battalion give up their arms'. A bootblack, a polisher and two casual labourers [gagne-petits] spent a week in prison for this, persisting in their claim that the Guards had provoked them with words and blows. The *commissaire de police*, in sending them down, had noted that such a statement about the grenadiers 'could excite the greatest uproar and the greatest uprisings'.[26]

The events of the Easter crisis show that the coalition of sentiments that was holding the revolutionary political order together was fragile at best, at

23 See *Ami du Peuple*, no. 444, 30 Apr.; APP, AB323:503, 28 Apr., Section de Ponceau. The man, François Feneau, was vouched for and released on 2 May. The *Journal* of the *Club monarchique*, 30 Apr., confirms that they were the publishers of *A nos camarades*. The other man arrested was the editor of the *Journal du Soir*, who compounded his crime by resisting the Guard and crying 'thieves' to 'stir up the people': APP, AB323:471, Section des Quatre-Nations, 26 Apr., released 29 Apr.

24 *Ami du Peuple*, nos 456, 461. This latter issue also reported that Lafayette's chief spy, Estienne, had been 'dismissed by the god Mottié' for embezzling the funds confided to him.

25 *Courrier*, 26 May. See Lacroix, *Actes*, iv. 43–7, 49–50, 59–65, 325–33. Lacroix suggests that one of the reasons for the original defiance of the troops was a long-standing grudge against their captain over purely material motives. Information on this *affaire* can also be found in Bourdin, *Sociétés populaires*, 213–16.

26 APP, AA182:199; AB323:533, Section du Louvre.

worst unsustainable. The issue of the king, whom radicals were now begin-ning to see as incompatible with the Revolution, still united those of less sophisticated views. Yet what this unity meant was that the 'crowd' and the Guard resisted both the court and the administration on 18 April, even if the Guard rallied hurriedly to oppose the supporters of the Cordeliers' declara-tions, going so far as almost to sell their souls to the general (a bargain that some would argue, of course, had been struck long before). The one tenet that all agreed on was the incessant activity of counter-revolutionary plots, and it was on this theme that the rulers of Paris were to lean to defeat the radicals. This process was to reach a climax in July, but before describing the events which led to that point, we need to consider some additional features of the political landscape of 1791, and how they contributed still further to the persuasiveness of the idea that destabilisation was being engineered by enemies of the Revolution.

The political clubs and their influence

Early 1791 had seen a significant addition to the radical dimension of Pari-sian politics – the formation of popular societies. From May 1790 the Corde-liers Club had stood alone as a political body admitting the common people to its discussions.[27] In late 1790 the 'Fraternal Society of the One and the Other Sex, sitting at the Jacobins', was organised to educate the people in the laws and Constitution. Its founder was a paternalistic schoolmaster, Claude Dansard, and the society seems to have soon attracted several hundred members. By the end of the year, the radical press was exhorting others to form similar clubs to promote civic virtue. The result was a stream of new foundations, reaching double figures by February 1791.[28] Of those new clubs which were to be most active, many drew their leadership from the educated cadres of the Cordeliers – even the original *Société fraternelle* had parted company with Dansard by April 1791, under a group of such men, including the journalist François Robert, who led it beyond its original modest aims.[29]

It would appear that this evolution was in line with the wishes of a membership which came largely from popular origins, and the tone of publi-cations and reported society meetings rapidly veered from a humble respect for the powers-that-be towards an extremely radical position. A pamphlet

[27] See Mathiez, *Club des Cordeliers*.

[28] For an extensive documentation of the clubs see Bourdin, *Sociétés populaires*, which covers the activities of the clubs into 1792. The same period is covered in less depth by Rose, *Making of the sans-culottes*.

[29] Bourdin, *Sociétés populaires*, 30–3, 171–7. Despite the societies' dual-sex character, the term 'men' for their leadership appears largely accurate, at least at this stage of the Revolu-tion, notwithstanding the probable contribution of Louise de Keralio, François Robert's wife and fellow-journalist, and author of, among other works, *The crimes of the queens of France*, one of the more learned texts to defame Marie-Antoinette in this period.

recording various communications of the *Société fraternelle* in late November and early December 1790 addressed Charles de Lameth as 'illustrious citizen', and proclaimed 'Long live our brave and generous defender!'.[30] We have seen some of this club's comments on the Easter crisis, and by early June 1791, the same society was publishing a sixteen-page 'Appeal to the nation on the unconstitutional decrees'. This pamphlet, while focusing on the decree of 10 May against collective petitioning, also denounced in passing the distinctions of active citizenship and eligibility, the executive powers afforded to the king, and the royal veto – the very agenda of Lameth and the 'Triumvirate'. It concluded that the May decree was 'to prevent you [the nation] from demanding the reform of anti-constitutional laws' such as these, having previously made clear its view on the relation of the Assembly to the rights of the people: 'if the National Assembly has decreed laws which attack the foundations of the Declaration of Rights . . . it does not have the right to demand that the nation recognise these laws and pledge obedience to them'.[31]

Quite clearly it was the educated adherents of 'Cordelier politics' who shaped this political discourse, but a large body of evidence suggests that the normal run of society business, and the bulk of club membership, was rapidly imbued with an intemperate and visceral interpretation of popular sovereignty.[32] As Isabelle Bourdin has observed, it was this doctrine, in its more moderate form, that the societies had originally set out to teach, and the results of its meeting with Parisian popular mentalities was dramatic:

> The people of the Revolution demanded the exercise of their sovereignty, and in their minds this quite naturally took on the character and prerogatives of that of the king which it had succeeded. It was absolute, and thus only took on the cover of principles in order better to deal with realities. . . .
> The right of verification that the people attributed to themselves developed in them the sentiment of mistrust, the natural fruit of the desire to do good allied with a lack of culture; they became jealous and tyrannical and made a constant association of virtue and hatred. Knowing no indifference or cynicism, but often unconscious of the evolution they were undertaking, they united a near-mystical respect for the law to the incessant transformations that they attempted to impose on it.[33]

In many ways, then, the popular societies, whose membership appears to have been drawn largely from genuinely popular circles, constituting a core of up to several thousand, could be seen as the 'shock-troops' of the radical demo-

---

[30] BN, 8–Lb40–849.
[31] BN, 8–Lb39–4989, *Appel à la nation des décrets inconstitutionnels.*
[32] Bourdin's work is filled with examples drawn from both the texts of the societies and from more-or-less hostile observers, all of which point in this direction.
[33] Bourdin, *Sociétés populaires,* 10–11.

cratic movement.[34] But to understand that term in any literal sense would be a mistake. Although a handful of the seditious persons arrested around the time of the Champ de Mars Massacre proudly admitted to society membership, as we shall see later, the vast majority denied this frequently-imputed affiliation, without, it would seem from their general tone, intent to deceive.

Even if the popular societies entered into correspondence with each other, and with the Cordeliers and the Jacobins, they do not seem to have ever formulated a positive common agenda beyond outraged responses to the increasing evidence of counter-revolution. In early May 1791 François Robert tried to organise a Central Committee of Societies, attracting, according to his own report, delegations from more than thirty groups to the initial meeting. Major difficulties over funds, premises and co-ordination, and possibly the jealousy of the Cordeliers, meant that by the end of the month the Committee was only just ready to begin functioning. Two weeks later a newspaper reported a session at which twelve delegations were present, after which there are no other signs of its existence.[35]

Nevertheless, at every incident from January 1791 onwards, popular societies can be found commenting, outraged, at the exploits of *aristocratie*, and making righteous demands for the authorities to act in the popular interest. However it must be said that there is no evidence of their having influenced political events, other than by contributing to a highly-charged rhetorical atmosphere. This in itself may not have been a negligible factor in the escalation of political tensions. Whether this function, allied to that of offering a certain radical education to some of *le peuple*, is sufficient to afford them the title of revolutionary vanguard, however, is a moot point.[36] Moreover, other aspects of the behaviour of the popular societies clearly undermine any attempt to view them as determined social radicals.

On occasions such as the abolition of the hated customs barriers around Paris, on 1 May 1791, the popular societies showed that they shared a certain unease at the potential reactions of the people. For months before this event, it had been feared that popular disorders would follow from it, for all the usual reasons that subversion was expected. On this occasion, the societies were fervent in their appeals for calm, a calm which did in fact follow, although probably not as a result of their exhortations.[37] The popular societies were quite capable of falling into the same distrustful view of the actions of the lower orders as that shared by the police and other authorities, although in

---

34 Ibid. ch. v, for membership analysis.
35 Ibid. 167–70.
36 Rose, *Making of the sans-culottes*, 89–93, is most eager to invoke this perspective, seeing the societies as the direct heirs of the Districts, denied the right to meet regularly [*en permanence*] since mid-1790, and using their existence as an explanation for the political quietism of the Sections in 1791: 'the locus of popular political involvement' had switched (miraculously) to the societies.
37 Bourdin, *Sociétés populaires*, 180–2.

their case it was mitigated by a contradictory belief in their ultimate goodness.

When, however, the situation became desperate, in July 1791, and real social conflict appeared on the cards, radical attitudes became even more ambivalent. On 15 July the *Cercle social*, not a genuinely 'popular' society but one with distinct radical sympathies, and which had regularly attracted large audiences to lectures on Rousseau, hosted a mass meeting of popular society members to discuss the decree exculpating the king over the Flight to Varennes. This meeting, a 'stormy session', ultimately voted to support calls for resistance and an appeal to the nation, but meanwhile, however, it was observed that,

> thanks to some trouble in the garden [of the Palais-Royal] and to the invita-
> tion sent to all the patriotic societies, some enemies of order and truth had
> inserted themselves into the assembly, where they did not carry it away, but
> this has alerted us to some inconvenient circumstances that it would be diffi-
> cult for us to prevent in these moments of ferment, as we have always done
> before. The new measures that we have taken in that regard, will prove again
> that the friends of truth are the most severe friends of the laws and of public
> tranquillity.[38]

This is all somewhat elliptical, and what the new measures were is not clear, but they were apparently ineffective, as a few days later the society announced that 'in this moment of trouble, the *Cercle social* is immediately closing its public forum'. Meetings would continue, they went on, in private, open only to *bona fide* members, and it was specifically noted that 'women shall not enter' – thus repudiating what had been one of the major innova-tions of this and other societies.[39]

The *Cercle social* quite clearly possessed an extremely jaundiced view of the kind of popular disorder that was being stirred up by the political tensions of the moment, and took refuge in social and gender exclusivity. In all fairness we have already observed that this group did not class itself among the popular societies, although it claimed kinship with them. Its attitude at this time might therefore escape being seen as excessively hypocritical. However, a document published by Gorsas on 2 August, with the apparent consent of the *Société fraternelle*, and signed by one of the police administrators, raises more serious questions.

The society was responding to what Gorsas called an 'execrable lie' being put about by its enemies to the effect that it had planned after 15 July to topple statues of kings around the city. Its leadership had turned to the police on 16 July, presenting the police administrator Jolly with a deliberation of the society in which they formally disavowed such activity, although it had

38 Report in *La Bouche de Fer*, newspaper of the *Cercle social* (of which the *Amis de la Vérité* was the public manifestation), no. 96, 18 July.
39 Ibid. no. 99, 21 July.

apparently been proposed by one or two hot-heads. On 24 July, barely a week after the mass petitioning meeting organised by the popular societies had been fired on by the National Guard, the society had returned to Jolly and obtained a certificate confirming the substance of their original statement, which Gorsas published in full. Jolly observed that he recalled to his satisfaction that the deliberation had been 'conceived in terms which announced the indignation which that proposition had caused to the society'.[40]

This evidence of a cordial relationship with the highest police authorities, at a moment when martial law was in full vigour and other popular societies were afraid to meet for fear of arrest, is quite remarkable. What it suggests is a concern for respectability among the cadres of the *Société fraternelle* (and perhaps, therefore, among the larger Cordelier network whence they originated), distinctly at odds with their image of political radicalism and appeal to the sovereignty of the whole people. Having already encountered the odd attitudes of some radicals when confronted with notions of the *populace* and social disorder, and the difficulties the revolutionaries clearly had in getting away from pre-revolutionary models of popular psychology, we might now suggest that the radicalism of the popular societies was not as unambiguous as its rhetoric appeared. While such clubs clearly constituted a force for advancing a radical political agenda in the Revolution, it must be questioned whether they were as socially radical as their language and the appearance of their membership would suggest. As we saw in considering the conceptual cul-de-sac of the press's position on popular insurrection, such profound ambiguities were widespread. They were to be further accentuated throughout the spring of 1791, as a wide variety of events triggered by socio-economic problems emerged to trouble the political arena.

Work, money and crisis

Reports that 'the workers are in ferment' had reached the press even before agitation over the 18 April affair had died down.[41] As early as 26 April the municipality had responded to stirrings among the workforce by publishing a *Notice to the Workers*, which principally sought to remind them how fortunate they were to be living now in a free labour market, and to warn them gently not to form restrictive associations.[42] On this very day, according to the *Moniteur* of 28 April, 'gatherings' of workers had been seen 'in several neighbourhoods of Paris', agitating for higher pay and stopping others' work

---

[40] *Courrier*, 2 Aug. Bourdin confirms this incident indirectly, noting that 'two women of colour' were expelled from the *Société fraternelle* in August 1791 for proposing such a demolition, and for claiming the society's support for their violent public *motions*. She passes no comment on the socio-political implications of this, and it comes in a general discussion of the disciplinary frameworks of the societies: *Sociétés populaires*, 40.

[41] *Courrier*, 1 May.

[42] Lacroix, *Actes*, iv. 8.

through intimidation. Bailly responded at once by ordering the Guard to monitor an assembly of carpenters meeting in the Archevêché palace, and to patrol the workplaces where coercion might be employed – such activities were described as 'acts of violence' and 'dangerous disorders' that could easily become general.[43]

The following week the Corps municipal published a formal order to forbid groups of workers from passing decrees or halting others' work. The next day a delegation from the workers on the Louis XVI bridge, a project of the public workshops, came to the Corps to request a pay-rise. They were told that they would be 'guilty if they persisted in their coalition', and that they should earn the sympathy of the municipality by returning peacefully to work. A delegation of the carpentry workers who had been meeting at the Archevêché received equally short shrift, and on 16 May the municipality registered a decree from the departmental Directory which reinforced its stand against coalitions.[44] By this stage the National Assembly, responding to the municipality's pleas for more powers, had added the weight of its infamous decree of 10 May against collective petitioning to this position.

These events drew the battle-lines for a 'wages movement' that began with apparently isolated events around Easter, such as a mason's labourer arrested for inciting a stoppage of labour in several workshops and threatening to hang his master.[45] The movement continued to expand into June, bringing in trades as diverse as blacksmiths, hatters and cobblers, and ultimately leading to the repressive measures of the Loi Le Chapelier of 14 June. As a 'movement' of economic grievance, this has attracted much attention from historians, particularly as some links seem to have been forged with the popular societies.[46] The conflict, as we shall see more clearly below, was initially sparked by the forced dissolution of the trade guilds, which had taken effect shortly before Easter. Workers and former masters were testing out their strength in a new economic context, which was also, however, highly politicised.

[43] Ibid. 20.
[44] Ibid. 123–4, 136–7, 139.
[45] APP, AB323:387, Section de la Bibliothèque, 18 Apr.
[46] See Bourdin, Sociétés populaires, ch. iv, and Rose, Making of the sans-culottes, 108–9. Early works include G. Martin, Les Associations ouvrières au XVIIIe siècle (1700–1792), Paris 1900, and G. M. Jaffé, Le Mouvement ouvrier à Paris pendant la Révolution française (1789–1791), Paris 1924. W. H. Sewell, Jr., Work and revolution in France: the language of labor from Old Regime to 1848, Cambridge 1980, has been widely seen as seminal, but among the many criticisms raised by L. Hunt and G. Sheridan, 'Corporatism, association and the language of labor in France, 1750–1850', Journal of Modern History lviii (1986), 813–44, is Sewell's neglect, amounting to narrative elision, of the context of the workers' movements in 1791 (see their discussion at p. 822, and Sewell, Work and Revolution, 100, for the passage referred to). It must be said, however, that Hunt and Sheridan's response (pp. 822–3), that politicisation as 'the people', and the (later) opportunities for organised collective participation offered by the sectional movement, negated tensions around 'work', is itself somewhat limited as an explanation.

Conflicts over wages and conditions arose in an environment deeply troubled by a variety of economic issues, from the unemployment provoked by the emigration, to a more general disruption due to political uncertainties, and to the nature and security of the money-supply itself. Since the beginning of the year the *assignat*, which despite the National Assembly's original intentions had become *de facto* a paper currency, had been failing to hold its value compared to coin. Its steady decline had bred a new species of social parasite, the *marchand d'argent*, a dealer who changed paper for coin with a variable mark-up. These men, in turn, had bred a new kind of fear. As early as mid-January 1791, when the newly-issued fifty-*livre* note was the smallest in circulation, and paper was discounted against coin by a mere 5 per cent, Gorsas was writing of an 'odious speculation' concocted between the clerks and administrators of the Royal Treasury and the *marchands d'argent* of the rue Vivienne.[47]

A few days before, the Police Department had warned *commissaire* Toublanc to be on his guard against 'ill-intentioned persons' who had disturbed the Stock Exchange and were suspected of planning to gather in the Palais-Royal 'with the intention of insulting the brokers who might be found there'. Such was their concern that Lafayette had been warned to have troops ready, and the police administrators themselves would be standing by in a nearby café. In the event no trouble was reported.[48] On 18 January, however, Gorsas reported that four or five *marchands d'argent* had been 'battered' by an irate crowd. The *Feuille du Jour* noted that 'the gentle proposals of the rope and the lamppost were put forward', and that a movement led by 'a gallows-fodder orator' to besiege a bar where the dealers were hiding had to be headed off by cavalry.[49]

On 21 January a man was stabbed in the Palais-Royal, and the consensus of opinion was that the *marchands* had revenged themselves on him for speaking out against them. The *Révolutions de Paris* carried a detailed account of how the man, a jeweller, had said, after learning that the price of coin had risen again, that 'until they have hanged a *marchand d'argent*, it will still rise', whereupon a crowd of forty or fifty of the latter had gathered and he had fallen to the blade of one of them. One individual, a doorman in the Palais, took the opposite view and the next day 'gave an inflammatory speech against the National Guard, saying that it was composed of nothing but pickpockets and thieves in epaulettes'; in his opinion the charges were false, because the *marchands d'argent* 'were all honest men'.[50] The *Révolutions* disagreed on this score, but demonstrated here the contradictory economic attitudes which were to plague this issue: 'We believe that the best way to

47 *Courrier*, 14 Jan.
48 APP, AA82:35.
49 *Feuille du Jour*, 20 Jan.
50 APP, AB322:949, Section de l'Oratoire, 22 Jan.; the man served a one-month sentence in La Force for his outburst.

halt this brigandage . . . is to liberate the trade in money; the honest man will not blush any longer to sell his own; and the competition of sellers will soon bring down the price.'[51]

On the 22nd, however, another incident further illustrates the popular hostility towards the dealers. A Guard patrol rescued three men 'whom the people wished to seize', an operation involving considerable reinforcements before it was successfully completed. Various witnesses recognised them as having been dealing in assignats and gold coins at 5 or 6 per cent discount on the paper. Rather than being the rapacious *bourgeois* that one might expect, they are rather a pathetic sample – an unemployed servant and a stocking-seller both surviving as *colporteurs*, and an unemployed journeyman perfumer from Normandy. They denied the charge of being *marchands d'argent*, and were released with the usual warning to be 'more circumspect' in future.[52] It appears from the testimony given that the arresting Guard and some of the witnesses felt the men to be guilty of trading in money, whereas this was not actually an offence – indeed, a few months later, on 16 May, the National Assembly was to specifically guarantee the liberty to deal in currency.

The social status of *marchands d'argent* seems to have been highly variable. All classes of society had recourse to them, and there were doubtless grada-tions among them. Some of those singled out for public vengeance may have been no more than messengers for more affluent dealers. The lower-budget variety persisted, however. On the day of Mirabeau's funeral, 4 April, an innkeeper who was also a National Guard 'had heard speeches against the *marchands d'argent*' on the way home from duty. He arrived at his establish-ment to find one such openly dealing at a table, and threw him out. A few days later the dealer returned, and a fracas ensued, in which virtue does not seem to have been wholly on the side of the bar-owner. His antagonist was, however, much more willing than the men arrested in January to admit that 'he buys and resells gold and silver'. Furthermore, one of the impartial witnesses the *commissaire* called on to unravel the fight was himself a *marchand d'argent*. Thus it would seem that respectability was creeping into the dealers' identity, even as they remained widely disliked.[53]

The shortage of coin, meanwhile, continued to press on ordinary people. Louis Hallet, for example, a journeyman baker, tried to change a fifty-*livre* assignat in a wineshop on 27 January, was refused, and went to complain to the nearest guardpost, where the unhelpful treatment he received led him to insult the Guards and thus spend three days in prison.[54] Two weeks before this an errand-runner was arrested 'for having sought to raise up the public'

---

51 *Révolutions de Paris*, 15–22 Jan. The *Feuille du Jour*, 23 Jan., on the other hand, thought the murder 'probably private vengeance', despite noting the wide circulation of the more dramatic version.
52 APP, AA82:149.
53 APP, AA83:85, Section du Palais-Royal, 9 Apr.
54 APP, AB322:994, Section de Notre-Dame.

after protesting to the crowd in the courtyard of the *Caisse extraordinaire* (the body charged with the official trade in assignats) that 'they had kept back his interest' on several notes he had changed.[55] By March pamphlets were abroad sowing panic by alleging 'that the municipality was going to declare a bankruptcy'.[56]

Florin Aftalion has attempted to blame the assignat for the decline of the Revolution into Terror. This is an extreme view, based on the improbable notion that politics were 'a prisoner of the mob' from the October Days onwards, and that the superficial demands of the semi-literate forced the Assembly down the paper-money road.[57] Had this been so, few of the events that make up our subject matter would have taken place, but none the less Aftalion makes some valid points about the revolutionaries' economic foolhardiness. Their response to the effects of Gresham's Law removing coin from circulation was to print more paper, and an attempt to put copper coin into circulation drove the commodity price of copper above its face value, so the coins were simply hoarded and re-sold to the mint.[58]

If Aftalion administers a corrective to the long-held view that the assignat 'saved' the Revolution, he is not the first to doubt its benefits. As long ago as 1925 one writer described the same situation – coin-hoarding, rising prices, discounts on paper, economic dislocation, and suspicion – so that 'the popular classes, refusing to suffer losses on every exchange, saw in each trader a speculator on the assignat'.[59] We have already seen some of the violent consequences of this perception. The assignats themselves were only one aspect of the complex money crisis that seemed to envelop Parisian life in 1791. Amongst the ramifications of this situation, economic realities and simple criminality met with, and reinforced, the darkest political suspicions.

Consider the example of the comte de Toussaint, denounced on 6 March for plotting to print counterfeit 500-, 1,000- and 2,000-*livre* assignats. He told his plan to a merchant, saying that 'he had enough paper to overturn every-

---

[55] APP, AB322:848, Section des Postes, 14 Jan. He was released the next day. This case may also demonstrate popular ignorance about the exact nature of the assignats; they were interest-bearing bonds, but the first payment was not due until April 1792.

[56] APP, AB322:1477, Section des Enfants-Rouges, 11 Mar., a *colporteur* arrested for crying this headline, released three days later with *passeport* to leave the city.

[57] F. Aftalion, *The French Revolution: an economic interpretation*, Cambridge 1990, 4–5, 55. A more judicious review of the French revolutionary economy can be found in F. Crouzet, 'Les Consequences économiques de la Révolution française: réflexions sur un débat', *Revue Économique* xl (1989), 1189–204. The historiography of the *assignat* is surveyed in M. Albertone, 'Une Histoire oubliée: les assignats dans l'historiographie', *Annales historiques de la Révolution française* cclxxxvii (1992), 87–104. E. S. Brezis and F. Crouzet, 'The role of assignats during the French Revolution: an evil or a rescuer?', *Journal of European Economic History* xxiv (1995), 7–40, decide in the end that the paper currency was a fiscal necessity, given conditions, and previous state decisions, in 1789.

[58] Aftalion, *Economic interpretation*, 98.

[59] J. Morini-Comby, *Les Assignats*, Paris 1925, 56.

thing', if only he could find a good enough engraver.[60] We cannot completely dismiss this as an idle boast, when we know that false notes were in circulation – their discovery seeming to accelerate through the year until, by late July and August, they were becoming a veritable plague. Most of them seem to have been what were called 'fifteen-livre assignats', and were in fact small interest-coupons detached from larger notes, paying thirty *livres* in April 1792. That they should even have been changing hands, and serving in fact as part of the currency, at half face-value, shows clearly the monetary plight of the Parisians.[61] By early August forged versions of these coupons were turning up regularly – the Section des Arcis noted four separate incidents in the space of two weeks, including one note that had passed through the hands of the *commissaire de police* of the Section du Faubourg-Montmartre – unwittingly, of course.[62] Forgeries of all types were reported regularly in the press – for example, the *Feuille du Jour* spoke of false six-*livre écus* in March, false twenty-*livre* louis in May and false 200–*livre* notes in August.[63]

The situation surrounding the assignats could give rise to complex fears. On 13 May the Director-General of Artillery Transport tried to change five 1,000–*livre* notes with a *marchand d'argent* near the Palais-Royal. One of the notes aroused some suspicion in the mind of the *marchand*, but before this could be resolved, his customer became alarmed:

> seeing the *marchands d'argent* gathering in front of the shop, and fearing to be ill-treated by them, which could happen, through the continual fear that they have of an insurrection on the part of the public due to the extraordinary rise in the cost of money, carried today to nine per cent . . . fearing for himself the fate of a young man who was assassinated in the square several months ago, which was related in several of the papers . . . he fled to the guardpost.[64]

There followed a complex interchange between the Guard, the customer and the *marchand d'argent* who came after him, before first the Section Justice of the Peace and then the police *commissaire* were roped in to smooth things over. The *marchand* finally decided that the note was probably good, but by then his customer no longer wanted it, 'in fear of passing for a carrier or maker of false assignats'.

The production of these fakes seems to have been a regular prison industry. Since these buildings were guarded by little more than gatekeepers, this posed little obstacle to such activity, while offering the forgers secure

60 APP, AA82:347, Section du Palais-Royal. The information was passed on to the Police Department.
61 See APP, AA85:146, Section du Palais-Royal, 28 July, where an actual example of such a coupon is attached to the *procès-verbal*. The five-*livre* coupons that the *Caisse patriotique* had put into circulation also seem to have been easy to fake: APP, AA85:151, 29 July
62 APP, AA57:8, 12, 33, 36.
63 *Feuille du Jour*, 20 Mar., 17 May, 1 Aug. On 29 August a false 200–*livre* note was handed to the Palais-Royal *commissaire*: APP, AA85:388.
64 APP, AA84:67.

premises to work from. On 15 April one errand-runner from the Châtelet was found trying to pass a forged coin. He admitted getting it from a prisoner, who was found with melted tin in the stove in his cell. On 22 April another prisoner's sister-in-law denounced him for giving her a false coin from within the same prison.[65] On 15 May the authorities of the Section de la Place-Vendôme apparently captured another coin-forger with plans to turn his hand to 1,000–*livre* notes – he was still in prison untried in August 1792, as the court had lost his papers. At the same time this Section apprehended one of the few gangs of assignat-forgers working outside the prisons – an ex-farmer, the former porter for the Venetian ambassador and a deserter who had come all the way from Languedoc. They were sent to the Conciergerie, where a month later the *commissaire* of the Section d'Henri-Quatre swooped on a gang of forgers of the fifteen-*livre* notes – nine names were dragged out of the men caught with the evidence, but apparently these were a different group altogether. On 6 June a raid on the Châtelet by the police of the Section du Louvre had also discovered plates to print these notes stuffed under a loose plank in a cell.[66]

Beyond the question of the authenticity of notes, we might also ask how it was that people of no social standing got into fights with *marchands d'argent* over the discount on large assignats – people such as the soldier Jean Michel Perrin who came to blows with a *marchand* on 14 March.[67] The exchange was of two 1,000–*livre* notes, and the dispute over whether it was to be at a 6 or 6.5 per cent discount. Thieves in the Palais-Royal area were tricking people, particularly women, out of sums in assignats, by offering to exchange them at a prime rate – on 7 June an unemployed cook gave 300 *livres* to a man who offered to get her face-value for them, and then vanished.[68] Servants began to disappear with the notes given to them to change or deliver – on 3 June the servant of a merchant currier went off with 100 *livres*, and on 4 July Mme Clermet de Villiers reported that one of her servants had robbed her of 500 *livres* by claiming to have lost the note, and on being dismissed after a second attempt at this trick, had stolen 890 *livres* from her strongbox.[69] The proceeds of such crimes had to be cashed, and the enormous sums that went into the gaming-houses around the Palais-Royal had to emerge somewhere too. Some of the stakes for these games themselves came from theft – on 5 May an unemployed servant came to complain that he had given 200 *livres*, the legacy from his dead master, to a *valet de chambre* to change for him, only to discover later that it had disappeared straight into a card-game.[70]

Out on the streets, everyone wanted coin, but the *marchands d'argent* had

65 APP, AA182:174, Section du Louvre; AA83:167, Section du Palais-Royal.
66 APP, AA206:257, 245–52; AA215:445; AA182:247.
67 APP, AB322:1504, Section de la Bibliothèque.
68 APP, AA84:207.
69 APP, AA56:224, Section des Arcis; AA85:15, Section du Palais-Royal.
70 APP, AA84:18–19, Section du Palais-Royal.

their agents out gathering it brazenly, including allegedly buying up the hard-currency takings from wineshops each day. On 25 February the *Feuille du Jour* observed that 'many retailers are suspected of delivering, each evening, the products of their sales to the money-sellers of the rue Vivienne'. On 15 August a water-carrier was arrested for starting a fight when a barman refused to change a note for his drink. He began to shout that 'the merchants are hoarders', but was later found to have over sixty *livres* on him, half in coin. He claimed to be departing 'to his country', but the *commissaire* noted that he 'merits without a doubt being rigorously punished'.[71] The collection of coin raised more than economic fears, as the *Feuille du Jour* intimated on 6 April: 'one of the symptoms of a coming insurrection is this: When small change is harvested from the bars, in exchange for écus, and this collection continues for three days, take it as certain that the funds for a gathering are being prepared, and that it is not far off'.

Meanwhile, the emigration continued, and if people could not always grasp the complexities of the monetary situation, it was not hard to blame the fleeing rich for absconding with the nation's wealth. Even those who did not criticise the fugitives were forced to acknowledge the situation: 'they remove a frightful amount of wealth from the capital', as the *Feuille du Jour* observed on 25 April. The Lille mailcoach held up by a crowd in February may not have contained the rumoured millions, but there were none the less several hundred thousand *livres* of coin aboard labelled as other goods, as well as a very great deal of money being moved out of Paris 'legitimately'. On 26 February, presumably because of this incident, a merchant made a declaration to *commissaire* Toublanc that he was sending a total of 24,000 *livres* to Lille on the next *diligence*, and on 1 March he sent a further 25,200 *livres*, all to various wholesalers.[72] Although the authorities may have accepted such business as honest and upstanding, to popular eyes it was probably indistinguishable from counter-revolutionary exportation.

To revolutionary journalists brought up on the economic theories of the Enlightenment, the way to halt this flight was 'to encourage commerce, to augment national industry . . . and above all to declare the liberty of charging to change écus against assignats'. For the same writers, however, when it came to the problems of internal circulation, 'There is no more doubt but that the three funds, the discount, the public treasury and the *extraordinaire*, are in league to block the sources of circulation for all kinds of currency.' The crowds that constantly blocked the doors to their offices could only be the agents of a cabal, forcing people to go to the *marchands d'argent* for their business – 'Would not the share-out from these extortions be done each evening between the posted speculators, the clerks and perhaps the administrators?'[73]

71 APP, AA57:15, Section des Arcis.
72 APP, AA82:296, 315. See AA74:414, Section de Mauconseil, for a *procès-verbal* of the mailcoach affair.
73 *Révolutions de Paris*, 2–9, 9–16 Apr.

As time wore on, despite such palliatives as copper coin and five-*livre* notes, paper continued to fall against specie, from 5 per cent in January, through 10 per cent at Easter, to 15 per cent in a panic in mid-May. The *Feuille du Jour* observed on 16 May that two days previously a *marchand d'argent* who had dared to sell at 12 per cent had been narrowly rescued from a lynch-mob. The Assembly decree of the 16th protecting exchange was a response to actions such as these, but as the same paper noted on 20 May, the result was unproductive:

> Yesterday coin was sold at 15, 18 and 20 per cent; and the persons who bought it were obliged to hide themselves as carefully as those who sold. All the groups are stirred up against the National Assembly, since the decree which put the *marchands d'argent* under the protection of the laws; they are not accustomed to consider money as merchandise.

Besides this, prices were rising – rural producers in particular, unhappy at paper payments, were avoiding the markets and provoking scarcity, while in the city, for want of change, prices were hiked to rounder figures.[74] It was in this climate that agitation over wages began, although this simple economic stimulus brought out issues of social and political identity that will require more careful examination.

One trade where these issues were particularly strongly felt was printing, as one case study has shown. The massive expansion in publishing under the Revolution had necessarily led to a similar growth in print-shops, from a tightly-regulated group of thirty-six shops concentrated in the Quartier Latin in 1788 to possibly in excess of 200 across the city by 1790. The pre-revolutionary printers had been a tight-knit body with 'a strong sense of collective power'. They clung to an ideology of corporate pride even while facing up in reality to the 'boss-caste' that their masters had become, and conducting 'effective rebel activity' under the cover of their confraternity of St-Jean-de-Latran.[75]

The explosion of the printing trade created a huge labour shortage, which made the workers' position both powerful and precarious. On the one hand, their average wages all but doubled, and 'poaching' of staff with offers of better conditions and more money was reportedly endemic; on the other, the corporate ideal was broken down, the employers now called themselves proprietors rather than masters, and in the words of the workers' own protests, had no respect for the ways of the craft – 'If they could, they would teach it to wooden men.'[76] To resist this breakdown, in late 1790 the workers

---

[74] See Aftalion, *Economic interpretation*, 98ff., and Morini-Comby, *Assignats*, 54–8.
[75] P. Minard, 'Identité corporative et dignité ouvrière: le cas des typographes parisiens, 1789–1791', in Vovelle, *Paris*, 23–33, citation at p. 24. G. Feyel, 'Les Frais d'impression et de diffusion de la presse parisienne entre 1788 et 1792', in Rétat, *Révolution du journal*, 77–99, contains some interesting information on the labour and costs involved in press production.
[76] Minard, 'Identité', 25–7.

organised themselves into a Mutual Aid Society. The title of the rules of this association, 'General regulations for the typographical *corps*, composed by the committee of the general assembly of representatives of the print-workers of Paris', illustrates their debt both to the corporate idiom and to the new modes of political action. Besides specific arrangements for sick pay and so on, the society stressed union and zeal in work, for the cause of fraternity and the honour of their trade and craft. Revolutionary political zeal was also on display, and the workers took great pride in laying out the link between the press and freedom – their banner for the Federation of 14 July 1790 read 'Printing, Torch of Liberty'.

By early 1791 the negative side of the growth in the industry was beginning to trouble them more severely. The society became embroiled in running campaigns for the recognition of craft skill and some control over the admission of apprentices to the trade, campaigns that the masters denounced as self-interested cabals. Arguing from their corporate background, the workers articulated a claim that 'we have become again the owners of our industry', having invested their time and skill in it, and going on finally to see the wheel of the corporate ideal turn full circle. Now they pressed claims for some new form of *police* of the trade that would safeguard what was precious in the *corps*, inviting 'bosses who truly love their craft' to join with them.[77] Ultimately, of course, they were whistling in the wind, as the Loi d'Allarde of March 1791 erased all trace of corporate life, and the authorities took violent exception to any attempt at workers' organisation.

It was not only the authorities that took this view. As early as January of 1791 the municipality received a petition from a group calling itself the 'Encyclopedic Assembly, composed of all artists, entrepreneurs, workers and contractors, sitting at the Grands-Augustins'. The petition concluded by denouncing the 'new society formed by the print-workers', as an iniquitous body: 'It was undoubtedly the most ingenious means imagined by the enemies of the fatherland to destroy the liberty of the press and consequently the individual liberty of all the citizens of this vast empire.'[78]

The *Assemblée Encyclopédique*, on the other hand, proclaimed itself dedicated to 'assuring to the poor labourer ever-certain aid' and 'giving greater activity to the genius of industry', while removing 'privileges . . . hoarding . . . rivalries . . . corporate spirit that is as fatal to individuals as to the public good'. If the print-workers could appropriate revolutionary rhetoric and forms to their own uses, evidently so too could this group, which, it transpired, was interested in obtaining a contract to oversee all municipal public works. They offered value for money, precision, speed and 'the eradication of all rivalry

---

[77] Ibid. 27–9. The printers' concerns can also be traced in their own newspaper, the *Journal du Club Typographique et Philantropique* [sic], particularly no. 20, 15 Mar., on their fears of de-skilling, and no. 25, 19 Apr., which contains an indignant rebuttal of the charge of being a seditious assembly intent on interfering with others' employment.

[78] Lacroix, *Actes*, ii. 57–8.

between all workers'. If such a large-scale undertaking did not attract the municipality, the *Assemblée* also had a proposal for a 'national laundry' in every Section, and a wood-distribution scheme for the capital. None of these offers were taken up, but this association seems to have survived for a while at least, establishing a Construction Bureau in February that offered credit for building work, and sold shares in the enterprise. In the same month, however, they were themselves denounced to the municipality by an 'assembly of citizens of the Section de la Grange-Batellière' as 'unconstitutional and harmful to the public good'.[79]

These confusions of economic and political intent, whether naïve or wilful, could generate intense bitterness, as the dispute of the Parisian carpenters proved between April and June 1791. The workers were seeking to impose a uniform wage rate for the trade, the self-styled 'entrepreneurs in carpentry' to prevent this. As we have noted, throughout April a series of petitions from both sides to the authorities and a series of decisions and decrees in favour of the employers had followed, all of which were equally scorned by the workers at their meetings in the Archevêché palace. Even the forcible closure of this meeting-place had not halted their campaign, and on 22 May the employers asked the National Assembly to act, reminding them of 'the irreparable dangers of corporate assemblies of workers' which could 'deal a most fatal blow to commerce'.[80]

On 26 May the workers responded with their own petition, which told a very different story. They claimed to have first sought mutual accommodation with the old employers, which failed; and then

> several amongst the workers found work to be carried out, took this on, and offered to give fifty *sous* as the lowest price for a day's work to those they employed, and asked to have fixed regulations, in order to be able to work from a solid basis in bargaining with the owners.

What the employers condemned as a 'deliberation' was no more in fact than 'one-to-one agreements [des conventions de gré à gré]', the approved revolutionary form of pay-bargaining. Regulations in eight articles had been drawn up to the satisfaction of all, agreed to by all the new employers and even 'the greater part of the old ones'.

The entire dispute, the workers claimed, was the work of 'a very small number of former carpentry entrepreneurs', who, deprived of the 'frightful right' to pay low wages and profit from the sweat and skill of their workers, were harassing them by defaming them to the authorities. They had no ill intent – as their own article seven said, 'the workers engage themselves never to profit from a master's urgent need to complete work to make him pay more than the agreed price'.

---

[79] Ibid. ii. 641. The last trace of the *Assemblée Encyclopédique* appears to be in April 1791.
[80] Lacroix, *Actes*, iv. 349–50, which reproduces in full the employers' *Précis* of their situation.

Yet again revolutionary rhetoric was pressed into socio-economic service – when the National Assembly had destroyed corporate privilege and declared the Rights of Man, it 'certainly envisaged that this declaration would serve some purpose for the most indigent class, which has for so long been the plaything of the entrepreneurs' despotism'. If denunciations were what was needed, the workers remarked, then they noted that the *ci-devant* masters 'assemble together daily . . . they form a coalition, and . . . they agree together to give the workers only the least they can' – they had even in some cases paid less at the end of a job than had been agreed at its start. The workers' conclusion condemned the employers as 'sworn enemies of the constitution, since they scorn the Rights of Man; they are the most zealous partisans of the most extravagant aristocracy and, consequently, enemies of the general good'.[81]

The entrepreneurs published a *Response* to the workers' claims, which has been lost, but which prompted a further *Refutation* from the workers, dated 2 June. Since they had gained no satisfaction from the National Assembly, this time they directed their claims to the wider public, addressing the 'Citizens', and rehearsing their grievances in more forceful and direct tones: 'that they [the employers] should beware that these great and rapid fortunes are not in the spirit of the Revolution, and that liberty desires that all men should enjoy the benefits that they have taken from us, and in which they wish to deny us participation!'[82]

The workers described how they had acted for the benefit of the trade and the *patrie*, their formation of a mutual aid fund, and a fraternal school – 'where is demonstrated all that is necessary to that art so useful to the fatherland and to individual citizens'. All these undertakings were 'schemes inspired by patriotism alone', but opposed by the *ci-devants* – 'people who, for the most part, have no talent except that of acquiring the rights of mastership and guild office [jurande]'. This document was signed by 120 names, four more than their previous publication, headed by the same four chosen *commissaires*.

The rhetoric of these documents, oriented around liberty, despotism and patriotism, might seem to echo that of François Robert, who around this time was organising a 'Central Meeting of Arts and Trades [Point central des arts et métiers]', intended to get the message of the popular societies, and of Robert's brand of republicanism, into the economic sphere.[83] There is, however, no direct evidence for such a link, and it might indeed be suggested that it devalues the workers' own grasp of events to imply one – the printers

81 Ibid. 351–2. Unlike the employers' document, there is no sign that this *Précis* was ever accepted by the National Assembly.
82 Ibid. 353–4.
83 See Bourdin, *Sociétés populaires*, ch. iv

and the carpenters, in their own words, were clearly capable of articulating their position forcefully and in relation to revolutionary aspirations.[84]

What is evident from other sources, however, is that across a wide spectrum of opinion the workers' movements were regarded with unease, and seen as factionally motivated. The *Feuille du Jour* noted on 9 May that 'The workers are disquieted; they form groups in the public places, and assemblies elsewhere. The friends of disorder take care to foment their discontent, and to slander before them the intentions of the municipality.' The report went on to observe that the workers would put themselves all out of jobs if they carried on prompting the flight of capital from the city.

Around the same time, the impeccably radical *Révolutions de Paris* was making a different, but equally unsympathetic, point about the carpenters' dispute:

> An assembly which can only admit men who exercise the same profession, injures the new order of things; it casts a shadow on liberty; in isolating the citizens, it makes them strangers to the fatherland. . . . We believe that in general it is not in the workers' interest to establish a uniform price: competition is the mother of emulation, and he who possesses a good grasp of his art, and who has the love of work, is always sure to be occupied and paid to his worth.[85]

Quite how this paper could reconcile its economic panglossianism with its political paranoia is unclear, but it is clear that the carpenters received no satisfaction from any quarter. On 18 June seventeen carpentry workers who had been among a group from their trade 'found assembled at the hôtel de Brigy, despite the order of the *Corps municipal*', were dispatched to La Force by the *commissaire* of the Section du Roi-de-Sicile. The police were continuing to operate on normal assumptions – 'the [seventeen] non-domiciled have been imprisoned, and . . . the domiciled have been released with a warning not to re-offend'. Thirteen of the former were released on 30 June, but the remaining four seem to have still been caught up in a tangle of referrals and re-referrals in mid-August.[86]

The breaking-up of a meeting of journeyman hatters on 5 July in the Section des Quatre-Nations shows that worker-solidarity was still attempting to operate, but not with entire success. The journeymen had called the meeting to raise strike funds for their fellows in Lyon, and to arrange sanctions against those who refused to contribute. As the report said, the latter would be 'by a very abusive custom, prevented from working in any shop'. Disagreement appears to have emerged over this, becoming a brawl in the street after one of the journeymen had been 'called a villain'. Guard interven-

---

[84] We may recall here the argument of Kaplan, 'Character and implications', that pre-revolutionary guild manoeuvrings had prepared the artisans for political contestation.
[85] *Révolutions de Paris*, 7–14 May.
[86] APP, AB323:1318, no final outcome noted.

tion seems to have restored unity rather too late, and the enraged hatters collectively made 'rebellion against the Guard', disarming several soldiers before eighteen of them were detained. All but two of them, including two who seem to have been moonlighting as salaried Guards (or vice versa), were released on 30 July – a relatively lengthy confinement for this period, reflecting again the unease with which workers' collective actions were viewed.[87]

Before considering the continuing development of socio-political tensions within the atmosphere created by the economic events of this period, it is worth recording the following observations from the *Révolutions de Paris*, which could be seen as a definitive statement of patriotic perception of the relation between the various forms of disorder we have noted:

> [The aristocrats] have spread false terrors to provoke the emigration which makes our money flow abroad; most of them have preferred, in collecting their charges, to lose a certain sum, and have coins . . . they have driven the timid capitalists far from Paris, frightening them with false proscription-lists; and their emissaries, in causing violence towards the sellers of currency, have necessarily driven up the price of exchange.

The aim of this activity, according to the writer, was clear:

> by hoarding our currency, they have nearly paralysed our manufacturing, they have put it in a precarious state; an infinite number of workers seek work, and work flees from them. . . . When the workers are deprived of necessities, the aristocrats regard it as simple to make them exchange their patriotism for bread.[88]

We have recorded the evident depth of the economic crisis, and its ability to destabilise relations on many fronts, exposing people to further exaggerations of pre-existing fears. The prevalent obsession with aristocratic plotting, coupled with the age-old vision of the working population as lacking in any kind of valid self-consciousness, and ignorance of both the strength of popular feeling and the principles of the economic situation, would tip the perception of this situation slowly but surely towards repression. The crushing of cabals of workers was a step on the road to the Champ de Mars, even if not all patriots could see the link.

---

[87] APP, AB323:1469. The fate of the final two is, again, not noted.
[88] *Révolutions de Paris*, 14–21 May.

6

Before and after Varennes: The Rise in Popular Hostility

Popular disorder and political challenges, May–June 1791

The situation in the capital after Easter was one of constantly aggravating social and political confrontation. Tensions created by the perception of the aristocratic and brigand threat, and exacerbated by the clerical challenge of the spring, now began to impinge, as we have seen, on all aspects of social relations – repression of disorder was swift and violent, and economic grievances provoked bitter rhetoric. A continued undercurrent of confrontation with *aristocratie* heightened the atmosphere of instability. On 2 May, for example, Clermont-Tonnerre made a speech to the National Assembly in which he condemned the idea of annexing Avignon, and two days later a mob hounded him from outside the Tuileries back to his home, where it lingered abusively all afternoon, not dispersing until Lafayette and Bailly had been called to the scene with reinforcements.[1] The actions of the clergy similarly continued to provoke unrest – we have already noted the alarming events in the Bonne-Nouvelle parish, and the complex response to the Ascension Day service at the Théatins.

Through all this, the police responded according to their predetermined model of the roots of disorder, but their interpretations of events and motivations were constantly threatened by the actions of the people. On 16 May a gauze-maker, 'for want of work labouring on the demolition of the quai d'Orsay', was arrested 'for having for no reason [sans aucun sujet] insulted and mistreated a cleric . . . whom he had firstly challenged to tell him if he was an aristocrat'.[2] The phrase 'sans aucun sujet', which appears as a formula in many cases of insult and assault, is often, as here, belied by the evident content of the incident. Once again, this demonstrates that the police could not believe that members of the common people might act out of non-personal, political motivation.

A variety of incidents make it clear that lowly persons had taken up at

---

[1]   See Lacroix, *Actes*, iv. 126, and *Journal de la Société des Amis de la Constitution Monar-chique*, no. 21, 7 May. This paper ceased publication shortly thereafter, having repeatedly appealed for re-subscriptions as its first semester expired. It seems the *Club monarchique* died of apathy as the king's own difficulties with the Constitution became more evident: see no. 26, 11 June.
[2]   APP, AB323:742, Section de Popincourt, released, vouched for, 21 May.

least some of the Revolution's rhetoric for their own purposes. Its possible use in even minor incidents can be seen as early as January, when an architect scuffled with four Auvergnat labourers carrying some poles in the rue Dauphine. They rounded on him, 'calling him an aristocrat and telling him to get on his way since at present everyone was equal'. The significance of this remark can perhaps be seen from the fact that when questioned, the men were prepared to admit that their antagonist had been struck in the clash, but not that any of them had spoken out in this way.[3]

When in February two brothers working in the public workshops saw a wagon nearly run down one of their comrades while a National Guard cavalryman stood idly by, they burst out with a furious round of denunciation and curses, which various witnesses differed over, but which all agreed indicated a criticism of the Guard – 'that they would not take up the interests of a citizen' or 'were not f—ing ready to support the citizens', and that generally 'there is no justice'. The tenor of the brothers' fury was exacerbated by their partial inebriation, which is perhaps why they were merely temporarily detained in the guardpost and reprimanded for their lack of respect.[4]

The claim that the new revolutionary order had given individuals more rights than the authorities were willing to allow extended into the *demi-monde*. *Commissaire* Deneux discovered this when on 12 May five prostitutes were brought before him at 11 p.m. for quarrelling in the street. Three of them claimed employment in garment trades and a fourth admitted being 'a bit of a whore [un peu putain] but an honest woman otherwise'. Questioned on their actions, they unanimously replied 'that since the liberty [depuis la liberté] they could go about in the night-time as in the day'. They then fell to 'the most obscene remarks', prompting a swift closure of the *procès-verbal* and detention in La Force.[5] None of these incidents show any inclination to regard as 'political' the statements from such elements, in which we may discern an alternative interpretation of the message of the Declaration of Rights; they were read simply as dangerous aberrations.

This harsh interpretation of the popular mind was echoed in an equally harsh approach to the physical needs of the common people. On 5 May an unemployed labourer was detained 'for having insulted lesieur Garson, *commissaire de section*, because he had refused to give him charity, being still of working age'.[6] By the middle of June the poor unemployed, flocking to Paris for want of work elsewhere, were being rounded up in batches, like the ten men found asleep in boats tied up in Section de la Fontaine de Grenelle on 12 June – 'the said individuals have been in Paris a little time, having

3   APP, AA215:367–8, Section d'Henri-Quatre, 22 Jan. Sent to La Force, released with warning, 26 Jan.: AB322:948.
4   APP, AA182:95, Section du Louvre, 24 Feb.
5   APP, AA56:168, Section des Arcis.
6   APP, AB323:603, Section de la Halle au Bled, released with *passeport*, 9 May.

neither trade nor domicile, and appearing suspect'.[7] The register of La Force shows that the numbers of people falling foul of the police swelled from April onwards – by June the overall total of prison admissions recorded was some 25 per cent above the relatively constant level it had displayed in the period January–March. It would remain significantly higher into August, even discounting the leap caused by arrests for sedition in late July.[8]

We have already seen the anger and harsh response that the 'crime-wave' of May–June induced in *commissaire* Deneux, and there is some evidence that the growth in indigence also heightened general social tensions, although the warmer weather might also have brought more disputes outdoors. When on 30 May a water-carrier 'threw water over a naked man to engage him to cover his nudity, the man struck him with a stone'. On 3 June a female stallholder on the Place de Grève hit a man sleeping outside her premises, and explained 'that the man wanted to piss in front of her stall, which is why she hit him'. In both cases the aggressor was imprisoned.[9]

The swelling ranks of the completely indigent do not appear to have expressed any interest in politics, their attentions doubtless being rather focused on survival, despite the prevalent fears we have seen of their suborna-tion. Others of *le peuple* continued to speak out, such as the cab-driver who said, in a bar on 12 May, 'that you could shit on the National Guard coat, and that the French constitution would be carried out in France like in England'.[10] Part of this at least is rather obscure, but the underlying senti-ment is clear, as was that of a innkeeper who was detained on 11 May 'for having insulted and made shameful remarks towards two salaried guardsmen, whom he reproached for having acted badly as former French Guards in the affair of sieur Reveillon'.[11] There is no indication of the context of this remark, but it suggests both a long memory and a reluctance to accept the reconciliations sought by the more orthodox revolutionaries. The French Guards had been whitewashed of their rather unsavoury past after their patri-otic stand in June–July 1789, but there is evidence to show that some of them had not renounced their previously well-known dubious morals. On 17 May Joseph Ficier, salaried guard, was arrested along with 'his mistress', Louise Bellinger, prostitute, for an assault on a second-hand goods dealer who had

7   APP, AB323:1108, all released on 16 June with *passeports*. See also AB323:1070, 1082, a total of twenty people found sleeping in the plaster-kilns at the Butte de Chaumont (Section du Faubourg St-Denis, 7, 10 June.)

8   A comprehensive analysis of the registers has not been attempted; however, extrapola-tions from dates and numbers recorded would indicate some 320 cases per month before April, reaching 360 in that month, and rising thereafter month-on-month to 400, 420, 560 and 490 by August. The July figure includes some 200 cases for the week following the 17th. It should also be noted that the actual rise in detentions may have been steeper since 'batches' of prisoners under the same number seem to have become more common in later months, these being mainly arrests of suspicious indigents.

9   APP, AA137:105, 110, Section de l'Hôtel de Ville.

10   APP, AA157:110, Section des Enfants-Rouges, sent to La Force.

11   APP, AB323:697, Section de la Place Royale, released 14 May.

been her client, while the 'lover' of Catherine Eubellione, one of two prostitutes arrested outside their lodgings on 31 May, was also a salaried guard.[12]

It was during this period that the Fayettist harassment of lieutenant Hion
reached the point where he made his allegations public, both in print and to
the police. The Fayettists, although probably the only true *parti* at this time,
were not the only people conducting a politics of insult, as we are by now well
aware. In an incident late on the night of 22 May the Guard reserve from the
Hôtel de Ville had to be summoned to break up 'tumult occurring at the door
of an inn on the quai Pelletier'. Two men were arrested for having said 'in a
mocking and derisive tone . . . ah here come the friends of the constitution, to
me the Nation'. They were hustled off for this, and compounded the Guard's
suspicions when one of them tried to write to a 'former chevalier' to vouch for
him. When they were interrogated in the morning, the would-be letter-
writer, a nineteen-year-old wigmaker and musician, could give no reason for
his words, while his companion, a former clerk in the parlement, openly
mocked the questions put to him. They were sent to La Force, although soon
freed.[13]

Another man was detained in the same disturbance, a journeyman shoemaker who, although he claimed he had been 'drunk and not to really
remember what he had said', seems according to the record to have made a
decidedly inflammatory statement: 'f— . . . we will break and burn the
municipality tomorrow, and if some of us are put in the Châtelet we shall do
the same to the Châtelet'. This is strong stuff for what started as a tavern-door
gathering, and it seems to have attracted popular sympathy: 'He was taken as
a precaution to the reserve [i.e. the barracks at the Hôtel de Ville] because the
people were making demonstrations towards taking him from the hands of
the Guard.'[14]

Clearly here it would seem that the alcohol had loosened this man's
tongue, but such an outburst of apocalyptic threats would have required a
background of basic hostility to the authorities to bring it into being. Even if
his statement, like that of the other two detainees, was only a response to the
Guard's interference, its awareness of what popular power might do, and its
willingness to invoke that outcome, show just the kind of popular sentiments
that the authorities were most afraid of – sentiments which seem to have
grown stronger since Easter, as nothing of this ilk can be seen before then
(excepting the extraordinary circumstances of the Vincennes expedition).
The press also reported this incident in alarmist terms: 'At ten p.m., an

---

12 APP, AA56:184, 219, Section des Arcis, and AB323:778 indicating that Bellinger was
vouched for on 24 May and that Ficier was referred to the Tribunal, the verdict of which is
not noted. See Mercier, *Tableau*, 200, for an earlier opinion of the *Gardes françaises*,
although he noted that reforms in the early 1780s had improved them somewhat.
13 APP, AA56:199; AB323:832. The first man was vouched for on 25 May, the second
released with a warning on 1 June.
14 APP, AA56:201; AB323:834. His papers were sent to the Tribunal, which returned them
'for lack of evidence' two months later. Released with warning, 1 Aug.

immense crowd arrived on the quayside across from the Place de Grève. They manifested the intention to burn down the Hôtel de Ville; before this, they had to make themselves its master. The siege began with a barrage of stones.'[15]

Although the Guard seems to have had every justification for breaking up this incident, in other cases the same fear of disorder led them into heavy-handed over-reaction. On 28 May a wagonner was arrested 'for having worn at his neck in derisive fashion, by his own account, a scarf which he had bought'. In other words, for satirising the sash of an official.[16] With people and authorities apparently looking for confrontation, one could be manufactured out of the most unlikely material. The *Feuille du Jour* reported on 31 May that a crowd had surrounded a carriage and prepared to lynch the occupants after 'a ruffian, selling flowers' had yelled 'aristocrat' after it. The intervention of a merchant ensured that this culprit was apprehended, whereupon he was 'recognised as having several times transformed himself into a woman. He is a most distinguished adjutant of the army of the disruptors [l'armée des perturbateurs]'. Whatever the truth of this particular charge, some odd incidents did occur – on 3 June a servant and an architecture student were held 'for having excited the greatest revolt amongst the citizens against the National Guard, relative to a gathering on the Pont-Neuf which took place when a horse collapsed with *la morve*'.[17]

Members of the population could use any issue to raise a protest against the troubles of the time. We have already noted the vehement protest outside the Théatins on 2 June and the harsh fate of one man arrested there. Another, Etienne Cassac, 'having no trade', was detained in the same incident, 'for allowing himself to utter inconsequent remarks against the operation or administration of the Royal Treasury, on the subject not only of Assignats, but again concerning the rarity of coin, claiming that it was the Royal Treasury that trafficked in it'.[18] This, of course, is the accusation already sustained for months in the press. Once again we see elements of the people associating all the actions of authority into an aristocratic conspiracy, while the press which had done much to inflame them, in this case as in others, blamed the resultant popular agitation on subornation.

Repercussions of this incident were felt elsewhere. François Jean Lebel, aged nineteen, journeyman goldsmith, was arrested in the Section d'Henri-Quatre for saying 'that M. Carle was a rogue, a beggar, a villain, and his damned Battalion as well'. A party of citizens who made the arrest was led by

15 *Feuille du Jour*, 25 May.
16 APP, AB323:895, Section des Quinze-Vingts, released 30 May.
17 APP, AB323:986, Section du Louvre. The servant, who had struck a Guard, was sent before the Tribunal, no sentence recorded. The other was vouched for. *Morve* is a form of respiratory disorder, apparently serious, since there were two 'experts named to verify the illness of horses with *morve*' on the municipal payroll: Lacroix, *Actes*, vi. 180–1, confirmation in office, 24 Aug.
18 APP, AB323:1002, Section des Quatre Nations, sent to Tribunal, no sentence noted.

a journeyman grocer who had been 'scandalised' by this outburst. In response to the usual queries, Lebel claimed that 'he had no motive' for his utterance, and 'he had not been incited by anyone'. He explained 'that having been that afternoon at the Théatins he had heard remarks being said against M. Carle, and that this evening he was repeating the remarks that he had heard'. At the time of his arrest he had simply been passing on his way home with a friend after a drink. His father, a joiner, was summoned, and was 'astonished' by news of the offence. His son was released into his charge, and he 'engaged himself to make efforts to prevent any such remarks in future'.[19]

While incidents such as this one indicate a fairly unsophisticated response to events, others show that some people had developed a more complex view of their position. One such individual was Pierre Jean Charles Chenant, aged twenty-nine, a journeyman baker reduced to working in the public work-shops. He was picked up on 5 June for declaiming against Lafayette in a street-corner group, and his questioning is worth recording at length:

> Interrogated as to why he was arrested, [he] responded because the persons surrounding him wished to oppress him. [Q] why he had insulted the Parisian National Guard, [A] because they had mistreated him. [Q] if he had said that all the National Guards were f—ing beggars [etc.] and that it was he who clothed them, [A] that it was all the public that clothed them, and that he had not made any insulting remarks to them. [Q] what motives had determined him to insult M. delafayette, [A] he did not understand what M le commissaire was asking him. [Q] if he had not been paid to excite some popular movement and uprising, [A] that he wished that someone would give him a hundred louis [2,000 *livres*], that he would come and declare anyone who made such a proposal to him. [Q] why did he say that M. delafayette bore a name that did not belong to him, [A] he had seen in the public papers that he was called "moitié" [*sic*]. [Q] if he had at some time been in prison, [A] he had been put in the guardhouse in the Section des Petits Pères for having supported his friend in the café Yon, who had a bonnet on his head instead of a hat.[20]

Chenant clearly read the radical press, the only ones to use the name Mottié; he knew the language of 'oppression'; he scorned the idea that he might be suborned; he gave a clear signal of his view of the relationship of the public and the Guard; he seems to have been involved in an earlier incident where he defended the right of a friend to wear worker's headgear in a café. All in all, a regular democrat. The authorities were probably glad to let him sit out the next few months in a cell.

As sentiments such as Chenant's were fermenting throughout Paris, the stage was set for the next major confrontation between radicals and authority when the case of Santerre versus Desmottes and Lafayette came before the

---

[19] APP, AA215:442, 2 June.
[20] APP, AA206:284. Chenant was sent to La Force, where the record indicates that he was given a one-month sentence on 20 August, by which time of course he had already served over twice that: AB323:1011.

Civil Tribunal near the Place Royale on 6 June. Santerre, popular commander of the Enfants-Trouvés battalion from the Faubourg St-Antoine, claimed that he had been defamed by the general and his *aide-de-camp*, who had alleged that the latter had been shot at on Santerre's orders as he rode from Vincennes to Paris on 28 February. Even before the hearing, tensions were running high. The newly-instituted journal the *Babillard*, which recounted the ravings of open-air democracy with a conservative commentary, noted on 4 June that 'it appears that many ragamuffins [va-nu-pieds] are disposed to go to the hearing on the day this case is heard. They have even announced the intention of *crushing the Tribunal*, if it pronounces in favour of the aide-de-camp'.[21]

This episode offers a particularly rich illustration of the confused and confusing discourses of the press. On 4 and 5 June, no less than five *colporteurs* were arrested on separate occasions in the Section des Enfants-Rouges, for selling a pamphlet entitled *Discovery of a great treason against the inhabitants of the faubourg St-Antoine, on the occasion of the trial of M. la Fayette and M. Santerre.*[22] The opening lines of this work seem to offer good reason to seize it:

> Citizens, be on your guard, distrust all that surround you; realise that you live amongst your greatest enemies; the most cruel and villainous enemies who will never pardon you for having broken the shameful yoke they had burdened you with; yes, so long as there is in France a single aristocrat, you may say that there is constantly beside you a monster ready to slit your throat, and to drink your blood.
>
> Those most to be feared are not those who make the most threats; but are those traitors to whom you have imprudently given your trust, whom you have honoured with public functions and charged with the care of your defence.

However, while thus appearing to incite popular vengeance against Lafayette and his supporters, the pamphlet went on to denounce rumoured plans for crowds to disrupt the court hearing as a plot by these very same Lafayette-led aristocrats to give them an excuse to crush the people – *mouchards* have been infiltrating the faubourg, inciting people to besiege the Tribunal and force it to render a verdict against Desmottes: 'What joy for the enemies of the nation, if the citizens of the faubourg committed then the slightest indiscretion!' So, as the pamphlet continued, if the *faubouriens* do come to the trial, it will be to bear witness to their 'probity', and to disappoint those it addressed as 'cowards, who burn to soak your sacrilegious hands in the blood of your brothers'. Another pamphlet, *New PLOT discovered, concerning the trial of M.*

---

[21] *Le Babillard, ou Journal du Palais-Royal*, no. 2. Emphasis in original.
[22] APP, AB323:1037, 1040–1, 1045, all released 14 June. Variations are noted in the title, but only one pamphlet matching this description can be found: BN, 8–Lb39–4681, *Découverte d'une grande trahison contre les habitans du faubourg St-Antoine, à l'occasion du procès de M. la Fayette avec M. Santerre.*

SANTERRE, contained much the same message, this time in an 'Address of the Fraternal Society of les Halles', which observed that, 'All means are employed to lead you astray, in order more easily to find pretexts to calumnify you. You have shown too much courage in this revolution not to have great enemies, and they can only defeat and destroy you by leading you into errors.'[23]

There was a significant popular presence at the trial sessions, matched by a concentration of National Guard forces, but no particular disorders. The *Babillard* announced on the 7th that a speaker in the Tuileries gardens, supposedly 'one of the authors of the so-called *Ami du Peuple by Marat*', called Vallé, 'excited the citizens to go on Thursday to the Minimes [the site of the Tribunal] to force the judges to pronounce in favour of Sr Santerre. Some sans-culottes supported him'. The same agitation was going on in the Palais-Royal, and on the 8th it reported a consensus that Orléans was backing the radicals – 'one is assured that M. d'Orléans will tomorrow have several persons at the Minimes Tribunal'.[24] On 10 June Gorsas published a letter accusing the comte de la Touche, chancellor of the duc d'Orléans, of going cloaked about the Faubourg, where he 'paid for the beer and sought to lead the citizens astray'. Thus Fayettists, Orléanists and radicals had all been blamed in advance for a disorder which never finally occurred. Calm was maintained despite the unsatisfactory outcome of the trial – the court declared itself incompetent in the matter, since the incident occurred between Guard personnel on duty, and should be tried in a court-martial. Such a trial was never held – Santerre let the matter lie, possibly because of business difficulties, and later events overtook it. Rumblings of popular dissatisfaction continued for a few days, but died away peacefully.[25]

From this point on, the *Babillard* offers a useful source for popular opinions, once its sardonic tone has been discounted. It appeared daily, with reports from the Palais-Royal and Tuileries of the public debate, as well as from the main cafés, the faubourgs and the popular societies. This was too large a field for any one author to cover alone, and the editor, Jean Pierre Sarrasin, employed agents to collect news from around the city. We know this because a former customs clerk he had taken on to record the debates of the *Société fraternelle* had him arrested on the Pont Neuf on 21 June. This man, Thomas Vanière, had gone to work, but had been seized by society members, his paper 'lacerated', and had been 'called a *mouchard* of the aristocrats'. Since then, Vanière said, 'He had learned that the individual who had charged him to take notes . . . was an enroller of *mouchards* that were spread through the various societies to spy on what happened there and he presumed that all these enrolled persons were to facilitate the escape of the king.'

---

23 BN, 8–Lb39–9962, *Nouvelle COMPLOT découvert, sur le procès de M SANTERRE*.
24 *Babillard*, nos 4, 5.
25 See BN, 8–Lb39–4682, 9971, two pamphlet accounts of the trial itself, and *Babillard*, nos 6–8. See also Bourdin, *Sociétés populaires*, 222.

Sarrasin was given the chance to explain himself, and justified his use of agents by his state of semi-invalidity. His journal, he said, was meant 'to calm the minds of the people concerning all the inflammatory speeches which are made every day in the Palais-Royal and at the Tuileries'. This was sufficient for the *commissaire de police* of the Section d'Henri-Quatre, who released him.[26]

Sarrasin's method of calming the public seems to have been to write off most of what he published as either naïve excess or the subsidised ravings of prostitutes and criminals. Despite this device, a reading of the first seventeen numbers of the *Babillard*, up to the king's flight, does not present a reassuring picture of the state of popular opinion. The Santerre trial occupied the public for a week, as we have seen, and general complaints about the municipality were a constant refrain, usually expressed as personal hostility to Bailly and especially to Lafayette. Against this background complaints were recorded in ten of the seventeen issues about money and speculation, in nine about the refractory clergy, and in the same number about the general aristocratic threat. In seven, discontent by or about the workers was noted, in six about gambling dens, usually linked with allegations of official collusion, and the same number about the threat of war, once linking this to a threat to the food supply. Of the seventeen issues, no less than fourteen included comments by the editor on the suspicious nature of speakers, but his evidence usually seems to have been no more than a dislike for certain vociferous groups of women.[27]

Many of these complaints could be rolled together in the public discourse, heightening the atmosphere of disquiet:

> Thursday 16 June, Palais-Royal . . . [Yesterday] there were complaints that the postal receivers, and the various offices of patriotic donations, were selling coin. . . . Several workers complained about the decree which gives to masters the freedom to reward talent and activity; this law opposes the do-nothings and the ignorant men who were forcing the entrepreneurs to pay them like good workers. . . . It is reported that brigands are spreading in the countryside, devastating crops, and will burn the châteaux if they are left to act. One is assured that they are stirred up by the enemies of the Constitution.[28]

> Tuesday 21 June . . . Palais-Royal, evening [20 June]. . . . Bitter and well-founded complaints against the municipality, which does nothing to reduce the price of goods, which allows and seems to authorise gambling-dens. . . . Tuileries, evening. . . . Much is talked about the multiplying gatherings of workers of all kinds, of their speeches, their threats and their designs. Most complain of lacking bread and want to dictate the law to their masters, concerning their wages.[29]

---

[26] APP, AA215:450.
[27] *Babillard*, nos 1–17.
[28] Ibid. no. 12.
[29] Ibid. no. 17.

On 16 June the primary assemblies were summoned to begin the process of electing a new Legislative Assembly. Although there was considerable enthusiasm for disposing of the old Assembly, the *marc d'argent* qualification for eligibility provoked some uncertainties. A patriot as moderate as Gorsas felt it was unacceptable, and along with other 'excellent citizens' who paid that much, he and they 'have excluded themselves voluntarily from these assemblies, where intrigue has overtaken patriotism, and will perhaps push it aside'.[30] The *Babillard* noted on this day in the Palais-Royal that, 'two ill-dressed individuals were of the opinion that all should be admitted without distinction to eligibility. It was gently represented to them that a man who was fit to make shoes, was not fit to make good laws'.[31] Even blinkered by this disdainful attitude, Sarrasin was able to record the ebb and flow of a massive popular interest and concern about contemporary events; and a more sympathetic observer might have found even more to say about the mind of the people.

The nearest Paris came to such an observer, however, was Marat, whose determined belief in the necessity for immediate insurrection tended to blind him to more tentative developments in popular consciousness. He did stand up for the participants in the Théatins riot: 'One would be very surprised to learn that this scene had been carried out by emissaries of the police', despite the consensus of 'the enlightened citizens' on the subject. In the same issue he mentioned the upcoming Santerre trial, with the inevitable plot to declare martial law and attack the people. He later reported his dissatisfaction with the outcome, and the popular acceptance of it: 'The people should have the good sense to hang you [Lafayette, the judges, etc.] high and dry. That's how all the villainy of the public functionaries, plotting with the king to re-establish despotism, must be ended.'[32] As the primary assemblies met, Marat published long lists of the *mouchards* and the 'sold' in them, while also denouncing the 'Indignity of citizens who desert the section assemblies through cowardice.'[33]

Turning to Audouin's *Journal Universel*, as fervent an enemy of aristocracy and counter-revolution as one could wish for, one still finds no great sympathy for the masses. In the first three weeks of June, he made no less than seven allegations of aristocratic subornation of the people, and stated his belief 'very firmly' that the Théatins agitation was thus inspired.[34] Audouin gave a picture on 1 June of his view of the fears of counter-revolution:

> there are first the fearful who think to see the enemy forever at their side, and who do not wish to get it into their heads that the French people, having become free, are invincible; next there are the ill-intentioned who, in

30 *Courrier*, 17 June.
31 *Babillard*, no.13.
32 *Ami du Peuple*, no. 479, 4 June; no. 491, 16 June .
33 Ibid. nos 493–6, 18–21 June.
34 *Journal Universel*, 4, 6, 8, 13, 14, 15, 21 June.

continually threatening France . . . have no other goal than to perpetuate anarchy, to make money disappear, in order to sell more dearly; there are also those citizens who, fearing always that the people might lose their energy, spur them on constantly, by displaying to them the counter-revolutionaries at the gates . . .; there are, finally, those same counter-revolutionaries, who dream only of war, of carnage.

This says a good deal about the mental world of the journalist, who was constantly inserting into the public discourse such images of disorder and menace, but it cannot explain why, for example, a merchant brushmaker from the Faubourg St-Antoine chose to risk arrest on 18 June, 'for having . . . made inflammatory speeches, having said loudly that the primary assemblies were composed entirely of rogues, thieves, etc'.[35] A master tailor who tore down a list of active citizens was prepared to admit that he thought 'that since everyone was a citizen there was no need for lists of active citizens'. Oddly, however, given that this occurred on the very day of the Flight to Varennes, he denied saying 'that one could tear down the notices because it was right to erase the word "royal" wherever it was found'. He was released with a warning.[36]

Figures in authority, witnessing such democratic stirrings, seem to have become hyper-sensitive to criticism. On 14 June one Sieur Beauregard, knight of St-Louis, captain of cavalry and *aide-major* of the National Gendarmerie, was walking with a friend in the Palais-Royal when two people, apparently beggars, came up to him and addressed him as 'comrade'. This is the same *aide-major* who had harassed lieutenant Hion, and in this incident he displayed another facet of his political attitudes. He dismissed the beggars, and remarked to his friend 'that if he wished he could have them arrested'. Jean Charles Brunet, a 'pharmacist taking courses', was strolling with a friend just behind them, heard this remark and 'did not believe himself to be committing an indiscretion in remarking to the knight of St-Louis that he believed that as an individual according to the new law he had no right to arrest, nor to have anyone arrested'. Beauregard said he did, Brunet repeated that he did not, their raised voices drew public attention to them, and Beauregard 'having found this language Extraordinary on the part of a man he did not know', took him by the collar and led him 'fairly peaceably' to the guardpost, and thence to the *commissaire*. Both men involved, and their respective companions, gave similar accounts of the incident. Beauregard's friend, Charles Beaupoil St-Aulaire, volunteer grenadier of the Filles St-Thomas battalion, noted that Brunet had added to his interpellation 'are we not all citizens?' There can be little doubt that the 'patriotic' nobles of the military

---

35 APP, AB323:1181, Section des Tuileries, referred to prosecutor. No outcome noted.
36 APP, AA157:135, Section des Enfants-Rouges.

command had a very different answer to that question than did the popular patriots.[37]

It seems that student chemists were not the only such group taken up with revolutionary fervour. Ten days before this incident, the *Bureau municipal* had heard from some law-abiding medical students 'that there reigns in the schools of surgery . . . a spirit of discord and of disunion . . . this evil has been brought to birth, and grows each day, through an assembly called the *Surgical Club*, held by a party amongst the students'.[38] A police investigation was instructed to restore order and union. The outcome of this is unknown, and no mention of this gathering can be found elsewhere. Evidently, however, the spirit of discord that flowed through Paris was not restricted to the suborned masses and the public speechmakers. Around this time the *Révolutions de Paris* was drawn to comment on another form of incipient conflict – 'these small divisions which exist between the people in uniform and the people in plain coats; divisions which enter into the calculations of the factious'. To call some of the incidents we have seen 'small divisions' may seem an under-statement, but at least this report acknowledges that such divisions reflected more than merely the line between citizens and vagrants. The author was remarking with approval on the scheme of one battalion-commander to invite all citizens to take part in drill-sessions, a move that he believed all battalions should emulate, but which he was sure that they would not, because the headquarters and officers 'would fear that the sworn men, mixed with those against whom they claim to arm them, would perceive at last that they have been deceived, and that the cause from which they wish to separate them is the better one'.[39] Meanwhile, according to one denunciation on 19 June, a Sieur Nadam had condemned the chiefs of his local battalion with various 'inflammatory remarks . . . notably that the said headquarters earned ten [écus?] per day'.[40] This apparently growing disenchantment with the Guard was to bear bitter fruit in the following month, as events replaced concern over the Assembly elections with a new and more critical agenda. How a city so obviously divided would have coped with the transition to a new constitutional order is impossible to gauge, and in any case the king chose to present all parties with a new conundrum when they awoke on the morning of 21 June to find him absent from the Tuileries.

37 APP, AA84:248. Brunet was allowed to go free after a grilling over his identity and intentions, and after producing a cousin who was a Guard sergeant to vouch for him.
38 Lacroix, *Actes*, iv. 478.
39 *Révolutions de Paris*, 4–11 June.
40 APP, AA157:129, Section des Enfants-Rouges.

Immediate responses to the Flight to Varennes

In the midst of the constant turmoil in the capital, the king's departure came as a shock to Parisians, but hardly as a surprise. On the 21st (and writing therefore on the 20th) Gorsas had announced that 'the rumour was spread yesterday that there had been an attempt to kidnap the king and queen two nights ago'. On the 22nd his stark headline was 'Escape of Louis XVI and his family'. Other journalists were equally stoic on this day. The *Feuille du Jour* reported that 'Yesterday through the evening, the arms of the king, his name and that of the queen were removed, erased, struck out from all the places they had appeared. . . . Nothing happened otherwise that was contrary to good order.' Audouin took a slightly more sardonic line – 'So he has gone, this patriot king, this king who so loved the people.' He asked if the people would now acknowledge the threat that the 'patriot journalists' had been warning them of for so long. The *Babillard*, however, while equally projecting calm – 'the movements of a few factious persons were stopped at their origins, and order was not troubled' – none the less took an opposite view: 'We even dare to say that the king would not have given himself over to such an ill-considered act, if these journalists had not constantly stirred up the people, on the pretext of enlightening them.' Marat and Fréron took the inevitable inflammatory line on the *affaire*, and were duly condemned on all sides.

The primary assembly of the Section de l'Hôtel de Ville happened to be in session when, as they recorded, 'the news of the escape of the king and the royal family was spread through all the capital'. They went into permanent session, and left their minutes in the police files.[41] A few hours later the official version of events arrived, in the form of a report that the municipality had just received a decree of the National Assembly 'bearing different precautions taken for the maintenance of good order, and the discovery and arrest of those who have co-operated in the kidnapping of the king and the royal family'.

This slide from escape [évasion] to kidnapping [enlèvement], and the priority of maintaining good order, had been determined very early in the course of events. Immediately after informing the other authorities of the king's flight Bailly had, 'conjointly with MM. the police administrators . . . taken precautions and given orders necessary so that property was not violated and public tranquillity might not be troubled'. Their next move was to order the printing of a proclamation beginning 'The king has been kidnapped.' The truth was evident to all, but, as the authorities must have instantly realised, this fiction was their only chance of saving the Constitution from this crisis.[42]

Meanwhile, if the people had not begun to riot *en masse*, the atmosphere was still not one of calm, despite what all parties interested in order noted,

[41] APP, AA137:139.
[42] Lacroix, *Actes*, v. 2–3.

148

and would recall later. While the *Babillard* observed that 'the people appear to place all their trust in the National Assembly', it also reported a few lines above that 'Marat and d'Anton [*sic*] appeared at the Tuileries; the people surrounded them near the large basin, and conducted them, as if in triumph, to the National Assembly.' Royal insignia were indeed being erased across the city, as the *Feuille du Jour* had reported, and on the 22nd the municipality had to decree that this should stop, and that people should not insult troops whose uniforms incorporated such emblems.[43]

On the 21st itself a crowd threatened the duc d'Aumont, a division-commander in the National Guard, who was spotted in civilian dress and seized by 'some ill-intentioned people . . . while making his way to the Hôtel de Ville; the people were led astray; seditious cries were heard; M d'Aumont was in peril'. It took four municipal officers and a Guard detachment to get him to safety. Labourers in the municipal construction works on the Louis XVI bridge attacked an *aide-de-camp* attempting to leave in search of the king's route, and a rumour ran through the National Assembly, possibly provoked by the d'Aumont incident, 'that M. de la Fayette had been arrested on the Place de Grève by the people'.[44] On the Place du Carroussel a casual domestic worker nearly got himself lynched by 'a large gathering' for having 'scorned the national cockade, and, having one in his hand, allowed himself to wipe his rear with it, throw it to the ground and step on it, saying that he stepped on the nation, and that he shit on the cockade'. In the context it seems likely that this outburst came from disgust with the National Guard and the authorities, rather than being an attack on the Revolution, although it was clearly a risky form of protest. A journeyman marquetry-worker and a journeyman locksmith were also accused in the Section du Louvre of having trampled on a cockade. They were harassed by the surrounding crowd, and finally arrested, although they protested that the cockade had fallen acciden-tally from the marquetry-worker's hat. They were detained as 'disturbers of the public peace'.[45]

While public response to isolated suspicious acts caused trouble in itself, a more general wave of fear concerning the dangerous lower orders was also present. Rumour had it that the prison population was stirring, and in particular 'the prison of Bicêtre has become in the last few hours the object of general concern in the districts of St-Jacques and St-Marcel'. This was inves-tigated by the municipality, as were murmurings of trouble in the quarries to the south of the city. The Section des Thermes-de-Julien informed the municipality that it had checked its lodging-houses for suspicious move-ments, and asked that this be generally ordered.[46] Despite the general consensus that the people were behaving themselves, the fears of a suborned

---

[43] *Babillard*, no. 19, 22 June; Lacroix, *Actes*, v. 46.
[44] Ibid. v. 3–4, 33.
[45] APP, AB323:1325, Section des Tuileries, referred to the prosecutor; AA182:258.
[46] Lacroix, *Actes*, v. 14, 25, 73, 89–90.

populace ran deep. None the less, in this crisis, a certain amount of social solidarity was on show. The commander of the St-Jacques-la-Boucherie battalion requested extra arms for the market-porters that had joined his unit, and received 100 muskets. The main preoccupation of the Hôtel de Ville Section assembly was with moving several piles of builder's rubble, that might have proved useful to a mob, from the Place de Grève, but they also recorded 'that permission had been given to non-active citizens armed with pikes to join the battalions of their areas'.[47]

However, despite its official sanction, even this movement to arm the wider citizenry led to some confusion and disquiet. In the Faubourg St-Antoine Santerre was particularly quick to take up this task, and seems to have drawn large numbers. Some of these, however, fell by the wayside. Four of them were arrested at 12.45 a.m. on the 22nd, armed with muskets but unable to give the password to a sentry, claiming that 'they had been put in the battalion of M. Santerre, but that afterwards they had fallen behind'. One, a cabinetmaker, resisted the Guard that disarmed them, and spent three days in prison as a result.[48] Elsewhere, the *Feuille du Jour*, recording the decision of the St-Roch battalion to admit 'every known citizen', observed that they would receive a certificate 'which will serve to legitimise them and to distinguish them from the vagabonds, who will not fail to profit from this occasion to spread throughout the city under arms'.[49] The Guard was alert for any signs of suspect behaviour, arresting two men in different parts of the city for making marks on buildings – which could have been signals between faction-members but were probably just born of idleness.[50] Meanwhile the rounding-up of indigents continued – including five boys aged between twelve and sixteen arrested while sleeping on the quai de la Megisserie on the 21st. All claimed to be working as errand-runners, and to have lodgings, but only one convinced the *commissaire* not to send him to La Force.[51]

Other arrests on the 21st, however, were motivated by more than a mere confusion of intention or general suspicion. For example Christophe Labbé, journeyman shoemaker, was 'arrested for having insulted M. Goujon commander of the third battalion of the sixth division, whose epaulettes he criticised, as well as [criticising] the National Guard'. Jean-Baptiste Duthy, waggoner, was detained 'for having dared to say that M. Bailly and M. Delafayette must be hanged'. While under arrest he 'committed acts of violence against the Guard and tore off an officer's epaulettes'. It was also alleged that he claimed to have done the same to several others, but he denied this in his

---

47 Ibid. v. 57, 76; APP, AA137:139.
48 APP, AB323:1212.
49 *Feuille du Jour*, 23 June.
50 APP, AB323:1208, Section du Roule; 1218, Section de Notre-Dame, 21 June. One man was a mason, now in the public workshops, the other was a 'maker of bullet-moulds'. Both were released on the 25th.
51 AA182:257, Section du Louvre.

interrogation.[52] The popular scorn for the notion of military authority symbolised by these adornments is clearly on display. Seditious remarks at this point seem particularly to have been directed towards officers, like those of René Valentin Pierson, journeyman pewterer, arrested near the Hôtel de Ville, 'for having made inflammatory remarks both against the commanding general and against M. Delaheu division-commander. This individual revolted against M. Leclerc, lieutenant . . . who wished to make him hand over a sabre that he was carrying'. Men were arrested in a further five Sections on the 21st for insulting the Guard relative to the king's flight, usually commenting, like Nicolas Beuzard, cab-driver, 'that they had let the king leave'.[53]

On the 22nd, as the deluge of immediate press reaction hit the city, dangerous popular comment seems to have been less widespread. One *colporteur* was picked up 'for having uttered inflammatory remarks against the citizens of Paris . . . amongst other things that the Parisians were f—ers to have let the king leave'. This arrest was demanded 'by public outcry', as was that of Leonard René Vaquier, public workshop supervisor, 'for having said loudly, that if the king had gone it was the fault of the General, who had [promised to] answer for him [i.e. for the king's good conduct,] on his own head, and that it was astonishing that his head was not on the end of a pike'. The witnesses who reported this, besides the president of the Section, were a journeyman grocer and three wives of artisans. As in other cases we have noted, it is clear that the conflicts of the city did not run along simple 'class' lines.[54]

The spontaneous angry reactions among the people were soon seconded by the observations of some sections of the press. As early as the 21st one *colporteur* had been arrested 'carrying seventy-eight copies of a publication entitled "Manifesto of the king", beginning . . . with the words, "Peoples have made kings and may destroy them" '.[55] It took until the 23rd, apparently, for more *colporteurs* to fall foul of the law. One was picked up for reading from *L'Orateur du Peuple*, 'saying that MM. Bailly and Lafayette were Traitors who must be killed'. Another was more generally guilty, 'for having hawked and distributed papers entitled *l'ami du peuple* and the *brave Duchesne*, which

52 APP, AB323:1206, Section du Temple; 1228, and AA206:305, Section de la Place-Vendôme. Labbé was released on 25 June, but Duthy was referred to the Tribunal. No sentence noted.
53 APP, AB323:1239, Section de l'Hôtel de Ville, released 27 June. AB323:1252, and also 1219, 1229, 1255, 1260. All were released by the 28th at the latest.
54 APP, AB323:1301, Section des Lombards, released 30 June. AB323:1210, Section des Postes, referred to Tribunal. No sentence noted.
55 APP, AB323:1295, Section des Lombards, a twenty-seven-year-old casual labourer, released 28 June.

contain calumnies against the General as well as against the National Guard, the mounted police, the National Assembly and others'.[56]

Other incidents continued to trouble the next few days, offering sufficient evidence to show that calm and order were not the mood of all Paris – a beggar made seditious remarks about the royal family on the 24th, a market-trader tried to get people to seize an army general on the same day, and there were several incidents of insults to the Guard, in one of which a whole patrol was set upon, 'of which several fusiliers were struck'.[57] In the midst of this the municipality put great effort into ensuring that the Fête-Dieu parades on 23 June passed off 'with a religious pomp that inspired respect', as Gorsas observed the next day. Lacroix notes that the authorities had in fact been planning to make this a great display for weeks, not for any motive of devotion, but 'to prove to the population that the installation of the oath-taking constitutional clergy had not diminished the splendour of the traditional religious ceremonies'.[58] Such was the zeal for conformity in the circumstances under which the processions finally took place that one man was arrested 'for having caused a scandal . . . having refused to remove his hat from upon his head, although invited to do so by the Guard on three different occasions, and having also made resistance to the Guard'.[59]

Some incidents can be examined in greater detail through the individual Sections' records. At 6 p.m. on the 21st in the Section du Palais-Royal two men were arrested for tearing down notices posted by the National Assembly. A master tailor testified 'that he had spoken to them about this reprehensible conduct, all the more so as he heard it said that they had already torn down several'. The culprits, a servant and a jeweller, refused to listen, and he and 'several Citizens' seized them while a friend went for the Guard. Under interrogation, the first offender explained that, 'having heard the word "kidnapping" inserted in the notice, he said that the king had not been kidnapped but had gone away of his own free will, and thus it was permissible to erase that word from the notice'. The second went further in his interpretation: 'that seeing the word "kidnapping" inserted in the notice, he was persuaded that these were further inflammatory notices and he had thought it right to suppress them, that indeed he had suppressed two, and was going on his way when the National Guard seized him'. This last phrase suggests that the tailor and his friends may have been in uniform off-duty, a common practice. The men's quite reasonable sentiment that the use of the term *enlèvement* was a falsehood, even an inflammatory one, passed for nothing, since

---

[56] APP, AB323:1237, Section des Gobelins, released 2 July; 1249, Section des Enfants-Rouges, released 25 June.

[57] APP, AB323:1289, 1270, 1312, 1292, 1296. All the culprits were released by the end of the month.

[58] Lacroix, *Actes*, iv. 552.

[59] APP, AB323:1300, Section des Lombards, 23 June. The detainee was a master tailor and managing tenant of a building, reduced to working in the public workshops. He was released on 30 June.

the authorities had another model of truth and order to pursue. As both men were domiciled, they were not imprisoned, but 'to make an example' they were put in the holding-cell at the Palais-Royal guardpost at the pleasure of the *commissaire*.[60]

On 22 June the Cordeliers Club posted a significant notice, in which they formally took up a republican position – '[The Society] can thus no longer conceal from itself [the fact] that royalty, hereditary royalty above all, is incompatible with liberty.'[61] One of the bill-posters was arrested by 'the public' in the Palais-Royal around 4.45 p.m., along with the activist François Robert, who was himself carrying a packet of the posters. A third man was detained for yelling 'that we had to pull them from the hands of the Guard', again after public outcry. The identity of the two unnamed men is unclear, as Robert's immensely verbose declaration monopolised the *procès-verbal*. He began by having 'le sieur' deleted from in front of his name, and persisted in discussing events in the 'Palais so-called Royal', after having listed the clubs and societies he belonged to, and noting his authorship of a work entitled 'Republicanism adapted to France', and of the motion which led to the notice. He went word-by-word through various exchanges in the open air, before and after his arrest, concluding with an account of events inside the guardpost which is both unintentionally amusing and very revealing:

> Reaching the guardpost, the insults recommenced with new force, a fat man with a flattened nose came up to him like a madman saying: 'you are an incendiary, a rogue, a bad subject, and f— you'll pay for it' [they use *tu* to him throughout]. This man wore the insignia of a captain of grenadiers of the National Guard: [Robert] answered him: 'I do not fear you, I fear no-one, neither group nor individual, do not think you can impose on me, I know my Rights as well as I do my Duties, I know only the Law, I have not violated it, and just so long as I do not violate it I shall walk with my head high and the attitude that befits a free man.' This speech produced an entirely other effect than that which one should expect, the captain seized [Robert] by the lapels: 'desist, Monsieur', [Robert] said to him, 'you should know how to respect me': 'respect you', they said, with one voice, 'you're a fine one you are, that we should respect you'; 'yes messieurs, respect, you must; and you broke the law when you apprehended me . . .' [Robert] was going to say *by the collar*, when the entire guardpost appeared beside themselves with rage; they had understood by the word *apprehend* that [Robert] meant that the guardpost feared him: [he] wished to explain his remark, but no, twenty or thirty armed men wanted to prove that they had some courage, and they said to him: 'wait, wait, we're going to prove to you whether we apprehend you': at the same moment, as a sabre was drawn out, [he] was assailed with punches, taken by the hair, hit in the stomach. . . .[62]

---

60 APP, AA84:270.
61 The full text is in Lacroix, *Actes*, v. 111–12.
62 APP, AA84:276–7, elision-marks in original text.

While one cannot help suspecting that he really was asking for it, it seems likely that he was going to get it anyway. Here we can see again the combination of insecurity and violence which made the Guard as much a volatile element as a force for order in social relations. Ordinary bourgeois armed and put in uniform, expected to deal not only with crime at saturation-levels, but also with political opposition of all shades, reacted without discipline to perceived threats. With this kind of conduct to judge them by, it is easy to see why they could be associated with hated *mouchards* and reactionary conspirators. It seems that Robert was not even making a formal complaint when he made this statement, as there is no attempt to record the names or even the unit of the Guards, and his indignation does not go so far as to ask that anything be done – perhaps he was merely acknowledging political realities on this point. He was allowed to go free, along with the two other men. The *commissaire* perhaps felt under pressure, since as soon as it was known that Robert had been arrested, the *Société fraternelle*, the Cordeliers, and the Section des Quatre-Nations all sent official delegations to ask for his release.[63]

While highlighting the Guard's excesses, it must also be pointed out that the population sometimes gave them reason to react aggressively, and to feel insecure. For example, a guardpost commander in the Section de la Place-Vendôme reported that at 10.30 on the morning of the 21st he had had to rescue 'an individual that the people wished to assassinate' from 'a considerable gathering on the Place Louis XV'. The apparent motive for the attack was simply that 'he had placed a blue riding-coat over his National Guard coat'. The final outcome, beyond that the man was saved, is not recorded; the details were 'dispatched to the Hôtel de Ville'.[64]

If this violence seems somewhat thoughtless, a more sophisticated, if little less hostile, relationship continued to develop between the Guard and the radicals of the popular societies. This is revealed by what happened to Jean-Baptiste Martin Chabrol, a sergeant of the St-Roch battalion, when, 'being in the Palais-Royal, he had been recognised as the one who had torn down the posters of the Société fraternelle . . . at that moment he was seized and arrested by individuals whose names he did not know, and at the same time a cry went up – "it's one of Lafayette's *mouchards*, string him up" '.[65]

Chabrol chose a conciliatory route, handing over two pistols to his captors, and although he claimed justification by order of the National Assembly, and asked to be taken to a guardpost or a Section, he offered no resistance as he was led instead to a meeting of the *Société fraternelle*. 'At the

---

63 APP, AA84:279–81. These are the credentials of the three delegations sent to Robert's aid.
64 APP, AA206:309.
65 APP, AA84:278. This is dated 29 June, but appears in the record between 22 and 23 June. *Babillard*, 23 June, indicates that there was trouble over an *affiche* of the *Société fraternelle* on the evening of the 22nd.

moment of his entry, when they were told that it was he who had torn the poster, he heard a general shout, "there's the *mouchard* of Lafayette and the Mayor".' Chabrol climbed onto a chair and unsuccessfully tried to justify himself to the hostile assembly, which was having none of it and eventually booed him from the room. They first decreed, as he reported, that he was 'unfit to wear the uniform of the nation' and that he would be denounced to the patriotic societies, the Sections and battalions, 'since he is a paid *mouchard* and enemy of the Constitution'.

What is most revealing in all of this is that before attempting to address the meeting, Chabrol had 'removed his sash and his epaulettes . . . in order to appear before the Society without any marks of distinction'. Not only, then, did this Guard sergeant recognise the radical patriots' distaste for such emblems, but he was willing to accommodate their prejudices in this regard. The radicals and the moderates found themselves sharing some symbols – most clearly the 'national coat [habit national]' – while being at loggerheads over others. Nor was it evidently a conflict of mutual incomprehension. Chabrol knew exactly why they disliked his insignia, and was prepared to take the initiative of removing them – under some pressure of circumstances, naturally, but without real peril. He allowed nearly twenty-four hours to pass before he made his declaration to the *commissaire*, suggesting that he had not fled from the scene in fear of his life, however much indignation he could summon over the 'menaces and insults' made to him.

None the less, in the general situation, fear of the population on the part of respectable citizens was a leading motif. Although the *Babillard* had reported initial calm after the royal flight, its issues of 23–5 June are filled with lurid recordings of dangerous talk from the Palais-Royal, the Tuileries, the Faubourgs, the cafés and elsewhere. By the late evening of the 22nd it was known that the king had been detained at Varennes, but the rumours of plots continued to redouble. On the 25th they were summarised thus:

A vague, but terrible ferment is spread throughout the capital; all citizens of any quality are alarmed: they fear the arrival of the king. Already it has been insinuated to the paid Guard companies that their pay is to be cut, but that they will be supported by the faubourg St-Antoine and the workers on charity if they wish to get justice for themselves. The faubourgs are in fact in turmoil; everyone says that the enemy powers are stirring them, and wish for the Guard to remain under arms to impose themselves on the madmen. It is said that Santerre is assailed by people who present themselves to him, and he receives everyone. The delirium has reached the height of raising the price of coin to 27 per cent; and, to embitter people's minds, the rumour has been spread that from the end of the month the assignats will no longer be valid. A thousand workers run through the streets in gangs. The market-women are assembling; their design is to fill the inns along the route of the king and queen, and not to go home until they have had satisfaction from them.[66]

66 *Babillard*, no. 21.

This was not the only paper to be reporting such things. Despite what we have seen of the relatively few cases of men detained for political outbursts, the *Feuille du Jour* reported on the 24th that 'many suspects are being arrested: the prisons are stuffed with them. Most of those taken in Paris are outsiders, they have been furnished with money and assignats'. The return of the king, of course, passed off without incident, except for some heckling of the queen outside the city limits. Some of the solemnity was by municipal order, but nevertheless a truly enormous crowd watched the royal cortège pass in digni-fied silence.[67] Regardless of the truth of this situation, it would seem that it had already been obscured in advance by rumour and suspicion. Radical agitation would accelerate in the weeks to come, as it became ever more clear that the authorities and the Assembly were planning to rehabilitate the king. The municipality and National Guard matched the pace with an elevation of suspicion, as both sides were primed for an explosive confrontation.

[67] See *Courrier*, 26 June, for a report of 30,000 Guards and a half-million crowd. S. Schama, *Citizens: a chronicle of the French Revolution*, New York 1989, 558, gives a reasonable account of the day.

7

The Constitution in the Balance: Events after the King's Return

The apparent calm which greeted the return of the king did not last long. The *Argus Patriote* reported that on 28 June 'a crowd of workers went . . . to the Abbaye, to ask that they should be given the Gardes-du-Corps who are confined there'.[1] This was not a rescue, but a lynch-mob, the dispersal of which required the summoning of the Guard by sounding the *générale*. It was in response to a 'false rumour' that the royal bodyguards, couriers for the Flight to Varennes, 'were to be set free by their comrades'.

Some smaller incidents, meanwhile, point to the continued high level of social and political tensions. On 26 June, at around 6.30 p.m., Simeon Charles François Vallée, a former master-painter and gilder, now a seller of pictures and prints, was seized by a group of citizens in the Palais-Royal for reading from a copy of the *Ami du Peuple*.[2] Two witnesses deposed that he had 'occasioned tumult' and had made 'several commentaries against Lafayette, the Lameths and several other deputies . . . as well as against M. Bailly'. He had been charging them with complicity in the king's flight and general perfidy. Three other witnesses confirmed the substance of this accusation.

Vallée said he had been passing on his way through the Palais-Royal when he had met 'around twenty women who were talking together and who asked him, "Hey brother, have you got today's Marat?" '. He had a copy in his pocket, and at their request read it out, but protested that this had lasted only 'half a quarter-hour' – not long enough therefore to have made the alleged 'commentaries'. After this time, 'the public stopped him, calling him a ragamuffin [va nus pieds], [and] he had been ill-treated by several individuals, arrested and handed over to the Guard'.

His answers and his social status secured his release with only a warning 'to be more circumspect in future'. However, Vallée returned to the Section *comité* on 29 June, apparently to get the address of the *commissaire* who had dealt with him, and while there launched into a complaint against Lafayette and Bailly. This scandalised the Guards present, and he was forced to be more explicit. He had two grievances. The first was that he was still owed 967 *livres* 10 *sous* by the municipality for premises he had provided for the salaried

---

1 *Argus Patriote*, no. 7, 30 June.
2 APP, AA84:295. It seems probable from the context that this was the 'Vallé' that *Babillard* noted as a supposed author of the *Ami du Peuple* at the time of the Santerre trial. If it was, then he may have been less innocent than he makes out in this case.

Guard from August 1789 to January 1791. Secondly, he had been burgled during the *Fête de la Fédération* of the previous July, while patriotically hosting two men from Rouen. Attempting to complain to the officers of the Section d'Henri-Quatre, where he lived, 'he had been verbally mistreated by M. Carle, commander of the battalion'. He had been unable to gain satisfaction 'From the Mayor or the commanding General'.[3]

These grievances suggest that Vallée was an active patriot, but had got on the wrong side of the municipal hierarchy. A week after this encounter, on 5 July, in the Section du Louvre, Vallée appears again, in an incident which suggests why this might be so. Florent Corps, merchant pork-butcher, was walking along rue de la Monnaye when he saw some prints on display. He particularly noted 'a caricature which represented the General as an elephant, and other personalities of our revolution there personified . . . he became enraged against the merchants who had so little patriotism that they sell objects so contrary to the new constitution'.[4] Another passer-by in Guard uniform told him that 'one must not idolise men', and that he thought Lafayette was treated as he deserved. This only enraged Corps further, and he tore up one print and threw another into the shop, telling the man he didn't think him fit to be a Guard. The latter vanished, leaving Corps to confront the irate shopkeeper, who turned out to be Vallée himself, and who 'called him a beggar, villain, thief and *mouchard*', despite his immediate offer to pay for the prints.

Vallée claimed to have seen Corps 'furtively grab two prints he had displayed before his door', and to have seized him 'in the name of the enjoyment of rights [la jouissance], possession and resistance to oppression'. His account was backed up by a 'sworn public functionary priest' who had been dining with him, and who noted that he saw Corps 'in defiance of the law which promises the security of the individual and of property' take the prints, and heard Vallée 'make use of the very expressions of the law borne in the declaration of rights, which permit any injured individual to resist oppression', after Corps's 'unconstitutional seizure'.

With all parties claiming to invoke the law, it is unclear just who called the Guard. The view that Vallée had been acting righteously towards a simple thief is somewhat overturned in the *commissaire*'s summing-up:

> in view of the above declarations, that the said Vallée sells unconstitutional prints, as personifying the first subjects of our revolution and potentially [thus] inflaming minds, and has moreover made in our presence several statements which do not denote a good patriot, that he even forgot himself in our secretariat so far as to say, upon seeing pass some gun-carriages driven by volunteers, that they will have need of cannon, we have thought it our duty to refer him to MM. the police administrators.

3 APP, AA84:297.
4 APP, AA182:286.

The latter officials released Vallée because of his domiciled status, but also observed that there had been no grounds for seizing Corps. Here as elsewhere, two interpretations of constitutionality and patriotism were brought into direct conflict, and the full weight of the administrative machine used to give victory to the more conservative version. Vallée was clearly incapable of keeping his opinions to himself, which may have led him to become branded as an opponent of the authorities, in the same way that men such as lieutenant Hion were victimised.[5]

Returning to the end of June, rumblings of discontent at the previous week's events could still be heard. A Breton doctor named Putod, rare in his open voicing of counter-revolutionary sentiments, was arrested on the 29th for declaiming in the Palais-Royal, 'we have sworn to be faithful to the nation, the law and the king, and above all to the king; I am Breton, we are forty thousand in my party, we shall defend him'. When someone remonstrated with him that the Assembly had now amended the oath to exclude the king, he went further: 'down, down with the decrees of the National Assembly, I know only the king'. Thus 'a crowd' of people of varying status seized him, but the outcome of his interrogation is missing from the record.[6]

Far more prevalent in public disturbances were those who saw the authorities and the court in league over this affair, however. On the afternoon of 27 June an adjunct *commissaire* and elector of the Section de la Place-Vendôme was sitting in a café with two other men, discussing 'in low voices' the departure of the king. A man 'who they were told was a cab-driver' intruded into the conversation 'and said loudly to them that if the king had fled via the Cour des Princes all the National Guards were rogues and bought with cash'. The elector told him 'that he should be more circumspect, not speak of the National Guard in this affair in bad terms, or speak of them in a respectful manner'. The 'invective' was repeated, however, and the encounter rapidly moved towards blows. The three men grabbed the cab-driver and would have brought him in, but they were set upon in the street 'by a multitude of persons' who helped him to escape. Among this group were another cab-driver who worked for the same carriage-hire merchant, and this employer's wife. The *commissaire* later discovered that the offender's name was Boucher, but he could not be tracked down.[7]

On 29 June, Joseph Mollier, 'seller of ribbons and bows in the streets', was imprisoned 'for having, mounted on a chair before the porte St-Denis, read before some three hundred persons a pamphlet entitled "Louis XVI and

---

5   Vallée seems to have remained marginally active throughout the Revolution: he was arrested as a *septembriseur* in germinal III, but acquitted. He does not seem to have held any responsible posts, but was reported as coming armed to Section assemblies, and once speaking of his readiness for 'patriotic expeditions'. As late as 1813 he was denounced for 'remarks against the emperor', but talk always seems to have outweighed action in his career: Soboul and Monnier, *Répertoire*, 120.

6   APP, AA84:306.

7   APP, AA206:325.

Antoinette treated as they deserve" '.[8] On the following day in the same Section, a doctor was arrested for having said various things about the Guard 'notably that they were villains who received six-*livre* ecus from those they were taking to prison', a notion which had sparked riot a year previously. A silver-worker was also detained 'for having said and cried aloud in the streets, the treason of M de Lafayette, which he denied'.[9]

To show that politics did not monopolise popular thoughts, there is the case of François Martin, domestic servant, detained on 30 June in the Section de la Place Louis XIV 'for having mistreated with blows of a stick one Porte, labourer, for being the comrade of an individual who sold money at ten per cent, the said Martin maintaining that he wished to sell it at 16 per cent'.[10] While such conflicts over the supply of money clearly continued to dog Parisians' lives, the major social drama of early July was the abolition of the public workshops. An investigation of their history will reveal yet another dimension of fear and suspicion in revolutionary Paris.

Rumours of the dissolution of the workshops had been abroad for several months, as it was well-known that their cost was ruinous to the municipality. A decision to shut them seems to have been taken in mid-May, although it was not immediately put into effect. None the less, some hints of this leaked out, as the *Feuille du Jour* reported on 23 May:

> A movement was greatly feared last Saturday [21 May]: the rumour had spread the previous day, that the directors were intending to dismiss a considerable number of workers attached to the public workshops. It is certain that this is planned, and that this determination causes fears of disturbance. The insurrectionaries [les insurrecteurs] will not let such a good occasion to agitate the capital escape.

Press discourse by this stage had long identified the public workshops as a site of actual or potential subversion and subornation. As early as April Marat had given this tale his own special treatment: 'For a long time the ministers and their agents in the provinces have drawn into the capital a crowd of indigents, the refuse of the army, and the scum of all the towns of the kingdom.' 'Agents of the old police . . . a crowd of *mouchards*' were running the workshops, excluding good patriots and recruiting others for a coming rising.[11] Three days later Marat published a letter from some workers, announcing that not all of them were bad, but going on to denounce various men employed as 'verifiers' as exactly the kind of *mouchards* he had talked about. On 27 May another letter began 'Be convinced, my dear friend, that almost all the workers occupied in the public workshops, are as patriotic, as their chiefs are aristocratic.' A list of some of the latter followed, along with other

8   APP, AB323:1359, Section de Ponceau.
9   APP, AB323:1372, 1373, both released 2 July, as was Mollier.
10 APP, AB323:1376, released with *passeport*, 4 July.
11 *Ami du Peuple*, no. 422, 7 Apr.

of their abuses, such as 'some *mouchards*' wives disguised as men who receive pay'.[12]

Marat's tone and his sweeping condemnation of the government were the only things which separated his view of the workshops from that of most of the press, as became evident once the workers were aroused by their final dismissal. The official order to dissolve the workshops was given on 16 June, but such was the reluctance of the workers to accept this that by 1 July the municipality was forced to reiterate its order in a decree:

> The *Corps municipal*, informed that, despite the orders given by the adminis-tration in execution of the law of 16 June last, which suppresses the works funded as assistance workshops, the workers employed on repairs to the quays and elsewhere have continued their work, which they have orders to halt; reit-erates to the said workers, in the name of the law, the order to cease their work.

The municipality warned that they would not be paid for work done since the 16th, and if they resisted legitimate authority, 'measures shall be taken against them as against disturbers of public order'.[13] The workers had not only been resisting by simply refusing to stop work. They had been gathering in large numbers on the Place Vendôme regularly over the previous weeks, and on 25 and 28 June petitions had been presented to the National Assembly in the name of more than 20,000 workers 'who have lost everything in favour of the Revolution, instructed of the decree which removes from them their only remaining resource'. On the 25th they came to 'offer their hearts, their arms, their faculties, and [to] beg you to suspend the execution of the decree which will make them starve to death'. On the 28th they proclaimed 'our love for your virtues and merit, and . . . our respect and entire submission to the just laws you have prescribed'. Their delegates swore in their name 'to be faithful to the nation, to love, respect and protect the laws decreed by the Assembly, to live free or die'. All the protestations were in vain, although on the 29th the municipality did put in hand, on a commercial basis, a small amount of general reconstruction work that might take up some of the excess work-force.[14]

With the toughening of policy on 1 July force was soon employed for the winding-up of the workshops. On 3 July Bailly wrote to Lafayette asking for infantry and cavalry to go to the Champ de Mars the next day for just this purpose, as some 2000 workers there 'are committing excesses against their inspectors', charged now with closing down the works. Bailly also noted that 'the Richelieu guardpost have already offered their services and would put themselves forward to assure order' – seeming to indicate a positive eagerness

---

12 Ibid. no. 425, 10 Apr.; no. 471, 27 May.
13 Lacroix, *Actes*, v. 223.
14 Ibid. v. 235–40.

on the part of some in the Guard to have done with this social menace.[15] On the same day, a high-level meeting was convened between National Assembly representatives of the *recherches*, *rapports* and *mendicité* committees, Bailly, Lafayette, the Directory of the *Département*, and police and public works officials. The most evident fruit of this was an explanatory *Notice to Citizens* published the same day, in which the current disturbances over the workshop closures were dismissed as 'a new pretext seized by the ill-willed to perturb the people and trouble their sensibility'. The *Notice* observed that

> The good citizens have complained for a long time against the establishment of the charity workshops; they lamented at the enormous sums of money supporting idleness and producing no useful work. At the start of the winter the number of workers had reached 32,000; through concern and research, the administration succeeded in reducing this to 20,000, although every day admitting new men. In this number were many outsiders . . . many earning a living elsewhere . . . a secret pact on the part of some chiefs favoured these abuses and cheated the surveillance of the administrators. Others still, whose labour was wanted in private concerns, in manufactories, preferred a lower wage in the public workshops.[16]

Every type of iniquity was thus poured on the heads of the poor workers of the public workshops, and if the municipality did not explicitly make the allegation that they were little more than a camp of brigands in the heart of the city, the journalists took to that task with gusto. The *Feuille du Jour* reported that on the night of 3 July 'workers from the assistance-workshops assembled outside the customs barriers with the aim of running to disarm the posts during the night. The surveillance of the National Guard broke up all these plans. Gatherings are frequent in the various districts of Paris'.[17] The same day, 5 July, Gorsas commented, in a rather convoluted example of suspicion:

> We said yesterday that . . . the constitutional committee had chosen the moment of Louis XVI's escape to dismiss the workers on the public workshops; we dare to announce today that all sorts of means are being employed to corrupt these unfortunates, in order to engage them to disrupt the festival of the translation of Voltaire [i.e. the installation of his remains in the Pantheon].

Even the representatives of the workers themselves, when they returned on 4 July for a third desperate plea to the Assembly, observed that 'hunger begins to work on them, and the counter-revolutionaries rejoice at this: they read only too much into their faces'.[18] The *Révolutions de Paris* commented on the

---

[15] Ibid. v. 260.
[16] Ibid. v. 252, 260–1.
[17] *Feuille du Jour*, 5 July.
[18] Lacroix, *Actes*, v. 262.

continued gatherings of the workers, and the violence with which the Guard had kept them under control:

> These assemblies, it is true, appear even more suspect, as within the crowd many white cockades have been noted; but, in any case, it is very dangerous to employ force. Either the workers are seduced, or they are not: if they are, it is not the blood of the unfortunate, blind instrument of traitors, that must flow, it is that of the corruptors. If they are not, is it with bayonets that one appeases the cries of indigence [la misère]?[19]

The simple answer to that question was in the affirmative, as far as the authorities were concerned, but overall, even in the comments of this radical journalist, we can see that 'la misère' gave grounds for suspicion. The workers had tried to enlist the popular societies in their cause, and indeed it is debatable whether the demonstrations and petitions up to 4 July were not at least partly orchestrated by the leadership or members of the clubs. Unfortunately, the patriotic journals and societies tended to have the same basic economic outlook as the authorities – that there was far more useful work the men could be doing elsewhere. In its *Notice* of 3 July the municipality had exhorted workers to go back to the land or into the army, and the radicals could only improve on this by suggesting that the surplus workers could be removed from Paris if funds were found for public-works projects such as canals and river-navigations.[20] On the 3rd the *Société du Point Central des Arts et Métiers*, Robert's attempt to unite patriotism and worker-solidarity, although petitioning the Assembly to suspend the decree of dissolution, stated that they sought this only to allow time for such provincial projects to be put in hand.[21] Even this petition stressed that they were concerned that 22,000 workers would gather on the 4th, and that 'various reports presage misfortune'. As it transpired, the starving workers seem to have drifted off into the economy, or into hunger, without any mass manifestations of wrath, although as we shall shortly see, not all went quietly.

Although the petitions of the public workshops' workers depicted them as honest patriots, one of the first things to emerge from a review of their encounters with the police is that this is not entirely a valid view. For example, on 24 February two brothers, Pierre and Louis Nostry, were arrested for insulting the Guard after one of their fellows had been nearly crushed by a carriage. Louis was a journeyman wigmaker who had been unemployed for ten months, and was working in the public workshops for twenty *sous* a day. His brother Pierre was a groom for a livery-stable, a job he had taken on a month before after eighteen months 'on the street'. With such an extended period of destitution behind him, it is perhaps unsurprising that, while

---

19 *Révolutions de Paris*, 2–9 July.
20 See, for example, Audouin's *Journal Universel*, 7 July, and the *Bouche de Fer*, 29 June, which at least proposed confiscating the civil list to fund such projects.
21 Lacroix, *Actes*, v. 259.

working with horses each morning, he also took the opportunity each day to catch the 1 p.m. roll-call at the Passy works. There, 'they ask no more than that from him', in return for fifteen *sous* a day from the municipal purse. He seemed to admit this quite openly, and the difference in the two wages suggests that municipal suspicions of co-operation between workers and foremen were well-founded.[22] As early as 10 January, a public workshops inspector had been arrested 'for corruption in his functions, in allowing himself to scratch out on the weekly sheets the zeros which state the absence of a sick worker'.[23]

Such criminal complicity was not the whole story of social relations in the public workshops, however. On 25 January a worker there was jailed for 'having insulted and injured le sieur Lachapelle his chief with several blows of a stick'. On 19 March another worker attacked both his foreman and the inspector, going on to vent more spleen on the Guard.[24] On 5 April an inspector was attacked by one man specifically because he 'reproached him for not working and only appearing at the roll-calls'. Not only did this worker insult and threaten the official, but he had 'sought to raise up the entire work-shop against him'. For this he was sentenced to three months in Bicêtre, followed by automatic expulsion from the city.[25] On the other end of the punitive scale, a worker who had 'insulted and threatened his workshop chief' on 7 April was released from La Force only two days later, vouched for by this same *chef*.[26]

Reviewing the arrests of public workshops' workers noted in the register of La Force from 1 January 1791 to their dissolution, we find a surprisingly low total of fifty-one individuals detained. It is possible that others were working there, but preferred to conceal the fact, but in general the police seem to have been very good at extracting details from their suspects. Compared to the legions of the unemployed who were not on relief and who litter the records with their acts of desperation, this seems to suggest that the social menace of the public workshops was far greater in the minds of the bourgeoisie than in reality. Of the fifty-one detentions, fifteen were for simple theft, three for assault, three for gambling, and two for threatening an admissions clerk of the workshops. Six were for disorders within the works, some of which we have just seen, and four were for generally suspect or criminal behaviour. The remaining nineteen, however, all involved some kind of resistance to the authorities or political statement.

This last category includes a number of cases we have already seen, such as

---

[22] APP, AA182:95. As was noted in ch. 6, the low status of these two did not prevent them voicing a 'political' rebuke of the Guard.

[23] APP, AB322:874. He was released on the 17th, but reported to the prosecutor.

[24] APP, AB322:978, sent to Tribunal, and AB323:16. In this latter case, the man was treated more leniently, being released after nine days in time to return to work.

[25] APP, AB323:245.

[26] APP, AB323:244.

the man threatening to have two nuns whipped for refusing to donate him tools, or the one who would not uncover for the Fête-Dieu procession on 23 June. Other cases hint at long-running disputes, such as that of Adrien Charles Hiver, a dismissed former salaried Guard of the Ste-Margueritte battalion. He sought to 'arouse the public' on 27 March against a sergeant of his old company, claiming that the latter had had him put in the Abbaye prison. The Abbaye was not the normal destination of petty offenders, so this may be some echo of the French Guards' mutiny of June 1789.[27]

Less ambiguously, public workshops' workers were to be found making radical statements at every turn of events in 1791. They were blamed *en masse* for the demolition of Vincennes, and one was arrested on 4 March for 'the most indecent remarks' against Lafayette on this subject. Incidents we have already noted at Easter, and around Santerre's court-case and the royal flight all involved these workers criticising the authorities, and Lafayette in particular.[28] At the height of the crisis over the abolition of the workshops, one André Le Blin insulted and threatened a sentry near the Tuileries on 3 July, going on to tear the epaulettes off a sergeant in the guardpost, and becoming so violent that the Guards broke two muskets while beating him into submission. Here again, the brutal over-reaction of the Guard emerges as apparent subversion produces disorder.[29]

It would probably be an exaggeration to say that radical opinions were particularly current in the public workshops, but they certainly seem to have been as evident there as in the general population. Another incident on 3 July indicates some of the feelings running at that moment. Jean Germain Devrin, a forty-year-old labourer, was arrested for saying, in a group on the Place Vendôme, 'that M. the Mayor was a beggar and a rogue and other invectives, that he must be hanged'. Moreover, 'if he was not armed at the moment, he would be when he wanted, that if blood was needed they would spill it, that one must win or die, and they would prefer to go to the Mayor's residence than elsewhere'. The Guard observed 'that those present applauded his words', and they arrested him when he was safely away from the group. One of the deposing Guards perhaps betrayed a slight sympathy for him, noting 'that the said individual said these things only because of the suppression of the public workshops'. He did however also note that Devrin had been making 'inflammatory speeches . . . standing on a chair' the previous day.

Devrin tried to deny any inflammatory remarks, but admitted that he had heard others speaking ill of Bailly, particularly because he had supposedly said that the surplus workers should 'put themselves on the streetcorners to run errands'. He reported that the gathering of workers on the Place Vendôme was due to a rumour 'that the National Assembly would have them given

27 APP, AB323:104, Section des Arcis. On the events of June 1789 see Godechot, *Bastille*, 150, 175–6, 183–4.
28 See pp. 111, 141, 151–2; APP, AB322:1431; AB323:427, 742, 1011, 1210.
29 APP, AB323:1420, Section des Tuileries.

work'. Devrin was there 'with his comrades awaiting their decision'. This may indicate that workers such as these had heard only indirectly of the petitioning taking place on their behalf. Devrin seems to have held similar views to those expressed in the petitions, saying 'if they want our blood here it is, it is for the interest of the nation', and that 'having no bread he could do nothing else but die'. He had served eleven years in the army, and may have been technically a deserter – 'he had a leave-certificate expired in October 1789', but he was enrolled in the Section de Bondy to leave for the frontiers. This patriotic admission did not save him from incarceration.[30]

With the fading away of this agitation, and as they awaited the outcome of the Assembly's negotiations with the king and queen, the citizens of Paris entered a brief interlude of strained tranquillity. The level of anxiety can be judged from two commentaries from either side of the moderate/radical divide. Audouin wrote on 6 July:

> I shall not end this issue, without warning the good citizens to always have to hand either their muskets, or sabres, or pikes, in a word their arms, in order to be ready at the first signal . . . for they manoeuvre, they cabal, they intrigue in every direction, to instigate a bloody quarrel in Paris, thanks to which they would pillage, burn, commit all sorts of horrors.[31]

'They' are of course the Revolution's enemies, whoever one might take them to be. On 8 July the *Feuille du Jour* reported the arrest of the eighteen journeymen hatters noted in an earlier chapter. Although the police record shows them being received without disorder into La Force, according to this account, they had been taken to the Abbaye, whereupon, 'an immense [crowd of] people assembled at the prison gates. They asked for the prisoners to be delivered to the multitude; one party wished to hang them, the other claimed to put them under its safeguard. The National Guard repulsed both parties, and the prisoners remained in the Abbaye'. What this indicates is unclear. The journalist, or the crowd, if one existed, may have confused this event with the continued detention of the Gardes-du-Corps noted above; in any case, it certainly shows a city in a state of high alarm.

The next day the same paper persisted with its concerns over the public workshops' workers – 'their number grows every day. M. Bailly appears to be the continual object of their threats and their resentment'. Furthermore, the lack of funds to see them safely out of the city meant that 'from whichever side we view the crisis we are in, it is frightful'. The *Feuille du Jour* had also reported on the 8th that 3,000 people had been brought to the Place Vendôme by a rumour that the king had fled again – 'it was a pretext for a

---

[30] APP, AA206:337, Section de la Place-Vendôme; AB323:1409, referred to Tribunal 9 July.
[31] *Journal Universel*, 6 July. One may suspect from the windiness of this passage that it was no more than a filler for the last page, but plenty of other editions had been 'filled' with less alarming pronouncements.

gathering, undone by prompt measures. The national cavalry cleared [nettoyé – literally 'cleaned'] the square in ten minutes'. Three days later it reported an attempt at a mass-meeting of the workers on the Champ de Mars, pre-empted by an occupation of the field with cavalry.[32]

As a decision on the fate of the king drew near, the authorities heightened their vigilance. One Louis George de St-Gilles had the temerity to remark to a deputy that a passing Guard's uniform 'was a storehouse of baton-blows', and proposed to demonstrate this with his own cane. He was sentenced to a year in Bicêtre after insulting the Police Tribunal with his 'affected' cries of 'Long live the king, the queen, the royal family'.[33] Such isolated outbursts of aristocratie no doubt helped to colour views of a continuing flow of more popular propos. A journeyman dyer was arrested on 11 July for 'inflammatory remarks against M. Lafayette and the National Guard' in the Section de l'Arsenal. A tribunal eventually decided that this offence was only worthy of an eight-day prison sentence, but he had remained in custody from his arrest until the hearing, on 7 September.[34] On the morning of 13 July, a cab-driver was arrested on the Place de Grève for saying that if he were arrested in the way the Guard were arresting a gambler on the square, 'he would have kicked the f—ing arses of the National Guard'. Those testifying against him included a horse-dealer, a cabinetmaker, a journeyman printer and a journeyman locksmith, once again showing the lack of a clear social divide in such incidents.[35]

On 14 July, as the Guard celebrated a relatively low-key Fête de la Fédération, several arrests were made around the city for insults and inflammatory comments to them. One, detained 'for having insulted M. Gaillot commander of the St-Victoire battalion' was a certain Jean Varlet, 'living from his property', who would appear to be the future Enragé leader.[36] Meanwhile, tensions were continuing to rise perceptibly. It was reported that Duport and d'André, architects of the evolving political compromise with the royal family, had been 'pursued with threats and invective by that populace suborned to yell against the king', upon leaving the Assembly on the 14th.[37] By the evening of 15 July news of the Assembly's decision to whitewash the king was abroad, and the guardpost on the Pont au Change had

---

32 Feuille du Jour, 8, 9, 11 July.
33 APP, AB324:1517, Section de Ponceau, 10 July, sentenced 16 July.
34 APP, AB324:1602.
35 APP, AA56:338, Section des Arcis. So indignant was the arrested man, Gabriel Tramu, about the charge, that he added in his own hand after his signature, 'do not recognise the depositions of those deposing against me'. He was released on his employer's avowal, 'in order not to harm the public service', as he had to drive to Clichy that day.
36 APP, AB324:1579, Section des Gobelins, released 15 July. Also, AB324:1580, Section de la Bonne Nouvelle, cab-driver and carriage-owner, fined six livres, 16 July; 1692, Section des Invalides, unidentified man, vouched for 20 July.
37 Feuille du Jour, 15 July. The 'high politics' of the post-Varennes settlement can be followed in Fitzsimmons, Remaking France, ch. iv.

posted an extra sentry 'to keep people moving who wanted to stop and talk, in order not to give rise to the smallest gathering'. As this sentry was telling two men who had stopped for just this reason to move on, a third arrived and 'found this bad, said that the hour was not unsuitable, that it was free for all men to talk where it suited them'. He was told to mind his own business, as the other two had moved on anyway, but he persisted. The sentry decided to detain him and took him by the collar, at which point the pervasive tension became manifest, as by his own admission the detainee had 'leapt on [the Guard's] musket in the fear that he would use the bayonet on him'.[38]

The offender was Jean-Baptiste Duclos, a bourgeois, which is probably why this incident resulted in no more than 'a lively reprimand' from the *commissaire*. Slightly earlier the same evening, two men had been arrested on the Boulevard du Temple for beating a drum, perhaps with the suspicion that this was a seditious false alarm. The men, however, had been 'inviting all the citizens to come to the Bastille to dance', as even the arresting Guard had to note. Nevertheless, a *bourgeois de Paris* had seized the hapless drummer, who turned out to be a clerk working for Palloy, the entrepreneur who had won the contract to demolish the Bastille. He had been touting for business on the great man's orders. His comrade was a journeyman mason from the site who had gone with him on Palloy's suggestion, 'believing that it would have no consequences'. They had borrowed the drum from a Guard drummer. 'Palloy, patriot', as he signed himself, arrived to vouch for them, and they and the drum were returned to their rightful places.[39]

If these two incidents seem to show the excesses of fear amongst the capital's population, others gave more cause for real alarm, like the tailor on the 15th who cried 'down with the bayonets and the cavalry' at the Opéra, or the 'Chief in the charity workshops' the next day who insulted the *commissaire* questioning him, after saying 'they needed a counter-revolution to put everything back in order because an innkeeper had not wanted to change a 25–*livre* note for him against [a bill of] 10 *sous*'.[40] In a world where all causes of popular disorder converged on counter-revolution, both these incidents were equally dangerous.

Meanwhile, as the *Feuille du Jour* noted, the 15th saw a mass presence at the Assembly – the deputies 'were besieged by an immense multitude which pressed around the doors. Insults and threats were addressed to the most estimable amongst the members'. This was apparently the result of the popular societies' first petition concerning the king, which, according to the *Argus Patriote*, had been 'sent READY-MADE' to the *Société fraternelle* – 'The supposed petitioners, who mostly can neither read nor write, having stopped

38 APP, AA56:340, Section des Arcis.
39 APP, AA239:94, Section du Temple.
40 APP, AB324:1629, Section de Bondy; 1637, Section des Invalides, both referred to Tribunal.

passers-by to get their signatures. . . . The guards have been doubled every-where because of this petition.'[41]

The petitioners met again the next day, and later on the afternoon of the 16th, a distiller and three 'engineers of the bridges and roads [authority]', passing down the rue St-Honoré, arrested a man 'dressed in a brown striped coat, bearing on his left arm a ribbon in the national colours, a similar ribbon on his chest, from which hung a medal'.[42] He was carrying a text entitled 'pet-ition to the National Assembly' and a further 'invitation to all citizens', and had been reading out this second document 'in a loud, intelligible voice'. It called on men, women and children 'having reached the age of Reason', to come to the Champ de Mars on the 17th to sign 'the said petition'. Here, we find the beginnings of the final clash between the radicals and the authori-ties, and within this *procès-verbal* a microcosm of the formation of revolu-tionary suspicions.

The concern aroused by this man's behaviour was compounded when one of the engineers recognised him as having been 'in the area of his Départe-ment and notably at Mantes [Seine-et-Oise] proclaiming and publishing various inflammatory papers'. This was sufficient for the *commissaire* of the Section de la Place-Vendôme to subject him to stern questioning, which he appeared to answer guilelessly. He was Jean-Jacques Larcher, aged twenty-three, a teacher, from Rouen by birth, and presently lodged in Paris. As he explained, he had been reading the *arrêté* of 'an Assembly of citizens at the Champ de Mars', this meeting having been formed to write a petition requesting the National Assembly to revoke its decree of the 15th 'on the person of Louis XVI', and the *arrêté* being an invitation for citizens to sign the completed work the next day 'towards two in the afternoon'. He could only name one other person who had been at the meeting, but added that deputa-tions from various societies were present, including the Jacobins, the *Société fraternelle* and the Cordeliers.

When the *commissaire* moved on to look at Larcher's circumstances, he revealed a history echoing the troubled times. Larcher was unemployed, living from the meagre remaining profits of a pamphlet he had had printed of his memorial oration to Mirabeau in Rouen's 'metropolitan church', given at Easter. He had been in Paris for twenty-two days, following up a verbal commission from a Rouen municipal officer to gather certificates from his previous places of work.[43] These had included the 'Brothers of the Christian Schools' in the rue de Lappe for two and a half years, six months in another

---

41 *Feuille du Jour*, 16 July; *Argus Patriote*, no. 12, 17 July. The popular societies' role in the events of this period can be followed in Bourdin, *Sociétés populaires*, ch. viii, esp. pp. 275–83 on the period 14–17 July. The unfolding of these events from the perspective of the munici-pality can be seen in Lacroix, *Actes*, v. 371–410.

42 APP, AA206:363–9.

43 From the context it must be strongly suspected that this officer had told Larcher to go away and not come back without better credentials.

convent at Auxerre, and various similar institutions for shorter periods. A young man of pronounced radical sympathies, therefore, who had taught in religious institutions for diminishing periods of time (two facts probably not unrelated), and now in Paris on uncertain business. All this was evidence to brand him a dangerous character, a label seemingly confirmed when his pockets were turned out, revealing two *Société fraternelle* tracts and a manuscript of the petition in question, along with a piece of paper saying 'we give powers to the said Larcher bearer and author of this petition to present it to the National Assembly, [signed] Larcher president, Groulon secretary, this 16 July the second year of liberty, done at the Champ de Mars'. The *commissaire* had made up his mind, the medallion Larcher was wearing was taken from him, and he was dispatched to La Force.[44]

Larcher had been detained with two other men, arrested for allegedly passing a hostile comment about the Guard as he was seized. Their identities would do nothing to improve his case. The first was a twenty-seven-year-old servant of the 'treasurer-general of monies', Damas Joseph Drecq. He admitted frankly to having said that 'beneath the coat of the National Guard there were some false brothers', a remark he felt was justified after one Guard had said that all the people who were making petitions deserved to be hanged. Was he one of these people, he was asked – no, he said. Why then, went on the *commissaire*, should he find the Guard's remark 'bad?'. Drecq replied 'that he thought that the public was authorised to make petitions by a decree of the National Assembly'. He had no 'interest' in the makers of petitions, however – he merely thought the remark wrong. He had been passing by and did not know either Larcher or the third man. A search revealed his membership card for the *Société fraternelle*, where he went 'fairly often'. Predictably, the next question was whether he had been paid to join the society, or had received money to 'support its views'. He retorted that on the contrary, it had cost him 24 *sous* for three months and 'he had never never received anything'. His master was to turn up and vouch for him, gaining his release, but not before the waters had been further muddied by the third detainee.

This man seems to have been no more than the passer-by to whom Drecq had addressed his comment, and claimed to have said nothing about the arrest, or about the Guard in general. None the less, the *commissaire* was suspicious. He had given his name as François Delatourat, aged forty, 'living from his property', lodged in Paris with a *restaurateur*, but having been in the city for eighteen years. While in the guardpost, he had tried to summon his wife with a note written on the back of a letter from his father, which had

---

44 Like the vast majority of those imprisoned for suspect activities from this point on, Larcher would be referred to the Tribunals, lingering in prison until the general amnesty marking the acceptance of the Constitution on 13 September: Lacroix, *Actes*, v. 486. This is the fate that should be assumed in all cases referred to from now on, unless specifically noted otherwise.

come into the hands of the *commissaire*. As was sharply observed from his father's signature, Delatourat was not his family name, and he explained that it was the name of 'a former fief' he had used since childhood. None the less, the *commissaire* pointed out, it was now illegal to pass under such an assumed identity. He responded to this reasonably enough, that having passed as Delatourat in Paris for eighteen years, to take on his 'true' name would be tantamount to adopting a false one.

Changing tack, the interrogation went on in search of culpable activities. He had not been to the Champ de Mars that day, but had passed by on the 15th 'for lack of anything to do'; 'he did nothing there', other than to have signed a petition 'which appeared very wise to him'. A search of his person revealed a pair of loaded pistols in his pocket, which he said was 'out of the ordinary' because he intended going to a dangerous place – the Champ de Mars, since 'he had been told that there was a great gathering of people, which might sometimes leave him surrounded by the ill-intentioned, and he had armed himself in fear of such events'. The arms merely added to the other suspicions about him, and he was sent to La Force. Were the *commissaire* inclined to believe what a great many of his fellow Parisians believed, including those who wrote the official account of the events of the next day, he could congratulate himself on laying hands on what looked like a conspiratorial cell: a shiftless provincial firebrand, the servant of a high official who criticised the Guard and belonged openly to a subversive assembly, and an aristocrat without a permanent address who carried loaded weapons, consorted with crowds and passed under an assumed name.

Furthermore, if he sought confirmation of suspicious activities around his Section, the *commissaire* had only to look to the next man the Guard brought in, barely a half-hour later. Two Guards had heard him on the Place Vendôme, saying that the nation was getting tired of the Assembly, 'that if the National Assembly continued further to give out f—ing decrees like yesterday's, then in a month it would be chased out by the people', and further that the Guard would not last much longer – three months at most. The man was detained overnight and hauled up first thing in the morning for questioning.

He was Anne Joseph La Porte, aged forty-seven, a law graduate, living in lodgings. He claimed to have said only that the decree of the 15th 'appeared not to be agreeable to everyone'. Following this, a Guard had told him he was an aristocrat in the pay of Bouillé, but he had not responded, and now said that the remark about the Guard's days being numbered was 'an atrocity' when it was quoted to him. He was further suspect for wearing a Guard uniform coat while not a member, and was accused of buying it illicitly. He responded indignantly, saying that it had been given to him by the Nation as a *Vainqueur de la Bastille*. He lacked certification of this status, but he had been one of the 'assailants', 'and he will be recognised by those that were there'. He lived, he said, 'by writings that he did for those to whom he was known', which led to questioning about any writings he might have done for the *Société fraternelle*, for example, or any mass petitions he might have had a hand in. All this he denied, having 'no knowledge' of the petitions of the 15th and 16th.

A search of his pockets revealed a sheet of paper containing an appeal to workers of the public workshops to meet on 1 July and ask the authorities 'with that submission, that prudence which marks out honest men', not to close down their workshops, but to offer 'the help we need, as much for our wives and children as for ourselves'. Given this document, La Porte had to admit that he had been enrolled in the workshops for some fifteen or sixteen months. The text's pathetic appeal did not stop it from contributing to suspicions about him, and he was sent to La Force.[45]

The records of La Force indicate that some detainees had gone beyond merely protesting the actions of the Assembly. Philippe Joseph Lefranc, 'former paid artilleryman, having his discharge four months before, ex-president and citizen of the Section du Théâtre-Français', was seized in the Section des Tuileries, 'for having formed a seditious gathering at the door of the National Assembly, having insulted M. Charles de Lameth, and having threatened an aide-de-camp, a salaried Guard, etc., with knife-blows'.[46] Meanwhile, at the Palais-Royal at 11 p.m. on the 16th, there was an almost unique instance of someone venting their spleen on the king personally. Pierre Toulin, an unemployed mathematics master, was in a group of people, where, as a witness observed, 'a great deal of alarm reigned' due to the nature of his words: 'that the decree of the National Assembly which declares that the king may not be tried was dangerous, that Louis XVI was an imbecile or a villain, he had to be dethroned or tried, he could not go against the will of the people who had flung him from the throne'.[47] He had added that the seven Assembly committees who had united to decide this issue were 'sold to our enemies and the foreign powers'. Toulin admitted that 'some rash expressions' may have escaped him, but denied that he had addressed the public with any 'intention'. He was sent to the Hôtel de Ville, and then to La Force.

The gatherings and agitation in the Palais-Royal continued into the small hours of the morning, reflecting the state of a city aroused by nearly a month of continued uncertainty over the place of the king in the Constitution, and by the sentiment of a significant minority that what had been decided among the political class was not in the interests of the people. Thousands who took that view would return to the Champ de Mars the following afternoon, and 6,000 people would sign a petition there to that effect. Some of them would pay for their opinions with their lives. Journals such as the *Babillard* had a predetermined view of the tumult, which they were happy to disseminate:

---

[45] APP, AA206:370.
[46] APP, AB324:1708, referred to *comité des recherches*, and thence to the Tribunal. If this was the behaviour of this Section's ex-president, it may help to explain why Théâtre-Français was one of only six Sections not to detain any seditionaries in July 1791.
[47] APP, AA85:68.

Palais-Royal [16 July]: Since the publication of the decree which declares that the king shall not be tried, the garden is covered with innumerable and very tumultuous groups: the wise notices which recall the people to the respect they owe to the law are torn down by brigands in rags and replaced by addresses from the *Société fraternelle*, in which every line breathes the spirit of sedition; from time to time, paid emissaries come to recruit for [the gathering on] the Champ de Mars, where credulous workers, playthings and victims of a few hundred factious men, swear to overturn the monarchy, to disobey the laws and to tear out the heart of the fatherland.[48]

The continued intensification of political awareness promoted by this extended crisis had reached the point where massive popular involvement was inevitable. Unfortunately, the governing discourse of suspicion also rendered it intolerable.

---

[48] *Babillard*, no. 34, 17 July. The address of the *Société fraternelle* referred to is probably one catalogued by the Bibliothèque nationale, but apparently missing. The text, however, was published in Gorsas's *Courrier* on 17 July, and is emphatic: 'Frenchmen, take up again the exercise of sovereign power, which so many of your mandatories abuse; forbid them, on pain of revocation, to pronounce upon the fate of Louis and his vile accomplices, before you have manifested your will on that subject.'

8

17 July 1791:
Massacre and Consternation

This account has now arrived at the point at which we began, the confused *journée* of 17 July. By now it will be apparent just how complex were the fields of political and cultural force surrounding that event. In the hours before and after the massacre, the police and National Guards detained a swathe of individuals, many, if not most, of whose offences were trivial. Their interrogations, however, illustrate three key facets of the political landscape of July 1791: the ability of individuals to critique the authorities in scathing fashion, the determination of the authorities to treat such dissent as illegitimate, factious and dangerous, and the desperate confusion of many 'good citizens' caught between these two positions.

Before the horror

At 1 a.m. on 17 July, the same sergeant Chabrol who had been humiliated at the *Société fraternelle* the previous month brought to the Palais-Royal *commissaire* a medical student (perhaps one of the Surgical Club), who had remarked to a group that it was 'abominable' to see patrols of Guards with fixed bayonets, and that 'all this would finish, that today they had made a deliberation at the Champ de la Fédération and tomorrow two hundred thousand men should gather at the field, and the National Guards had only to turn up'. When challenged on this by Chabrol, the student, Felix Nicolas Traisuel, claimed to have orders from the municipality allowing the meeting, despite Chabrol's objection that all gatherings had been banned. Concluding that the group Traiseul was in must be 'bad citizens', he seized him with the aid of two Guard officers.

Traisuel claimed that what he had meant was that the Guard would be met 'with fraternity' if they came to the meeting. He stated his belief that the meeting was 'following the invitation of the Jacobin Club authorised (supposedly) by the municipality', but it is not clear if the parenthesis is his or that of the *commissaire*. He had called out for 'patriots' to come forward and corroborate his explanation, but none had done so. He went on to complain that he had been seized by 'an individual out of uniform' – something we have seen before. Traiseul was, however, a member of the *Société fraternelle*, and he had placed enough suspicion upon himself to be put in the detention-cell at the Palais-Royal until his father could claim him. It seems that the latter did arrive, but by then 'he had escaped' and was not seen again by the authorities. One hopes he was not unfortunate enough to come to a bloody end in the day's events.[1]

The next *séditieux* of 17 July was also found in the Palais-Royal, an hour later at 2 a.m. The Guard noted that he had been arrested an hour before, but released 'at the request of several citizens'. He had, however, repeated his 'inflammatory speeches', leading two off-duty Guards to detain him again. He was Dominique Joseph Billot, *bourgeois de Paris*, and former mail-coach driver. He had been heard to say, 'why do they applaud the National Guard which behaves so badly?' Several Guards of various battalions had chased him outside the Palais, where he had claimed that on his first arrest he had been bayonetted in the face – a manifest untruth, they protested. Moreover, he had made a more serious political comment,

> That the Decree of the National Assembly which acquits the king would not stand, that he had dined [and presumably therefore discussed this issue] with individuals from various *départements*, that he answered that the said decree would not pass, and the National Guard must not be allowed to carry out such excesses against the citizens.[2]

Billot tried to cover himself regarding the words about the Guard, claiming to have asked only 'why are they applauding', but he was forthright in his radical opinion on the validity of the decree, stating that 'the eighty-three *départements* alone had the right to confirm it, which sentiment he would maintain to the last drop of his blood'. He was fortunately able to find a merchant dyer to vouch for him in the morning, and was released despite his trouble-making attitude.

No further incidents seem to have cropped up until 8 a.m. when a master jeweller and a master hatter brought a young man to the *commissaire* of the Section du Louvre. They had found him tearing down 'a notice posted on the corner of the rue St-Germain l'Auxerrois by the département relative to the decree issued yesterday evening which invites the French to vigilance'.[3]

The culprit was Claude Gros, aged twenty-one, pharmacy student. He claimed only to have 'put his finger on' the poster, which 'being too damp . . . had torn'. He was asked if he had been 'incited' to tear it by someone, and answered 'that having heard several individuals say that the word "king" must be suppressed from the said notice, he put his finger on it . . . but he was not incited by anyone'. The suspicions of the authorities were not wholly satisfied by this explanation, and the *commissaire* 'observed to him that it appeared that he was disposed to the annihilation of royalty, since one observes that the word "king" has been scratched out on the buttons on his coat. [He] answered that it was on the day of the king's departure that he had

---

1 APP, AA85:71.
2 APP, AA85:72.
3 APP, AA182:311.

been constrained to erase it'. Despite the evident desire of the authorities to forget the episode of the king's flight, such an obvious explanation had to be accepted, and Gros was allowed to go free after his master had testified 'that he was a good patriot'.

As the city began to come fully awake on this Sunday morning, the *colporteurs* were out plying their trade. The *commissaire* of the Section de la Place Louis XIV arrested one at 9 a.m. he had heard crying 'the great anger, the rage, the fury of the Père Duchesne against the infidel Louis Capet'. After reading the man's wares, he concluded that not only were they 'contrary to public tranquillity, to the respect due to royalty and to the principles decreed by the National Assembly', but also 'contained insults against the National Assembly, the public officers and against the National Guard'. He marched the man to the Hôtel de Ville, where no more is noted of him.[4]

By 10 a.m. *colporteurs* were causing disquiet in several areas. One was detained on the rue de Popincourt for crying 'the great treason of the Popincourt battalion commander', which he admitted to a Guard was not the title of any of his wares. 'This perfidy' brought him to the *commissaire*, where he confessed his crime, but said he had heard the substance of the accusation in 'all the areas he had passed'. The papers he had for sale included Audouin's *Journal Universel*, the *Journal de la Révolution* and two versions of the *Père Duchesne*. He was sent to La Force.[5] This hour also saw the arrest in the Section des Enfants-Rouges of the *colporteur* selling the pamphlet from the Imprimerie de Tremblay, whose gratuitously incendiary production we surveyed in an earlier chapter.

Tensions continued to rise throughout the morning. At 10.30 a.m. a Guard detachment was moving through the Place de Grève with some cannon when Pierre Sallandrous, a painter, said 'ah here's some of them already come to fire on the citizens'. A citizen told him to be quiet and he replied, 'is it that one is no longer free to speak one's mind?'. This 'repeated remark' led to his arrest. Sallandrous admitted the second comment, but claimed that, concerning the cannon, he had only said that if they were going to fire, his nearby home would be in danger. This was a fine point of distinction, and *commissaire* Deneux of the Section des Arcis was inclined to ignore

---

4 APP, AA167:61.
5 APP, AA219:11, Section de Popincourt. His name was Louis Auguste Vellière, aged thirty, a former port labourer. Lacroix, *Actes*, v. 355–9, clarifies the issue of the 'treason'. On the 14th the Battalion commander, Colin de Cancey, and the captain of the centre-company, Thouvenin, had been denounced to the Section committee for saying that Louis would be re-enthroned the next day, there would then be a massacre and that they would keep one of the first shots for a republican like Vialle, the Guard captain they spoke to, and who denounced them. They were detained, and an investigation reduced the *affaire* to an imprudent remark by Thouvenin to the effect that if the republicans won the day he would take to wearing a white cockade. Meanwhile, naturally, threats had been issued to lynch them and burn their houses, but any consequences of this were lost to view in the larger events of this time.

it, and to lock him up, the remarks being 'of a nature in the present circum-stances to excite an infinitely dangerous ferment'. However, one of Deneux's fellow Section *notables*, in attendance due to Sallandrous's domiciled status, felt that this status meant that he should be freed, which view prevailed, regardless of the danger of his comments.[6]

At 11 a.m. the grande rue du Faubourg St-Antoine saw two incidents. The first was a *colporteur* who allegedly 'cried out loud . . . here's the unworthy decree of the National Assembly, and made an invitation to the citizens to go to the Champ de Mars where there were twenty thousand citizens who would protest against this decree'. A *citoyen de Paris* seized him, and was joined by 'several passing citizens who were outraged at the insult to the National Assembly'. These were a master gardener, two glass-workers, a joiner and a printer, all of whom testified to the man's words.

The *colporteur*, Denis Billiette, formerly of the public workshops, claimed however to have only said 'here's the *Journal Universel*, here's twenty thou-sand citizens who will go to the Champ de Mars to protest', and that the man who had seized him denounced him to the passers-by, putting the words about the 'unworthy decree' into his mouth. Even so, he could not show where in Audouin's paper anything was written about 20,000 citizens, since he was illiterate, and admitted to having heard it from someone selling a different paper.

Hence subornation rose in the mind of the police, and he was 'interrogated as to whether someone had not led him to call out . . . to stir trouble in the Faubourg St-Antoine and persuade the citizens that the National Assembly might be wrong'. He denied this, but was sent to La Force for insulting the 'legislative body' and encouraging protest against 'the sovereign authority'.[7] In the liberal pluralist stage of the Revolution, it was still a crime to suggest that the National Assembly might have erred.

Further along the same street André Etienne Primery, aged twenty-one, marquetry-worker, was arrested by a group of citizens for 'having presented himself in various shops along the grande rue du Faubourg St-Antoine with a blank piece of paper in his hand on which he asked for signatures'. A joiner and two shop-boys explained to the *commissaire* that Primery had announced himself as a member of the 'society of the Halles and Liberty' and was looking for the Society of the Enemies of Despotism; not being able to find it he had resorted to asking for their signatures and their presence at the Champ de Mars that afternoon. The witnesses decided that he must have 'some suspect intentions' and took him in.

Primery explained that the *Société des Halles* had heard the previous

---

6 APP, AA56:346. Deneux had to be satisfied with reporting the matter to the mayor and the Police Department.

7 APP, AA173:24, Section de Montreuil. When searched, he was happy to show 'that he had nothing in the place where he put the papers he hid and which were forbidden', yet another example of the absurdity of policing this trade.

evening that there was to be a general rally of popular societies at the Porte St-Antoine at 10 a.m. Upon his arrival, 'the quantity of individuals not being consequent', he and some others had been sent to find the *Ennemis du Despotisme* and ask them to join them. He insisted 'that he had not demanded any signatures from anyone' in the street. None of this diminished the initial suspicion, however, and he was taken to the Hôtel de Ville, though his fate from that point on is not recorded.[8]

Meanwhile, suspicion was equally on display in the heart of the city, in the Section d'Henri Quatre. At 11 a.m. a Guard sergeant-major, leaving his house to go on duty, 'saw several people gathered together', and heard 'an individual repeat several times that the National Guard would lose France, and many other inflammatory and evil remarks'. He remonstrated with him, and tried to detain him at the same time, having to chase him in order to do so. In the guardpost the detainee repeated his central statement, and the Guard concluded 'that he had a premeditated design to sow discord and to excite the citizens to an uprising'.[9]

The individual was Etienne Boinet, aged thirty-one, a journeyman tailor. He admitted at once that 'I have been arrested because I said that it would be a misfortune that the National Guard should lose France.' He claimed, however, that this was just a reply to two passing women who had said 'that the National Guard was too good', whatever that may be taken to mean. Following up the Guard's suspicions, he was asked if he belonged to 'any society or club', and responded 'that he did not have the time, that he was at work from five in the morning until nine at night, that this fact might be attested to by all the people who live in the house where he resides'. Likewise he did not serve in the Guard because he was 'alone and that would prevent him from working'. However, although he was living in a furnished room at the moment, at a previous address (when presumably his circumstances were easier) 'he had formerly paid his guard' – that is, presumably, made the financial contribution of non-serving active citizens. With this evidence of (former) status to support his honesty, despite another witness testifying to his repeated use of the phrase 'the National Guard was losing France', he was released with a warning 'to be in future more circumspect in his remarks'.

This parade of minor incidents serves to show that, before any word of lynchings at Gros Caillou, the situation on 17 July was one of extreme tension and suspicion. In this variety of cases, we may speculate on who was genuinely an 'incendiary', if such a phrase has any meaning, and who was wrongly accused thanks to the over-active imagination of those who were inflamed, by the press and their own institutional assumptions, in an anti-radical direction. In any case, the scene was being set ever more precisely for massacre and repression, even as the radicals stirred themselves to ever

8 APP, AA220:142, Section des Quinze-Vingts.
9 APP, AA215:455.

greater heights of oratorical indignation. Two further incidents show this clearly.

At 12.30 p.m., three artillery volunteers, another Guard, a worker in the subsistence department and a student arrested a man on the Place de Grève. The first *canonier* testified that he had seen him eight days before, 'wearing some kind of uniform', making 'the most inflammatory remarks, saying that M de la fayette had to be hanged'. Just now he had seen him again, making a speech on the Place 'in a manner such as to enrage anyone, that he said that the king should be judged, and that today there were two parties, and the strongest would win'. The witness noted 'with pleasure' that the crowd listening 'told him he was wrong on everything', but still arrested him as 'infinitely suspect', particularly as the uniform he wore was the same as the Guard's except for the buttons. This, the witness thought, suggested an intention to 'render the patriotism of the National Guard suspect, giving it to be believed that it was divided into two parties'.

The suspect, Jean Allais, aged twenty-five, *sans état*, explained that he had been in the Netherlands, serving with the 'Brabançons', from where he had deserted. The uniform's original yellow facings had been 'absolutely worn out', so he had replaced them with blue ones he had bought. He had been in Paris for six months, and employed until recently in the Ste-Geneviève public workshops. He was happy to admit having said 'that the soldiers were there to go to the Champ de Mars in order to stop those there from signing to have the king judged', but protested that he had never said he wanted Lafayette hanged – 'nothing is more false'.

He may have been *sans état*, but he had a silver watch, the origins of which were probed by the *commissaire*. Allais said he had bought it recently, as he was living from the proceeds of the sale of 'some property at Noisy le sec' which he had come into at his majority on 6 May. He also offered an uncle, a clothes-dealer, to vouch for him. However, the *commissaire* was in no doubt as to what to do with him:

> considering to what extent this individual is guilty, who, wearing a coat almost identical to that of the Parisian National Guard, made inflammatory remarks . . . considering how far, for the public security and tranquillity, it is important to punish this orator severely, and that this man brought before us appears to belong to the unfortunately considerable number of the ill-willed who desire only trouble in order to make a *coup de main*.

He was sent to La Force with a recommendation that he immediately be interrogated further.[10]

At 1 p.m. in the Section d'Henri Quatre, a miniature-painter was passing down the rue de la Vieille Bouclerie, when 'he saw many people assembled,

10 APP, AA56:348, Section des Arcis. Perhaps Deneux was still aggrieved at having to release Sallandrous.

amidst whom were two individuals who were haranguing the public and who found it bad that the assembly at the Champ de Mars had been prevented yesterday, and that the National Assembly had decreed that no club or society might meet without a certificate'.[11] He spoke up at this point, saying 'that they had published a false fact, since such a decree did not exist'. One of the speakers responded 'with fury' that the municipality had, that very morning, posted an order to prohibit citizens assembling, 'and that it had put at the head of this order *Louis by the grace of God king of the French*'. At this, the painter answered 'that the order of which they surely spoke was to prevent the factious, those suborned people, from stirring up a rising amongst the people, and to make the laws respected'.

At this, the speaker and his comrade 'cried with fury that they wanted to enslave them, [but] they were ready to massacre all the Royalists', and one of them punched the painter in the stomach. A weaver, a surgeon and a tailor, all members of the Guard, and an apprentice joiner seized the two, and later confirmed the nature of their remarks and action. The culprits were Jean-Baptiste Morel, aged eighteen, and Pierre Joseph Henry, aged twenty-five, both *colporteurs*. Morel claimed to have met Henry only at the place where they were found, but Henry said 'that he had drunk all morning with his comrade'. Neither had funds that might indicate they had been suborned, but Morel had stocks of the *Orateur du Peuple*, Audouin's *Journal*, and a 'lettre du Père Duchesne'. They were sent to La Force. Their fate is unremarkable, but the interchange with the painter indicates just how confused ideas of who were patriots and who 'factieux' could be in practice. The painter who sparked the men's assault appeared to assume that anyone he was talking to would agree that the factious had to be kept down, not seeming to appreciate that others could view the situation in an entirely different light.

During the afternoon of 17 July no seditious individuals were detained in those Sections whose records survive – in the hours when the crowd on the Champ de Mars grew and the Guard marched to put them down, it seems everyone's attention was focused there. The records of La Force indicate that a certain Busse, 'nicknamed Glasson, former actor in Rouen' was arrested on the order of an *aide-major général* 'going to the Champ de Mars at noon at the head of a group, holding two women by the arm'. He was also found to be carrying a pair of pistols. His explanation in later interrogations was that he was leading the group to the Champ de Mars 'to engage those who were there to return, since there might be danger'.[12] Besides this, however, reactions waited on the news of the massacre, which reached the heart of the city by the early evening.[13]

---

11 APP, AA215:456.
12 APP, AB324:1889, referred to the Tribunal.
13 It should be noted here that apparently no effort was put into capturing and interrogating in any detail actual participants in the demonstration: a mere dozen men were

First reactions

At around 7 p.m. in the Section d'Henri-Quatre, the thirty-nine-year-old language-teacher Jean-Baptiste Rotondo was detained by a sentry as 'the cause of a gathering, by all appearances dangerous in the present circumstances'. The Guard said that he had picked him from among 'a group of people amassed outside the café Conti . . . making inflammatory speeches against the National Guard and the public good', saying, 'amongst other things, that the National Guard would not be able to prevent them from assembling'.[14]

Rotondo's account was rather different. He claimed to have just arrived at the café when he heard word that the martial law flag was being flown, and was merely standing at the door in a group of people 'unknown to him' when 'a National Guard whom he did not know came up and put his hand on his collar, asking him if he was M. Rotondo [he said yes] . . . he gripped him tighter and arrested him despite the persons present wishing to oppose this'. Rotondo also complained of 'ill-treatment', despite having offered no resistance – 'striking him in the head, causing him to bleed, which has stained the front of his shirt'. No further comment was made about this; after cursory questioning, the *commissaire* consulted with the Section President and two other Section *notables*, and sent Rotondo to the Police Department, along with a sealed packet of the papers he had been carrying.

The *commissaire* was summoned to the Abbaye prison on 29 July to witness the opening of this packet in the presence of Rotondo and Administrator Perron. The papers included three letters from Marat, a ticket to the Cordeliers' meeting of 10 July and a card from an unknown popular society – 'the society of support for liberty, of the Rights of Man and the Citizen'. There was also a receipt for 'notes confided to Sr Maillard bearing the sum of three hundred and twenty-six *livres*', and 'four pieces relative to the affair of Pierre Kabert nicknamed Louvain'.

Recalling that the Guard of the Section d'Henri-Quatre was commanded by Carle, whose feud with Stanislas Maillard dated from Rotondo's court appearance in late 1790, and had been exacerbated at the trial which led to the Kabert riot, Rotondo's arrest, and all these papers, may appear somehow significant. However, as the National Assembly's *comité des rapports* ordered Rotondo's release on 2 August, all they may signify is a continuing vendetta between men who viewed each other as members of determined opposing *partis*.

A rather more banal incident occurred at 7.30 p.m. outside the Royal

---

detained, but no record of their interrogation survives, and they were mostly released shortly thereafter, for reasons discussed in ch. 9.

14 APP, AA215:457.

Stables in the Section de la Place-Vendôme. Louis Honoré Grisel, aged twenty-three, a self-employed wigmaker, had been seen tearing down a poster headed 'Département of Paris, law'. He was seized by Claude Michel le Roy de Fontigny, major of the Veterans battalion, who had seen him from a window along with 'M. de Gouvion, major-general', second in command of the Parisian National Guard. Le Roy went down and grabbed Grisel, helped by a passer-by, and had heard several people say as he led him away, 'that's well done, it's that rogue who was making speeches in the Palais-Royal this morning'.

Grisel admitted tearing the poster, claiming that 'an individual having stirred him up to it, telling him that the National Assembly was making itself despotic, he had got so angry', that he tore it, saying 'that since this act was tyrannical, it must be torn down'. However, he went on, 'without departing from his principles which had directed him up to now in his speech, he still placed all his trust in the National Assembly'. Le Roy apparently pointed out the contradiction in this, and Grisel admitted on the spot 'that he had done wrong, and said then to he who asked the question and arrested him, that he had committed an involuntary act'. The authorities, however, were not inclined to treat it so lightly. Although he denied belonging to any 'Société Fraternelle' and said that the people who accused him of *motions* 'were lying about it', indignantly demanding that this should be recorded, Grisel was sent swiftly off to La Force.[15]

These last two incidents appear as appendices to the general tensions which had led to the massacre. As we saw in the introduction, Philippe Chapelle, himself a *Vainqueur de la Bastille* and former National Guard sergeant, was among the first to carry word of the massacre into central Paris. By around 8.30 p.m. in the same Pont-Neuf area, the news was spreading rapidly, and acquiring further interpretations. The 'controller at the department of clothing of the National Guard' reported

> that passing along the quai de l'horloge at the Palais he had heard a woman who said she came from the Champ de la Fédération say that they were firing on the citizens with artillery, and then an individual came forward and asked who had been seen to give that order, and another individual answered it was Lafayette, that villain Lafayette.

He followed this third person until he was within sight of several Guards, then had him arrested. Augustin Michel Riottot, journeyman goldsmith, frankly admitted the exchange – 'that having heard that they had fired on the public without flying the red flag he had answered that only a villain could have given such an order'. By this, he confirmed, he meant Lafayette. He went to the Conciergerie.[16] The idea that the Guard had opened fire without

[15] APP, AA206:376, released by 20 Sept. when reclaimed possessions.
[16] APP, AA215:461.

the proper declaration of martial law was to be one of the central charges in the public condemnation of the massacre voiced over the following days. It would be condemned wherever it was met as a vicious falsehood, but we shall see that matters were not as simple as that.

While the critics of the Guard might appear to exaggerate its perfidy in such accounts, the defenders of order were now, even more than before, zealously pouncing on any hint of social insubordination. At around 8 p.m., two 'citizens of Paris' and one of Bordeaux grabbed a man in the rue Royale, one of a group of four they reported as having said of the massacre 'that if they had met there they would have done much violence to the officers and the National Guards'. The one they detained was 'armed' with a black cane with a polished metal top. He was Pierre Forgon, aged eighteen, braidmaker, who said

> that he had only seen an officer of the National Guard, who was hitting with his sword all the persons who were protesting before him . . . being with three of his comrades [he] had found that extraordinary, he had said to his comrades that if they did the same to him he didn't know what he would have done; that in anger he might have defended himself.

He could only name one of his 'comrades', and was sent to La Force.[17]

Turmoil at nightfall

By 10 p.m. the news of the massacre, with attendant distortions, had spread across the city, parts of which were in ferment. As people gathered to discuss the events, they fell foul of martial law, which prohibited the Parisian habit of street-corner gatherings. In the Section de la Fontaine-Montmorency, the Guard dispersed one such *attroupement*, arresting a man 'wearing a blue coat' who was reported to have said that 'if they had hanged M. Lafayette all this would not have happened'. His words were denounced by two servants, one of a Guard division-major, the other of the 'First *aide-major* of the Parisian National Guard'. Jean-Baptiste Legris, clothes-merchant, explained simply that 'coming back from the Boulevard he had heard the remark and had repeated it'. He did not say why, preferring to emphasise that he had not been in the illegal gathering, but merely passing it at the time, and that he had not been 'engaged to make this remark'. He went to La Force none the less.[18]

At the same hour, a patrol in the Palais-Royal picked up Jean Etienne Wors, aged thirty-eight, journeyman farrier, for saying that 'if the laws were just he could obey them, which he cannot resolve to do because by his judgement they were not just'. His brief interrogation revealed only that he, too,

17 APP, AA206:375, Section de la Place-Vendôme.
18 APP, AA172:50.

had not been 'incited' to this speech and 'that he did not know the law'. He was held overnight, and vouched for in the morning by the secretary of the Section des Enfants-Rouges.[19] Meanwhile, outside on the rue St-Honoré, Jean Le Gueulx and Alexandre Caguy were each receiving their separate beatings for alarming the good citizens of the Guard with their protests and admonitions. Another, less dramatic, episode, but redolent of the sensibility of the Guard, took place not far away in the Section du Roule. A group of *chasseurs* brought in a man who had called to them 'by the right, ha! That's good, by the right forward march, ha!, aren't they bollocks! [comme ils sont les couillons!]'. He was a valet named Jean Pierre Huet, who claimed only to have said 'forward march!' This had been 'without intention and as he would say "bonjour mon ami" '. To La Force he went, trailing an unmentioned but definite hint of alcohol.[20]

Of all the cases from the evening of the 17th, perhaps the most revelatory is that with which we began our account, in the rue Tirechappe, and it is worth reviewing here at greater length. The incident arose from a disturbance between 9 and 10 p.m., caused by a group of journeyman shoemakers, which resulted a day later in the arrest of one of them – Louis Oré, 'nick- named Normand', aged thirty-one, originally from Calvados, and working for a master in the aforementioned street. After the trouble on the 17th, he had fled the scene, and returned in the morning to walk into a storm of neigh-bourhood wrath from which his arrest saved him. The record does not indi-cate how serious the threat was, however, but tempers were running high. On the 17th the Guard had detained four men over the incident, whom witnesses now agreed were innocent – for a start the detainees were jour-neyman tailors, not shoemakers – and they were released without even a note of their names being kept.[21]

The group that caused the disturbance had numbered a dozen or more, and was gathered on the doorstep of the house containing Oré's master's shop. Merely by their presence they were in breach of martial law regulations for *attroupements*, and they compounded the offence by insulting two salaried Guards who were passing, asking if they were coming from killing flies on the Champ de Mars, and remarking that that was all they were good for.[22] Since the Guards fled, the tone must have been menacing.

Next, a volunteer sergeant and a cavalryman passed by, and received a heavier barrage of insults, including the hefty political judgements we remarked on previously:

---

19 APP, AA85:83.
20 APP, AA224:92; AB324:1634, vouched for 18 July.
21 APP, AA153:9–15.
22 There is an obvious play on words between *mouche* [fly] and *mouchard*, and they were sometimes used interchangeably. From the second-hand reports here it is impossible to tell what exactly is meant by the phrase, but it was clearly not complimentary.

claiming that they came from the Champ de Mars, where they had committed horrors, that all the National Guard had assassinated people, that they were beggars, villains, that their uniforms must be torn off them and not one left alive. . . . [The Guard say] that it was outsiders spread through Paris who do ill, while it was the National Guard itself who did it, and was paid to do it.

The man who, with Oré, was accused of most of the *propos* said they should take cobblestones up in the houses and throw them out onto passing Guards, but Oré countered that it was better to lie in wait for them and stick the *bougres de cochons* in the stomach with knives when they left their houses. He went on to say that if the Parisians had the sense to follow his opinion, they would not leave a single one alive.

The witness who described this last outburst was Marie Anne Butot, *femme* Courroye, whose husband was a merchant clothes-dealer in the same street. She was present along with several other merchants and master artisans' wives and the forty-year-old servant of a draper, Mlle Marie Geneviève Raget. All of these gave overlapping and confirming testimony of the incident. When the shoemakers had done with the two Guards, who withdrew in search of support, they clashed verbally with these women, one of whom had spoken to a journeyman chandler, telling him to leave their bad company. The women were showered with sexual insults after remarking that the group were speaking ill of better men than themselves. One answer was that 'workers like them were better than a piles of sluts like them, and that they took the side of the bluecoats because they f—ed them'.

After a pause, they retracted the remark as it applied to the married women, but said it was meant for Mlle Raget, 'that damned slut Javote', as they called her. Raget said that at this point the men also threatened to kill her master – 'your fat pig, your fat belly, we'll choke him'. She also noted, along with Marie Lionnais, *femme* Houdain, another of the artisans' wives, Oré's remark about having searched for arms in July 1789, and seeing these turned against the people now.

Watching from the sidelines of this drama was François Girard, the journeyman chandler. A fourth woman, Mme Rennion, alleged that he had said to her 'here's a fine blow that the National Guard have just struck, it's premeditated murder'. She thereupon told him to shut up, that he was a fool and that if he didn't go back inside she would slap him. His widowed mistress called him in at this point. He was, we may note, twenty-seven, and in his deposition claimed to have inserted the crucial words 'they say' between the two phrases he admitted uttering.

Oré could add little detail in his interrogation, since he rested his defence on having been drunk at the time, and now remembering nothing of it. The *commissaire* was dogged in his attempts to trap him into an admission, but none was forthcoming. He named his partner as one Manceau, the only name he knew him by, a man who had been his workmate up to that day, but had now vanished. Oré could not say where he might be found, and nor could their master, Claude Cornullier. The latter could testify, however, that Oré was a good worker who had been with him for three years, but he could (or would) not vouch for him. This no doubt disconcerted Oré, since he had been at pains to point out that he was 'known in the neighbourhood' and that he had never had a complaint against him in all the time he had been in Paris. He claimed the insults against the women would never have left his mouth, although he did remember one woman saying something to him, but not what it was. This admission led into complexities, and he fell back on amnesia. He could not sign his name, and Cornullier's reluctance led to his imprisonment.

This incident seems to set up an opposition between the 'workers' and the female stalwarts of the artisan establishment, but against this we can place the denunciation we also saw in the introduction of the clearly formidable Dame Garpant, and her view that the authorities were suborning support. Equally interesting, but for different reasons, is another incident which occurred in the Section de la Fontaine de Grenelle, between the Invalides and the Quartier Latin. This was home in 1791 to Constance Evrard, whom George Rudé chose to quote in *The crowd in the French Revolution* to illustrate 'the influence [that radical agitation] might exert on . . . many ordinary Parisians'.[23] She was a twenty-three-year-old cook from the Vosges, in service with the 'former Treasurer of France M Foulard' at 64 rue de Grenelle. She was also a woman who already had an impressive record of activism. In January of that year she had visited the offices of the *Révolutions de Paris* to offer her condolences for the death of its editor, and went into print to praise its stance on tyrannicide – 'if you are short of a tyrannicide to make up the battalion, count on me; I would soon quit my woman's garb to take on that of a sex all of whose courage I feel in myself'. She would willingly shed her blood, she went on, to spill that of the 'enemies of the fatherland'.

In the *procès-verbal* it is noted that 'the Dame and the Demoiselle Léon were her only company' on a daily basis. The 'Demoiselle' is none other than Pauline Léon, her neighbour, but also one of the five so-called leaders of the *Enragés* in 1793 and founder in that year of the Society of Revolutionary Republican Women, which Evrard also joined. In the meantime she had joined Léon in the smashing of a bust of Lafayette in February 1791 at Fréron's house, and in a confrontation with some royal bodyguards on 21 June. She had been with the two others at the Champ de Mars on 17 July, and was also known to the *Babillard*, which mocked the radicalism of this trio several times, introducing them as 'the three ladies, who are paid to come . . . to rip apart MM Bailly, Lafayette, the National Assembly and all the holders of office'. It also noted their place of residence, when 'several citizens proposed to make them take a bath next Sunday' on 20 June.[24]

The actual events leading to Evrard's arrest were not particularly dignified.

---

[23] See Rudé, *Crowd*, 86–7, where he quotes from her interrogation.
[24] AA148:30; other information from Godineau, *Citoyennes tricoteuses*, 372. See also *Babil-*

Among the other inhabitants of 64 rue de Grenelle were the Mullers, a pharmacist and his wife who were evidently no friends of Evrard's trio. At 10 p.m. on the 17th, the three women got into a stand-up fight with Mme Muller, having seen her husband marching with his battalion. They returned home to confront her, calling him 'an assassin, an executioner, a scoundrel who killed everyone at the Champ de Mars', and threatened 'that within three days they would stab him'. Evrard then hit Mme Muller, but if she started the fight, she did not get the best of it, since M. Muller senior, a 'bourgeois of Metz' staying with his son, grabbed her by the throat, telling her he would strangle her for threatening his son, salting this with the customary designations of *garce*, *pute* and *salope*. A short time after, his son arrived to do much the same thing, before they all trooped off to the *commissaire*.

What is perhaps most remarkable in this case, aside from Evrard's fiery personality, is that after referral to the *Département de Police*, she was released the very next day. Despite her avowed radicalism, which included trips to the Cordeliers, readings of Marat and her regular presence at the Tuileries and the Palais-Royal, her age and three years service with a distinguished gentleman seem to have merited lax treatment. We must observe that Rudé's use of her as an example owes more to the strident tone of her words than to any typicality in her pattern of behaviour. Even if several members of popular societies did get arrested at this time, Evrard remains undoubtedly the one with the most dedicated radical history up to this point.

None the less, more typical incidents continued to arise throughout the city later into the evening. At the inner end of the rue St-Honoré, a man was brought to the *commissaire* of the Section de Mauconseil at 11 p.m. for having said 'that half the Guard were all f—ing beggars'. The witness, a M Picot, had asked him then if he was a Guard, 'he answered, that if he wore the uniform, he would tear it into a thousand pieces'. Picot noted that he was 'astonished at such remarks at a moment when [the city] is in danger through popular riots which multiply everywhere to excite the trouble that the National Guard hastens to disperse', and arrested the man. Two other witnesses confirmed the words that had left them 'scandalised'.

The detainee, one Jean Pierre Barthelemy Marchand, employee of the letter-post, did not try to deny his words, claiming only to have been 'moved to see passing by his eyes some corpses killed on the Champ de Mars'. He said also that he had seen a Guard who had torn his coat, driven 'beside himself' at these events. He mentioned what Picot had not, that in the course of his arrest 'he had received from Sr. Picot a kick in the rear'. In questioning him the *commissaire* noted the establishment view of the current activities of the Guard – 'they expose their lives for the common cause' – and justified

---

lard, no. 16, 20 June; no. 18, 22 June; no. 29, 12 July. It had the address as 74, but this would be easily misheard.

sending Marchand to La Force by observing that 'the fatherland is in danger ... the smallest contrary opinion may trouble public order'.[25]

The complexities of the various positions people could take up on the role of the Guard are well-illustrated by a case from the Section des Enfants-Rouges. At some time in the evening, a Guard lieutenant encountered a group of fifteen to twenty people in the street, among whom was Jean Langreny, a volunteer grenadier. It seems that opinion in the group was divided on the Champ de Mars *affaire*, but not heated. When, however, the officer moved on, Langreny came after him and said 'that up to now he had worn the National Guard uniform but that after what had happened today he would wear it no longer as the National Guard had acted too ill'. At this, the lieutenant had him arrested. Langreny fully admitted the exchange, but said that the comment was made 'effusively' and not 'with a bad intention', and also that the two of them were alone at the time (i.e. that he was not trying to stir trouble.) To establish his respectability, he said that he had been at Gros Caillou earlier in the evening, and had been robbed of several items of uniform by 'a group of people'.

With all this borne in mind, Langreny was released, but he fell under deeper suspicion two days later, when a fellow Guard named Marcellot reported that he suspected a grenadier of their battalion of having fired a shot at Lafayette on the Champ de Mars. There is no substantiation for this incident ever having occurred, but it was widely mentioned in accounts of the provocation leading to the general firing. Marcellot did not know this Guard's name, but had met him in a café on the morning of the 16th, where he had asked if Marcellot would be going to sign the petition against the 15 July decree. Marcellot had replied that he thought the decree just, and 'that he would be a f—er and a damned ball-brain [sacré couillardin] to go there'. The grenadier replied 'I don't give a f—, I'll go', but Marcellot thought he had then changed his mind after being told 'you are a triple *voulele* [volaille: fowl?] f—er of a *couillardin* if you go there' – a ciceronian political argument.

None the less, Marcellot now charged him with this crime, and after his description Langreny was recalled and questioned. He acknowledged the conversation, but unsurprisingly disclaimed any attack on Lafayette. He elaborated on his conduct on the 17th, saying he had been at Gros Caillou between 4 and 7 p.m., and had gone there principally to see the two men who had been lynched that morning. He had been with a friend and had spent most of the time in a café. As he left this café, a mob crying 'down with the National Guard' had set upon him, departing when the more tempting target of a cavalryman presented itself, although they did not catch the latter. For their pains, both Langreny and Marcellot were sent to La Force pending further inquiries, although each was freed within a few days. Later, on 10 August, they returned to the *commissaire* and made a retraction and apology,

25 APP, AA74:468.

in Marcellot's case, and a guarantee of no further action, in Langreny's. Whether this was a genuine resolution, or just an expedient end to the matter, is of course impossible to tell.[26]

Whatever the complications of this individual case, the prison record of detainees from Sections whose own records do not survive confirms the picture of widespread popular revulsion and inflammatory remarks we have been building up. Men were arrested in four other Sections for attacking the *affiches* of laws – a tailor in the Section des Innocents, a *colporteur* in the Section du Luxembourg, a woollen-worker in the Section des Lombards and an actor from the Théâtre-Français in the Section des Gravilliers.[27] Jean Denis Olivier was arrested in the Section de Bonne-Nouvelle for crying that 'the Guard was paid to use their sabres on people, as they had done at the Champ de Mars'. In the Section du Roi-de-Sicile Adelaïde Dufresne, *sans état*, seems to have put a female slant on events, saying that 'Marie Antoinette Queen of France was a slut and she wanted to hang her'. An errand-runner had 'stirred up a considerable number of individuals around him . . . made inflammatory remarks and . . . insulted the National Guard' in the Section de la Grange-Batellière.[28]

South of the river in the Section des Quatre-Nations, a journeyman boot-maker said 'very loudly, that M. Delafayette was a beggar and he had to be hanged'. A caster, a gilder and his wife said that 'all the cavalrymen were f—ing beggars and had to be strung up'. Again in this Section, another man was detained for unspecified 'inflammatory remarks against the National Guard'.[29] The same offence generated arrests in the Sections de la Place Louis XIV, de la Halle aux Bleds (two incidents), des Gravilliers, de la Place Royale and de Beaubourg. The culprits were a journeyman mason, a hair-dresser, a dressmaker, a journeyman candlemaker, a fruit-seller, a coachman and a former journeyman baker.[30]

Actual violence seems to have been relatively limited, although as we have seen, it would appear that in the immediate vicinity of the Champ de Mars, some attacks were made on the Guard. In the nearby Section de la Croix-Rouge, a wood-gilder was detained for disarming and mistreating a Guard as a member of a mob. Besides that, there was only a reported 'brawl

---

26 APP, AA157:140; AB324:1732, Langreny released 21 July, Marcellot 25 July.

27 APP, AB324:1653, 1675, 1715, 1640. The actor and the tailor were sentenced to 15 days' detention on 23 July, the other two, one of whom had publicly thrown the law in the gutter, the other having repeated his offence several times, were referred to the Tribunal.

28 APP, AB324:1643, 1672, 1678. The first was released with a warning on 20 July, the other two were referred to the Tribunal.

29 APP, AB324:1703, 1691, 1676. The first was vouched for on 21 July, the others were referred to the Tribunal.

30 APP, AB324:1630, 1635, 1661, 1684, 1685, 1698, 1704. Of these, one was simply released on 19 July, four were vouched for, and two were referred to the Tribunal, but no reasons are given for these differences.

[rixe]' in the Section de Ponceau for which a journeyman carpenter, who claimed to be in the Guard, though he could not give his unit, was arrested.[31]

One last case on the 17th, from the furthest corner of Paris from the Champ de Mars, firstly confirms the continuing aggression of the Guard, but also shows something of the distortion possible in the rapid oral transmission of news. The *commissaire* of the Section du Temple, making a round shortly after midnight, found in a guardpost two detainees, with a written report from a patrol: 'at half past eleven, a patrol from St-Martin, composed of twenty men . . . overheard a woman carrying a child, accompanied by a man who says he is her husband . . . the said woman said there go those villains who assassinated the Bourgeois, they are scoundrels; the said patrol quickly ran to them and seized them'. Catherine Nuller, wife of Nicolas Guillaume, porcelaine-sculptor, admitted having heard 'that a detachment of cavalry and one of customs-guards [chasseurs des barrières] had fired on the bourgeois', and that she had commented that 'they could only be villains to thus assassinate the bourgeois'. They were released, as she was a nursing mother.[32] Nuller's interpretation of the news into something like a rerun of the La Chapelle 'massacre' of January might have made it more comprehensible, and possibly less socially divisive. Over the next days, however, accounts would emerge in the public arena which emphasised precisely that feature of the events, and decisively challenged both official and journalistic attempts to erase such divisions.

---

[31] APP, AB324:1705, referred to Tribunal; 1701, released by Police Tribunal, 25 July.
[32] APP, AA239:96. The less said about the courage of twenty armed men confronting a dangerous nursing mother, the better.

9

After the Bloody Field: Commentaries, Narratives and Dissent

The initial perception of the journalist Gorsas, that the massacre signified a fundamental breach in the body politic, could not be sustained for long within the prevailing political climate. By 19 July as we saw, he would be driven to recant his initial suspicions of the Guard fulsomely, by which time other journals had already developed multiple levels in their arguments for an explanation based on brigandage. The *Feuille du Jour* was already taking the argument a stage further on that day: 'All appear convinced that the movements which agitate us are fomented by outside instigators.' Such 'missionaries of all the powers' apparently filled Paris, scattering gold and sowing discord. According to the *Patriote François* on the 20th, the affair was a plot among such agents, including 'the jew Ephraim . . . an emissary of Prussia', and various aristocratic officers, a plot concerning which the municipality and *comité des recherches* 'have a great deal of information'.

This more convoluted plot construction seems to have been peripheral to the general understanding of the massacre, but the theme of brigandage ran through all sides' accounts. To reiterate the extent to which this was true even of the radical press, here again is how Marat put it in his own fashion on the 20th:

> They had to use trickery, to make them appear to be so many mutineers, seditionaries, rebels, assassins. For that, a crowd of cut-throats, paid by Mottié, had taken the lead, and mixed with the citizens in a corner of the Champ de Mars. On the arrival of the cavalry and the armed henchmen, they threw stones at them, and fired a few blank pistol-shots at them.[1]

The *Révolutions de Paris*, appearing after nearly a week had passed, stayed with the same basic explanation, claiming first that brigands had committed the Gros Caillou murders, and continuing in the same vein:

> if force had been provoked by brigands, it is against the brigands that it needed to be used. But no, they knew them, the brigands, and had them left alone, and the blind fury of the National Guard was directed against the authors and subscribers of a petition which was going to have its effect, and which is a

---

1 *Ami du Peuple*, no. 524.

crime that the committees of the National Assembly find it impossible to pardon.[2]

As we shall see, the population at large would not be entirely convinced by this interpretation, particularly not in its more conservative forms, but the pursuit of possible brigands clearly figured among the police's preoccupations as they set about pacifying Paris. In one case at least, a patrol came up with some genuine *gens sans aveu* upon whom to foist their suspicions. Three men were dragged out at 2 a.m. on the 18th from the riverside booths in the Section du Louvre, where they had been asleep. One offered few grounds for suspicion, but the second, Joseph Cellier, an 'oil-maker . . . [now] seeking alms', admitted to having been on the Champ de Mars, not to protest, but to gamble, at which he had won fifty *sous*. That he should be sleeping rough with this sum in his pocket was suspicious to the *commissaire*, who found among Cellier's papers a certificate attesting to residence in Paris for five months, though he had already admitted arriving only in June. He also had a *passeport* dated for the 18th, suspicious at 2 a.m. on that same day. He even finally admitted that he had wanted to sign the petition 'but that being a minor he had not signed'.

The third man, François Vignier, an unemployed bootblack, admitted freely 'having been at the Champ de Mars, having eaten there some pears and sausage given to him by a National Guard, and having seen the start, that is all the wigmaker's workers and others come in order before the cannons . . . that the National Guard having been hit with some stones had fired and he fled'. All three were sent to La Force, Cellier noted as 'suspect', and Vignier as 'able to give information on the affair of the Champ de Mars'.[3]

The subject of the massacre was inevitably prominent in public discussions on 18 July. When Bernard Maltelte, shoemaker, and his worker Antoine Lhullier fell into conversation with a man outside their shop, Lhullier was provoked into saying 'that the Parisians were f—ers if they didn't disarm the National Guard today'. The *commissaire* of the Section de la Fontaine de Grenelle was prepared to release them with an injunction to future circumspection, as he was again an hour later when a forty-eight-year-old journeyman farrier admitted 'that he had said that among the National Guard there were surely some ill-intentioned men, and that they needed gallows to hang all of them'. In the latter case the testimony of several domiciled citizens that he was 'a very honest man' aided the decision.[4] This Section's *commissaire* was clearly a man who understood the virtues of leniency, as the

---

[2] *Révolutions de Paris*, 16–23 July, note the wishful thinking about the possible results of the petition.

[3] APP, AA182:312. The mention of 'wigmakers' workers' has intriguing possibilities, as Mercier observed (*Tableau*, 95) that these flour-covered 'merlans' were often student surgeons, funding their studies – the Surgical Club? This rather complicates Rudé's use of this quote as 'evidence of the attendance of wage-earners at the Champ de Mars': *Crowd*, 91.

[4] APP, AA148:32, 33, 7, 8 a.m.

Constance Evrard case has already illustrated. Given that the Fontaine de Grenelle area was immediately adjacent to the Section in which the massacre had occurred, such examples remind us that responses to these events very much depended on the individuals who held positions of authority, and on their propensity to either panic, or believe the tales of subversion circulating around them.

Less-considered responses increasingly became the rule as groups gathered to discuss the events of the 17th in the harsh light of day. Public discussion seems to have stirred up fierce sentiments in the open spaces of the city, and in general it was from working people that alternatives to the official explanation emerged. Such narratives centred upon accusations that the Guard had acted precipitately, firing without warning, according to some accounts without provocation, and clearing the field with great brutality, even with relish. Pierre Gery, aged seventeen, an unemployed journeyman goldsmith, gave a mild version of this. Having gone to the Champ de Mars 'out of curiosity' with his father, he reported in the Palais-Royal the next morning 'that yesterday there were . . . some cavalry that moved too quickly and there was not time to escape'. Even this was enough for an angry group of citizens to seize him.[5]

Near the café Conti, in the Pont-Neuf area, Nicolas Clement Goidou, aged thirty, shoemaker, made 'the most seditious remarks' as he recounted his tale of the massacre to a group. He had seen stones thrown at an officer, the Guard advancing, 'the public having cried out, down with the weapons, down with the red flag, down with martial law'. Next, 'the National Guard had opened fire . . . an individual had been killed next to him, which had revolted him . . . he then left peacefully'. All this remains within the boundaries of the official version of the event, but he went on to voice an opinion: 'that if the National Guard had grounded arms for only two minutes which would have given time for the good citizens to withdraw such misfortune would not have occurred, and that there was much indiscretion in the conduct of the National Guard'. When he was seized, he had further cried 'to me, my comrades', words which signified 'a coalition with the factious' to the *commissaire*. For this he was sent to La Force.[6]

Further divergence still from the official line came from Philippe Moisson, aged thirty-four, engraver, arrested in the Palais-Royal by several citizens for saying that martial law had not been proclaimed when the firing started. He indignantly supported his version of events: 'that he was a good enough citizen to have withdrawn if he had heard such a proclamation . . . he had been obliged to pass over the bodies of several persons to get himself out of danger, that since the beginning of the revolution, he had served as a

5 APP, AA85:105, vouched for by his father.
6 APP, AA215:462, Section d'Henri Quatre.

National Guard . . . that his conduct was irreproachable'. The *commissaire* allowed him to be vouched for.[7]

René Valentin Pierson, journeyman pewterer, was seized by several people with whom he had been talking near the rue de Montreuil guardpost, after they claimed he had said he saw the Guard fire without warning. Under questioning, on the other hand, Pierson claimed to have been at the Champ de Mars between 6 and 7 p.m. on the 17th, and to have heard there that a peaceful meeting had been authorised by 'nine *commissaires* from the municipality', but had retired when the red flag arrived. His account of the discussion that led to his arrest was contrived to suggest that he had been supporting the official view. The *commissaire* thought little of this, and Pierson was about to be imprisoned when his 'sincere repentance . . ., having promised never again to depart from the principles of the Constitution, for the maintenance of which he swears to die', earned him his release.[8]

The seizure of such individuals derives quite clearly from their attempts to circulate any alternative versions of the events which did not place the National Guard in a favourable light. Official and conservative discourses had already defined such approaches as seditious by their very nature – the entire Champ de Mars episode, in the words of the municipality, was the work of 'factious men', 'seditionaries' and 'brigands'. On the 18th itself, the National Assembly made the point clear beyond a doubt, specifically criminalising elements of 'sedition' in public discourse and printed publications. Speech likely to provoke riot or disorder was made punishable with three years' hard labour, and it was decreed that 'any cry against the National Guard or the public force in the performance of its duties, tending to make it lower or abandon its arms, is a cry of sedition and will be punished with imprisonment not exceeding two years'.[9]

Nevertheless, such alternative accounts could not immediately be suppressed, and as if it were not enough to have eye-witnesses contradicting the official story, second-hand versions also contributed to the uproar. Jean Vigoureux, aged twenty-eight, 'buckle-seller on the Pont Neuf', told a group in the Palais-Royal that he had just come back from exploring the site of the carnage, and 'that he had found it stained with blood and the trees riddled with bullets'. A witness denounced his lurid account of events:

> that the salaried Guard had not fired a shot, that the massacre was made by the Bourgeois . . . that a young man was shot and fell down, and getting up again they had run to him to fire another shot and he had been killed . . . that a grenadier from St-Marceau had killed his own pregnant wife, that in a word

[7] APP, AA85:97.
[8] APP, AA173:25, Section de Montreuil. Pierson had been picked up in a different Section for a seditious clash with the Guard at the time of the Flight to Varennes, but this *commissaire* could not have known that.
[9] See Lacroix, *Actes*, v. 400, 441.

the National Guard chased them from one side to drive them back on the points of bayonets.

The *commissaire* made Vigoureux explain these remarks, which he denounced as being 'as false as they were calumnious'. Vigoureux said that he himself had seen 'very much blood' and damaged trees on the field. Someone who had picked up the body of the 'young man' told him his tale, while a salaried *chasseur* had said that only the volunteers had fired. The rest was 'hear-say'. A 'doctor and National Guard' vouched for him, as an 'honest and peaceable man'.[10] The idea that only the *bourgeois* Guards had fired persisted – Marat on 29 July asked his readers to 'Give a thousand thanks to the brave, the generous French Guards, the [salaried] centre-companies, who did not fire on the citizens.'[11] On 2 August the *Argus Patriote* reported (perhaps in the light of Marat's comment) that this story was being spread around by 'the enemies of public tranquillity . . . to prepare means to trouble it again'.[12]

At this point it is worth turning to the accounts of the massacre collated by Albert Mathiez, many of which come from the testimony of Guard officers in the official judicial inquiry. This inquiry of course did not in any way set out to inculpate these figures, but rather sought to pursue the 'authors of the crimes and the chiefs of the riots [des chefs des émeutes]', as a municipal decree put it on the 18th.[13] From the various witnesses' testimony, Mathiez established the following clear account. As large bodies of National Guards approached the Champ de Mars from several directions the municipal representatives were behind them, unable to control events; as troops neared the crowd, a shot struck a cavalryman in the thigh – some said it was a pistol-shot from the crowd, while others said a musket had been fired accidentally. After this shot, the crowd began to throw stones at the Guard, and, as several senior officers agreed, 'the troops could not be contained'; no verbal proclamation of martial law was made to the crowd. Firing broke out from the Guard lines, and the crowd broke and fled, some towards the river, others towards the Invalides. The Guards broke ranks and pursued them with shots and bayonets.[14]

The testimony of Raphael Carle himself, notorious commander of the Henri Quatre battalion and of the second Division of the Guard, reveals a great deal about the relative responsibility of volunteers and professional Guards. 'Amongst the salaried grenadiers of the second Division', he stated, 'there were some who did not advance as quickly as [he] would have wanted.' They also let go a prisoner whom he put in their hands, and 'he heard

10 APP, AA85:88.
11 *Ami du Peuple*, no. 525, 29 July.
12 *Argus Patriote*, no. 16, 2 Aug. This of course may only be a retort to Marat, but the idea will turn up again in the mouths of the people: see p. 205 below.
13 Mathiez, *Club des Cordeliers*, 193.
14 Ibid. 146–7. The phrase directly quoted comes from the testimony of Jean-Baptiste Boyer, *aide-major* of the Saint-Marcel battalion. See also ibid. pp. 275–6.

amongst these grenadiers various mutterings and even saw some demonstrations against good order'.[15] Jean Charton, who commanded the first Division, was more graphic about the behaviour of some salaried Guards:

> he saw some salaried grenadiers of the second Division who were ill-treating a National Guard, that throwing himself amongst them, he pulled out that soldier, that then these grenadiers insulted him and one of them . . . uttered the most insulting remarks against the municipality, the headquarters and the chiefs of the National Guard, that he pushed his audacity so far as to raise his musket by the barrel to strike with the butt at [Charton]; as he withdrew . . . [the Guard] came at him again and this second time was stopped by M. Carle.[16]

Reviewed in this light, it is apparent that the witnesses who spoke out and were detained for their pains had a rather more accurate recollection of events on the field than the authorities were prepared to make public. Yet those who did speak made every effort to get their version across.

André Klauser, aged twenty-seven, hairdresser, informed a group in the Palais-Royal that 'martial law had not been published yesterday at the Champ de Mars and nevertheless they had assassinated a considerable quantity of citizens there without warning'.[17] Pierre Philippe Augustin Poitevin, aged sixteen, an unemployed journeyman goldsmith, was alleged to have said in 'a fairly considerable group' near the Louvre that 'the National Guard were beggars who had fired on their brothers and that they had even done so before the proclamation of martial law, that it was not true that stones had been thrown at the Guard before they fired'.[18] Pierre Fontolivé, aged seventeen, water-carrier, was seen by two Guard witnesses on the Place de Grève 'running from group to group, and saying loudly that the National Guard . . . at the Champ de Mars, had been most wrong, had acted very badly, that they had fired on the people without being provoked, even before martial law was proclaimed'. All Fontolivé would admit was having repeated what one of his friends had told him, that no-one threw any stones where he had been. He claimed to have actually offered his services to the local guardpost on the previous evening. Somehow the *commissaire* was persuaded of this and allowed him to go, noting none the less that the arrest had resulted from 'the zeal and

15 Ibid. 249–50.
16 Ibid. 280.
17 APP, AA85:93. Two self-defined 'patriot citizens' seized Klauser, and he proved far less able to justify himself than Vigoureux, at first trying to deny his speech, and only admitting that 'an old woman that he did not know' had told him she knew a woman who had been shot in the arm. He went to La Force.
18 APP, AA182:313, Section du Louvre. Poitevin admitted hearing both this and the opposite point of view in groups that day, but claimed to have said nothing himself. His uncle, with whom he lived, was allowed to vouch for him.

vigilance of the National Guard, always very laudable in such circumstances'.[19]

The trick of remorse and submission we saw used earlier by Pierson also
worked for another man, Jean-Baptiste Joseph Delvaux, stocking-maker, who
was overheard by a Guard saying that 'if we wanted we'd sweep out the Parisians in an instant, that they were all for the Republic at home, and that three
quarters of the merchants were beggars and villains'. He claimed 'that he was
only discussing remarks, which were indeed inflammatory, which had been
made in a group', and 'that his wish was always to be in submission to the
law'. He was warned and released.[20]

Two further cases illustrate the arbitrary fashion in which severity or leniency might be meted out to alleged seditionaries. Nicolas Joseph Raboulais,
aged twenty-eight, 'clerk to the consuls', had been in a gathering that had
begun to form on the quai du Louvre, and that several Guards were independ-
ently trying to persuade to disperse. A Guard accused him of criticising the
authorities' conduct on the 17th. Raboulais claimed to have been appealing
for calm and denouncing Danton, 'an impetuous and quick-tempered man',
for his part in the Champ de Mars petition, and claimed that the witness
against him must have heard him abusing a public figure and assumed much
more. Despite the fact that a subsequent witness observed that Raboulais had
previously been 'arrested in the Palais-Royal for various speeches', a long
recital of his patriotic motives won his release, aided no doubt by the 'chief
secretary to the consuls', who arrived to vouch for him.[21]

The encounter of François Louis Valentin, aged fifty-six, *sans état*, with the
authorities was more abrupt. He was picked up by the *commissaire* of the
Section de la Fontaine Montmorency for allegedly shouting 'down with the
motion' in a group on the rue St-Martin. Valentin denied this, or even having
been stopped in the group – just as he denied, of course, having been 'solicited by anyone to unite with his comrades and friends to trouble public
order'. None the less, the alleged shout was called an 'inflammatory remark',
and he was sent to La Force.[22] Valentin's status, or rather lack of it, may of
course make this severity less arbitrary than his actions seem to suggest.

This assumption is reinforced by the case of Sixte Leclerc, aged fifty, a
saddler, who was arrested for resisting the Guard clearing the Place de Grève
at 11 a.m. on the 18th. The Guard reported that he had said 'that if all those
on the square thought like him, they would not withdraw'. There is no elabo-
ration on what this meant, but Leclerc seems to have become hysterical when
he was arrested, crying 'that they were hanging him', and had apparently
'sought to destroy himself with his knife'. He explained this by saying 'that he
would as much like to be hanged as to be led away like a criminal by the

19 APP, AA137:179, Section de l'Hôtel de Ville.
20 APP, AA153:8, Section de l'Oratoire.
21 APP, AA157:144, Section des Enfants-Rouges.
22 APP, AA172:52.

Guard'. Although he denied uttering the phrase in question, when the matter of subornation was raised, he seemed to contradict himself, saying 'it was wholly by his own motivation and he had no evil design'. He was sent to La Force, with the comment that 'it appears essential to seize the persons of all these homeless vagabonds who seek to promote an uprising of the citizens against each other'. Since Leclerc had a job, a home and a master, this attitude seems a little unfair, but it does account for the harsh treatment of those who actually were *sans aveu*.[23]

The records of La Force offer less detail on the views and responses of detainees, but they leave little doubt but that the echoes of the massacre were heard across the city, and that the Guard in general was condemned by many of the common people. The Section des Quatre Nations was particularly troubled on this day. A journeyman mason, a hat-seller and a cane-seller made incendiary remarks from inside a cab; a journeyman locksmith made an 'inflammatory and insulting speech against the National Guard' and struck an officer; a cab-driver said the Guard were 'f—ing villains and rogues who had the baseness to fire on the people'; and a journeyman shoemaker made a similar speech in a bar.[24]

Other incendiaries included a journeyman carter in the Section de Ponceau who said the Guard 'were beggars because they had fired on the people'; a labourer in the Section des Tuileries who had 'wished to interfere with a drummer beating the alarm and upon his resistance had punched him'; a master joiner from the Section de Popincourt who said he 'shit on the blue coats'; and a vegetable-seller in the Section du Temple who similarly said 'that she wiped her backside with the grenadiers'.[25] In the Section de la Bonne-Nouvelle a journeyman marble-worker insulted passing Guard cavalry, while in the Luxembourg, a merchant perfumer and Guard in the Bonne-Nouvelle Battalion tore down a 'notice of the law, and threw it to the ground'.[26] In the Tuileries, a joiner made an 'inflammatory speech' from inside a cab, and followed this by 'acts of violence towards the National Guard whom he called the hangman of the nation'. In a bar in the Section du Jardin-des-Plantes, a 'former joiner' made remarks 'against MM. Bailly and Lafayette and against the National Guard, all on the subject of what had happened at the Champ de Mars'.[27]

By the next day, the 19th, it would seem that the outrage over the massacre was beginning to die down, or at least that fewer people were willing to voice their recriminations. The situation, however, had by no means

23 APP, AA137:176, Section de l'Hôtel de Ville.
24 APP, AB324:1722, 1730, 1754, 1755. All referred to the Tribunal except the locksmith, vouched for on 22 July.
25 APP, AB324:1700, 1659, 1656, 1743. All vouched for except the carter, referred to Tribunal.
26 APP, AB324:1665, vouched for 20 July; 1679, vouched for 21 July by a 'numerous deputation from his Section'.
27 APP, AB324:1682, 1731, both referred to the Tribunal.

become calm. One Guard witness related an incident in the Palais-Royal at 5.30 p.m.: 'he approached several groups, where speeches were being made, that in one of them he noticed a man who spoke to him about a fairly [illegible] motion, saying to him, "the National Guard, if they don't behave differently, we are ten thousand workers, we'll turn to the side of the Aristocrats, and then the blue coats will have a fine time" '. The Guard, 'in civilian dress', along with a 'comrade and . . . several irritated citizens', arrested the man. Thomas Tanquerey, aged thirty-six, joiner, said in his defence 'that he is in despair at what he said, and that if such a remark escaped him it was the effect of the wine . . . that he loved his fatherland, that he is French in his soul and he will defend the constitution at the peril of his life'. This seems to have had the desired effect, as the *commissaire* ordered him merely to be held for the rest of the evening to cool off, and even agreed to let him spend the night in the guardpost 'as a measure of economy', rather than have to find a room for the night.[28]

On a number of occasions like this, drink has already appeared as an alibi, and the proportion relying on this to alleviate their guilt or evil intent seems to have risen sharply from here on – probably as the sober saw the virtues of silence. Pierre Gabriel Menager, aged thirty-two, journeyman roofer, was unfortunate in running into the hardline Arcis *commissaire*. Even the patrol that arrested him at 10 p.m. noted he was 'a little drunk, it is true' when he 'allowed himself to cry, "down with the uniform" '. This 'insulting remark' got him into La Force, the *commissaire* grudgingly conceding that his drunkenness was worthy of recording for the administrators, though he personally gave it 'no regard'.[29] Earlier that day *commissaire* Deneux had put away another drunk, François Gougaud, journeyman tailor, who had walked from the Pont Notre-Dame to the Place de Grève saying repeatedly, 'Yes, Lafayette is a beggar, yes Bailly is a rogue, they should be hanged the both of them, it's they who have brought out the red flag, and had the unfortunates massacred at the Champ de Mars.' Little sense could be got out of him – he initially claimed 'that M. Lafayette is his cousin'. His landlady vouched for his normally impeccable character, but despite this note in his favour, he was sent to La Force.[30]

A stone-cutter working on the new church of the Madeleine also said 'that he had drunk' when asked to explain himself, but in this case there is more than just a random drunken remark at stake. The stone-cutter, François Corte, had remarked to a corporal who was passing through the site, 'you're going to kill someone, you're going to do like the others', adding later that 'the National Guard are f—ers'. The corporal, in seeking reinforcements to arrest the man, thought that the local guardpost held too few men to risk the operation 'in a location where there were at least two hundred workers', but

28 APP, AA85:117.
29 APP, AA56:352.
30 APP, AA56:353.

reinforced by 'several citizens passing on the Boulevard in uniform', they proved enough. In such concerns the state of high social tension once again makes itself clear. Although Corte was forced to admit that not only had he spoken to the corporal, but that the previous day he had told two teachers from the 'Christian schools' that the Guard were 'f—ers and they should watch out for themselves' because of what they had done, his ability to produce a second Guard corporal, who in this case was prepared to vouch for him, was enough to end the matter.[31] The Guard's fear of the unknown workers is tangible here, and yet in the end, the individual who was actually culpable evaded responsibility through the simple means of an *aveu*.

Moreover, not all the outbursts of the 19th were attributable to drink. Two Guards were conversing about martial law in the Palais-Royal at 11 a.m. when Jacques Marie Joux, polisher, interrupted their talk,

> saying that last Sunday during the supposed proclamation of martial law, he was himself on the Altar of the Fatherland, that martial law was not proclaimed, and none the less he had seen the National Guard surround and fire on the people, that he even saw the drummers, with their drums on their backs, draw their sabres and mount the Altar to chase off the people that were there.

He then added 'ironically', according to the witness, 'what then is your National Guard, and this loudly enough to gather his partisans'. As he thus imputes malice, the witness noted that Joux was disappointed, because the people around him said he was courting arrest. His arrogance in then saying 'that no-one could arrest him' provoked another man into saying he had seen Joux 'make . . . inflammatory speeches' on the Champ de Mars on the 17th, and elsewhere since. A clamour arose, and Joux was seized. Although he made some effort to distance himself from his remarks, the testimony of the official inquiry reveals that his version of events was indeed accurate, despite his later denials. The commander of the Saint-Marcel battalion observed that six men from his unit, including three drummers, had scattered the group of protestors on top of the *Autel*, an incident confirmed by the Division commander Charton.[32]

Earlier that morning, Charles Joseph Hoffmann, aged thirty-two, tailor, had been arrested on the Pont Neuf for looking at a sentry 'with a menacing air' and making 'some insults, the words of which [the sentry] had not heard'. This was after the sentry had told him to 'keep quiet' for saying 'that the

---

31 APP, AA206:378, Section de la Place-Vendôme.
32 APP, AA85:113. The *commissaire* took Joux point-by-point through his supposed account, and he responded at each point by retailing the official version of the course of events. Realising later that this still put him at the heart of the seditious gathering, he amended it to say he had been moving away when the first shots came, and had heard from others all about what followed. La Force received him forthwith. See Mathiez, *Club des Cordeliers*, 147.

National Guard did not look out for the citizens and fired on them like game'. Hoffmann explained that he had been talking with two or three strangers, discussing what they had heard about the Champ de Mars *affaire*. He had at that moment been saying 'that they had fired on some workers who were helping to pick up a man who had just been killed, thus they fired on the workers as if at game'. His remarks had all been without 'intention', for he was passing peaceably with his wife, and had no idea how he could have been construed as threatening the sentry. He was released, 'since Sr. Hoffmann is domiciled . . . [and] there was no cause for his arrest'.[33]

This is a case that seems to cross the line between a methodical crackdown and an hysterical over-reaction, as does the arrest of Antoine Olivier Harant, aged sixty-three, 'former verifier of customs on the entries of Paris'. He had been in the Palais-Royal as a patrol passed, and remarked, as several witnesses affirmed, 'there's a good f—ing guard'. One witness noted the addition 'they're in no condition to impose themselves'. The Guard was actually summoned by a twenty-five-year-old locksmith who had only heard the incident at second-hand. Harant explained that 'seeing the Palais-Royal in a state of frightful tumult, he desired to have an imposing guard there', and thought little enough of the passing patrol to say to himself, though out loud, the words with which he was charged. He was enjoined to circumspection and released.[34]

It seems fairly clear that there was indeed tumult in the Palais-Royal that day – the arrests of both Joux and Tanquerey show that frenetic public discussion was under way. Madeleine Lorin, aged thirty-three, kitchen-maid, was arrested there at 4 p.m. for 'very inflammatory remarks'. Two witnesses described her words, the first as that 'the king was very unfortunate and that the National Guard was wrong to act with such rigour towards him'. The second witness, however, thought the remark about the Guard had been about 'what it did regarding the people'. He at least had followed her and testified that she had repeated these words to a group of 'four other women like her', and upon this 'recidivism' he 'allowed himself to arrest her'. She denied all she was charged with, admitting only to have remarked in passing to two people 'who were talking about the king's flight . . . that it was very difficult to change small notes and that having presented one of a hundred *sous* a few days before to a baker to get bread she could not get any because the baker could not make change'. Despite contradicting the men who spoke against her, she was released with a warning.[35]

If Lorin seems to have been given the benefit of the doubt, as was Constance Evrard on the 17th, later in the evening of the 19th the full force of public opprobrium would fall on another woman. One witness, an innkeeper, explained:

33 APP, AA215:463, Section d'Henri Quatre, 8 a.m.
34 APP, AA85:118, 7 p.m.
35 APP, AA85:115.

that being in the Palais-Royal, several persons meeting him said, there's a woman who makes the most inflammatory remarks in various places, such as the Tuileries, the cour du Manege, place du Carrousel and the garden of the Palais-Royal . . . that also she said that the National Guard would not exist for much longer, that upon this [he] and several other witnesses seized this individual.

Another witness noted her last comment, and had often heard her speaking 'against all the authorities, excepting only in these factious remarks MM. Roberspierre [sic], Reubel, Petion, Danton and Marat'. Two other witnesses mentioned the Cordeliers Club among those she had been 'lauding very much', while a third noted that she had said 'that if she had been on the Altar of the Fatherland on Sunday evening she would not have got away and that it was shameful that the National Guard had fired on the patriots, and a thousand other remarks of a factious nature'.

She was Lallemande Loisy, aged forty-nine, 'doing nothing' and claiming to live from 600 *livres* in *rentes* 'for which she could produce the titles'. None the less, the next question was whether she was a 'macquerelle' – a procuress. She denied this, and all other comments, except making a remark on the Terrasse des Feuillants earlier that 'it was a very unhappy revolution and one no longer saw silver [i.e. coin, as opposed to assignats]'. This raises the point of whether it was somehow felt legitimate for women to comment on the economic situation, as Lorin claimed to have done. It served Loisy less well, however – she was 'more than suspect' and was sent to La Force. Here the suspicion continued, and on the 27th the Police Tribunal ordered an enquiry into her means of support. These were presumably verified, however, as she was released on 6 August.[36]

Lallemande Loisy seems to have been something of a minor celebrity in the world of *motionnaires*, since prior to her arrest 'Madame Lallemande' had been mentioned no less than five times by the *Babillard*. On 9 June it recorded her presence in the Tuileries gardens with 'several women' who 'vomited a thousand curses against all the authorities'. Two days later she was claiming personal knowledge that Lafayette 'would order fire against the patriots, as soon as against the aristocrats', if there had been trouble at the Santerre trial. In the same issue she is noted as a 'matrône de profession' – another term for a procuress. On 16 June she was reported in a group of 'shrews suborned by the enemies of the constitution', reading *libelles* on 'the disunity of the National Guard, insubordination, scorn of every type of authority'. On 23 June she had moved to the Palais-Royal, where she joined in calls to hang those who interfered with radical posters. On 5 July she seems to have been meeting more opposition – 'no longer daring to perorate against the authorities', she was now accompanied by an old woman who 'apostrophised against all the men in

36 APP, AA85:121; AB324:1783.

office'. However, it was observed that 'they were chased out of all the groups'.[37]

Her arrest on the 19th was reported with glee – 'it is good to observe that her courage abandoned her' in front of the *commissaire*, and 'she asked very quietly . . . if she would be hanged'. We have, of course, no evidence for the authenticity of this remark. When she reappeared in the Cour du Manège on 11 August the journalist marked this with an intimation of just who he thought she was. A bystander was reported as having taken her by the arm and warned her, 'if you did not have some obliging friends, you would be risking an unpleasant time: believe me, be wise, and don't compromise them'.[38]

With this suggestion of friends in high places, we are reminded yet again of the supposed link between popular agitation and court subornation. Two Guards must have had this in mind when someone reported to them on the evening of the 19th, that in a nearby café a man was not only making 'inflammatory speeches against the National Guard', but also 'sought to hoard wheat to make a party . . . said that he could not be arrested . . . [and] offered four *livres* ten *sous* per day' for unknown work. They seized a man, having burst into the café, and marched him out despite his insults. Jacques Barre, aged forty-two, miniature-painter, indignantly denied all these charges, and insisted that 'he had been arrested no doubt in place of another'. The *commissaire* showed no inclination to believe this, and Barre's admission that 'he had arrived in Paris from Brussels' six weeks before was underlined heavily in the *procès-verbal*.

Everything changed, however, when an 'office clerk from the Secretariat of M. Bailly mayor of Paris' appeared and vouched for Barre. This was presumably the son-in-law he claimed to be staying with. All the dark suspicions melted away, and he was released without further ado.[39] Once again the police seem to be assuming that anything was believable about a person *sans aveu*, but that once that crucial avowal is found, all must be well. In no instance does it appear in the records that further action was taken against a person for whom a domiciled male citizen was prepared to vouch. This may seem obvious, since the avowal would not be recorded if it was inoperative,

37 *Babillard*, nos 6, 8, 12, 19, 23 (break in publication, 26 June–3 July).
38 Ibid. nos 38, 21 July, and 59. Loisy reappeared in the pages of the *Babillard* on 17 October, when she was sighted on the Terrasse des Feuillants in the Tuileries, 'declaiming, as usual, against royal authority, the constituted powers and the person of the king'. Four days later the journal took the time to describe some of the leading 'paid agitators' at length. One of these was 'Mdme [*sic*] Lallemand, famous personage, interesting woman, on more than one count, a mare for every saddle, athlete for all comers. The job committed particularly to her care is to decry the National Guard and to render them odious to the non-armed citizens.' To which end she travels the city constantly retelling a venomous version of the events of the Champ de Mars. See ibid. no. 126, 17 Oct; no. 129, 21 Oct. What meaning such characterisations had is an open question.
39 APP, AA206:380, Section de la Place-Vendôme.

but the records sometimes break off, as here, in the midst of harsh interrogation, or even the committal process, when a claimant arrives. The simple fact
of producing such a person changed the authorities' entire view of a suspect.
The mythical outlaw elements of the population were on the outside of a
circle drawn with some very blunt strokes, within which all was well, and
outside of which almost anything was credible.

Beyond these various exercises in convoluted suspicions, resentment at
the events of the 17th continued to be felt and expressed more directly across
the city. A journeyman joiner in the Section de l'Arsenal said in a bar 'that
being on the Altar of the fatherland M. Delafayette had struck at him with a
sword and hit his hat, that he had riposted with stones and if he had not
killed him it was not his fault'. In three other Sections the Guard was accused
or insulted (in Beaubourg, by a servant, by a second-hand dealer in the
Section des Innocents, and in Notre-Dame by a casual labourer).[40]

Trouble continued south of the river. In the Section des Quatre Nations a
miniature-painter was detained for 'insulting remarks to the National Guard
in the middle of a gathering'. In the nearby Section des Gobelins, a journeyman starch-maker was found in possession of 'a carbine no. 1777
belonging to a National Guard cavalryman pulled from his horse on the
Champ de Mars'. A furbisher in the same Section had 'caused trouble' as he
read an 'announcement of an assembly' in the streets, making 'remarks
tending to compromise M. Acloque, commander of the St-Marcel battalion'.[41] Acloque had been prominent in recent events, in command of troops
who barred access to the Tuileries for a crowd of protestors on 15 July and, by
his own testimony, at the forefront of the troops of his battalion, who had
fired on and charged down stone-throwing protestors near the *Autel de la
Patrie*.[42]

After 19 July, however, the number of sedition-related arrests declined
dramatically, and of those who were detained between then and the end of
the month, many could blame their behaviour and remarks on overt inebria-

---

[40] APP, AB324:1702, 1723, 1745, 1768, casual labourer sentenced to one month in Bicêtre
by the Police Tribunal, 27 July, others referred to the Tribunal. Meanwhile, in the Section de
l'Hôtel de Ville, two journeyman masons and a third man who shared a surname with one of
them were arrested 'suspected of having thrown stones and fecal matter onto the National
Guard and moreover as suspect persons'. Much to the regret of the Guard, no doubt, they
had to be released on 23 July for lack of evidence: AB324:1664.

[41] APP, AB324:1734, 1724, 1697, furbisher released 22 July, others referred to Tribunal.

[42] Mathiez, *Club des Cordeliers*, 273–5, testimony of André-Arnoud Acloque, aged forty-
three, 'native of Paris, brewer and commander of the Saint-Marcel battalion'. See also (at
pp. 275–9) the several testimonies of members of the same battalion. Lafayette had ridden at
their side as they entered the field, and they had received the first volleys of stones, before
charging and mounting the steps of the *Autel*. Acloque (or Aclocque) had been prominent in
local politics in the Faubourg Saint-Marcel for some time, and had even published his
own, physiocratically-inclined, *cahier* in 1789. Garrioch, *Formation*, 141, calls it a 'stereo-
typical *bourgeois*' document, 'utilitarian, humanitarian, and stressing the benefits of free
trade'.

tion. One case that is less clear is that of Joseph Noiriel, aged twenty-seven, a public writer who slept in his booth near the Sainte-Chapelle. At 5 p.m. on 20 July, a group of Guards 'drinking a glass of wine . . . in an inn' heard him say 'that he would assassinate M. de la Fayette . . . and that M. de la Fayette had renewed . . . the Nancy affair'. One of them slapped him, and he told them 'that they were brave like the Regiment of Navarre, when they were four against one'. They arrested him.

Noiriel claimed he had been saying, hypothetically, that if Lafayette had acted as badly as Bouillé had at Nancy, he should hang, but that he had not judged the matter. He was sent to La Force. While on the general subject of alcohol, we should note that the corporal who deposed first, one Vernot, said he was drinking at the time of the incident, whereas two other witnesses described him as the leader of a patrol that came to arrest Noiriel. They may just be confused, or perhaps they had more scruples than Vernot about the fact that he had been drinking in a bar when he was 'on patrol'. No-one troubled to mention the slap Noiriel had received – he was, after all, just an 'undomiciled bad subject'.[43]

The next day, Sulpice Bernardet, chocolate-maker, insulted the Guard, the municipality and Lafayette in a bar, and admitted saying that he thought the Guard on the Champ de Mars could have surrounded and captured the *factieux* without firing. His plea of drunkenness was accepted after referral to the municipality, and he was released. A tobacco-shredder was less lucky, since his drinking led him to express republican sentiments, and then to hit a passing priest: he was imprisoned. A journeyman joiner who sang ribald songs about the Guard, Bailly and Lafayette was also locked up for his pains, despite pleading drunken amnesia.[44]

On the 22nd a coachwork joiner managed to get a *commissaire de section* to vouch for him after he had drunkenly insulted the Guard on the rue Montmartre, and on the 25th a drunken German-teacher claimed to be repeating the sentiments of the citizens of Le Havre when he insulted a patrol. He was vouched for by a furbisher.[45] On 30 July Jean Raimond Berthaud, porter at the Halls and song-seller, was less fortunate. He too claimed inebriation as a defence for having stopped outside a guardpost manned by salaried Guards and said 'that the volunteers who had fired on the Champ de Mars were f—ers, but that the [paid] soldiers were brave boys'. Upon this, they arrested him. A potter who commented on this was also taken in, but released. The *commissaire*, however, seems to have vented his spleen on Berthaud, 'since the peace of the neighbourhood is perpetually troubled by the threats made to the National Guard, and the spirit which wishes to establish itself in the

43 APP, AA182:324, Section du Louvre.
44 APP, AA182:326, Section du Louvre; AA157:147, Section des Enfants-Rouges; AA206:386, Section de la Place-Vendôme.
45 APP, AA167:65, Section de la Place Louis XIV; AA85:132, Section du Palais-Royal.

neighbourhood would have the fatal consequence of sowing division between those who should be united'. He sent him to La Force, as one who 'goes with the help of his songs spreading trouble and disorder'.[46]

By now we are deeply familiar with the harsh spirit in which Paris was policed. Of all the arrests for sedition after 19 July, in only one case is there a realistic possible threat to public order – a *colporteur* on 20 July who had been gathering a crowd by publicly reading and orating against the authorities in the rue de Charonne, Faubourg St-Antoine.[47] On the 24th a journeyman tailor was arrested for saying 'these damned — of bluecoats'. The blank may have been 'villains', as this is what he admitted to having said after the Guard had hit him with a musket-butt and knocked him down, for the crime of not clearing the way fast enough as they came through with a prisoner. For this crime, he went to La Force.[48] Paris seems to have been so heavily patrolled that perhaps only drink or such blatant provocation gave people the courage to speak out.

An extraordinary case from 29 July shows how far the suspicions of the Guard could be stretched. Two unemployed cooks were in a café in the Section du Roule when a number of 'citizen National Guards' heard one of them, Antoine Guillet, say that he was a Guard *chasseur*, and that on the night of the 17th 'he had on the orders of his superiors helped to carry a corpse to the Palais-Royal'. The citizens rounded on him – 'that deed was infamous . . . against the law . . . no superior would have given such an order', and the two were arrested. After Guillet retracted his claim that he was a Guard, his attempt to stick to his basic story grew increasingly suspicious, and he finished in La Force, although his companion was freed. Guillet ended up claiming that he had been one of four volunteers solicited by an officer after a corpse had been brought into the Palais-Royal, in order to move it away, but that he personally had declined after seeing the bloody state of the body. While there is nothing inherently implausible in this, the Guards clearly found the whole concept outrageous.[49]

Yet there is every reason to think it likely that just such an episode occurred that night. At 10 p.m. on the 17th Jean Le Gueulx had been arrested, as we saw in the introduction, distraught at the sight of a corpse carried 'by four urchins on some tree-branches coming from the side of the Palais-Royal'. Jean Marchand also claimed to have been 'moved' to see such

46 APP, AA198:62, Section de l'Observatoire. Note that this is on the Left Bank, where although few records survive, tension seems to have been particularly high. It is worth remarking here that, despite the prevalence of song in pre-revolutionary culture as a political/satirical device, not once in this period does an individual appear in the police record for actually singing sedition. See Isherwood, *Farce and fantasy*, esp. ch. i. For what the Revolution did with song see L. Mason, *Singing the French Revolution*, Ithaca 1996, esp. ch. ii.
47 APP, AA173:27, Section de Montreuil, sent to La Force.
48 APP, AA182:332, Section du Louvre.
49 APP, AA224:110.

corpses passing by at 11 p.m.[50] Furthermore, we have the report of a *commissaire de section* from the Palais-Royal, who at eleven that night, along with two other officials, supervised the identification and removal of 'an individual who had been brought from the Champ de la Fédération where he had been killed'. Not only did this involve moving him around the Palais, eventually putting him in a coach destined for the morgue, assisted by various 'porters' roped in from those present, but even at this stage the suspicion was strong that the body had been left there to cause trouble – it 'might excite some rumours' and 'had no doubt been brought from the Champ de la Fédération for that'.[51]

While we are on the subject of the actual victims of the massacre, recalling how vigorously the Guard put down any unofficial version of the events of the afternoon of the 17th, it is worth quoting the account of a man actually wounded in the charge of the Guard. Nicolas David, another unemployed cook, was found on the field and taken to the *commissaire* of the Section du Luxembourg. Somewhat disingenuously, he claimed to have been there to copy the inscriptions from the *Autel de la Patrie*:

at the approach of the troops, the persons near him had escaped, and [he], wishing to do the same, [but] finding himself face-to-face with the troops, had been knocked over by several volunteers of the National Guard and had received a small cut from a bayonet in his right side and another above his left eyebrow.

A doctor certified his wounds as 'very superficial' and he was apparently allowed to go, despite the lack of popular provocation in his account of the murderous, but rather inefficient, charge of the enflamed bourgeoisie.[52]

Assembling an overall picture of the Champ de Mars repression is not entirely possible. The patchy survival of the records of the Section police *commissaires*, a result of the destruction of the Prefecture during the Paris Commune of 1871, means that a full correlation between detainees arrested and those imprisoned cannot be obtained – for the latter, we have the full register of La Force prison, which was the destination of the vast majority, and which shows prisoners received from over 80 per cent of Sections for seditious offences at this time.[53] With only twenty-two of the forty-eight Sections' records surviving, and some of them fragmentary, some arrests have

---

50 APP, AA85:85; AA74:468 (Section de Mauconseil).
51 APP, AA85:76. It will be recalled from the introduction that Gorsas had labelled the carrying of bodies through the city as a factious device: *Courrier*, 19 July.
52 APP, AA166:14, 10 p.m., 17 July.
53 The only exceptions are the backwaters of the Champs-Elysées and the Île-St-Louis, the radical enclave of the Théâtre-Français, and the distant northern Faubourgs: Montmartre, Poissonnière, St-Denis.

been lost to us, since the surviving records indicate that at least as many were detained and released as were imprisoned.

The prison register indicates 105 detainees for the period 10–31 July with relevant offences, including thirty-seven on the 17th alone and twenty-four on the next day, twelve the day after and only four on the 20th – clearly Paris rapidly learnt to keep its head down under martial law. We have records of a further forty-eight non-imprisoned detainees among the ninety-six cases which survive from the Section records. As our examination of these cases has shown, arrests were often made for offences which cannot be clearly said to indicate radical sentiments, amounting more to merely saying the wrong thing at the wrong time. Nevertheless, while it is hard to assign a definite value to the social profile revealed by these cases, it remains worth stating.

The identities of these documented detainees range from five men who are simply *sans état*, through nine *colporteurs*, five of whom offer previous occupations lost in the economic crisis, eight domestic servants, and nine unskilled workers; on to thirty-four artisans who still describe themselves as journeymen, twenty-eight who merely give the title of the trade, and eight who call themselves merchant or master in a trade. At the upper end there are three teachers of various descriptions, three painters, two clerks, a postal employee, a student chemist and a student surgeon, a former mail-coach driver, an actor and three men living on private means. In addition, two were listed as volunteer grenadiers of the National Guard and, as we have noted, several detainees, some of whom were quite clearly given to radical expressions, recorded active or previous Guard membership along with another occupation. A breakdown according to age of the sixty-four cases for which there is information reveals that only seven detainees were under twenty, and fifteen between twenty and twenty-five. Eleven were in the twenty-six to thirty age-group, and eight between thirty-one and thirty-five. Fully fifteen were aged between thirty-six and forty, and eight were over forty, including two over sixty. Speaking out, then, was not the preserve of impetuous youth.

The identities of the 180 people who acted as witnesses against these detainees form a significant comparison. Excluding those on-duty Guards who were evidently acting only as formal 'arresting officers', this sample comprises twenty-two who designate themselves simply as citizens, bourgeois or similar formulae; thirty who were at the mastership level in a trade, or independent merchants; thirty-eight who gave a trade but did not specify their social level; fourteen who were at the 'wage-earning' end of the trades – journeymen or workers, plus two apprentices; and seven servants, including one female. There were also three artisans' wives, a female innkeeper, a student, a church singer, a merchant's son and an eleven-year-old boy. Within the bourgeois category, two noted that they were also Guards, as did seven of the masters and eleven in the non-specific trade group. No less than sixty-one witnesses felt that their identity was adequately expressed by the fact that they were Guard volunteers, and gave no other social status. Thus, while a certain social disjuncture between this sample and that of the detainees is evident, it is a matter of differently-weighted hierarchies rather than of two distinct social groups.

Our commentary on the social distribution of witnesses and detainees from this period can be carried further by a comparison with the sectional personnel of the Year II inventoried by Albert Soboul and Raymonde Monnier. From this summary of the surviving records, it emerges that while none of our sample of seditionaries from the Champ de Mars episode appears to have been a later *sans-culotte* (or at least one who made it into the records), some eight of the 180 witnesses can be matched with reasonable certainty to their later identities as *sectionnaires*. These are:

Jacques Sulpice Carré, who appears on 18 July 1791, a National Guard clearing the Place de Grève, describing himself as 'former sub-lieutenant of the volunteer chasseur company of the Popincourt Battalion'. In the Year II he was a gunsmith with five employees and a militant in the Section de Popincourt, having been wounded on 10 August 1792, and was later arrested for involvement in the prairial days of the Year III.[54]

Etienne Cochois, weaver and National Guard, witnessed at 1 p.m. on 17 July the seditious remarks of Morel and Henry in the Section d'Henri Quatre. He was president of the revolutionary committee of this Section in frimaire II, and was arrested in floréal as an *hébertiste*. It was noted that he had fought on 14 July and 10 August, been a member of the Commune of 10 August, been in the *journée* of 31 May and served as an assessor for the local magistrate and as a captain in the Section's armed force. Released in prairial, in Year III he was persecuted as a *septembriseur*.[55]

Antoine Pierre Poupart witnessed Jean Allais's seditious outburst in the Section des Arcis on 17 July, and was at that time a volunteer corporal in the local artillery company. In the Year II he had become captain of the same unit, and was arrested on 14 thermidor, suspect for having been seen shaking the hand of the robespierrist commander Hanriot on the night of the 9th. Although released, he was still being 'noted as dangerous' in Year IX.[56]

Mathieu Tamisier, dyer and volunteer grenadier, arrested a drunk who insulted the Guard on 22 July in the Section des Arcis. He was later an elector in 1792, and a member of the local popular society's purification commission. In the Year III he was hunted down for participation in the prairial days and for a massacre of prisoners at Versailles.[57]

---

54 Soboul and Monnier, *Répertoire*, 279. See also APP, AA137:176, Section de l'Hôtel-de-Ville.
55 Soboul and Monnier, *Répertoire*, 417; APP, AA 215:456, Section d'Henri Quatre.
56 Soboul and Monnier, *Répertoire*, 229; APP, AA56:348, Section des Arcis.
57 Soboul and Monnier, *Répertoire*, 231; APP, AA56:360, Section des Arcis.

Jacques Boucher, sergeant of salaried Guards, testified in the Section de l'Observatoire on 30 July against a drunk who had praised them in comparison to the bourgeois. A man of this name from this Section served three months in detention in the Year III for unspecified political offences, and was rehabilitated in Year IV.[58]

Jean Baptiste Fleury, engraver and citizen-soldier, arrested a man on 18 July in the Section d'Henri Quatre for telling his version of the Champ de Mars events. He later served on the revolutionary committee of the Section des Gardes-Françaises (Oratoire), and was also a clerk in the war office. He was arrested in Year III, accused of participation in preparations for the *journée* of 31 May and of being a leader of his sectional popular society, although he was later released.[59]

Sebastien Bolback, a corporal of salaried Guards in the Place-Vendôme Battalion, arrested a stoneworker on 19 July for his derogatory comments on the Guard. A Bolbach was arrested in this Section in prairial III as a militant.[60]

Jean Fleury, finally, a locksmith in the rue des Gravilliers, who involved himself in an arrest in the Palais-Royal, had become a gunsmith by the Year II, and had presided over the general assembly of the Section des Gravilliers. He was arrested for participation in the germinal troubles in Year III, and further accused of being a self-confessed *septembriseur* and a leader of the rue du Vert-Bois society.[61]

Several other witnesses could be matched more tentatively to later *sans-culottes* by name or location, but this sample of eight are sufficient to illustrate the point that the men of that era could not all honestly claim a spotless record of advanced opinions.[62] While it is clearly impossible to establish a direct correlation between the forces of order in 1791 and the *sans-culottes* on

---

[58] Soboul and Monnier, *Répertoire*, 510; APP, AA198:62, Section de l'Observatoire.

[59] Soboul and Monnier, *Répertoire*, 125–6; APP, AA215:462, Section d'Henri-Quatre. His address, rue des Mauvaises Paroles, also matches.

[60] Soboul and Monnier, *Répertoire*, 87; APP, AA206:378, Section de la Place-Vendôme.

[61] Soboul and Monnier, *Répertoire*, 319–20; APP, AA85:118, Section du Palais-Royal.

[62] Tentative matches include Pierre Joannis, who testified against Constance Evrard in the Section de la Fontaine-de-Grenelle, and a Joannet who served on the revolutionary committee of the neighbouring Section de Luxembourg: Soboul and Monnier, *Répertoire*, 481; APP, AA148:30. Robert Grevin, a salaried grenadier in the Section du Roule, and a Grevin listed in the same role as Joannet in the neighbouring Section des Champs-Elysées: Soboul and Monnier, *Répertoire*, 57; APP, AA224:99. Louis François Lecamus, miniature-painter from the quai des Augustins, and a Lecamus *jeune*, 'artist painter' in the Section du Faubourg-Montmartre whose lengthy and complex career ended with an arrest as a *babou-viste*: Soboul and Monnier, *Répertoire*, 241; APP, AA215:456. Expecting a greater match between the Guards of 1791 and 1793–4 would be perhaps unreasonable, given the huge drain that the war imposed on Parisian manpower, and all the possible trajectories individuals might take in a time of extreme upheaval.

the basis of such a small sample, two other pieces of information may help define a link. The first is the way in which on 10 July 1791 Pierre Maurice Cardinaux talked himself out of trouble at the Bastille. This cook-shop keeper was arrested for saying in a crowd 'that the chiefs of the National Guard were swine, and the cavalry should be pulled down'. One Guard cavalryman swore Cardinaux was the speaker, and a grenadier sergeant said that he had 'the same sort of voice' as that which had uttered the remark he had heard.

Cardinaux claimed under questioning to have said something about the height of the porte Saint-Antoine, and that a wagon could not get through unless the workers aboard got down. Anything else 'is not him'. This rather contrived denial was accepted as 'sufficient proof', since 'le sieur Cardinaux is domiciled and known'.[63] The dismissal of the charge against him, then, relied completely on his social status. This is given a certain piquancy by the later career summarised by Soboul and Monnier:

> Elector in 1792, standard-bearer of the armed force of the Section, member of the revolutionary committee, the fraternal society, lieutenant of the revolutionary fusiliers in the Section's company, then attached to the Committee of General Security, as a *surveillant*. Disarmed in floréal III; arrested on 9 prairial: 'a raving terrorist', accused of inflammatory remarks on 10 germinal, of having attended the illegal assembly of 2 prairial. His café, on the place de l'Estrapade, was the meeting-place of the babouvistes, the exclusives.[64]

He was to be exiled to the Seychelles by the *senatus-consulte* of 14 nivôse IX, where he died around 1809.

The second piece of evidence is the fact that of the twelve men actually arrested on the Champ de Mars on 17 July, no fewer than five can be matched to activists in left-bank Sections in Year II: Claude François Germain (Section du Jardin-des-Plantes), arrested in nivôse III; Noel Pierre Gillet (Section des Quatre-Nations), arrested in Year III, released vendémiaire IV, and member of a 'constitutional circle' in Year VI; Joseph Lafonds [Lafon] (Section du Jardin-des-Plantes), arrested in Year III as a *septembriseur*; Pierre Mainvieille [Mainvieux] (Section du Théâtre-Français), served on his Section's revolutionary committee, denounced in floréal III; and François Millière, (Section de la Croix-Rouge) who served on the Commune of 10 August and in Year II, was arrested in vendémiaire III, but served the Directory in Year IV and as an elector in Year VI, before deportation in Year IX.[65] All of these men were released without charge in 1791 because they were

---

63 APP, AA205:52, Section de la Place-Royale.
64 Soboul and Monnier, *Répertoire*, 499. Besides the identity of name and profession, information also matches Cardinaux for age, place of birth and Section of residence.
65 Ibid. 444, 459, 466, 515 n. 1, 520. Names in square brackets are as recorded in APP, AB324:1850. Mainvieille was referred to the non-political *tribunal de police*, but released without charge on 24 August.

vouched for by other active citizens. No evident attempt was made to explore their role in events, despite the note of their detention 'as seditionaries and disturbers of the public peace and ill-intentioned men'. Quite possibly here, as evidently for Cardinaux, a respectable social identity was sufficient to override the suspicions of the authorities, and indeed even the *prima facie* evidence of seditious participation. This reinforces the point which all our evidence makes clear, that the model of sedition which the authorities were operating – a few leaders such as Danton and Marat and a horde of rootless 'suborned persons' – did not match the actual picture of Parisian opinion. It achieved a partial match, enough to keep a large number of people in prison until September, because political opinions were being propagated throughout the population, amongst individuals both *domicilié* and *non-domicilié*, in a way that made such a distinction meaningless. However, this sort of prejudice constituted one of the primary social distinctions operated both by the authorities and by the population at large in the eighteenth century. Its strength and persistence enabled commentators from all sides to shape their version of the July events to match their preconceptions, and thus to abandon the people who had stood, and fallen, on the Champ de Mars.

Conclusion

Popular assertion and political exclusion in revolutionary Paris

The Champ de Mars Massacre did not, in the end, change very much. In terms of the constitutional crisis ignited by the Flight to Varennes, it was a mere postscript, as the leaders of the Jacobin Club understood when they withdrew from the petitioning process. The train of events launched by the massacre itself, most notably the tortuous judicial inquiry dissected by Albert Mathiez, expired in the amnesty of September 1791 as France supposedly turned her back on past troubles. Insofar as the event lived on during the revolutionary era, it was thanks to its revival as part of a republican heritage after 10 August, going along with the municipal persecution of Marat as part of the infamous history that led Bailly to the guillotine in November 1793, and many of his colleagues to rather less formal deaths in September 1792. Here its value was largely symbolic, the specifics of the event and its antecedents absorbed into a generalised picture of monarchist misdeeds and aristocratic plots. For us, however, if we choose to see the massacre not as a finger pointing to the future, but as a culminating point in a long series of events, almost a catharsis, we can suggest it holds a deeper significance.

Of course the *leitmotif* of aristocratic plot had already shaped the events themselves, but the issues which need to be addressed more closely here go beyond that generalised concern. The fear of *aristocratie* infested the political and cultural structures that had formed in Paris by the beginning of 1791, and through the influence of that fear, some of those structures would be perpetuated into the republican era, and others snuffed out or driven underground. Most important to stress in our discussion of popular actions and responses, and the treatment of those by the revolutionary authorities, is the complex interchange between the old and the new in the attitudes displayed on the streets.

The clearest, or most blatant, example of *bricolage* in the mixing of positions and attitudes comes from the carpenters and their dispute of April–May 1791.[1] Their profession did not superficially appear to be a particularly 'revolutionary' one, unlike for example the printers with their defence of free speech, but the carpenters were none the less able to deploy a full panoply of revolutionary rhetoric against their employers. Seeking essentially to secure,

---

1 By *bricolage* I refer to one of the notions of Claude Lévi-Strauss, that people work with what they have to hand when they formulate their ideas. Robert Darnton has rephrased this in his idea of people being 'street smart': 'they think with things, or with anything else that their culture makes available to them': *Great cat massacre*, 12.

and indeed reinforce, the influence that journeymen had exercised over collective work-practices, their rhetoric enabled this activity to be offered up to the legislators and the public in the light of a concern for liberty and the public good. The employers' concern to drive down wages (or to resist the inflation of wage-claims) was in the same light an echo of the 'old ways' of the guilds' restrictions, and at the same time the exercise of 'aristocratic' domi-nance in the economic sphere. The terms in which the workers condemned the employers left no doubt of the sweeping nature of the accusation: 'sworn enemies of the constitution, since they scorn the rights of man; . . . the most zealous partisans of the most extravagant aristocracy and . . . enemies of the general good'.[2]

From this denunciation it is clear that there has been a complete appro-priation of revolutionary language in the interests of this group. No gap is left between the perceived ill-treatment of the workers and the threat to the 'general good [bien général]'. It is this feature, perhaps less clearly-stated, but none the less implicit, which underpins the even more turbulent concerns that Parisians voiced (or acted upon) when projected into the political arena. Thus the demonstrations of 28 February at Vincennes and the Tuileries were direct appropriations of revolutionary activity, a term in which we must see more than just 'actions', but the principle of being *active* – people acting in the name of the people. This appropriation could of course descend to levels at which it is hard to see more than a faint echo of political purpose – in pros-titutes who parade their deviance before the police 'since the liberty', or indi-viduals who treat the accusation of *aristocratie* as a pretext for assault. The developing course of popular action against non-juror clergy is a clearer illus-tration of the political application of this principle, associated with the concept, gleaned from long experience, that 'violence is sovereign, because sovereignty is eminently violent'.[3] We need not pretend to approve of this association, but we should recognise that it was commonplace to the eight-eenth century, and that those who combatted 'popular violence' were scarcely less violent, for all they clothed their actions in legal forms or the requirements of 'public order'.[4]

The ability to use revolutionary language for personal assertion, of one kind or another, underlines a fundamental difference between those who

---

2 Lacroix, *Actes*, iv. 351–2.
3 P. Viola, 'Violence révolutionnaire ou violence du peuple en révolution?', in M. Vovelle and A. de Baecque (eds), *Recherches sur la Révolution*, Paris 1991, 95–107, citation at p. 97. As Viola adds, 'What the people recollect most directly about sovereignty [as they had expe-rienced it under the Old Regime] is the right to punish.' The right to 'high justice', and to one's own gallows, was central to seigneurialism, and the state's use of overt violence as social control was endemic, as we have seen. Michel Foucault, of course, most famously theorised on this in *Discipline and punish: the birth of the prison*, London 1977, pt i, 'Torture', at pp. 3–69.
4 Which comes first, a violent population or violent repression, is of course a chicken-and-egg question, best answered, like all such questions, with 'neither'.

followed certain beliefs and languages, and those who used them. This is not to suggest a pattern of demagogues and those they managed to lead astray, and indeed the evidence suggests rather an inverse pattern. It is strongly to be suspected that the likes of François Robert were far more clearly attached to certain beliefs and principles than were those who used the same terminology in street-corner fracas. Attention to the patterns of pre-revolutionary popular life should alert us to the extent to which contestation and assertion from amongst the population were affairs of tactical response. Put bluntly, a great deal of popular concern with revolutionary politics might fairly be seen as a necessary concern for pursuing the conditions of everyday life. This should not, however, be seen as reducing popular political concern back to the 'hunger thesis'. The conditions of everyday life in the Old Regime had included a great deal of necessarily 'political' involvement, and the Revolution did not noticeably amend this, other than indeed to increase such concern.

Thus, for the carpenters of Paris, the language of Revolution was another way of pursuing their pre-existing interests, a new tool for a new situation. The Revolution had licensed new forms of assertive popular response to the troubles of the times, forms which individuals and groups took up and moulded to their own needs. However, out of this came a popular response that, evolving through the confrontations of the spring, was prepared to face down the National Guard on the Champ de Mars, and to expose itself to musket-fire in the name of a constitutional petition. In such a confrontation one might well claim that new identities were being forged, and tactical moves being subsumed in the evolution of ideological positions. However, such claims require further dissection.

The appropriation of revolutionary rhetoric, at the economic, political or purely interpersonal level, provides a backcloth for a wide range of individual and collective actions, in which a number of further dimensions of common understanding become evident. These tie in to emerging and pre-existing structural conflicts, not merely of the type exemplified by the carpenters, but also with more direct consequences for the interaction of politics and popular culture. The first dimension, which will already be evident from the foregoing, is the continual alarmist reflection on the nature and presence of *aristocratie* in the city. It is difficult to stress enough the extent to which discourse emerging from all elements of the political structure, side-by-side with the flood of press discourse, coloured the public arena red with the terror of massacre and invasion.

The oratory of a journalist such as Fréron gives the extreme example from the side of the radical press, in that little that happened in Paris was not made a portent of destruction in the pages of the *Orateur du Peuple*. However, the less extreme press were no less eager to invoke the same fears, though in a less dramatic tone: the *Révolutions de Paris* saw no problem in conflating all aspects of the economic crisis of the spring to a deliberate effort at destabilisation, as we have seen. Moreover, as the same example shows, such publications dispensed alarm into the public arena while simultaneously harbouring deep-seated fears about the political reliability of the lower orders. The circularity of this type of argument is one of its essential features – alarm was broadcast to the population at large, yet what was feared about the aristocracy was less its open face in the 'capucins' and 'monarchiens' whose activities were known and notorious, than the supposed hidden machinations of aristocrats amongst the common people themselves. Any actions or concerns expressed by such people in the light of what they were being continually told were thus susceptible to reinterpretation as the very destabilisation that journalists and authorities feared. Action against the clergy, although sometimes escaping such characterisation, as with the flogging of nuns in April, was more often fitted into such patterns, both by commentators and by the police. One may suspect that the brutally sexual connotations of the assaults on nuns somehow elevated them (if that can be the right word) to the status of revolutionary acts in an environment where the feminine and the deviant already went hand-in-hand with perceived counter-revolution.

Journalistic suspicion represents the 'macro' level of the destabilising consequences of mistrust of the populace. The everyday practices of the police serve to show the 'micro' level, which is also the level at which most individuals might actually experience the consequences of such views. This has already been discussed at length as a topic in its own right, so we may merely restate our basic conclusions. The arena of policing makes it clear that there was a considerable amount of quite open hostility to the organs of public order from elements amongst the population. At the same time, the police were heirs to the developing eighteenth-century tradition of intervention in popular life, and to the role of the Châtelet *commissaires* as arbiters of neighbourhood life, or at least, incontrovertible witnesses to claims of probity or insult. This was intermixed with the active presence of the National Guard as the uniformed police of the city, who in their civilian capacities, as well as through their duties, were exposed to, and clearly absorbed, a complex cocktail of alarm and suspicion which was reflected in their policing practices. The more clandestine practices of policing were in themselves able to unleash another, even more explosive, cocktail, which echoed back through the realm of spies, agents, criminals and factions to the folkloric beliefs about policing that dominated eighteenth-century perceptions.

Taking this collection of influences as a whole, we may draw up a summary of the structural elements of social relations contributing towards the events of the summer of 1791, before going on to consider the effects of the rapid evolution of those events themselves on their outcome. The general population was exposed to alarmist messages from multiple levels of public discourse. Pre-eminent amongst these was the press, which regardless of overt political intention did little other than scare-monger for much of the time. Influenced by this discourse, the organs of local censitary democracy in the committees and assemblies of the Sections responded in kind, as the alarms of February in particular show. Meanwhile, the population was providing an audience and sounding-board for this debate, and sometimes springing to centre-stage in a series of collective manifestations. The intermittent presence, and lurking threat, of popular collective action animated the anxieties of the municipal authorities and National Guard hierarchy, whose concerns over aristocratic subornation were manifested as heavy-handed public-order policing. This rested uneasily with the continued presence of police informers and *observateurs*, of whom the population were only too aware, and whom some radicals were coming to associate with another branch of the counter-revolutionary threat.

The events which followed the revelation of royal doubts about the legitimacy of the constitutional clergy illustrate once again the possibility of dramatic political action by the general population, and the evolution of sentiments that could derive from such events. The actions of the crowd itself on 18 April, and the widespread rumour that people had been killed by the forces of order, show the extraordinary level of tension already existing between the population (or elements thereof) and the supposedly revolutionary authorities. The scandal of Lafayette's withdrawn resignation, leading as it did into the brief *cause célèbre* of the Oratoire grenadiers, and intersecting with the more substantive charges levelled against the king by the Cordeliers, set a determined seal of opposition on relations between National Guards loyal to their general and a growing segment of the population. This is the atmosphere in which tensions provoked by economic difficulties began to overlap with direct political confrontation, and elements such as the ongoing currency-conversion problems acquired new significance as wage disputes and accusations of forgery mounted. Once again, the perennial accusation of complicity with aristocratic plotting provided the overt text of denunciations on all sides. The situation also prompted the municipality into a statement on the concerns of the population which merits re-examination:

> For a long time, the enemies of the constitution have placed their hopes in anarchy; they have counted on the exaggeration of patriotism and on the excess of that impatient ardour produced by the rapid conquest of liberty. They have calculated on the habit of mistrust in a people always abused; that hatred so-long compressed for an oppressive government; those movements of fear and of scorn inspired by all acts of authority, when it is usurped. They have employed these sentiments, which they must have found everywhere, with the most fatal cunning against all the legitimate powers conferred by a free people.[5]

We find here an assessment of the underlying attitudes of the population that is quite remarkable in its perceptiveness, yet at the same time both entirely naïve about the popular response to authority, and deeply authoritarian in itself. The desire of the municipality is to have everything its own way, to

---

5 Lacroix, *Actes*, iv. 6–7, joint appeal, 26 Apr. by municipality and departmental directory to National Assembly, requesting further public-order powers.

laud the patriotism of the masses, while dismissing it as untutored, which also licenses the dismissal of any qualms such groups may raise about their revolutionary 'betters', all the more so as their fears are merely fodder for aristocratic destabilisation. In short, the municipality here, like so many other revolutionary actors, finds itself able to simply look past what elements of the population are actually doing and saying, to find refuge in its own preconceptions. When the Flight to Varennes produced open conflict, these attitudes were given free rein in action.

It is tempting to do as Mathiez and Rudé did, and extract some social significance from the clashes in July. Various elements in that situation and its aftermath would licence us to do so, not least the efforts to make the National Guard a consistently propertied force, and the overt pursuit of *gens sans aveu* in relation to the disorders. However, examination of detainees and witnesses clearly shows that such rupture as there was in the social body ran along far more jagged lines than those of 'class'. Indeed, one of the remarkable features of what we might term the radicalisation of sentiments in the summer of 1791 is the individualism of its participants. There are all manner of claims put forward as to relative revolutionary merit and membership of the revolutionary people, in which a variety of social distinctions are drawn. While such distinctions can be supported, to a certain degree, by the evidence provided by detainees and witnesses, it is more clear that there were not two social groups set against each other in this episode. Individuals from *bourgeois* to *colporteur* took a radical line, while artisans, apprentices and even labourers might freely testify against them. In other words, in the conditions of political controversy that flourished in 1791, the question of who belonged to the revolutionary collective was answered in an entirely individual way.

Of course, this individuality was constrained and acted upon by the prevailing sets of political and discursive forces, and thus lost to sight beneath the various forceful interpretations of the massacre. The extent to which there was an almost incredible refusal to register popular political consciousness of any type can be seen in the history of the *Chant du Coq*, an anti-radical periodical placard developed by the authors of the *Babillard*, the journal that had begun to report on popular speech in early June 1791. The *Chant du Coq* began to appear on the walls of Paris in late July, shortly after the Champ de Mars Massacre, when it appears that the editors of the *Babillard* had decided to intervene still more directly in the political situation. An announcement appeared in the edition of 22 July:

> While the intriguers, the factious, the foreign and domestic enemies of the constitution spread their gold around to produce an uprising amongst the people, a society of good citizens (the editors of the *Babillard*) join together their resources and their efforts to enlighten them; [this society] will consecrate to the conservation of peace, the money others spend on exciting a civil war.

The product of this expenditure, the *Chant du Coq*, would carry a message of political good sense to the population, and encourage them to avoid excesses, while lifting 'the veil that conceals their dangerous enemies from them'. The announcement ended with an appeal to the National Guard, 'intrepid avengers of the law', to watch over these posters to avoid them being 'removed by obscure factious men'.[6]

The exact contents of the early editions of this poster are unknown, but by 28 July the *Babillard* was reporting the controversy they had stirred up – a man offended by the insults offered to Brissot in the third *Chant* alleged in a café that the poster was funded by the court. His fellow *habitués*, according to the report at least, gave him short shrift.[7] The *Coq*'s language becomes clearer from its number eleven on, when they began to be attached as appendices to the *Babillard* whenever space allowed. From the argument of this number, it can be seen what the poster's general line was:

> The enemies of the public good seek to embitter those who are not active citizens, in recalling to them this axiom: *men are born and remain equal*; they refrain from adding what follows, and explaining to these ardent, but honest men, how it is that the equality of rights is real, [but] the equality of fact chimerical, in society. This is to expose the people to drawing very dangerous and very absurd consequences from the most august and true principle.[8]

The argument ran to its already-obvious conclusion, that to admit to political activity those with no interest in society would deliver public life up to a 'credulous and easily-led crowd, that intrigue and ambition would strive to lead astray', and which would choose representatives who were 'perfidious' or 'ignorant'. Some of the results of such language may be surmised from the *Chant* number thirteen, which sings the praises of the National Guard at length, and ends with another request to watch over the posters and to prevent their destruction by 'those who would not dare to combat the principles enunciated in the poster'.[9]

Much of the output of the *Chant* was taken up with political calumny on radical figures, and most particularly on Brissot, by now well-established as a radical voice in journalism and the Jacobin Club, and seeking election to the Legislative Assembly. The *Babillard* had already from time to time broken away from its views on street-life to attack him – on 25 July it published a special supplement that ran to eight and a half pages of denunciation.[10] Brissot's journal, the *Patriote François*, did not trouble to retort to such things, but the *Courrier de Paris* of Gorsas, later a Girondin colleague of Brissot, rapidly took up arms against such calumny, and the perceived motives behind it. This

---

6 *Babillard*, no. 39.
7 Ibid. no. 45.
8 *Chant du Coq*, no. 11, printed in *Babillard*, no. 50, 2 Aug. [emphasis in original].
9 *Chant du Coq*, no. 13, in *Babillard*, no. 52, 4 Aug.
10 *Babillard*, no. 42.

would further reveal the convoluted attitude of such commentators to the people.[11]

On 2 August the *Chant du Coq* was described by Gorsas as one of the 'thousand atrocious productions, in which ignorance, the pleasure of doing harm, and stupidity all dispute for the glory of blackening talent and virtue'. Its authors were 'unknown suborned beings' who 'pile insult upon insult, and lie impudently before the eyes of the whole capital'.[12] Reports and accusations against the *Chant* continued to appear regularly.[13] Gorsas clearly believed the *Chant* and its parent publication to be the corrupt propaganda of the ministerial party – the next best thing to open counter-revolution, attempting to falsely allay fears of aristocratic court influence while stirring trouble, particularly between the common people and the National Guard. The *Courrier de Paris* of 19 August carried a particularly involuted example of this logic – printed threats left in several guardposts, referring to 'you and your singing cocks', oppression of 'the non-armed people' and 50,000 ready to destroy them, were denounced for being clearly part of a plot to enrage the Guard against the population, aided by the 'disgusting eulogies of the citizen soldiers' printed by the *Chant*, designed to vaunt the Guard, humiliate the population, 'and consequently to provoke them against the National Guard'.

It is evident from this response that the *Chant du Coq* caused a considerable stir in Paris, and the reporting of the *Babillard*, whatever prejudices may underlie its tone, shows that its words created dispute on the streets. On 7 August a *Chant* posted near the Pont-Neuf was provoking praise for its good sense from a group of citizens when an orator struck up in response. His discourse on republicanism and the need for genuine equality, reported at length, enraged the respectable elements – 'one amongst them even raised his stick against the temeritous orator who was attacking, in the midst of the capital, the constitution of his country'. However, 'the workers and women' who had gathered in 'considerable numbers' surrounded the latter, and it required a passing patrol to break up the confrontation.[14] Such disputes con-

---

11 The *Patriote*'s silence was broken briefly on 13 September (no. 764), when it reproduced a piece from the *Courier François* on the ever-growing number of wall-posters, and their fascination for the population, with the comment that 'we do not speak of the *Chant du Coq*. The people, who customarily cover it with mud from early dawn, hardly permit anyone to read it except those who soil their hands with *Le Babillard*'.

12 *Courrier*, 2 Aug. The pretext for this venom was in fact the accusation from the *Chant du Coq* about the *Société fraternelle* which had sparked its visit to police administrator Jolly: see ch. 5. above. Murray, *The right wing press*, 270, asserts that the *Chant du Coq* was 'almost certainly' funded by the king's civil list as part of a concerted effort to support a socially-conservative version of the Revolution. This, of course, was a contemporary accusation, and there is hard evidence to link a number of right-wing journalists to court funds in this period. Murray makes such links, but the comment on the *Chant du Coq* remains a supposition.

13 *Courrier*, 11, 15, 17, 19 Aug.

14 *Babillard*, no. 55. The length at which clearly-expressed republican principles were reported here is another ironic tribute to the journalists' belief that those principles were

tinued until the autumn weather began to clear the streets of spontaneous gatherings.

The episode of the *Chant du Coq* can be held to illustrate several points, not least of which is that journalists associated with the municipal or Fayettist position did not hesitate to tell the urban population to its face that it was just too stupid to have a place in political life. Similar sentiments had of course been on display in Fayettist propaganda a year or more earlier, but the tone in 1790 had been fond and paternal – no 'credulous and easily-led crowd' then, and a year of rising abuse had clearly taken its toll. Even more significant, perhaps, is the response of those we might call future Brissotins. Rather than retort that the people did have just such a political role, and were justified in the angry responses that the posters clearly produced, Gorsas and others seemed to feel it necessary to envelop those responses in the tenebrous fingers of plot.

This reaction echoes that which we have already laid out in connection with the Champ de Mars Massacre itself. The individuals and groups of people who acted in contradiction to basic assumptions of the leading strata of revolutionary society were thereby excluded from 'the people' as that term operated as a concept in revolutionary politics. This comes as no surprise, when we are considering the general Fayettist approach to politics, but it is echoed across the radical spectrum, from Gorsas to Marat, and hints of it are visible within the structures of the popular societies as well.

The Champ de Mars Massacre as retold by some of its contemporaries was an exercise in the suppression of the popular will by a violent and oppressive elite, one that some would go so far as to call 'bourgeois'. However, it will now be apparent that, although it invoked responses sufficient to support such a view superficially, the clash on 17 July also brought together conflicting interpretations of the politics of Paris, and the identity of 'the people', which at the same time had enough in common to make the clash not merely inevitable, but tragic. If the massacre was almost a catharsis, it is the fact that the necessary unleashing of tensions and subsequent re-evaluation of positions of a truly cathartic moment did not occur then, which redoubles its tragic dimension.

Rather than bemoaning with the revisionists the supposed 'violence of the people', we can see here that it was the presence of a complex of educated beliefs about that very concept which provoked conflict. Observers on each side were convinced that brigands abounded in the city, that the anonymous crowds of the Palais-Royal, the Tuileries gardens, the squares and quaysides of the city, were impregnated with dangerous men, drawn from outside society, primed to ignite plots, treachery and massacre. For constitutional monar-

patently absurd, and that one need not worry that repeating them might actually encourage such views.

chists, it was the Jacobins, Cordeliers and new-founded popular societies who formed the spearhead of anarchy preached for the purpose of restoring despotism.[15] For radicals and newly-declared republicans, however, the municipality, and especially the headquarters and wealthier battalions of the National Guard, planned to compromise the people's liberty in order to make peace with aristocracy. For them 'a moral and egalitarian *peuple* had developed, who were opposed by a selfish and self-indulgent *aristocratie*'.[16] Although there is a hazy sense of 'haves' and 'have-nots' floating around this discourse, the forces ranged against the radicals were not conceived of by them in explicitly social terms – *aristocrate* was a category of moral denunciation, which fitted Bailly as precisely as it did Lafayette.[17]

For all sides, however, 'the people' as such had to be pure. Thus there could be no question of recognising the existence of the apparent social antagonism displayed on the one side by the unrestrainable Guards, and on the other by the shoemakers of the rue Tirechappe. Indeed one might well say that for those Guards themselves, attacking radical agitators was simply attacking dangerous subversives, 'factious men' who had no real social identity. As we have seen, those detained who were found to have such an identity were released. Gorsas may have feared that the socio-political unity of the citizen-body was about to cave in, but when that, to all appearances, happened, it had to be rewritten so as to preserve just that unity. This furthered no particular political agenda, rather it was central to a broadly-shared conception of the revolutionary process. Accounting for all this requires that we acknowledge the perspectives of the revolutionaries, and the import of their own discourse, and not proceed with simple social explanations in mind. As Sarah Maza has pointed out, trying to account for the terms in which the revolutionaries thought through the use of concepts such as 'bourgeois universalism' is merely assuming what one is claiming to prove.[18]

This almost-universal misrecognition of popular activity by the educated strata still leaves us with the question of defining that activity itself. Beneath the particular responses to circumstances that mark the pretexts for arrest, there is in what individuals have to say for themselves evidence of a concern for the revolutionary body politic, or, to put it more simply, the revolutionary

---

15 Mathiez, *Club des Cordeliers*, 191ff.
16 Censer, *Prelude to power*, pp. xii–xiii.
17 See P. Higonnet, ' "Aristocrate", "aristocratie": language and politics in the French Revolution', in S. Petrey (ed.), *The French Revolution, 1789–1989: 200 years of rethinking*, Lubbock, Texas 1989, 47–66.
18 S. Maza, 'Languages of class in the French Revolution: the problem of the absent bourgeoisie', unpubl. manuscript 1998, 16–17. I should like to thank Professor Maza for allowing me to read, and cite, this piece. It takes issue with Patrice Higonnet's use of 'bourgeois universalism' in his *Class, ideology and the rights of nobles during the French Revolution*, Oxford 1981, esp. pp. 8–36, a theme more recently restated in his 'Cultural upheaval and class formation during the French Revolution', in F. Fehér (ed.), *The French Revolution and the birth of modernity*, Berkeley 1990, 69–102.

people. The defence of the people marks out a position perhaps acquired from radical language, perhaps condensed from the vast expanse of 'pro-popular' written and spoken rhetoric that coloured 1789, but overall something that is a definite position, with an Other – court, aristocracy, counter-revolution – to oppose. The crowds that lynched thieves in 1790 and battered Kabert in 1791 certainly lacked an overtly sophisticated political analysis, but they marked the most extreme end of a range of popular assertions that requires recognition. It might well be argued that the patriot journalists prepared to label a crowd as brigands for stoning the National Guard understood far less well than that crowd just what was at stake in the summer of 1791. In the end, however, the amorphous hopes for popular assertion on the revolutionary stage lacked any realistic prospect of achievement.

The events of July 1791 reveal the need for new complexities in the understanding of popular attitudes during the French Revolution. The outspoken dissent and its repression made manifest the divisions present in the urban body politic, divisions which, none the less, do not correspond to any of the previously-assumed lines of conflict within the political sphere. This book has attempted to decipher a division which ran jaggedly through the population of Paris, where artisans, Guardsmen or bourgeois might be found on either side, and where membership of the revolutionary people was fundamentally in doubt. In 1791 the pernicious consequences of that doubt for the fate of popular assertion served to turn even the popular societies and the most radical journalists against the alleged violence of the crowd. The later triumph of the 'popular movement' need not be seen to reflect any straightening-out of this jagged division, since, as we have seen, some of those who defended order in 1791 would later appear amongst the ranks of the *sans-culottes*. Historiography has now moved well past the point at which we need still accept a simple social categorisation of this movement, and it may not be going too far to see it as the conjunction of a pre-existing radical rhetoric with the concrete political needs of a neighbourhood elite.[19] The same spokesmen as in 1791 a year later led a wider alliance of interests, the same language of rights and popular action now responded to a more critical decay of the political system, and the monarchy fell. With such a clear political target, the alarms over the reliability of the lower orders could be temporarily put aside, but they need not have vanished entirely.

If we were to look forward in time to the perils of the Republic in 1793, might we not see the same processes at work in the triumph of *sans-culottes* over *enragés*? The process whereby Hébert's journalism and the political rhetoric of the Jacobins removed the food crisis of the summer of 1793 from the sphere of legitimate protest, and made bread queues into signs of aristo-

---

19 For the strongest expression of such a view see Andrews, 'Social structures, political élites'. Sonenscher, 'Sans-culottes of the year II', and 'Artisans', is less forthright on such 'social' questions, but does demand a rethinking of the link between language and identities.

cratic subversion, laying the grounds for the imprisonment of the radical priest Jacques Roux, might be held to parallel the spurning of the stone-throwers on the Champ de Mars.[20] The political agenda that demanded an effort at social consolidation, palliating the Federalist menace with the promise of the new Constitution, made uncompromising demands for action against hoarders and speculators into a destabilising influence. By the time of the *journée* of 5 September 1793, however, the views of the *enragés* had become the views of Hébert and Robespierre: the recuperation of radical views for political uses had accelerated since 1791. From that point on, the structures and policies of the Jacobin Terror would steadily erode the space for any popular assertion at all. By the time that Bailly went to the guillotine on the Champ de Mars, the popular forces that he had sought to contain, and in whose name he died, had already been reined in far more tightly than he could have hoped.

Popular assertion in the Old Regime had functioned by occupying the cracks and crevices of a political façade held up to reflect the glory of a distant power; when it became more directly challenging, as it had appeared to do in 1757 with Damiens's attack, dissent was persecuted out of sight. Power in the Revolution began much closer to the lives of the people, and while the similarity of radical rhetoric to their assertions of liberty can only have encouraged that expression, the reality of life when radicalism came to power was of a far more complete surveillance than the *lieutenants-général de police* had ever achieved. Popular assertion had used the gaps between the perspectives of employer and guild, guild and police, police and community, to make itself felt. The rule of the *sans-culottes*, and still more the regime that tamed even them, closed those gaps down to nothing. Under the circumstances, it is more remarkable that people should still have spoken out in bread queues, and that workers should have protested their wage-cuts in thermidor II, than that they should otherwise have been so quiet. In the end, then, might we not argue that the greatest tragedy of the Revolution was not its fall into a pattern of violence too easily condemned as 'popular', but rather its continual failure to admit the varieties of popular experience as legitimate in politics?

---

[20] See J. Roux, *Le Publiciste de la République française*, repr. Paris 1981, and Hébert, *Le Père Duchesne*, viii. This episode is discussed in A. Mathiez, *La Vie chère et le mouvement social sous la terreur*, Paris 1927, esp. pp. 200–88, 339–65, and R. B. Rose, *The enragés: socialists of the French Revolution?*, Sydney 1968. See also J. Guilhaumou, 'Les Journaux parisiens dans les luttes révolutionnaires en 1793: presse d'opinion, presse de salut public et presse pamphlétaire', in Rétat, *Révolution du journal*, 275–84. Guilhaumou notes that while 'For the Père Duchesne ... the existence of queues outside bakeries constituted proof of action by the ill-willed, by agents of Pitt', the *enragé* Leclerc's *Ami du Peuple* observed that 'the attitudes which were displayed there make evident the difficulties of the "labouring class" ' (pp. 281–2).

Bibliography

Unpublished primary sources

Paris, Archives de la Préfecture de Police

The following cartons from the AA series (*commissaires de police, procès-verbaux*), contain material covering the events of July 1791. They are catalogued alphabetically by the name under which the Section was known for the longest period. Where this differs from its name in 1791 I have indicated the catalogued name in brackets:

AA56	Arcis
AA74	Mauconseil (Bon-Conseil)
AA76	Bonne-Nouvelle
AA85	Palais-Royal (Butte-des-Moulins)
AA134	Postes (Contrat-Social)
AA137	Hôtel-de-Ville (Fidelité)
AA148	Fontaine-de-Grenelle
AA153	Oratoire (Gardes-Françaises)
AA157	Enfants-Rouges (Homme-Armé)
AA166	Luxembourg
AA167	Place-Louis-XIV (Mail)
AA172	Fontaine-Montmorency (Molière-et-Lafontaine)
AA173	Montreuil
AA182	Louvre (Muséum)
AA198	Observatoire
AA205	Place-Royale (Place-des-Fédérés)
AA206	Place-Vendôme (Piques)
AA215	Henri-Quatre (Pont-Neuf)
AA219	Popincourt
AA220	Quinze-Vingts
AA224	Roule
AA239	Temple

For all or some of the preceding six months, useful information was obtained from the following cartons:

AA56	Arcis
AA82	Palais-Royal (Butte-des-Moulins), Jan.–Mar.
AA83	Palais-Royal (Butte-des-Moulins), Apr.
AA84	Palais-Royal (Butte-des-Moulins), May–June
AA137	Hôtel-de-Ville (Fidelité)
AA157	Enfants-Rouges (Homme-Armé)
AA182	Louvre (Muséum)
AA206	Place-Vendôme (Piques)
AA215	Henri-Quatre (Pont-Neuf)

Isolated pieces of interest concerning this period were found in:

AA74   Mauconseil (Bon-Conseil)
AA76   Bonne-Nouvelle
AA174   Grange-Batellière (Mont-Blanc)

For August and September, in addition to scrutiny of cartons already listed for July, material was examined in:

AA57   Arcis
AA86   Palais-Royal (Butte-des-Moulins)
AA207   Place-Vendôme (Piques)

The registers of the prison of La Force were used to supplement this information:

AB322   (1 Nov. 1790)–18 Mar. 1791
AB323   20 Mar.–12 July 1791
AB324   12 July 1791–(12 May 1792)

Published primary sources

The following journals (in political order, left to right) furnished material for the whole period examined:

L'Ami du Peuple, par Marat
  Daily, extreme violent radicalism, but with evidence of a certain epistolary contact with elements of popular opinion.
Les Révolutions de Paris (Prudhomme)
  A weekly, hence less occupied with day-to-day events unless of a certain level of significance. Well to the left politically, but suspicious of popular agitation.
Le Journal Universel, ou Révolutions des Royaumes, par P.-J. Audouin
  The daily equivalent of Prudhomme, but with less flair, almost exclusively political news; occasional comments on local agitations.
Le Courrier de Paris dans les LXXXIII Départements, par A.-J. Gorsas
  Daily, mainly political news, reported with a centre-left stance, including comments on its reception on the streets of Paris and 'low-level' news of Parisian events and controversies.
Le Moniteur Universel (anon.)
  Highly respectable centrist daily, mainly occupied with foreign news and Assembly debates; occasional news of significant Parisian events.
La Feuille du Jour (anon.)
  Right-of-centre daily, containing information on everything from stock prices and theatre performances to country-house lets and bankruptcy sales, but also a fair amount of caustic comment on Parisian events, especially crowd disturbances.

Various other journals were examined, although most do not have the coverage of Parisian events which marks those above. Of these, the following (in the same order) furnished isolated material:

L'Orateur du Peuple, par Martel (Fréron)
Sub-*maratiste* incendiarism.
Le Père Duchesne (Foulhioux)
A short-lived, and politically-anodyne, version of this great revolutionary caricature [BN, 8–LC2–517]
La Bouche de Fer
Intriguing 'open forum' for radicals associated with the *Cercle Social*.
Le Patriote François (Brissot)
Radical politics, but coverage of popular activities dominated by plot mentality.
L'Argus Patriote (Charles Theveneau-Morande)
Patriotic high-mindedness from one of the greatest of the pre-revolutionary smut-merchants.
Le Babillard, ou Journal du Palais-Royal (anon.)
From early June, a rich source on popular outbursts in public places, with critical comments from a centre-right perspective.
Le Journal de la Société des Amis de la Constitution Monarchique (anon.)
House-journal of the *monarchiens*.

Two revolutionary journals were consulted in modern reprints:

Hébert, J.-R., *Le Père Duchesne*, repr. in 10 vols, Paris 1969
Roux, J., *Le Publiciste de la République française*, repr. Paris 1981

A number of ephemeral anonymous news-pamphlets were examined from the Bibliothèque nationale collection; place and date of publication is Paris 1791:

8–Lb39–4681, *Découverte d'une grande trahison contre les habitans du faubourg St-Antoine, à l'occasion du procès de M. la Fayette avec M. Santerre*
8–Lb39–4682, *Détail exact de tout ce qui s'est passé hier au tribunal de l'arrondissement des Minimes, à l'occasion du procès de M. SANTERRE contre M. LAFAYETTE et le nommé DESMOTTES, son aide-de-camp*
8–Lb39–4828, *Journée du 18 avril, 1791*
8–Lb39–4867, *Démission de M. de la Fayette, acceptée par l'Assemblée nationale, et les 48 sections de Paris, avec l'arrêté du Club des Cordeliers*
8–Lb39–4868, *Grande révolution causée par la demission de M. Lafayette*
8–Lb39–4925, *Grand détail de la révolte arrive hier et les jours derniers au Palais-Royal, occasionée par les marchands d'argent*
8–Lb39–4989, *Appel à la nation des décrets inconstitutionnels*
8–Lb39–8172, *Grand détail d'une sédition occasionnée par un vicaire de Paris*
8–Lb39–9869, *Détail de la grande révolution arrivée aux Thuileries pour le départ du roi*
8–Lb39–9962, *Nouvelle COMPLOT découvert, sur le procès de M. SANTERRE*
8–Lb39–9971, *Détail de tout ce qui s'est passé aux Minimes, au sujet du procès de M. de Lafayette, et de M. Santerre, avec la decision du tribunal*

8–Lb40–849, *Discours imprimés par ordre de la Société fraternelle des patriotes, de l'un et l'autre sexe, de tous âge et de tous état, séante aux Jacobins, rue St-Honoré*

8–Lb41–2553, *Grand détail de la révolution arrivée hier au faubourg St-Antoine, dans laquelle un mouchard a été massacré par le peuple*

Secondary sources

S. Lacroix, *Actes de la Commune de Paris*, 2nd ser. ii–viii, Paris 1902–11

This must be accorded special notice, as it contains a vast wealth of contemporary administrative and journalistic material, collated, correlated and elucidated with remarkable sensitivity.

Aftalion, F., *The French Revolution: an economic interpretation*, Cambridge 1990

Albertone, M., 'Une Histoire oubliée: les assignats dans l'historiographie', *Annales historiques de la Révolution française* cclxxxvii (1992), 87–104

Andrews, R. M., 'The Justices of the Peace of revolutionary Paris, September 1792–November 1794 (frimaire III), *Past and Present* lii (1971), 56–105

——— 'Social structures, political elites and ideology in revolutionary Paris, 1792–4: a critical evaluation of Albert Soboul's *Les Sans-Culottes parisiens*', *Journal of Social History* xix (1985–6), 71–112

——— *Law, magistracy and crime in Old Regime Paris, 1735–1789*, I: *The system of criminal justice*, Cambridge 1994

Baecque, A. de, *The body politic: corporeal metaphor in revolutionary France, 1770–1800*, Stanford 1997

Baker, K. M., *Inventing the French Revolution: essays in French political culture in the eighteenth century*, Cambridge 1990

Beik, W., *Urban protest in seventeeth-century France: the culture of retribution*, Cambridge 1997

Blanning, T. C. W., *The French Revolution: class war or culture clash?*, London 1998

Blum, C., *Rousseau and the republic of virtue: the language of politics in the French Revolution*, Ithaca, NY 1986

Bosher, J. F., *The French Revolution: a new interpretation*, London 1989

Bourdin, I., *Les Sociétés populaires à Paris pendant la Révolution*, Paris 1937

Bouton, C. A., *The flour war: gender, class and community in late ancien régime French society*, University Park 1993

Brezis, E. S. and F. Crouzet, 'The role of assignats during the French Revolution: an evil or a rescuer?', *Journal of European Economic History* xxiv (1995), 7–40

Burstin, H., 'La dynamique de l'assemblée: de l'expérience démocratique à la démocratie abusive', in Vovelle, *Paris*, 123–35

Castelot, A., *Philippe Égalité le régicide*, Paris 1991

Censer, J., *Prelude to power: the Parisian radical press, 1789–1791*, London 1976

Chartier, R., *The cultural origins of the French Revolution*, Durham, NC 1991

Clifford, D. L., 'The National Guard and the Parisian community', *French Historical Studies* xvi (1990), 849–78

——— 'Command over equals: the officer corps of the Parisian National Guard, 1789–90', *Proceedings of the Annual Meeting of the Western Society for French History* xviii (1991), 152–65

Cobb, R. C., *The police and the people: French popular protest, 1789–1820*, Oxford 1970

——— *Reactions to the French Revolution*, Oxford 1972

Cocquard, O., 'Le Paris de Marat', in Vovelle, *Paris*, 173–84

Cranston, M., 'The sovereignty of the nation', in Lucas, *The political culture of the French Revolution*, 97–104

Crouzet, F., 'Les Consequences économiques de la Révolution française: réflexions sur un débat', *Revue Économique* xl (1989), 1189–204

Cubitt, G., 'Denouncing conspiracy in the French Revolution', *Renaissance and Modern Studies* xxxiii (1989), 144–58

Cullen, L. M., 'History, economic crises, and revolution: understanding eighteenth-century France', *Economic History Review* xlvi (1993), 635–57

Darnton, R., 'The high Enlightenment and the low-life of literature in pre-revolutionary France', in D. Johnson (ed.), *French society and the Revolution*, Cambridge 1976, 53–87

——— *The literary underground of the Old Regime*, Cambridge, Mass. 1982

——— *The great cat massacre and other episodes in French cultural history*, Harmondsworth 1985

Devenne, F., 'La Garde nationale: création et évolution, 1789–Août 1792', *Annales historiques de la Révolution française* cclxxxiii (1991), 49–66

Doyle, W., *Origins of the French Revolution*, 2nd edn, Oxford 1988

——— *The Oxford history of the French Revolution*, Oxford 1989

Ducoudray, E., 'Bourgeois parisiens en Révolution, 1790–1792', in Vovelle, *Paris*, 71–88

Duprat, C., 'Lieux et temps de l'acculturation politique', *Annales historiques de la Révolution française* ccxcvii (1994), 387–400

Echeverria, D., *The Maupeou revolution: a study in the history of libertarianism, France, 1770–1774*, Baton Rouge 1985

Eisenstein, E. L., *Grub Street abroad: aspects of the French cosmopolitan press from the age of Louis XIV to the French Revolution*, Oxford 1992

Elyada, O., 'La Mère Duchesne: masques populaires et guerre pamphlétaire, 1789–1791', *Annales historiques de la Révolution française* cclxxi (1988), 1–16

——— 'L'Appel aux faubourgs: pamphlets populaires et propagande à Paris, 1789–1790', in Vovelle, *Paris*, 185–200

Farge, A., *Vivre dans la rue à Paris au XVIIIe siècle*, Paris 1979

——— *La Vie fragile: violence, pouvoirs et solidarités à Paris au XVIIIe siècle*, Paris 1986

——— *Dire et mal dire: l'opinion publique au XVIIIe siècle*, Paris 1992

——— *Fragile lives: violence, power and solidarity in eighteenth-century Paris*, Cambridge 1993

——— *Subversive words: public opinion in eighteenth-century France*, Cambridge 1994

——— and M. Foucault, *La Désordre des familles: lettres de cachet des Archives de la Bastille*, Paris 1982

——— and J. Revel, *Logiques de la foule: l'affaire des enlèvements des enfants, Paris, 1750*, Paris 1988

Feyel, G., 'Les Frais d'impression et de diffusion de la presse parisienne entre 1788 et 1792', in Rétat, *Révolution du journal*, 77–99.

Fitzsimmons, M. P., *Remaking France: the National Assembly and the Constitution of 1791*, Cambridge 1994

Forrest, A. and P. Jones (eds), *Reshaping France: town, country and region during the French Revolution*, Manchester 1991

Foucault, M., *Discipline and punish: the birth of the prison*, London 1977

Furet, F., *Interpreting the French Revolution*, Cambridge 1981

—— and M. Ozouf (eds), *A critical dictionary of the French Revolution*, Cambridge 1989

—— and D. Richet, *La Révolution française*, Paris 1965

Garrioch, D., *Neighbourhood and community in Paris, 1740–1790*, Cambridge 1986

—— 'The police of Paris as enlightened social reformers', *Eighteenth-Century Life* xvi (1992), 43–59

—— 'The people of Paris and their police in the eighteenth century: reflections on the introduction of a "modern" police force', *European History Quarterly* xxiv (1994), 511–35

—— *The formation of the Parisian bourgeoisie, 1690–1830*, Cambridge, Mass. 1996

—— 'The everyday lives of Parisian women and the October Days of 1789', *Social History* xxiv (1999), 231–49

Genty, M., *Paris, 1789–1795: l'apprentissage de la citoyenneté*, Paris 1987

—— 'Controverses autour de la garde nationale parisienne', *Annales historiques de la Révolution française* ccxci (1993), 61–88

Godechot, J., *The taking of the Bastille*, London 1970

Godineau, D., *Citoyennes tricoteuses: les femmes du peuple à Paris pendant la Révolution française*, Paris 1989

—— *The women of Paris and their French Revolution*, Berkeley 1998

Gough, H., *The newspaper press in the French Revolution*, London 1988

Gross, J.-P., *Fair shares for all: Jacobin egalitarianism in practice*, Cambridge 1997

Gruder, V. R., 'Whither revisionism?: political perspectives on the *ancien régime*', *French Historical Studies* xx (1997), 245–85

Guilhaumou, J., 'Discourse and revolution: the foundation of political language (1789–1792)', in Levitine, *Culture and revolution*, 118–33

—— 'Les Journaux parisiens dans les luttes révolutionnaires en 1793: presse d'opinion, presse de salut public et presse pamphlétaire', in Rétat, *Révolution du journal*, 275–84

—— *La Langue politique de la Révolution française*, Paris 1989

—— *Marseille républicaine*, Paris 1992

Hampson, N., *Danton*, London 1978

Hardman, J., *The French Revolution sourcebook*, London 1999

Hesse, C., *Publishing and cultural politics in revolutionary Paris, 1789–1810*, Berkeley 1991

Higonnet, P., *Class, ideology and the rights of nobles during the French Revolution*, Oxford 1981

—— ' "Aristocrate", "aristocratie": language and politics in the French Revolution', in S. Petrey (ed.), *The French Revolution, 1789–1989: 200 years of rethinking*, Lubbock, Texas 1989

—— 'Cultural upheaval and class formation during the French Revolution', in

F. Fehér (ed.), *The French Revolution and the birth of modernity*, Berkeley 1990, 69–102

Hunt, L., *Politics, culture and class in the French Revolution*, London 1984

—— and G. Sheridan, 'Corporatism, association and the language of labor in France, 1750–1850', *Journal of Modern History* lviii (1986), 813–44

Isherwood, R. M., *Farce and fantasy: popular entertainment in eighteenth-century Paris*, Oxford 1986

Jaffé, G. M., *Le Mouvement ouvrier à Paris pendant la Révolution française (1789–1791)*, Paris 1924

Jones, C., *The Longman companion to the French Revolution*, London 1988

Kaplan, S. L., 'Réflexions sur la police du monde du travail, 1700–1815', *Revue historique* dxxix (1979), 17–77

—— *The famine plot persuasion in eighteenth-century France*, Philadelphia 1982

—— 'The character and implications of strife amongst masters in the guilds of eighteenth-century Paris', *Journal of Social History* xix (1985–6), 631–47

—— 'Social classification and representation in the corporate world of eighteenth-century France: Turgot's "carnival" ', in S. L. Kaplan and C. J. Koepp (eds), *Work in France: representations, meaning, organization and practice*, Ithaca, NY 1986, 176–228

—— 'La Lutte pour la contrôle du marché du travail à Paris au XVIIIe siècle', *Revue d'histoire moderne et contemporaine* xxxvi (1989), 361–412.

—— *Farewell Revolution*, Ithaca, NY 1995

Kaplow, J., *The names of kings: the Parisian labouring poor in the eighteenth century*, New York 1972

Kates, G., *The Cercle social, the Girondins, and the French Revolution*, Princeton 1985

—— (ed.), *The French Revolution: recent debates and new controversies*, London 1998

Kelly, G. A., 'The machine of the duc d'Orléans and the new politics', *Journal of Modern History* li (1979), 667–84

—— *Victims, authority and terror: the parallel deaths of d'Orléans, Custine, Bailly and Malesherbes*, Chapel Hill 1982

La Marle, H., *Philippe Égalité, 'grand maître' de la Révolution*, Paris 1989

Lefebvre, G., *The coming of the French Revolution*, trans. R. R. Palmer, Princeton 1947

Levitine, G. (ed.), *Culture and revolution: cultural ramifications of the French Revolution*, College Park, MD 1989

Lewis, G., *The French Revolution: rethinking the debate*, London 1993

Lucas, C. (ed.), *The French Revolution and the creation of modern political culture*, II: *The political culture of the French Revolution*, Oxford 1988

—— 'The crowd and politics', in Lucas, *The political culture of the French Revolution*, 259–85

—— 'Talking about urban popular violence in 1789', in Forrest and Jones, *Reshaping France*, 122–36

Luckett, T. M., 'Hunting for spies and whores: a Parisian riot on the eve of the French Revolution', *Past and Present* clvi (1997), 116–43

Luttrell, B., *Mirabeau*, Hemel Hempstead 1990

McMahon, D. M., 'The birthplace of the Revolution: public space and political community in the Palais-Royal of Louis-Philippe-Joseph d'Orléans, 1781–1789', *French History* x (1996), 1–29

Martin, G., *Les Associations ouvrières au XVIIIe siècle (1700–1792)*, Paris 1900

Mason, L., *Singing the French Revolution*, Ithaca 1996

Massin, J., *Marat*, first publ. Paris 1960, Aix-en-Provence 1988

Mathiez, A., *Le Club des Cordeliers pendant la crise de Varennes et la massacre du Champ de Mars*, Paris 1910, repr. Geneva 1975

——— *La Vie chère et le mouvement social sous la terreur*, Paris 1927

Melzer, S. E. and K. Norberg (eds), *From the royal to the republican body: incorporating the political in seventeenth- and eighteenth-century France*, Berkeley 1998

Ménétra, J.-L., *Journal of my life*, ed. and comm. D. Roche, trans. A. Goldhammer, New York 1986

Mercier, L.-S., *Le Tableau de Paris*, textes choisis par J. Kaplow, Paris 1979

Minard, P., 'Identité corporative et dignité ouvrière: le cas des typographes parisiens, 1789–1791', in Vovelle, *Paris*, 23–33

Monnier, R., 'La Garde citoyenne, element de la démocratie parisienne', in Vovelle, *Paris*, 147–59

——— *L'Espace public démocratique: essai sur l'opinion à Paris de la Révolution au Directoire*, Paris 1994

Morini-Comby, J., *Les Assignats*, Paris 1925

Murray, W. J., *The right-wing press in the French Revolution, 1789–1792*, London 1986

Nathans, B., 'Habermas's "public sphere" in the era of the French Revolution', *French Historical Studies* xvi (1990), 620–44

Nora, P., 'Nation', in Furet and Ozouf, *Critical dictionary*, 742–53

Payne, H. C., *The philosophes and the people*, London 1976

Popkin, J. D., *Revolutionary news: the press in France, 1789–1799*, London 1990

Rétat, P. (ed.), *La Révolution du journal, 1788–1794*, Paris 1989

——— 'The evolution of the citizen from the *ancien régime* to the Revolution', in R. Waldinger, P. Dawson and I. Woloch (eds), *The French Revolution and the meaning of citizenship*, Westport 1993, 4–15.

Richet, D., 'Revolutionary *journées*', in Furet and Ozouf, *Critical dictionary*, 124–36.

Robiquet, P., *Le Personnel municipal de Paris pendant la Révolution*, Paris 1890

Roche, D., *Le Peuple de Paris*, Paris 1981

——— *The people of Paris: an essay in popular culture in the eighteenth century*, trans. M. Evans and G. Lewis, Leamington Spa 1987

——— *The culture of clothing: dress and fashion in the Old Regime*, Cambridge 1994

Rose, R. B., *The enragés: socialists of the French Revolution?*, Sydney 1968

——— *The making of the sans-culottes: democratic ideas and institutions in Paris, 1789–1792*, Manchester 1983

Ruault, N., *Gazette d'un parisien sous la Révolution: lettres à son frère, 1783–1796*, ed. A. Vassal and C. Rimbaud, Paris 1976

Rudé, G., *The crowd in the French Revolution*, Oxford 1959

Schama, S., *Citizens: a chronicle of the French Revolution*, New York 1989

Sewell, W. H., Jr, *Work and revolution in France: the language of labor from Old Regime to 1848*, Cambridge 1980

——— 'A rhetoric of bourgeois revolution', in Kates, *The French Revolution*, 143–56.

Shapiro, B. M., *Revolutionary justice in Paris, 1789–1790*, Cambridge 1993

Singer, B., 'Violence in the French Revolution: forms of ingestion/forms of expulsion', in F. Fehér (ed.), *The French Revolution and the birth of modernity*, Berkeley 1990, 150–73

Slavin, M., *The making of an insurrection: Parisian Sections and the Gironde*, London 1986

Soboul, A., *Les Sans-Culottes parisiens en l'an II: mouvement populaire et gouvernement révolutionnaire*, Paris 1958

———— *The Parisian sans-culottes and the French Revolution, 1793–4*, trans. G. Lewis, Oxford 1964

———— and R. Monnier, *Répertoire du personnel sectionnaire parisien en l'an II*, Paris 1985

Sonenscher, M., 'The sans-culottes of the year II: rethinking the language of labour in revolutionary France', *Social History* ix (1984), 301–28

———— 'Journeymen, the courts and the French trades, 1781–1791', *Past and Present* cxiv (1987), 77–109

———— *Work and wages: natural law, politics and the eighteenth-century French trades*, Cambridge 1989

———— 'Artisans, sans-culottes and the French Revolution', in Forrest and Jones, *Reshaping France*, 105–121

Sutherland, D. M. G., *France, 1789–1815: revolution and counterrevolution*, London 1985

Tackett, T., *Religion, revolution and regional culture in eighteenth-century France: the ecclesiastical oath of 1791*, Princeton 1986

———— 'Women and men in counter-revolution: the Sommières riot of 1791', *Journal of Modern History* lix (1987), 680–704

———— *Becoming a revolutionary: the deputies of the French National Assembly and the emergence of a revolutionary political culture (1789–1790)*, Princeton 1996

van Kley, D., *The Damiens affair and the unravelling of the ancien régime, 1750–1770*, Princeton 1984

———— *The religious origins of the French Revolution: from Calvin to the Civil Constitution, 1560–1791*, New Haven 1996

Viola, P., 'Violence révolutionnaire ou violence du peuple en révolution?', in Vovelle and de Baecque, *Recherches*, 95–107

Vovelle, M. (ed.), *Paris et la Révolution: actes du colloque de Paris I, 14–16 avril 1989*, Paris 1989

———— and A. de Baecque (eds), *Recherches sur la Révolution*, Paris 1991

Wahl, E. and F. Moureau, 'Les Nouvelles à la main en 1788–1789: idéologie et contrastes des gazettes manuscrites', in Rétat, *Révolution du journal*, 139–47

Weir, D., 'Les Crises économiques et les origines de la Révolution française', *Annales. Économies, Sociétés, Civilisations* xlvi (1991), 917–47

Whaley, L., 'Political factions and the second revolution: the insurrection of 10 August 1792', *French History* vii (1993), 205–24

Williams, A., *The police of Paris, 1718–1789*, Baton Rouge 1979

Wills, A., *Crime and punishment in revolutionary Paris*, Westport 1981

Unpublished theses etc.

Andrews, R. M., 'Political elites and social conflicts in the Sections of revolutionary Paris, 1792–an III', unpubl. DPhil. diss. Oxford 1971

Maza, S., 'Languages of class in the French Revolution: the problem of the absent bourgeoisie', unpubl. manuscript 1998

Index

Printed and bound by CPI Group (UK) Ltd, Croydon, CR0 4YY

09/06/2025

14685716-0003